D0989658

TRANSLATING HISTORY

THIRTY YEARS ON THE FRONT LINES OF DIPLOMACY
WITH A TOP RUSSIAN INTERPRETER

IGOR KORCHILOV

Whitaker Library
Chowan College
Murfreesboro, North Carolina

A LISA DREW BOOK

SCRIBNER

114988

A LISA DREW BOOK/SCRIBNER
1230 Avenue of the Americas
New York, NY 10020

Copyright © 1997 by Igor Korchilov
All rights reserved, including the right of reproduction
in whole or in part in any form.

SCRIBNER and design are trademarks of Simon & Schuster Inc.

A LISA DREW BOOK is a trademark of Simon & Schuster Inc.

Set in Electra

DESIGNED BY ERICH HOBBING

Manufactured in the United States of America

1 3 5 7 9 10 8 6 4 2

Library of Congress Cataloging-in-Publication Data

Korchilov, Igor.
Translating history: the top Russian interpreter's twenty-five years on the front line of
diplomacy/Igor Korchilov.
p.   cm.
"A Lisa Drew book."
1. Soviet Union—Foreign relations—1985–1991. 2. Gorbachev, Mikhail Sergeevich, 1931–   .
3. Korchilov, Igor. 4. Summit meetings—History—20th century. 5. Translating and interpreting—
Soviet Union. I. Title.
DK510.764.K67   1997
327.47'009'048—dc21   96–51575 CIP

ISBN 0-684-81418-8

For my mother,
ANNA BESEDINA,
with gratitude, love and affection

ACKNOWLEDGMENTS

This book could not have been published and the story in it could not have been told but for the efforts and determination of some people to whom I wish to offer my heartfelt thanks. My appreciation and special thanks go Ms. Lisa Drew, Vice President and Publisher of Lisa Drew Books/Scribner at Simon & Schuster. With her keen mind and critical eyes she could see certain merits in this work. Her belief in the project served to sustain me through some of the most difficult moments. My warm and sincere thanks also go to Ms. Mary Yost, the literary agent at Mary Yost Associates, who graciously agreed to take a look at what was an unknown author's manuscript in its original daunting version of over 1,300 pages, and who later shepherded it through the byways and corridors of Simon & Schuster. To Olga Seham, the talented former Random House editor, assigned to pare the original manuscript down to some four hundred manuscript pages—no mean feat in itself—I wish to express my admiration for having succeeded so well in what appeared to be a mission impossible. Her astute guidance improved the book's structure and her thin pencil its readability. My sincere thanks to her.

There are two persons to whom I owe a sincere debt of gratitude: Ambassador Joseph Verner Reed, and Ambassador Sergey Lavrov, whose support and assistance were a great encouragement to me.

I also owe a very special debt of gratitude to Dr. Menard Gertler, M.D., P.C., who literally saved this author and, consequently, this book from imminent death, from a heart failure. Without his timely professional interference and subsequent ministrations, this book would never have seen the light of day. He really went beyond the call of duty. To his lovely wife, Anna, I owe many, many thanks for her moral support and encouragement in the hour of trial. I stand in awe to Dr. Alfred Culliford, M.D., P.C., the surgeon who, on Dr. Gertler's strong recommendation, boldly rushed in where angels fear to tread, inside the heart, that sanctum sanctorum, to take corrective action and put me back on my

ACKNOWLEDGMENTS

feet. I thank him from the bottom of my heart for giving me a new lease on life, thereby making it also possible for this book to appear. I am also very grateful to Sergei Oleinikov, my good friend, for his understanding and for lending a helping hand.

Whatever the shortcomings of this book, they would have been much greater without the generous support, advice, and encouragement of many people, friends and colleagues, who shared with me the benefit of their wisdom and provided me with moral support and encouragement throughout. I would like to mention especially Monique Corvington, Lisa Heyward, Marcia and Nelly Hill, Elena and Fred Howard, Sergey Mikheyev, Brigitte Andreassier and Stephen Pearl, Sasha Shtanko, Guy Struve, Lynn Visson, and Hans Yanitchek.

I owe many thanks as well to Steven Boldt for the eagle-eyed and painstaking copyediting of my manuscript. And finally, my thanks go to Igor Khripounov, for his unfailing interest in and concern over the fate of this book, and to Marysue Rucci, the stellar and sterling assistant to Lisa Drew, for her guiding help.

Last but certainly not least, I am very grateful to my wife, Inna, for her infinite patience, forbearance, and invariable encouragement and support which sustained me throughout the years of my involvement with this book project.

CONTENTS

PREFACE   15

PROLOGUE: INTERPRETATION, IT'S NO MONKEY BUSINESS   19

1. FIRST IMPRESSIONS: My First Encounter with Gorbachev   27

2. TRUST-BUT-VERIFY SUMMIT: Gorbachev-Reagan Washington
   Summit, 1987   41

3. SLAYING-A-FEW-DRAGONS SUMMIT: Gorbachev-Reagan Moscow
   Summit, 1988   141

4. ROMANTIC SUMMIT: Gorbachev-Thatcher London Summit, 1989   187

5. END-OF-THE-COLD-WAR SUMMIT: Gorbachev-Bush Washington
   Summit, 1990   233

6. EMERGENCY SUMMIT: Gorbachev-Bush Helsinki Summit, 1990   309

7. REAGAN'S SOVIET REUNIONS: Ex-President's Nostalgic Journey
   to Moscow, 1990   333

   EPILOGUE: THE SUN HAS SET ON GORBACHEV . . . OR HAS IT?   379

   INDEX   385

He isn't going to change the system. . . . He'll throw curves, knuckleballs, and spitters if he can get away with them. Of course, Reagan has played a pitcher, too, in that movie *The Winning Team*.
—RICHARD NIXON on GORBACHEV in 1985

I like Mr. Gorbachev. I think we can do business together.
—MARGARET THATCHER in 1994

Words and illusions fade away, facts remain.
—DMITRI PISAREV

It is not my wont
To use cant
I can't
And I won't
—a diplomat's vow

TRANSLATING
HISTORY

PREFACE

I am grateful to fate, which threw me together with Mikhail Sergeyevich Gorbachev, who appeared on the political scene at a critical time in world history and changed its course. The idea of writing a memoir to describe my experiences as an interpreter for this extraordinary man had been germinating in my mind even before I actually began to work for him, and when I did, I started keeping notes in the form of diaries or journals in which I recorded, "hot on the heels" of events, my observations, impressions, and reflections. I realized that I was in a unique position to observe this man, at close range, interacting with world leaders. I wanted to record what I saw and heard, hoping that one day it would be possible to share my observations with the public.

These journals are a product of the four years in which I worked for Gorbachev, first while he was general secretary of the Communist Party of the Soviet Union and later president of the Soviet Union. It covers the pivotal period between 1987 and the fall of 1990, which saw an unprecedented number of East-West summits and the end of the Cold War. It is my hope that the inquisitive reader with a probing mind who is keen on history will enjoy being taken behind the scenes in those crucial days, be it at the Kremlin or the White House or 10 Downing Street or elsewhere, to observe for himself some of the history-making events whose impact on mankind will be felt for a long time to come.

Some of the things I describe in this memoir may already have been described in the mass media, but not from the specific privileged angle from which I was able to observe them. I have included excerpts from some of the discussions and conversations between Gorbachev and Reagan, Bush, and Thatcher, among others, as well as between Yeltsin and Reagan, in the belief that this will help interested readers gain a better insight into the frame of mind of these leaders at the time described and their evolving attitudes toward the crucial issues they grappled with, with the caveat that no interpreter will reveal everything that was said in those private discussions and conversations, for this is clearly outside his prerogative. Such disclosures of sensitive secrets are for the leaders themselves to make in their own memoirs, should they choose to do so. As someone aptly remarked, "The secret of boring a reader is to tell him everything."

In my portrait of the Soviet-U.S. summit milestones that brought about an end to the Cold War, I trace the evolution of Gorbachev's thinking, his attitude to and interaction with his foreign counterparts, showing above all his human side: from being self-confident and in command to becoming humble and more pliable—all in a space of some four years.

I wish to stress here that while the West in general and America in particular were indulging at the time in what was called Gorbomania, I, for my part, like so many of my compatriots, initially was rather skeptical about Gorbachev's true intentions in declaring *perestroika* at home and new thinking abroad. Not until 1988 did I gradually begin to change my mind about this man as I saw the growing resistance to his reforms by the system and those who embodied it. Only then did I come to believe that his intentions to carry out the reforms were genuine and serious. In retrospect, his almost seven years in power now seem to have been filled more with hope and promise than performance on the domestic front. But the hope and the promise that he held for the Soviet Union were real and have resulted in the rise of democracy and a return to common human values in that long-suffering country.

"Journalism is just the first draft of history," the late Philip Graham, journalist and newspaper publisher, once said to emphasize the fact that journalists could never know the whole truth right away. The whole truth takes too long to emerge, and it consists of too many strands. But what makes journalism so interesting and biography and memoirs so fascinating is, as the late President Kennedy remarked, "the struggle to answer that single question: 'What's he like?' "

Few of us become involved in history-making—in whatever capacity—and when it happened to me, it understandably dominated a good chunk of my life. When all is said and done, this memoir is a recording of history in the making, as seen through the eyes of this author, who was lucky enough to participate.

And so I hope that my record, even though I am an interpreter, not a journalist or historian, makes up at least a few but essential strands of the whole truth that was Gorbachev, and the leaders with whom he made history, and answers, albeit partially, the question on the minds of many: "What was Gorbachev *really* like in 'doing business' with his counterparts: Reagan, Thatcher, and Bush?" "What was that 'special chemistry' between them all about?"

For the personality of Mikhail Sergeyevich Gorbachev has left its indelible mark on history—he changed our destinies.

—IGOR KORCHILOV

INTERPRETATION,
IT'S NO MONKEY BUSINESS

In a world where international communication is a daily fact of life, interpretation is a vitally important field. Without interpretation and translation no meeting between world leaders is possible, no international agreement or treaty can be signed, and no business deal concluded if the parties involved speak different languages. From the times of Babylonia and ancient Greece interpreters have always been regarded as people who facilitate the restoration of peace by helping the parties involved—who speak different languages—to resolve conflicts. Anyone who regularly watches television news, especially CNN or C-SPAN live coverage of international events, has seen or heard interpreters. They stand between kings, presidents and prime ministers, foreign ministers, and other dignitaries. They are the "unidentified" men (or women, as the case may be) in the middle, or the anonymous "voice of interpreter." Their job is to interpret each word or phrase uttered by their principals. They strain to hear every word, however trivial, and they do their best to render everything they hear seemingly effortlessly and smoothly so as not to attract too much attention to themselves, following the unwritten rule "The interpreter is supposed to be heard, not seen."

In fact, when they are doing their work well, they receive no notice. Only when they make a mistake do they find themselves in the spotlight—or a hot spot. Many may recall the flap over interpretation when Jimmy Carter visited Poland in 1977. He told the welcoming crowd in Warsaw that he had come "to learn your opinions and understand your desires for the future." The next day the press alleged that his American interpreter had conveyed the final phrase into Polish as "your lusts for future." (The interpreter, whom I later met, denied any such mistranslation. He claimed Carter's visit simply did not arouse much interest, and so the press invented the story.)

In another amusing incident, an interpreter at a major international conference got some notice when he heard the Soviet delegate solemnly say in Russian in his speech, "V *ogorode buzina, a v Kieve dyad'ka*" (an elderberry grows in the kitchen garden and my uncle lives in Kiev). This Russian saying means that something is incompatible with something else and is akin to the American idiom *mixing apples and oranges*. But the interpreter in question didn't know the word *buzina* (elderberry) and hadn't the foggiest notion what the idiom meant, and besides, the speaker was already on his next sentence. With no time to think or to look it up in the dictionary and with no one to ask, the interpreter gambled. The delegates whose earphones were tuned to the English interpretation channel heard, "Something is rotten in the kingdom of Denmark." The interpreter was quite pleased with what he thought was a serendipitous translation until the delegate of Denmark grabbed the floor to protest the Soviet delegate's "unwarranted slur on Denmark" and to lecture him on the virtues of democracy in his country, which, he said, was "a paragon compared to the inhuman, totalitarian system in the country which the Soviet delegate represented. . . . We do not deserve this kind of treatment," concluded the Danish delegate. The Soviet delegate sat dumbfounded. He had never mentioned Denmark. So he interrupted the Danish delegate to express his resentment at what he called "a provocation."

When it became clear that it was all the interpreter's error, he nearly lost his job. Such are the occupational hazards interpreters face. A list of similar examples of interpreters' faux pas could be extended ad infinitum.

Speaking of occupational hazards, an amusing story is attributed to Richard Nixon. The way Nixon told it, Prime Minister Churchill sat up all night drinking with Stalin at the Yalta Conference and said to him the next morning, "I hope I didn't say anything indiscreet last night." "Don't worry," Stalin supposedly replied, "I had the interpreter shot."

One hopes it was only a story.

But while they are occasionally in the limelight, interpreters and their work are not, I suspect, well understood by the general public or even those who make use of them. A few explanatory notes therefore seem in order. Suffice it to say, while the translator writes, the interpreter speaks. A translator works with written materials, while an interpreter renders oral statements (which are often nothing but written speeches read by a speaker) uttered in one language into oral statements in another language. The translator can consult dictionaries or his or her colleagues, while the interpreter, of necessity, has no time to do so and must instantly react to what he or she hears, relying totally on his or her linguistic knowledge, training, skills, and experience. Also, while the translator ponders in private in the quiet of his office or cubicle, the interpreter works in public and must therefore be something of a performer.

There are basically two types of interpretation: simultaneous and consecutive. The simultaneous interpreter renders a speech from one language into another almost instantaneously while the speaker is delivering it. In consecutive interpretation, the interpreter first takes notes while listening to the speaker and then, after the speaker pauses, reproduces, relying on his memory and notes, the meaning of the words and phrases in another language. Simultaneous interpretation was first tried, rather unsuccessfully, in the late 1920s in the Soviet Union and abandoned. It was used in a meaningful way on the world scene for the first time in 1946 at the postwar Nuremberg trials. The obvious advantage of simultaneous interpretation was that it saved time. A one-hour speech now took just that—one hour, instead of the customary two, if interpreted consecutively into one foreign language only, or more than two hours if interpreted into more than one. The new method made possible interpretation in *real time*. And it prompted Hermann Göring, referring to the simultaneous interpreters, to exclaim, "They are shortening my life!" Found guilty, this top Nazi war criminal was hanged.

Most interpreters can work *into* or *out of* their native language. At major international organizations such as the United Nations, where simultaneous interpretation was introduced in 1946, interpreters normally work into their native language—that is, they translate from a foreign tongue into their own. The opposite principle is used in bilateral meetings, especially at U.S.-Soviet and Anglo-Soviet summits, ministerials, and talks. Both methods have their pros and cons, but whichever way the interpreter works, what he or she needs is what in Russian is called *perevoploscheniye*, or the ability to put oneself in the speaker's shoes, to become his döppelganger, as it were, to catch the essence of his message and not simply repeat what he is saying in another language.

In the late 1940s and the early 1950s, when simultaneous interpretation was still a novelty at the U.N., visitors asked to see three things: Mrs. Roosevelt, the ranking Soviet delegate, and the simultaneous interpreters, not necessarily in that order. They thought the interpreters had two brains: one for listening and one for speaking—often at a mind-boggling speed of as many as 250 words per minute. The incredible ability of the interpreters to coordinate their hearing in one language and speaking in another at the same time made them an eighth wonder of the world. American visitors especially were said to marvel as some foreign gibberish was instantly converted into cool English.

Friends have asked me many times what an interpreter feels when he works at a high-level meeting, what happens inside him. Well, nothing really happens beyond an occasional sinking feeling in the pit of the stomach and a sense of . . . loneliness. The sinking feeling comes when the interpreter senses that the meaning of his principal's utterances is beginning to elude him or when the latter interrupts his train of thought to wonder if he is being "got across" correctly. Early on in my career as a diplomatic interpreter in the 1970s, I was once interpreting for Brezhnev and the prime minister of India, and at one point Brezhnev used a deceptively simple word in Russian that nearly stumped me in the context in which he employed it. He was speaking about the Soviet Union's desire to strengthen further its relationship with India, which he described as *prochnyi soyuz druzhbi* (a solid bond of friendship).

Now, anyone who speaks Russian and English knows that *soyuz* means both "alliance" and "union." However, in that particular context neither was politically correct because the word *alliance* is strongly associated with military alliances such as NATO or the Warsaw Pact Organization, while the word *union* has an implication of a political nature (union of Soviet republics) and in the context of the Soviet Union's relationship with India could be misconstrued as an attempt to bring it within the Kremlin's orbit of influence. So on the spur of the moment I chose what I felt was the correct word in the context, a *bond*. But Andrei Gromyko, the foreign minister, who spoke good English and who attended the talks, interrupted me in the middle of the sentence to ask if I was sure it was the right word to use. I remember saying—rather presumptuously, I am afraid—that yes, indeed, I *was* sure. Gromyko was satisfied, but now Brezhnev—whose knowledge of foreign languages was limited to just one German phrase, *auf Wiedersehen* (good-bye), which he occasionally used both to greet his foreign visitors, including English-speaking dignitaries, and to bid farewell to them—looked at me sideways, then at Gromyko, clearly unsure about my reliability as an interpreter, and finally asked Gromyko bluntly and loudly if he was being "got across" correctly. That was when I had that sinking feeling for a moment. But Gromyko assured him that I was doing all right, and Brezhnev, now relieved, proceeded to read from the text in front of him.

The sense of loneliness comes from the fact that the interpreter is alone in the crosscurrents of ideas and in the midst of a sea of words. He has no one to help him and he just does his level best to interpret well.

At first at top-level meetings, whether they were private talks between two leaders or expanded talks across the negotiating table, I had to will myself to overcome the nervousness I felt. But almost immediately after a meeting got under way, I was so absorbed in the work that I did not see or notice the others around me—it was as if I had an audience of two people only: my principal and his opposite number. So much so that during those moments I seemed to have no existence of my own; the words I heard were all that mattered. I gave myself entirely to the job, as if I were indeed in my principal's shoes—that was *perevoploscheniye* in practice.

How does one become a summit interpreter? The general answer would be less by design than by sheer happenstance. One will never see, for example, in the Help Wanted section of the *New York Times* or in the *Times of London,* or in *Pravda* for that matter, an advertisement for a summit interpreter for the White House, for 10 Downing Street, or for the Kremlin. It goes without saying, of course, that only interpreters with a solid background in interpretation make it to the top. But beyond that, every interpreter who has made it to the top has a different story to tell of how he or she did it.

How I fell in love with and learned English, and came to work as an interpreter in the world of high politics, is different, I am sure, from the stories of other colleagues of mine in that I am not bilingual, nor have I had any formal schooling in English in an English-speaking country, or even at home for that matter. I did not have a chance to learn English at school at all. In fact, I did not begin to study it until after I finished high school, where I had studied German for six years, and then I started from scratch, with a little inspiration from Elvis Presley.

I grew up in Kislovodsk, a spa town in the southern part of Russia, in the Caucasus, with Stavropol, where Gorbachev's career was launched, as the regional capital. It was a pleasant enough town, I suppose, but my family was poor, my prospects were limited because we were not Party members, and by the time I was a teenager Kislovodsk had come to seem small and provincial, even stifling. A romantic by nature, I had since childhood devoured the few books and films of faraway places that had come my way, and now I was restless. I was ready to strike out on my own, but I didn't know how. I had no one to guide me.

Then one day in 1959, somebody—I think he was a dancer with a Georgian folk-dance company that had just returned from a tour of the United States—brought an Elvis Presley record to the movie theater where I worked as a projectionist and asked if I could play it on a turntable we had in the projection room. I said, why not? After hearing Presley only once, I instantly became his ardent fan. Then the dancer asked me if I could pipe the sound into the auditorium. I still remember that night well. It was a Saturday night—the time when the theater management turned the auditorium into a ballroom for young people. On those nights I usually doubled as a kind of DJ, and on that particular night, after playing some waltzes and polkas to satisfy the manager, who left soon thereafter, I decided to put on the Elvis disk. The crowd on the dance floor went absolutely wild, writhing, wriggling, and gyrating to the sounds of "Tutti Frutti," "Blue Suede Shoes," and "Jailhouse Rock." It was very exciting. I had seen nothing like it before. After it ended, the dancing public wanted more. So I spun the disk again, and again and again.

The following Monday I was called on the carpet by the manager and warned that if I ever played that kind of music again, I would be fired. Rock simply did not fit within the ideological straitjacket of unwritten rules prescribing what kind of music, among many other things, the Soviet people should listen to. Its effect on me and on all the other young people I knew, however, was magical. It was devastatingly different from anything else we had ever heard. It was a mind-blowing experience, to use the slangy expression that was popular with the flower children in the late 1960s.

I was so taken by this music that I wanted to find out what those rock lyrics were about, and one day I decided to start learning English. I was two months shy of my nineteenth birthday. The next day I went to a bookstore and bought all the primary textbooks of English covering the standard six-year school curriculum. On January 7, 1960, I sat down on the cot in my six-by-nine-foot room, pulled up the wooden stool that served as my desk, opened a textbook, and tried to read lesson one out loud. Easier said than done. I didn't even know how to pronounce those strange letters. And so I began to learn the English alphabet.

Six months later, after thousands of hours of intensive studies on my own, twelve hours a day, I completed what was designed for a six-year high school curriculum. I made it an iron rule to learn one hundred new words and expressions every day and to repeat them the next day at work, so as to memorize them better. Studying by myself, without a teacher or tutor, was hard. But I had an even harder time trying to master the tricky English pronunciation. A friend who spoke a bit of English gave me a couple of lessons in pronunciation, for which I was very grateful. Basically though, I had no one else to turn to for help. At home we had no radio, no television, no tape recorder to tape myself speaking, no telephone, and in fact, no electricity. Being very determined, however, after more intensive study on my own, and in spite of long odds, I won a coveted place at the best college in the country for learning foreign languages—the First Moscow State Institute of Foreign Languages, or Inyaz, in the nation's capital.

For the next six years I toiled my way through all the intricacies and hidden traps of English and Spanish, which I added as my third language. All the while I was studying with an eye to becoming an interpreter so that I could realize my dream to travel and see the world. In the summer of 1967 I passed the college finals and enrolled in the U.N.-sponsored courses for interpreters and translators, which operated on the Inyaz premises. I chose to be trained in simultaneous interpretation rather than translation because it seemed more challenging, more exciting, more promising. I was not disappointed later. The courses were for ten months, but in the spring of the next year a vacancy arose at the U.N. headquarters in New York. And so, on April 29, 1968, I was sent to New York, several months ahead of time, as a simultaneous interpreter at the beginner's level.

Thus, eight years and almost four months since I had begun a love affair with English, I found myself in New York—a city I had dreamed of seeing one day with my own eyes ever since I had read Maxim Gorky's *The City of the Yellow Devil*. Now my dream had come true. I remember being dumbfounded and rather mystified by the very first question the immigration officer asked me when I stepped on American soil at Idlewild, as the JFK airport was called in those days. After saying "Welcome to the United States" and inquiring about the purpose of my coming, the officer suddenly gave me a wink and asked, "No monkey business here?" Just in case, I said, "No," although I didn't have a clue as to what on earth he was talking about. I realized that I still had a long way to go to improve my English.

Working as a simultaneous interpreter with the United Nations turned out to be superb schooling for a diplomatic interpreter. Soon after my return to Moscow from the five-year tour of duty (in those days we were not allowed by our government to stay longer), I was invited to work for the Ministry of Foreign Affairs of the USSR, or the MFA for short.

My first hands-on experience there was to act as an interpreter for Foreign Minister Andrei Gromyko. To interpret for Gromyko was considered a special honor and a great challenge. He was a difficult and demanding man, and he understood English pretty well, but more importantly perhaps, he had been "spoilt" by the brilliant interpreter

Viktor Sukhodrev and, consequently, was used to the highest standards of interpretation. Fortunately for my professional ego, I came out of that experience intact. Later on, I was often given assignments to interpret for Brezhnev, Kosygin, Podgorny, and other officials of lesser standing.

By the time I left the MFA in 1980 for a second tour of duty at the United Nations, I had become a full-fledged interpreter with a solid background in both consecutive and simultaneous interpretation, and in 1985, when my fixed-term appointment expired, I was recalled to Moscow again to rejoin the government diplomatic service. But not before I was put through a course at the MFA Diplomatic Academy to master the subtleties of the art of diplomacy.

Now, for the first time in my life in the Soviet Union, I felt winds of change beginning to blow across the vast expanse of the entire country, clearing the stifling atmosphere. By the time I graduated from the Academy, the new Soviet leader Mikhail Sergeyevich Gorbachev and his close comrade-in-*perestroika* Eduard Amvrosiyevich Shevardnadze were putting a new foreign policy in place. It came to be known as the new thinking.

And so, upon completion of my academic studies in the summer of 1986, rather than pursue a purely diplomatic career, I decided to return to my old department in the Ministry of Foreign Affairs in my former capacity as a senior diplomatic interpreter, in the hope that sooner or later I would be called upon to interpret for that brave and courageous man who had started the great cause of *perestroika*—the quiet revolution.

My hopes were soon to be realized.

FIRST IMPRESSIONS

My First Encounter with Gorbachev

MOSCOW. JUNE 27, 1987, SATURDAY.

The first opportunity for me to interpret for General Secretary Gorbachev presented itself on this warm Saturday afternoon. Robert Mugabe, the prime minister of Zimbabwe, formerly Southern Rhodesia, and the chairman of NAM (the nonaligned movement), was in Moscow on a short, one-day visit, and Gorbachev was to receive him in his Kremlin office. I was assigned to be the interpreter.

Actually, it was not my first meeting with Gorbachev. I had met him in person eight years earlier, during the signing of Soviet-Indian agreements in St. Vladimir's Hall of the Grand Kremlin Palace. On that particular day, June 12, 1979, the entire Politburo turned out, as was the custom at the time, to demonstrate to the Soviet people and to the world at large their "unanimity" and the "unbreakable unity of their monolithic ranks." Before proceeding to St. Vladimir's Hall, the Politburo members gathered in a room known to Kremlin insiders as the Winter Garden. Because I was assigned to interpret for Brezhnev that day, I was instructed to meet him at the entrance and follow him closely wherever he went.

The Winter Garden is a large, brightly lit room that resembles a greenhouse because of its many exotic plants and palm trees in tubs, and it was used as a kind of drawing room for informal gatherings of the top Soviet government and Party elite before their public appearances.

I was already inside the Winter Garden when Brezhnev walked in, shuffling his feet, as usual. He was already slipping physically and mentally. In keeping with the instructions from protocol people I joined him as he started to move down the receiving line formed by the Politburo members, shaking their hands, one by one. They were arrayed along the wall in a strict pecking order: Prime Minister Alexei Kosygin; Mikhail Suslov, who was the ideology chief; Andrei Kirilenko, second to Brezhnev in seniority; Foreign Minister Andrei Gromyko, KGB chairman Yuri Andropov; Konstantin Chernenko, chief of Brezhnev's staff; Defense Minister Dmitry Ustinov; and so on. All of them were full members of the Politburo. Most of them were septuagenarians.

Next in the receiving line were alternate or nonvoting members of the Politburo, followed by Central Committee secretaries. At the very end of the line stood a stocky man of medium height. He wore a charcoal-gray, single-breasted, two-button suit of Soviet cut and a plain wide-collared shirt and tie with wide stripes. On the left lapel of his jacket he sported a red, flag-shaped badge of *deputat* (deputy, or member of parliament) of the USSR Supreme Soviet. When Brezhnev came up to him to shake his hand, an affable smile illuminated the man's round face, in stark contrast to all the others in the group, who habitually wore either dour or obsequious expressions, especially Chernenko. They were all gray old men in gray suits, and this man's relative youthfulness made him stand out. What struck me most, however, was a large reddish-purple blotch on top of his balding head. I had never seen anything like it before. The man's eyes were intensely dark brown and had an intelligent appeal to them.

After exchanging handshakes with Brezhnev, the man extended his hand to me and said simply but affably, "Gorbachev." I shook the proffered hand, mumbling my name in response. For a Soviet leader of such a high rank to introduce himself to an interpreter just like that was very unusual. Little did I realize then that this was the man who, years later, would shake the world by changing so radically the destiny of my country, and indeed the course of world history.

The next day I learned from the newspapers his full name and rank: Mikhail Sergeyevich Gorbachev, secretary of the Central Committee. He had been elevated to this position several months earlier, after he was brought to Moscow from Stavropol by his powerful mentor, Yuri Andropov, who was then chairman of Komitet Gosudarstvennoi Bezopasnosti, or the Committee for State Security, better known by its Russian acronym, the KGB.

Still, Gorbachev appeared at the time to be just another typical apparatchik, albeit much younger than the rest of them and certainly more amiable in his manners. He was forty-seven years old.

*   *   *

I remembered that first encounter as I was getting ready to meet Gorbachev again—eight years later. Only now he was no longer a newcomer to the Kremlin. He was very much in charge. Gorbachev had been the general secretary of the Central Committee of the Communist Party of the Soviet Union, or CC CPSU for short, for two years and three and a half months. That top job in the Soviet Union carried a lot more clout than that of a president or prime minister in most other countries. It was like being a king, a president, and a prime minister, all rolled into one. Despite Gorbachev's impressive record to date, not everybody in the world, and above all in the Soviet Union itself, was yet entirely convinced of the sincerity of his announced intention to change drastically the image of the country, to turn its failing economy around and to get rid of nuclear weapons. A lot of people, including this author, still thought it was all just a ploy, a ruse, to boost his popularity, like the ploys his predecessors had used so many times. Would he be bold enough to act on his words? There were quite a few doubting Thomases at that time, both at home and abroad.

Still, internationally, by then Gorbachev had some impressive accomplishments to his credit, that proved he was indeed serious in following *perestroika* at least in foreign policy. The word *perestroika* itself, which literally means "reconstruction" or "rebuilding," was not yet part of the world's vocabulary. In fact, the people in the Soviet Union did not have the slightest notion what stood behind it. And *glasnost*, i.e., "openness" or "transparency," or even "exposure of official lies," was an idea that had only barely begun to germinate. Even though used by Gorbachev publicly as far back as December 1984, *glasnost* was hardly a household word yet. True, it was now increasingly gaining currency, thanks in part to *Time* magazine, which had featured the word prominently in a cover story earlier in the year, and in part to the American TV talk-show host Phil Donahue. Donahue was instrumental in popularizing *glasnost* through a series of unprecedented TV programs that he televised from Moscow and Leningrad in early 1987 together with his Soviet co-host, Vladimir Pozner.

However, Gorbachev clearly did not have a master blueprint for radically rebuilding the country. There was no clear-cut concept or program of *perestroika*. Gorbachev seemed to be playing everything by ear. Hopes were high and he was riding their crest. Yet, most Soviet people were largely apathetic, skeptical, and even cynical about the reforms that he said he would carry out. This was understandable enough, considering the countless false promises they had been given by all the previous Soviet leaders, starting with Lenin himself, who had promised to turn land over to the peasants but never did. All the leaders who followed Lenin had issued more promises, the chief among them being to build communism in the USSR, whatever it meant, by the early 1980s. The latter promise was issued by Khrushchev as far back as 1960.

The ostensible purpose of Robert Mugabe's visit to Moscow was to attend an international congress of women, but his real goal was to meet with Gorbachev. Their meeting was scheduled for one o'clock in the afternoon. I had left myself ample time to get to the Kremlin, but because the MFA had failed to give my name to the KGB guards at the Kremlin, I was delayed at the security checkpoints and arrived breathless at Room 3 of the three-storied, yellow building that housed the Office of the General Secretary of the Communist Party of the Soviet Union, barely five minutes before the meeting.

I looked up at the small, black, unpretentious glass plate with the number 3 fixed over the entrance, pushed open the double doors of dark brown wood, and walked inside. I immediately recognized the room—a reception area that adjoined the main office itself. It was rather cramped, dark, and gloomy, like the rest of the government building. I had last been here eight years before, when Brezhnev occupied the Kremlin. The room also led into the famous Walnut Room, so named after its wood paneling. There, confidential matters of state were discussed at a large round table by a tiny group of men who were members of the Politburo and who, after reaching a decision, would then proceed through yet another door into a conference room where, together with other men, somewhat less powerful than they, alternate Politburo members and Central Committee secretaries, they would vote for formality's sake on the matters just decided.

I paused to catch my breath and introduced myself to one of Gorbachev's personal secretaries. He ticked off my name in the register on his desk and asked me to wait a few minutes. The waiting room was already full of photographers, reporters, people with TV and video cameras, who were being watched over by Kremlin security guards. Two photographers came up to tell me to step aside when they took Gorbachev's picture.

I was not surprised at this request. Generally, the photographers, who represented major national newspapers such as *Pravda* and *Izvestiya*, did not like the interpreters getting in the picture, and sometimes they would go to great lengths to prevent it from happening. In the not too distant past, even under the early Gorbachev, to say nothing of the Brezhnev era, they would simply airbrush the interpreter from the pictures showing Soviet leaders with their foreign guests, making it seem as though in their infinite wisdom Soviet leaders conversed with their counterparts from whatever country in that foreign language. The mentality behind such a ruse was hard to understand. I vividly remember one comic example of such misguided zeal. An official photo in *Pravda* showed Brezhnev seated in his Kremlin office facing his foreign guest across the table. In between them, at the end of the long T-shaped table, the observant reader could clearly see an open notebook and a pencil that was suspended at a precarious forty-five-degree angle with no visible means of support. A minor miracle, so to speak! The photo editors had obliterated the face of the interpreter, but forgot his notebook and the pencil.

Promptly at one o'clock, the double doors opened and Robert Mugabe walked into the reception room. A tall woman, said to be his wife and personal secretary, accompanied him. No sooner had I introduced myself to him as Gorbachev's interpreter and reminded him that we had already met in New York the year before than the other set of doors to the general secretary's office were thrown wide open, and following closely on Mugabe's heels, I found myself inside a large and spacious room—roughly sixty to seventy feet long and thirty to thirty-five feet wide. The familiar figure of the man with the famous purple birthmark on the top of his head suddenly materialized seemingly out of nowhere and started to move toward us with his right hand stretched out and a big, affable smile on his face.

He looked a little older, or I should say more mature, more solidly built than eight years earlier. He was now fifty-six. He wore a dark gray suit that looked smarter than the one in which I had seen him before, but on the left lapel of his jacket he sported the same Supreme Soviet deputy's badge in the shape of a red flag. His face was now a little more rounded, and he had a slight double chin. His graying hair was neatly combed back on both sides. His posture was erect, he held his head straight, yet he appeared quite at ease. His manners were plain, but pleasant and dignified. And his striking eyes had not changed. They were the same dark brown, still appealing, intelligent. Oh, yes, the eyes. His were not ordinary eyes; they had a special gleam that conveyed an intensity of thought. He appeared much more genial and lively in real life than on television. If one had to describe him in just one word, that word had be charismatic. In fact, it was this charisma that had perhaps prompted Margaret Thatcher, who met him for the first time in 1984, to describe Gorbachev as a man she could "do business with." On the other hand, Andrei Gromyko, in his characteristically sardonic manner, was said to have described him once privately as "a man with a nice smile and iron teeth."

To round out my first impressions of the new general secretary, I should mention his handshake. To paraphrase the old saw, let me shake his hand and I will tell you what kind of person he is. Gorbachev's handshake was strong and vigorous, and most importantly, it was reciprocal. Brezhnev, for instance, would just thrust his hand in yours and wait for you to shake it, as though he were doing you a great favor. You even had the feeling that he rather expected you to kiss it, as if he were Pope Leonid I, not the proletarian "Comrade Brezhnev." Well, come to think of it, it was no secret that some in the Soviet Union were more equal than others.

After exchanging hearty handshakes with us, Gorbachev motioned Mugabe and his secretary-wife (if indeed she was his wife) to take a seat across the conference table, then asked me if I minded sitting next to him, rather than at the head of the table, as had been customary for interpreters until then. I was pleasantly astonished at this change and took a seat to his left. Then, he pulled up a chair for himself and sat down with his back to the curtained windows. The thought crossed my mind that this same chair had been occupied by Chernenko, Andropov, and Brezhnev before him, and probably Khrushchev, too.

The Kremlin office of the general secretary of the Communist Party of the Soviet Union was basically used to receive distinguished foreign visitors. The general secretary had another, working office in the Party Central Committee complex on Staraya Ploschad, or Old Square, where he conducted day-to-day business. The one in the Kremlin was located on the third floor of the sprawling yellow building that also accommodated the offices of the Council of Ministers of the USSR, and it was one floor above Stalin's former office, which was now occupied by the chairman of the Council of Ministers, Nikolai Ryzhkov. Just a few steps from where I now sat was the office that had once been Lenin's and was now a museum.

As far as I could see, the general secretary's office had not changed in any way in the eight years since I had last been here. It was the same huge, cavernous room with a domed ceiling, the three big windows with the same white, ruffled curtains, and the light-colored parquet floors covered with the same flower-patterned carpets. The walls were decorated with the same off-white damask panels trimmed in what appeared to be teakwood. The same two huge crystal chandeliers illuminated the office. The same plain, square-shaped clock hung above the doorway. The same long T-shaped conference table covered with green baize stood close to the windows. And, of course, the same three obligatory official portraits of Lenin, Marx, and Engels hung on the wall.

In short, everything in this room reminded me of the past times of stagnation. To complete the picture of sameness and as if to emphasize the truthfulness of the maxim "The more things change, the more they remain the same," standing to the side and behind Gorbachev was none other than Vladimir Medvedev—the same personal bodyguard and aide-de-camp to Brezhnev, whose services had obviously been retained by Gorbachev and who had once rudely pushed me away from Brezhnev when I was assigned to interpret for him.

For a moment, the sense of sameness overwhelmed me. Shouldn't this new and obviously innovative and dynamic leader have gotten rid of all those trappings of the times of "stagnation"? After all, symbolism *was* important, if he truly desired to dissociate himself from the less than glorious past. But I was not there to indulge in idle musings, and I had to concentrate on the task at hand.

After the clicking of cameras amidst blinding flashes, the reporters were ushered out of the room by Medvedev and the doors were closed. The stage was now set for serious business. The Third African Desk at the MFA had prepared detailed talking points for Gorbachev to guide him through the conversation with Mugabe. As far as I know, no previous Soviet leader—least of all Chernenko and Brezhnev—had ever disdained to use such "prompt books." They were like verbal crutches to them. In the last years of his rule, Brezhnev was simply unable to put together coherently even a few words on his own without referring to talking points. In sharp contrast to him, throughout the entire conversation Gorbachev would not even open the folder with the papers.

The moment the doors closed, he briskly plunged into a conversation. Having paid a glowing tribute to the nonaligned movement in general and to Mugabe in particular, both as its chairman and as the prime minister of Zimbabwe, he then turned the floor over to his visitor. Since Mugabe did not have an interpreter, I had to interpret both ways—from Russian into English and from English into Russian. Fortunately, he spoke slowly, although in a soft voice.

He spoke for over an hour about several topics, including the importance he attached to a promised Soviet sale of a squadron of the latest MiG-29 fighter jets to his country and the situation in South Africa, which he described as "ripe for a revolution." Mugabe said he was ready and willing to "give it a push" by providing more military thrust. Nothing short of an armed struggle would overwhelm the 250,000-strong South African army and topple the Pretoria regime, he declared with conviction. All through Mugabe's lengthy exposition Gorbachev listened carefully, occasionally making notes in his small notebook.

After Mugabe finished, Gorbachev literally sprang into action. He spoke forcefully, if not always eloquently, frequently gesticulating and chopping the air karate style. Sometimes his remarks became somewhat rambling and disjointed, and then, on top of having to interpret and take notes, I was compelled to do some editing "on the run," so to speak. But overall, I must say his performance was very impressive. He was a veritable powerhouse of energy and dynamism. What a contrast to Brezhnev!

Responding to Mugabe's insistent plea for speedy deliveries of MiG-29s, Gorbachev assured him that the Soviet leadership adhered to its fundamental policy of supporting the frontline states in every way, including militarily. The Soviet Union, he said, was making its contribution to the strengthening of the [Marxist] regimes in Mozambique, Angola, Ethiopia, and in other countries. Analyzing the situation in Southern Africa, he said, "We see that the United States and Western countries have a stake in African affairs in general and in the South in particular. Therefore, they need the apartheid regime there as a support base to preserve their positions in Africa so as to continue exploiting the continent in the interest of their metropolises."

His views did not seem to differ much from those of his predecessors. Gorbachev lambasted "Western imperialist countries" for continuing "to use developing nations as a raw-materials appendage to support the high living standards of their people."

Then he turned to disarmament matters, and it was immediately clear that this subject was uppermost on his mind. What he said was rather curious in light of the subsequent evolution of his views:

"I, for one, Comrade Mugabe, appreciate especially highly the fact that the nonaligned movement now has a much better understanding of the relationship between disarmament and development. Really, if we halt the arms race and proceed with disarmament, we'll have enough resources to help the developing countries in solving many problems, especially those that are most pressing. . . . There is currently a growing trend in the world in favor of détente, cooperation, and disarmament. In this connection, it should be pointed out that the forces of reaction and the ruling circles of imperialist countries are trying to prevent this trend. They feel more comfortable with confrontation because then they find it easier to hold on to their positions that can help the imperialists achieve their goals. They fear any improvement in the situation, as this will lead to intensified struggle for independence of all peoples, and this, in turn, will undermine the basis for imperialist activities. . . .

"Nevertheless, there *are* factors that make it possible to take an optimistic view of the prospects for solving this problem, including the question of disarmament. I am talking first of all about the mighty socialist camp with its vast defense, economic, and moral potential. Secondly, the expanding forces of the nonaligned movement. And thirdly, the processes in capitalist countries themselves, where social conflicts are on the rise and the economic situation is getting worse, and where a reduction in military spending and reallocation of the funds thus released to meet the social needs are part of the agenda.

"In a word, the foreign policy of the Soviet Union in questions of disarmament and relations with other socialist countries, the active position of the nonaligned movement, and the public sentiment in Western countries are producing results and restraining the actions of these circles. Still, they have the maneuverability and react to events accordingly. This must be taken into account. And so, an increasing pressure has to be brought to bear on them. This is the essence of our philosophy."

This kind of rhetoric was odd and perplexing coming from the chief architect of what was proclaimed as the new thinking in foreign policy, the leader whose breathtaking proposals in Reykjavík eight months earlier had taken the world by surprise. There, on October 11–12, 1986, at a summit conference with President Ronald Reagan, he had called for total elimination of all nuclear weapons to achieve a nuclear-free world before the end of the century. Now, with Mugabe, he seemed to be quoting chapter and verse from the famous Stalinist propaganda "Short Course of the History of the CPSU." I had heard exactly the same kind of anti-imperialist rhetoric from Brezhnev in this very room eight years earlier, and I had even had to interpret it. I was bewildered and confused.

At that summit in Reykjavík, Gorbachev had told Reagan that no treaty cutting long-range nuclear arms by 50 percent was possible unless the United States abandoned its cherished Strategic Defense Initiative—SDI, or "Star Wars," as its critics labeled it—a program to develop an antiballistic-missile system with space-based components. Gorbachev remained adamant, as his predecessors had been, that all nuclear arms reduction issues must be linked to the abandonment of SDI. Reagan refused to accept the linkage and wanted to negotiate arms cuts while continuing to pursue SDI.

The general secretary continued, "To be more specific, we call on the United States and the West to develop the process started in Reykjavík. We favor radical reductions in strategic offensive arms, provided that the ABM Treaty is preserved and an arms race is prevented from outer space. But the main obstacle is that the United States believes that it has left us behind technologically and is now in a position to achieve military superiority via outer space. This is the principal obstacle in the way of reducing strategic arms.

"So we ask ourselves the legitimate question: If we radically reduce and subsequently eliminate nuclear weapons on earth, why then begin an arms race in outer space with its unforeseen consequences? If the United States continues to press ahead with it, this will mean that they don't want disarmament. . . . They are now doing some pretty fancy footwork [*pletut kruzheva*, he said], although they find themselves in a quandary, because they have demonstrated that they are not being serious about disarmament. It was a bluff! We have shown it to the whole world for what it is. Still, we hope that progress in this direction is possible, and we'll do everything we can to bring it about. We are ready to move across the entire disarmament board, including in the field of chemical and conventional arms. There's a great deal that can be said about what we have done. But no real steps have been taken by the West. They are anxious to save face before the public in these circumstances. So the situation is not that simple."

I thought the meeting was about to end, but the expression of Mugabe's face showed he had something else on his mind. After a moment's hesitation, he said, "Tomorrow, I will be meeting with Margaret Thatcher in London. How did you find her on disarmament issues?"

Gorbachev and Thatcher had last met here in Moscow just a few months before, in March, and had had a heated discussion, particularly on nuclear weapons. Their positions on the issue were diametrically opposite. Gorbachev replied to Mugabe's question, "As far as her position on disarmament issues is concerned, first, she has elements of realism. She understands that the arms race must be halted. She realizes that mountains of weapons have been piled up in the world and that everything must be done to avert military confrontation and to develop political dialogue. She wants to see a successful completion of the Geneva [START] talks. This is good. But on the other hand, nuclear weapons for Thatcher are a means of ensuring peace. She stressed this in Moscow so much so that we were amazed to see such attachment to nuclear arms. Third, Britain will continue to develop and improve its nuclear weapons. Fourth, she has numerous reservations regarding the ways of starting disarmament and advancing it. Moreover, Thatcher's response to the Soviet Union's proposal to abolish nuclear arms by the year 2000 is to say that it is a utopia. Such is the political portrait of Thatcher. . . . Such is the real British policy and especially the position of Thatcher."

As Gorbachev said this, Mugabe tapped his fingers on the table. His secretary-wife was furiously scribbling in her pad Gorbachev's remarks through my translation. After a brief pause, Gorbachev continued, "She believes that as the positions of the American president and Chancellor Kohl of the FRG become weaker, Britain must take over to lead the Western world. She has an anti-Soviet mind-set. . . . She is the vanguard of imperialist policies and a staunch hard-liner who believes that capitalism is the supreme achievement of human civilization. What she has embraced as the basis for her government's foreign policy is actually the philosophy proclaimed by Churchill forty years ago in his Fulton speech, and also by Truman.

"But forty years have passed since, and the world has radically changed. The train has left the station. One should see the world as it is—Western countries, socialist countries, countries that accelerate their development, and the nonaligned movement. They comprise great masses of people who follow their own independent path. This is something to be reckoned with. Otherwise, one may lose one's way in foreign policy. We had a heated discussion all the time."

"She is a difficult woman," Mugabe interjected.

"On the other hand," Gorbachev summed up, "she is straightforward. She says what she thinks. She does not mince her words. She has a dislike for diplomatic fog."

I found Gorbachev's political portrait of the British prime minister curiously unflattering, if for no other reason than her own assessment of him as "a man we can do business with." His remarks seemed to belie her assessment. On the other hand, he never once derogated her as the "Iron Lady," as Soviet newspapers so often did, and spoke of her in respectful tones.

With this exchange the meeting was over. After Gorbachev escorted Mugabe to the door and they said their final good-byes, he turned to me, took my hand in both of his, warmly shook it, and said simply, "Thank you very much for a job well done."

I had miscalculated: instead of a one-hour session, as planned originally, or two hours, as I had assumed, it had lasted exactly three hours and three minutes. I was glad I had brought two extra notepads with me. Gorbachev had been so carried away by the discussion that he had all but forgotten about a reception where the delegates to the women's congress had been waiting for him for over an hour. His total immersion in whatever he was doing at the moment was an interesting trait that I found endearing.

Toward the end of the meeting I was physically and mentally

exhausted, even though I got my second wind sometime after the second hour of nonstop work. The fingers on my right hand were totally numb from the three hours of uninterrupted furious note-taking. Gorbachev's speech was pretty straightforward, except that at one point, blaming the Western countries for being reluctant to go ahead with disarmament, he threw me a curve when he said *ony pletut kruzheva*. Translated literally, the phrase means "they are weaving elaborate lace." But such literal translation would not have thrown light on the real meaning of Gorbachev's words, and besides, he had coined the phrase himself— I have never heard any such metaphor in Russian either before or since. On the spur of the moment I understood it then to mean "they are now doing some pretty fancy footwork," and translated accordingly. The dictionary later confirmed that my translation was politically correct.

I think I would be remiss in my professional duty as an interpreter if I did not say a bit about Mikhail Sergeyevich Gorbachev's language for it is part and parcel of his personality. The world may have forgotten it, but in the now rapidly receding past, before Gorbachev's time, the language, as spoken by the previous general secretaries of the Soviet Communist Party, and Brezhnev in particular, was a mockery of Russian. As a rule, they never spoke in public extemporaneously, but always read from a piece of paper that they would invariably pull out of their breast pocket whenever the occasion demanded. Thus the senescent Leonid Brezhnev, toward the end of his life (and career as general secretary), became a virtual hostage to texts as they were written for him by his numerous aides. This generated quite a few political jokes, one of which captured his inability to say even a few words or phrases without consulting a text. Brezhnev meets Margaret Thatcher at the airport and reads the welcoming remarks from a piece of paper: "Dear and deeply respected Mrs. Indira Gandhi!" "Leonid Ilyich," his aide whispers into his ear, "this is Margaret Thatcher.!" "Dear and deeply respected Mrs. Indira Gandhi!" repeats the general secretary, mumbling and readjusting his spectacles. In despair, the aide again attempts to correct Brezhnev. "I know myself that this is Thatcher," he says, "but it's written here in the text, 'Indira Gandhi.'" The conspicuous exception was Khrushchev, of course; but his impromptu remarks invariably gave headaches to his stenographers and interpreters, who were expected to make sense of them and render them in coherent form.

But when, in 1985, the Russians suddenly heard normal Russian vernacular spoken by the new man in the Kremlin, Gorbachev, they could hardly believe it was for real. His animated language, devoid of clichés, was spoken with a lively intonation, natural slips of the tongue, repetitions, and yes, even mistakes. In a word, he revived Khrushchev's traditions of speaking extemporaneously, if not so colorfully. For the second time in my generation, a top Soviet public official's language was capable of expressing joy or frustration, interest or resentment, or other human emotions.

With the advent of Gorbachev's *glasnost* and the *human factor*, the dam broke. At first, no one but his interpreters noticed when he put the wrong stress in some words. We, his interpreters, concerned as we always were with providing as precise and accurate a translation of his locutions and words as we were capable of, even thought up a joke among ourselves that when M.S. (i.e., Mikhail Sergeyevich) says, "NAchat' protsess" (to begin the process), stressing the first syllable instead of the last, as it should be in Russian, we, too, should say in English, "BEgin the process," also accenting the first syllable. The idea was that stressing thus the wrong syllable in English would accurately convey this peculiarity of Gorbachev's speech and its flavor. Never mind that it sounded like the name of the former prime minister of Israel. It was only a joke, of course, but we enjoyed telling it to one another and to our friends—something we could never ever have contemplated doing in the old, pre-Gorbachev days.

Naturally, any off-the-cuff speech has its fair share of slips of the tongue or awkward turns of phrase. A few of Gorbachev's favorite locutions were *nam podbrasivayut* (literally, to toss up, throw up, or place something surreptitiously)—without specifying the object but apparently meaning "to insinuate" or "to spring something on someone"; *davaite opredelimsya* (literally, let us define ourselves), i.e., "let's get something clear"; *seichas obmenyaemsya* (we are going to exchange now)—without specifying the object of exchange, but meaning "we are going to exchange views now"; *nado pribavit* (literally, we have to add)— again, without specifying what it was exactly that had be added, but obviously meaning "we have to step up our efforts" or "work harder"; *podvizhki* (slight shifts, i.e., adjustments in one's position or policy); *raschistit' zavaly* (to clear away the obstruction or barriers); *pozitiv* (the gains, the accomplishments, or the credit side of something); *vyiti na soglasheniye* (to reach agreement); *protsess poshel* (the process has started); and so on and so forth.

The locutions cited above are not immediately translatable into adequate English. If their meaning was to be made clear to the English-speaking listener, they had to be first grasped, mentally edited, and only then translated. Many of them are characteristic of the speech of people from the southern regions of Russia, as is Gorbachev. He is truly a man of the people with his roots deep in the Stavropol region. Toward the end of his presidency, however, his speech would become noticeably more sophisticated and polished. Like his political views, his speech and language would undergo a remarkable evolution.

During that three-hour meeting with Mugabe, I was also exposed, for the first time, to Gorbachev's body language. I must say it was lively and expressive. His gestures were natural, spontaneous, and frequently involuntary. They expressed vexation, disappointment, bewilderment, anguish, but more often than not they conveyed the desire to persuade, to prevail, or to insist on having it one's own way. He liked to emphasize a point by tapping rhythmically with the edge of his hand. Sometimes he would resort to finger-pointing or spreading his arms wide in a gesture of helplessness. He could be provoked, but he could control himself (for example, the early Gorbachev was easily provoked into anger whenever Reagan or Shultz raised the subject of human rights). He was good at atmospherics and very different from the other Soviet leaders I had met in my professional career.

And, he was a great challenge for us, his interpreters.

Still, I came away from that first meeting with mixed feelings. On a personal level, I liked the new general secretary very much. He seemed to be an approachable leader, one with whom I felt at ease. But listening to what he had to say to Mugabe about Soviet foreign-policy philosophy, I could not shake off the impression that he was doctrinaire in his views when he was out of the range of TV cameras. He seemed to be still anchored in the past, the two years of *perestroika* notwithstanding. Nonetheless, it was a useful reference point against which to compare the subsequent evolution of his thinking and conduct.

That first meeting with Gorbachev also reinforced my conviction that he himself was very good at what he elegantly called "weaving elaborate lace."

CHAPTER TWO

TRUST-BUT-VERIFY SUMMIT

Gorbachev-Reagan Washington Summit, 1987

WASHINGTON, D.C. NOVEMBER 29, 1987, SUNDAY MORNING.

I was in Washington, D.C., a full week before Gorbachev was to arrive there for a summit with President Reagan. I had been assigned to interpret for Foreign Minister Shevardnadze throughout the summit, but I was in Washington early to help break down language barriers between the Soviet and American teams involved in the extraordinary, vast summit preparations. In the midst of the frenzied activities it was interesting to note that this summit almost didn't happen.

When Reagan and Gorbachev met in Reykjavík in October 1986, they were to set a date for a full-scale Washington summit, but the Reykjavík meeting ended at such a standoff over SDI that none was set. Then in September 1987 when Shevardnadze was in Washington, he unexpectedly asked for a private meeting with Secretary of State Shultz. I was their interpreter for it. Sitting on a soft couch at a coffee table in Shultz's office, Shevardnadze unveiled a surprise. He said for the first time ever that all Soviet troops were going to get out of Afghanistan. The troops had been there since Christmas 1979 and had been a hindrance to improved Soviet-U.S. relations ever since. The earnest tone of Shevardnadze's confidential disclosure, the twelve-month schedule for Soviet troop withdrawal that he outlined, and the good and close relationship between the two ministers must have convinced Shultz that the Soviet foreign minister meant business. Apparently in deference to Shevardnadze's request to keep it confidential for the time being, Shultz said nothing publicly about this disclosure, but Moscow's decision to get out of Afghanistan was among its most important of the Gorbachev era and clearly had a powerful impact on the United States, to say nothing of the major repercussions it had inside the Soviet Union itself.

The other important subject Shevardnadze and Shultz discussed in Washington was the INF treaty concerning the two nations' intermediate-range and shorter-range nuclear missiles. (INF stands for intermediate-range nuclear force.) These were missiles with a range of 500 to 5,500 kilometers. The U.S. missiles were based in Western Europe and targeted on the Soviet Union. The Soviet missiles were based inside the USSR and in Eastern Europe (Czechoslovakia and East Germany) and targeted on Western Europe. Negotiations to eliminate these missiles had been going on in Geneva since 1981, three years after the USSR first began to deploy its SS-20 missiles. In 1983, the U.S. deployed Pershing-2 missiles in Western Europe, and in retaliation the Soviets walked away from the negotiating table in Geneva. The world held its breath. Thankfully, in January 1985 talks resumed. The talks, however, might have gone on indefinitely and inconclusively, or even stopped altogether, had it not been for the new leader of the Soviet Union, Gorbachev, and his closest associates in *perestroika*, who introduced new thinking in foreign policy and manifested sufficient political will to conclude the treaty in question.

Now after six years of incredibly intense and difficult negotiations the text of the treaty was nearly complete. Under its terms the Soviet Union was to destroy more missiles than the United States and much more in terms of warheads on those missiles. The Soviet Union agreed to this seemingly unequal deal because Gorbachev reasoned that the end result would be equal both to the USSR and the United States: no INF missiles.

After three days of intensive talks and discussions, Shultz and Shevardnadze announced "agreement in principle to conclude a treaty" eliminating all short-range and intermediate-range missiles. It was also announced that to sign the INF treaty and to discuss the full range of issues in the relationship between the two countries, Reagan and Gorbachev would meet in Washington "in the fall." All in all, it was a rather successful and productive session, although no specific date was set as yet for the full-scale summit. In fact, the summit dates, December 7–10, were not announced until near the end of Ocotber. The delay was caused by strong doubts in Moscow about the wisdom of doing business with the Reagan administration, which, doubters said, did not show any signs of being willing to accommodate them on SDI. Even most of Gorbachev's closest advisers were opposed to a full-scale summit in Washington at this time.

As a matter of fact, Gorbachev himself was assailed with doubts.

When Shultz came to Moscow on the twenty-third of October to discuss the dates for the Washington summit, Gorbachev told him there would be no summit until Reagan renounced the SDI program and that the INF treaty alone was not a good enough justification to hold the summit. But right after Shultz left the Kremlin, Gorbachev convened a meeting of his advisers. His inner circle included Foreign Minister Eduard Shevardnadze, Chief of General Staff Marshal Sergei Akhromeyev, Politburo member Alexandr Yakovlev, Deputy Foreign Minister Alexandr Bessmertnykh, Gorbachev's personal aide Anatoly Chernyaev, and others. Gorbachev wanted to hear what they had to say on the subject of the summit. Almost everyone present said that no business could or even should be done with the Americans as long as they insisted on carrying out SDI and that it would be wiser to wait until a new administration was installed in Washington to resume any serious dealings with the Americans. The only dissenting opinion was ventured by Chernyaev, a man of uncompromising principle. He said firmly and unequivocally that Gorbachev should not back out of the summit now only because Reagan was not ready to give up SDI. He said it made no sense to have spent so much time and effort to prepare the INF treaty and then retreat at the last moment and urged Gorbachev to reconsider.

The next day Gorbachev sent Shevardnadze to Washington with a personal letter for Reagan in which he proposed the summit begin on December 7. It was a courageous manifestation of personal goodwill by Gorbachev to act over the objections of his entourage. He knew that "the buck stopped with him," and he made a wise decision. But while he decoupled the issue of medium-range missiles and Star Wars, the linkage between a START treaty—having to do with long-range or strategic offensive nuclear arms, such as land-based missiles, nuclear-armed submarines and aircraft, capable of reaching in excess of 5,500 kilometers—and SDI remained.

And so, on October 30, Shevardnadze came to Washington again with a letter for Reagan, and that day a simultaneous announcement was made in Moscow and Washington that "President Reagan and General Secretary Gorbachev have agreed to meet in the United States beginning on December 7, 1987."

Since the end of World War II until 1987 there had been only fourteen summit meetings involving the leader of the Soviet Union and the president of the United States. This summit in Washington would be the fifteenth. Like previous Reagan-Gorbachev summits, it would cover the topics of human rights, regional issues, bilateral issues, and arms control. But on the issue of arms control the continued Soviet linkage of SDI and START would be a major hurdle to be resolved if any progress was to be made. This issue would keep the actors involved and the world audience on edge to the summit's end.

NOVEMBER 29, SUNDAY.

The Soviet summit delegation had the good fortune to be put up at the Madison Hotel. This five-star establishment was conveniently located on the corner of Fifteenth and M Streets just a few steps from the Soviet Embassy's chancellery. In this sumptuous sanctuary in the very heart of the American nation's capital, rooms offered such nice touches as heated towel racks and thick, white terry-cloth robes, and the public spaces were filled with deep-pile carpets, rosewood paneling, Czech crystal chandeliers, and period furniture. In the lobby, a Louis XV writing table sat near a Louis XVI desk, each gleaming with gold leaf and ornate woodwork.

Every room in the Madison had a well-stocked minibar containing all kinds of pretty miniature bottles of liquor, which the Soviets cleaned out in no time, either drinking them on the spot or stashing them in luggage to take back to Moscow as souvenirs. The liquor was included in the price of the room and the guests could freely help themselves to it. The Americans hardly had time to replace them before Chaplin (not Charlie, but the Soviet deputy foreign minister, "Comrade" Chaplin, in charge of logistic supplies) arrived from Moscow and, upon hearing the stories of hard-drinking Soviet guests, asked the hotel management to turn off the flow of free liquor. All the liquor in the minibars was replaced with fruit juices and mineral water. The drinking problem of the two-hundred-odd Soviet guests in the hotel was thus solved very simply—by means of the old tried-and-true Soviet command and administrative method.

The Mount Vernon Restaurant on the second floor of the hotel with its superb French-American cuisine was placed at the exclusive disposal of Soviet participants in the summit. No wonder that after trying their first meal at this truly excellent restaurant the Soviets started to joke about how much they enjoyed "living under communism, American style." The scene at the hotel reminded me of the classic Greta Garbo movie of the late 1930s *Ninotchka*, in which a group of Russian officials learn to love capitalistic pleasures on an official trip to Paris. Just as in the movie, the Soviets were now seen happily being interviewed in the plush, tapestried surroundings of the hotel, and feted, wined, and dined at its restaurants. What a remarkable transformation! They did not seem at all like the dour and dowdy officials they were back home.

I decided to check out for myself if "living under communism, American style" was really what it was made out to be. Well, I was not disappointed. The splendid smorgasbord buffet-style service was sufficient proof that America had indeed reached a stage in its development that fit the description of what communism was supposed to be, as touted by Nikita Khrushchev some thirty years earlier, in his famous "kitchen debate" with Vice President Nixon. Like most of my compatriots, I remember very well to this day how the Soviet premier had then boasted that the USSR would "catch up with and surpass America in material abundance by the year 1980." Well, it was now 1987 and that goal was not anywhere near in sight, quite the contrary. The sad fact was that living standards in the Soviet Union continued to decline despite the *perestroika* initiated by Gorbachev while America enjoyed an unprecedented prosperity under Reagan. This brought to mind the joke about Khrushchev that had made the rounds in Moscow a good quarter of a century earlier:

When the Americans learned about Khrushchev's resignation, they decided to invite him to work for them. They said they would give him a nice job: to sit on top of the tallest skyscraper and wait for the decline of capitalism. To spite them, Brezhnev, who had ousted Khrushchev, immediately made a counteroffer for him to stay in Moscow, sit on top of the Ostankino TV tower (which was and still is the tallest structure in Moscow), and signal the advent of communism. "Accept our offer, Nikita Sergeyevich," the new general secretary tried to persuade him. "After all, their job is temporary and ours is permanent."

NOVEMBER 30, MONDAY.

The complexity and scale of preparations for the summit—security, scheduling, guest lists, etc.—were truly mind-boggling. The first Soviet advance team, made up exclusively of MFA (Soviet Ministry for Foreign Affairs) protocol people, headed by Deputy Chief of Protocol Igor Scherbakov, and KGB security officers, had arrived in Washington on November 10. The second, larger Soviet advance team arrived on November 27. Among them were communications experts with 350 pieces of equipment and Deputy Foreign Minister Chaplin, who was responsible for logistics, as I have mentioned, and the deputy chief of the KGB's Ninth Directorate, General Dokuchayev, who was in charge of security. The communications team put in more than two hundred additional phone lines, special microwave communications facilities on the roof of the hotel, and forty-two special *vertushka* telephones or scramblers. At this time the Soviet guest list already totaled more than three hundred people.

One of my first assignments came when I was asked to help interpret at a meeting between a certain Kirillov and a certain Mike concerning security arrangements. Kirillov turned out to be a Soviet KGB squad leader responsible for ensuring the security and safety of the top Soviet guests who would be staying in the Madison. As to Mike, he was a special agent of the Treasury Department's Secret Service, charged with the same mission from the American end. They wanted to discuss the security in the hotel, but were unable to communicate because neither spoke the other's language.

Five suites had been reserved in the Madison on the fifteenth floor for the highest-ranking members of Gorbachev's party, including one suite (just in case) for Gorbachev himself, who would be coming with his wife, that is, if he chose to stay there (in the end, he stayed at the Embassy). Kirillov insisted that two Soviet KGB security guards be posted at the door to each of the suites round the clock. The elevators were to be switched to a special mode of operation one day before the arrival of the top guests. The first one, nearer the entrance from the street, would be used to service floors one through seven; the second and third elevators would be servicing floors one through eight and would stop automatically to enable security men on the eighth floor to check the identity of anyone using them. Thereafter, those two elevators would travel all the way up to the fourteenth floor. If a principal guest wanted to go up to or down from his suite on the fifteenth floor, a special secret agent would "zip up the elevator there in no time, nonstop." The Americans were thorough, methodic, and pragmatic in their approach to security. "Ours" were a little excessive: some of their suggestions were extreme and were rejected as such by the Americans.

Furthermore, a magnetometer would be set up on the fourteenth floor and in the lobby to screen those entering the hotel. Teams of armed agents would be stationed in the lobby and also on the eighth and fourteenth floors. Sharpshooters with powerful binoculars and scope rifles would be posted on the roof twenty-four hours a day for the duration of the visit. On the night before the arrival of Gorbachev and his party, heavy concrete barriers would be set up in the center of the two streets around the hotel in such a way as to help speed traffic along, not disrupt or obstruct it. The hotel had two entrances to a parking garage under it, and agents would also be deployed there. A special control room, Suite 1524, would be reserved on the fifteenth floor for metropolitan police units and Treasury Department Secret Service agents, whose duties included protecting the president of the United States and foreign heads of state or government.

Altogether, Gorbachev would be protected and escorted by about a thousand Secret Service agents and policemen. The Secret Service also planned to weld shut every manhole along the route from Andrews Air Force Base, where Gorbachev would land, to the Soviet Embassy. The Americans were assigning several teams of ninety uniformed cops each to guard the short stretch—some nine hundred feet—between the Madison Hotel and the Soviet Embassy. In short, according to them, this stretch of land would be the safest place in town, and perhaps in the whole of America, for a few days.

As to the cost of all those security arrangements, suffice it to say that the special operation of the hotel elevators would alone cost $15,000.

DECEMBER 2, WEDNESDAY.

I had been busy with the not-so-exciting work of helping the security forces communicate when I had the chance to attend a decidedly glamorous cocktail party hosted by Mrs. Katharine Graham, the *Washington Post*'s owner and publisher. During the party, prodded by Bob Woodward to tell him "a secret or two," one of the Soviet guests, Col. Gen. Nikolai Chervov, who was chief of the arms control directorate of the Soviet Armed Forces General Staff and a top arms control expert, intimated, in a seemingly casual manner, that the summit might reach a framework agreement on basic provisions of a future treaty on 50 percent reductions in strategic nuclear arms. As to the treaty itself, he said he thought that it could be signed as early as at the next summit in Moscow between Gorbachev and Reagan. I came away with the distinct impression that Gorbachev was perhaps ready to delink a START treaty from the SDI issue already at this summit in Washington. If that happened, it would be a major shift in the Soviet position.

DECEMBER 6, SUNDAY.

With the Gorbachevs due to arrive the next day, many final details were still to be taken care of. In the afternoon, I participated, in my capacity as designated chief interpreter, together with Igor Scherbakov, deputy chief of MFA protocol, in a meeting with our counterparts from the State Department and the White House. The meeting was held at a stately government mansion, 736 Lafayette Square, within sight of the White House. Since the world of high-level interpretation is small indeed, I knew all the other interpreters there, including Bill Hopkins, a State Department interpreter with whom I had worked in tandem several times before, both in Moscow and in Washington. Unlike most other American interpreters I know, Bill was not a native speaker of Russian. He had learned the language in college and spoke it fluently and idiomatically, albeit with a slight accent. He had an excellent memory, which enabled him to interpret without making detailed notes.

The other two principal American interpreters, Dimitry Zarechnyak and Peter Afanasenko, were bilinguals and had Russian backgrounds. I had collaborated with both of them, too. Carolyn Smith was assigned to interpret for Nancy Reagan in tandem with Oleg Krokholev, who was Raisa Gorbachev's Soviet interpreter. Carolyn was another brilliant example of an American who had a perfect command of Russian and spoke it almost without accent. She and I had worked together many months in a row for several years in the 1970s, at arms control talks in Geneva.

Also in attendance was Ms. Stephanie R. van Reigersberg. She was the chief of interpretation at the Language Division of the State Department and had been instrumental in introducing simultaneous interpretation to the State Department and eventually to the White House. As far back as in 1981, when Reagan became president, she had convinced him to try simultaneous interpretation at one of his meetings with a Latin American leader. The president tried it and liked it, and ever since simultaneous interpretation had been used in the White House, but not in Soviet-American top-level meetings. Until now that is. According to her, it would be the first time this method would be used in a Soviet-U.S. summit meeting in the White House. Simultaneous interpretation was to be used even at what was known in diplomatic lingo as "four-eyes meetings," i.e., one-on-one or tête-à-tête meetings. I didn't need any convincing. I was an ardent partisan of simultaneous interpretation because it would not only save precious time, which could be better used for a more thorough discussion of the leaders' positions, but would also ensure the immediacy of communication between them. I welcomed the decision as "a small step for interpreters and a giant leap for simultaneous interpretation."

At the meeting we were given a list of "possible U.S. participants" in the summit talks. It was impressive: President Ronald Reagan, Vice President George Bush, Secretary of State George Shultz, Secretary of Defense Frank Carlucci, White House Chief of Staff Howard Baker, National Security Adviser to the President General Colin Powell, U.S. Ambassador to Moscow Jack Matlock. The list of their advisers included Chairman of the Joint Chiefs of Staff Admiral William Crowe, Assistant Secretary of State Rozanne Ridgway, Ambassador Max Kampelman, Ambassador Paul Nitze, and Ambassador cum General Edward Rowny.

Late at night the indefatigable and irrepressible American security agents, together with their Soviet counterparts from the KGB, did what they called "a bomb sweep" of the suites and rooms in the Madison, and they asked me once again to help with interpretation. Although it was close to midnight (they didn't want to attract unnecessary attention), I agreed. I had never seen a bomb sweep before. Before the sweep, one of the Secret Service agents told us a story from what must be the agents' folklore, concerning superpower one-upmanship. In advance of Nixon's 1974 trip to Moscow, it had been determined that Nixon would travel in Brezhnev's car when the two leaders left the airport. Security rules demanded that a Secret Service agent accompany the American president, but a KGB general informed the American lead agent that his place had been taken in the crowded car and that he would have to follow. The agent argued to no avail. Just as the car was about to pull away, the agent jumped into the front seat—and onto the general's lap. According to the storyteller, the general was "a little guy" and the agent "pretty big."

The sweep began with Suite 1531 on the fifteenth floor, the Presidential Suite, reserved for the Gorbachevs, even though it was now almost certain they would be staying at the Embassy. It had a white, fluffy wall-to-wall carpet and looked chic and impressive, fit for a king or a president, his wife, and perhaps a platoon of their bodyguards, who could easily lose themselves in the many rooms of the suite. The other principal suite, the Royal Suite, was reserved for Shevardnadze.

The two star "inspectors," Pinsky and Minsky, turned out to be beautiful, specially trained Alsatian police dogs, trained to sniff out bombs. The dog trainer explained that like any human being, but unlike his "comrade-in-sniffing," Inspector Pinsky had his foibles: he was a heavy beer drinker and would not do his duty unless he was reassured that he would be rewarded with beer afterward. So, before starting out, Pinsky was shown a can of Budweiser, and when he saw it, he wagged his tail in recognition. Now, he was ready and raring for action, satisfied that he would get his reward.

During the inspection of the five suites reserved for the Gorbachevs,

Shevardnadze, Yakovlev, Akhromeyev, and Dobrynin, the two dogs sniffed all the nooks and crannies as well as the closets, under the beds, and in any suspicious place where explosive devices could be hidden. The dogs were followed by an alert, young-looking, short, skinny albino with a crew cut and a military bearing. Like Pinsky and Minsky, he, too, sniffed things, looked under the lamp shades, then at the ceiling, closed his eyes, listened to something, sniffed again, and generally conducted himself in a most unusual manner. It was absolutely fascinating to watch him. I had never seen anything like it. I had been forewarned to keep completely silent so as not to disturb his concentration. Agent Mike, who was with the sweep party, whispered in my ear before we entered the first suite that the albino was a Pentagon guy who was a clairvoyant and a psychic with a sixth sense—he had the unique ability to sense explosive devices from a distance.

The KGB and the Secret Service also combed through the boiler room and the engineering room. The hotel's senior engineer noted that even as a soldier at Fort Knox he had never seen security as heavy and thorough as this. Fortunately, no bombs were discovered, but Inspector Pinsky still got his reward—a can of Bud. And so did I—five hours of sleep that night.

The eve of the summit was a time of promise but also caution within the Soviet Union and in its relations with the United States. In Moscow, there was disillusionment and frustration. By now, Gorbachev had been in power nearly two years, but the expectations he had raised were not being met. Since the summer of 1986 Gorbachev had turned sharply critical of the Communist Party bureaucracy—he was convinced even then that the political power centers of the existing Soviet system were standing in the way of the economic and social reform he espoused. This reform was essential if the country was to get out of the morass into which it had been plunged by decades of the economically inefficient Soviet partocracy. But Gorbachev was having a hard time convincing his Politburo colleagues (with the exception of Shevardnadze and Yakovlev, his two most staunch and loyal allies from the very beginning), the Communist Party leadership, and bureaucrats in general even to consider diluting their entrenched power and privileges. He had to tread lightly. He remembered the experience of Khrushchev, who was ultimately ousted and his reforms reversed when he stepped too hard on the Party's toes. If Gorbachev's intentions to reform the Soviet system were genuine, he had to be careful so as not to precipitate his own downfall. But then, there was no confidence that his reforms would go that far.

Still, change was in the offing. By 1987, the beginning of Gorbachev's third year as general secretary, the Soviet Union was in some respects already a fundamentally different nation. With the beginning of Gorbachev's policy of *glasnost* the people were exposed for the first time in many decades to much more realistic news and fewer official lies about their country's condition. This in itself was no mean accomplishment. At the Central Committee plenum that had convened in the Kremlin earlier that year, on January 27, 1987, Gorbachev for the first time used the word "crisis" to describe the country's social and economic predicament. Having failed at the 27th Party Congress in 1986 to persuade the Party apparat to support sweeping changes, Gorbachev at the January plenum shifted to democratization as a way of getting the bureaucrats to shape up or ship out. He did an unheard-of thing: he proposed introducing multiple candidacies and secret-ballot voting for local government and Party officials, including Party secretaries. "We need democracy like air," he stated. The attitude of the average citizen toward the reforms was still skeptical and lukewarm. Many thought that the much-talked-about changes were more propaganda than substance. A wicked joke was making the rounds in Moscow in those days that went like this: "*Segodnya perestroika, zavtra perestrelka*" (today *perestroika*, tomorrow a shoot-out). Little did anybody know then that the joke would become a grim reality some years later.

Abroad, nearly three years into the Gorbachev era, much of the world was still unsure what to make of the Soviet leader and the unmistakably different style he had brought to governing his country. That Gorbachev had captured international attention was without doubt. From London to Tokyo and from Washington to Harare, government officials and diplomats endlessly compared notes on their encounters with "new thinking" Gorbachev emissaries, swapping opinions on whether reforms inside the Soviet Union would expand and last, and what it all meant for long-term international stability. In many countries, and within many individuals, the Soviet leader and his policies provoked contradictory reactions. Hope, caution, curiosity, and cynicism were all expressed by a wide range of government officials, journalists, academics, and other opinion-makers. There was widespread reluctance around the world to make long-term predictions about where his new thinking would lead. However, much of the world agreed that the Soviet Union under Gorbachev behaved profoundly different, both at home and abroad.

In foreign policy, the powerful troika of Gorbachev, Shevardnadze, and Yakovlev had to decide how and when to pick up the threads of negotiations with the United States following the Reykjavík summit.

Gorbachev needed international prestige and international calm to help him overcome the resistance at home to the increasingly difficult changes he wanted to make. Gorbachev and his closest allies in the Politburo realized they had to do something to turn around the economy, which hovered on the brink of a crisis. That state of near collapse had been brought about primarily by the stupendous arms spending over the decades and the inefficient management of the economy. The true size of the military budget, however, was still carefully hidden from the public, 4.2 percent of the GNP being the official figure. Because of the multi-level falsification of the statistical data, the Soviet leadership itself had no clear idea of the real cost of its modern military hardware produced in the ambitious and ruinous arms race. Some years later more serious and realistic estimates of Soviet military spending would begin to appear, until it was finally admitted by some Soviet scientists that the real figure was as high as 30 percent of GNP, or even higher. That was just to maintain a rough parity with the United States in nuclear weapons and to surpass NATO considerably in quantities of chemical weapons, armored equipment, artillery, and some types of missiles. To build those missiles, the Soviet Union had spent, according to some Western calculations, a mind-boggling $600 billion. Some five thousand military plants continued to churn out mountains of weapons. No wonder the economy was on the point of bursting. By comparison, U.S. military spending amounted to 6.1 percent of its GNP, and even so some American experts thought it was too high.

With all this in mind, Gorbachev asked Shevardnadze to undertake a major review of Soviet policy toward the United States. The review was launched in Moscow in late 1986, in the wake of Reykjavík, to assess the advantages and disadvantages of continuing, among other things, to negotiate further with Reagan. As he had concluded in the meeting with his advisers, there was no real alternative to moving ahead. But while he decided to delink the issue of medium-range missiles, or INF, in Europe from SDI, the linkage between SDI and the START treaty remained. The important thing, however, was that Gorbachev had begun shifting the emphasis from military power to political accords as the basis for Soviet security. He introduced, among other things, the concept of "reasonable defense sufficiency," according to which armaments should be reduced to a level necessary for strictly defensive purposes. Moreover, he said publicly that the side with the greatest number of weapons—and it was the Soviet Union—should make asymmetrical reductions to achieve meaningful cutbacks.

By mid-1987, Gorbachev had imposed or announced a number of

policies like this that cut against the grain of traditional military thinking. To this point, his relations with the career military had been tenuous. With the exception of Marshal Sergei Akhromeyev, chief of the Soviet Armed Forces General Staff, with whom he had forged a close relationship, the other members of the military high command had been slow to back the general secretary's policies. Some warned him that he was moving much too fast to change the strategic concepts of the USSR. Taking advantage of the bizarre episode where a young West German, Mathias Rust, landed a single-engine airplane in Red Square in May of 1987, Gorbachev shook up the high command, replacing many top military officials. He appointed Dmitryi Yazov, an obscure general from the Soviet Far Eastern Military District, as the new minister of defense, in the belief, mistaken as it would turn out, that Yazov would support him in all of his new undertakings. Also, after the mid-1987 military shake-up, the Soviet Union produced increasingly promising proposals for on-site inspections of missile installations and missile-manufacturing plants. In fact, Gorbachev's proposals went so far that by late 1987 even U.S. officials began to resist some of those proposals when they realized the extent of Soviet access to U.S. military sites that would be required.

In the meantime, the possibility of doing business with Moscow was widely viewed by political commentators as a lifesaver for Reagan, who was being besieged from all sides in the most serious political scandal of his administration—the Iran-contra affair. By Soviet calculations, delaying arms control decisions until a new president was elected would mean waiting not only for his inauguration in January of 1989 but for new policies to be formed, a process that might put off serious talks until 1990. For Gorbachev, the arms control treaty that was to be signed on Tuesday, December 8, would be his first dramatic international accomplishment after more than two years in office.

DECEMBER 7, MONDAY. DAY ONE.

So the Big Day, Day One of the first full-scale Soviet-American summit since Gorbachev took office, had finally arrived. Gorbachev and his entourage were to land at Andrews Air Force Base at 4:40 P.M. Washington time. At 2:30 P.M. I went down to the hotel's lobby and found it literally teeming with people, mostly security agents communicating with one another through all manner of walkie-talkies and tiny earphones. Washington old-timers, that is to say the hotel staff, said they had never seen such a massive presence of Soviet KGB men and American Secret

Service agents and police in their capital. They did not complain, though. They felt they were about to witness history. I went out into the street and could not recognize it. The hotel had been surrounded overnight with heavy concrete barricades, impregnable even to tanks, and looked like a besieged fortress.

At 2:35 P.M., I got into car 42 together with two Soviet protocol officers, and some thirty minutes later we reached Andrews Air Force Base. It was warm for an early December day—sixty degrees Fahrenheit. At the entrance gate Soviet and American security agents stopped the car to check its special ID number displayed in the front window, and a couple of minutes later we were inside the modestly-appointed VIP Lounge building. Some ninety minutes still remained before Gorbachev's arrival, and gradually the lounge began to fill with people.

Outside, on the tarmac, about three hundred feet from the front of the arrivals building, was a long platform made up of several specially designed trucks. The platform held hundreds of TV, movie, and photo cameras and powerful klieg lights. A long red carpet runner extended from the platform to a ramp about a hundred feet away. Hundreds of reporters on the platform were already jostling for the best spot. As the time of arrival neared, I could feel a growing excitement in the air. Vladimir Chernishev, chief of Soviet state protocol, sought me out to confirm that I was to be attached to Foreign Minister Eduard Shevardnadze "at all times and never leave him alone in public." He said the minister knew I would be his interpreter and expected me to join him the moment he stepped off that plane with Gorbachev.

Shortly, a tiny dot appeared in the darkening skies; it rapidly grew into what resembled a bird, which soon assumed the outline of a plane. At 4:40, on the nose, the plane touched down and immediately began to taxi up to the ramp at the end of the red welcoming mat. With no special lettering or seal on its fuselage—in contrast to the U.S. presidential seal on Air Force One—the blue and white Aeroflot IL-62M jetliner had nothing to distinguish it from any other passenger plane, other than the sign on its tail "CCCP-B6540." It brought the Gorbachevs and a handful of top-rank *amerikanisti*, or Soviet experts on America, such as Yakovlev, Dobrynin—the former venerable ambassador in Washington—and others. Three more airplanes landed soon thereafter. They carried a large group of more *amerikanisti* of lesser rank and more KGB security agents. And then a fifth plane flew in as a backup aircraft for the general secretary.

After Gorbachev's plane came to a complete stop, Yuri Dubinin, the current Soviet ambassador to the United States, and Mrs. Selwa Roosevelt, White House chief of protocol, rushed up the ramp and disappeared inside the plane. A few seconds later Gorbachev, followed by his wife, Raisa Maximovna, emerged to a tumultuous welcome from the crowd on the tarmac. Wearing a gray overcoat with a scarf and a gray fedora, Gorbachev, arm in arm with Raisa Maximovna, slowly descended the steps of the aircraft ramp to the red carpet. He looked alert and cheerful, even though it was almost one o'clock in the morning Moscow time and he had just crossed eight time zones. They were greeted first by Secretary of State Shultz who was chairman of the welcoming committee. Then, a young girl selected from the Soviet Embassy school in Washington and various officials presented them with the obligatory bouquets of flowers.

Gorbachev was followed down the ramp by Shevardnadze, Yakovlev and Dobrynin. The latter had spent twenty-four years in Washington as Soviet ambassador and dean of the diplomatic corps; he was now Gorbachev's adviser. All three were without their wives.

Shultz had greeted the Gorbachevs on the tarmac by saying simply, "Welcome to the United States of America. We are delighted to have you here." Gorbachev, wearing spectacles, stepped up to the microphone. He first waited for Shultz to finish his brief welcoming remarks, then began mostly ad-libbing, although he held prepared remarks in his hand. As he spoke, I moved closer to where Shevardnadze stood, right next to Gorbachev. I realized that I was following instructions a bit too literally, but I knew from my previous experience that the interpreter had to stay next to his principal at all times unless, of course, he wanted to get separated from him.

Now that I was standing practically next to the Soviet first couple, I could get my first close look at Raisa Maximovna or simply Raisa, as the Americans called her. "The first Soviet first lady who had burnt her babushka"— that was how the American mass media had described her on the eve of the summit. The fifty-five-year-old wife of the General Secretary was stylishly outfitted in a knee-length silver-fox fur coat over a dark grey skirt and high-heeled boots. Her upswept red hair was uncovered.

While the foreign press zeroed in on any scrap of information about the Soviet first lady, much was still a mystery, especially to those inside the Soviet Union who had no access to the foreign press. Little about her was written in the Soviet Union itself where even a photograph of her beside her husband, which had recently appeared in some of the central newspapers, stirred up complaints that "she pushes herself forward too much." When asked why no personal information was available about the general secretary's wife, official Soviet spokesmen usually answered that Soviet society had no tradition of focusing on leaders' personal lives. But in actual fact, in the Soviet Union, as in the United States, there was tremendous interest in the personality of Gorbachev's wife. Indeed, many Soviets, especially young people, were eager for their top women to shed the stereotypical image set years ago by the plump, dowdy, babushka-wearing wife of Nikita Khrushchev during the Khrushchevs' visit to the United States in 1959. When a reporter asked Nina Khrushcheva what kind of influence she had over her spouse, she quickly responded, "None."

Not so with Raisa Maximovna Gorbacheva.

In the male-dominated society that the Soviet Union still was, Raisa Maximovna was an educated woman with a Ph.D., teaching until recently Marxism-Leninism at Moscow University and getting involved in her husband's work. During the television interview he had given to NBC's Tom Brokaw, which aired in America just one week before his arrival, Gorbachev admitted that he and his wife discussed everything, meaning that he consulted her on matters of state policy—something unheard of in Soviet society. But in Moscow's version of the interview, Brokaw's question to Gorbachev whether he discussed "national policies, political difficulties, and so on" with Raisa became *voprosi obschestvennoi zhizni* or "problems of public (or social) life." That deliberate change in translation was made to appease Soviet critics of their leader's unusually visible wife. Not since the last Russian czar, Nikolai II, had any Soviet leader been known to lend his ear to his wife's opinions and advice. Until now, that is.

The latest sign that her visible role was causing rumbling in the Kremlin was the recent demotion (in October) of Moscow Party chief Boris Yeltsin. A strong rumor was making the rounds in Moscow that Yeltsin had criticized, among other things, Gorbachev's wife for being present at all high party meetings and for appearing constantly on television. Raisa Maximovna herself denied any self-aggrandizement. She said that she acted naturally and did not exaggerate her role in any way—she was "only the wife of the general secretary, not a political creature, and a doctor of philosophy," and she had "[her] own interests and [her] own wishes." Yet the new general secretary often referred to her affectionately as "my general." In any case, historically speaking, behind every successful man there is always a woman.

In this regard, Raisa Maximovna had a close affinity with Nancy Reagan, who was said to have a not inconsiderable influence in the White House. In other ways, though, the two first ladies were poles apart. It was said that when—during their first meeting in Geneva, in 1985—Nancy Reagan wanted to chat about their children, Raisa Gorbacheva wanted to discuss Marxist theory. They had not met at the previous year's summit in Reykjavík—and that was a problem in itself. Nancy stayed home, thinking Raisa would, too. She didn't—and as a result had the spotlight all to herself.

Raisa Maximovna was said to have a taste for jewels, expensive perfume, and designer fashions. She was gaining increasing notoriety as a conspicuous consumer while on trips abroad. On her first two trips to Europe, for example, she was said to have delighted British and French capitalists—and scandalized the dour and dowdy proletarians back home—by "cruising, Imelda Marcos style," as some newspapers wrote, "through such luxury stores as Cartier, Pierre Cardin, and Yves Saint Laurent." Moreover, it was also intimated that in so doing, she used her American Express card. In London, it was said, she even canceled a visit to Karl Marx's grave to see the crown jewels in the Tower of London and buy diamond earrings at Cartier.

What the gullible Western public eager to hear such lurid stories did not know, however, was that most of them were either planted or grossly exaggerated by the KGB. In Moscow, I had heard that footage of her shopping excursions abroad had become a part of an underground video film made by some disgruntled elements within the KGB and circulated earlier that year in the Soviet Union. Their aim was to portray the Soviet first lady as extravagant and vain, and thereby to arouse antipathy among the Soviet people toward her and, through her, toward her husband, whose new policies were not to the liking of some in the KGB. The KGB was good at manipulating public opinion. In the meantime in Washington, such adventures, whether true or not, were fodder for jokes about Raisa: "Department stores are glad that Mikhail Gorbachev never leaves home without her" was one such joke. Another went something like this: "Nancy and Ron invited the Gorbachevs to their ranch to show them how the average capitalist lives, and the Gorbachevs invited the Reagans to Tiffany's to show them how the typical Marxist lives."

Raisa seemed destined for criticism regardless of what she did. In her trip to Paris in 1985 she had been criticized by the French for wearing the same outfit more than once. On the other hand, she raised eyebrows for changing outfits four times in one day when the French first couple—President and Mrs. Mitterrand—visited Moscow in July of 1987. Fashion became a focal point when the Soviet and American first ladies met at the Geneva summit in November 1985. Interest in the so-called Style Wars held its own against the Star Wars talks in which their husbands were engaged. The media outside the Soviet Union had dubbed Raisa "Red Little Star," "Bo Derek of the Steppes," "The Gucci Comrade," "Gorba the Sleek," "The Ambassadress of Charm," and other such flattering nicknames, including "Soviet Realism's Answer to Princess Diana."

Raisa Maximovna was such a personalty in her own right that she would pique anyone's curiosity. And now as she stood there on the tarmac next to her husband, right in front of me, all those stories came to mind and understandably I gave her more than a cursory glimpse. And what I saw was a thoroughly modern and intelligent woman of pleasing appearance, who conducted herself with dignity as any first lady should.

In the meantime, Gorbachev had finished his short remarks in Russian, and then, in friendly but forceful tones, he added that strategic arms would be at the center of his discussions with President Reagan and hoped that he would hear "new words" from the Americans about prospects for cutting long-range strategic weapons. He took the bull by the horns right away. As he finished his remarks, Secretary Shultz turned to him and said informally, "That was a good start." Replied Gorbachev, "The visit has begun, so let us hope. May God help us." That was an unusual thing for a leader of the world's largest atheist nation to say publicly. Later, Reagan would remark on Gorbachev's allusion to the Supreme Being, saying, "I have to believe that if he is talking to God, we ought to get along, because so am I."

After the brief welcoming ceremony, the Gorbachevs and their entourage climbed into sleek black armor-plated Zil limousines, flown in especially from Moscow, which were lined up on the tarmac in a long motorcade. Gorbachev's vehicle followed the two lead cars, then Shevardnadze's. Accordingly, I made my way through the thick crowd of Soviet and American officials and security agents and joined the foreign minister as he was about to get into his car. Shevardnadze's chief personal bodyguard, a short, solidly built Georgian by the name of Dima, held the door open for me in a welcoming gesture and I dived inside onto a jump seat, opposite Eduard Amvrosiyevich Shevardnadze and Selwa Roosevelt on the backseat. Mrs. Roosevelt had been tapped as the White House chief of protocol way back in 1981 by President Reagan himself, and now she was here to accompany the Soviet foreign minister during the ride to the Soviet Embassy. The foreign minister greeted me by saying, "And I was already beginning to think that I'd never be able to communicate with this charming lady." No sooner had I got in the car than the motorcade began to move.

It was an immense, impressive caravan—some fifty vehicles. Gorbachev's Zil was flanked by about a dozen police motorcycles and protected from behind by a Secret Service armor-plated pickup, actually a Ford station wagon with its tail part open showing the tense faces of Secret Service agents armed to the teeth with Uzi submachine guns, grenades, pistols, and other paraphernalia. All of them wore bulletproof vests. These people took their job seriously. I'd had a chat with some of them, and they all confirmed they would not hesitate for a second to use their weapons if necessary. The station wagon was followed by a Soviet armor-plated Zil limousine with *devyatchiki*—Soviet security agents from the KGB Ninth Directorate responsible for the safety of the general secretary wherever he went. The route had been cleared of traffic, and from time to time I heard the whirring of helicopters overhead. The scene may have been familiar to Washingtonians, what with hundreds of high-level officials visiting each year and motorcades zipping through their capital almost daily, but probably never before on this scale and with such pomp. After all, Gorbachev was a special visitor.

It was now quite dark. As the motorcade sped toward downtown, the loquacious Mrs. Roosevelt, ever a gracious hostess, did most of the talking. She fretted that it was already too dark for the general secretary "to see America," if only "out of the car window," if only "just a little slice of it." After all, "he's never been here before," she exclaimed with what seemed like genuine regret. It was too bad he didn't have enough time to see Washington, to say nothing of the rest of the country. It was so important to see a country through the eyes of its people. It helped to understand better their spirit. Hopefully, she concluded, on his next visit the general secretary would have time to travel around her country to get firsthand impressions. She was right, no doubt, but as I would see for myself, summiteers generally get to see few sights, if any. What with arms control negotiations in the morning, appearances before groups of exalted people in the afternoon, and state dinners at night, the Gorbachevs might never even see the real Washington.

Shevardnadze responded that he was sorry they could not "do any sight-seeing" now, but promised that next time Gorbachev would make it a point to visit other parts of the United States. He said Gorbachev expected President Reagan to come to Moscow next May on a return visit. He would make him this offer the next day. Generally, Shevardnadze did not seem disposed to keep up the small talk—he looked pensive and tired and responded basically in monosyllables. It was not surprising, for I knew from having observed him at close range so many times before that he wore himself down by working almost round the clock when necessary. He was always on an extremely tight and gruelling schedule. Most importantly, he was Gorbachev's most loyal supporter and fellow thinker, and that was an exhausting role. So now on the way to the Embassy only once did he smile and muster the energy to make a joke, when Selwa Roosevelt waxed enthusiastic about the Zil limousine, saying, "It is so spacious and comfortable inside." Said Shevardnadze, "I will give you this car, I will leave it to you, if you like it so much." It was a joke, of course,—the car was government property.

At one point, when we were already somewhere in downtown, I glimpsed a tall Trojan horse made of wood being wheeled around by some people. "The INF treaty is a Trojan horse," said the sign on its side. Another group of people held up the sign "Death to Communism." As we passed the Holiday Inn, though, I saw a different sign on its marquee, which proclaimed, "Welcome, Mr. Gorbachev, to the United States." Well, it was pluralism of opinion in action. Different people had different views, and they expressed them openly and without fear. There were coffins, flowers, black and red balloons. One lady carried a tattered umbrella with "Nuclear" painted on its front, apparently to symbolize what had become of America's nuclear umbrella. Another held up high the sign "I love Gorby." So many people, so many causes. They flashed by like a kaleidoscope as our motorcade bore down the streets toward the Soviet Embassy where the Gorbachevs would rest for tomorrow's big day at the White House.

December 8, Tuesday. Day Two.

At 9:20 A.M. I pinned to the lapel of my suit the coveted small blue security identification button with a red stripe running across its middle and took the elevator to the fifteenth floor of the hotel to meet my "charge," Foreign Minister Shevardnadze, at the Royal Suite, to accompany him to the White House for the official welcoming ceremony. The security buttons had been issued on the eve of the summit by the American Secret Service to all the Soviets who had to have access to the White House. The button had a magic effect on the four Soviet security officers who were guarding the suite entrance: they let me through without a question. Eduard Amvrosiyevich came out of the room at precisely 9:25, as per schedule; Yakovlev and Dobrynin caught up with us when we were already inside the elevator.

The minister was in a serious, solemn mood. He was reserved, silent, lost in his own thoughts. In contrast to him, the sixty-eight-year-old

Dobrynin was positively bubbling; he kept smiling and joking all the way. By nature, he was clearly an extrovert, and he conducted himself with utter self-confidence. For all his height and corpulence, he was surprisingly nimble. Unfortunately, when it came to speaking, his diction left much to be desired. Sometimes, when he got carried away, he would become incomprehensible, no matter whether he spoke in Russian or in English. Fortunately, most times he did not need an interpreter—his English was fluent enough, and he used it freely, without inhibition. When he bantered with Americans in English in the presence of Shevardnadze, he usually interpreted himself for the minister's benefit. That made my life a bit easier.

As for Yakovlev, my first impressions of him were mixed. He struck me as a rather dull and unimaginative apparatchik who used his position in the Party hierarchy to exaggerate his importance. Well, appearances are deceptive, as the adage has it. A year and a half later, when I would come to know him much better, acting as his interpreter during Gorbachev's visit to Britain, I would revise my opinion drastically. At that first encounter I didn't know, for instance, that he was the éminence gris of *perestroika*, the brain behind it and one of the principal architects of Gorbachev's effort to make Soviet society more open and democratic.

In fact, Yakovlev had been a closet liberal for a long time. He had been banished as ambassador to Canada by Brezhnev and did not resurface on the political scene until Gorbachev tapped him to be his adviser. He moved up rapidly in the Communist Party power structure under Gorbachev. In 1985 he became head of the Central Committee propaganda department. In January of 1987 he became a candidate member of the all-powerful ruling Politburo, and some five months later, in June of the same year, he was promoted to full Politburo status.

Shevardnadze's limousine was waiting at the exit from the garage, its rear door held open by the driver. I got in the car from the other side, and as I began to pull down the jump seat, the minister invited me to sit next to him. This democratic gesture that spoke volumes about the man did not surprise me. Whenever opportunity permitted, he would invite me to share the backseat, whether in Moscow or abroad. In contrast, during the fourteen years of my association with Gromyko, he never once asked me to sit next to him in his car, even when he was alone. Clearly, the new powerful troika, Gorbachev, Shevardnadze, and Yakovlev, had a different mind-set and treated their subordinates accordingly.

Selwa Roosevelt, who had joined us in the car at the Embassy gate, was elated. As we sped past the crowds of people gathered to watch the

Gorbachev motorcade, she drew the minister's attention to their sheer numbers, exclaiming that Washington had not seen so many people turn out to see a distinguished foreign visitor since the visit of Prince Charles, and even he hadn't drawn such large crowds as Gorbachev and his entourage. She observed that Americans were delighted to see Gorbachev "live and in person." They talked and wrote about him so much that his presence in Washington aroused enormous interest and curiosity. The people came out on the streets at their own volition, she continued, no one coerced them.

I don't know if Shevardnadze caught her drift. In the past, in the Soviet Union, the authorities usually required that people come out on the streets to welcome foreign VIPs, especially if they were from "fraternal socialist countries," to show their "love and solidarity" with them. Such practices had been discontinued under Gorbachev.

As our Zil approached the South-West Gate, I saw that both sides of the entrance to the grounds of the White House were lined with hundreds of American and Soviet security agents. This locus of power had probably never seen such an invasion of so many gun-toting KGB officers. The short space through which we drove was filled with dozens of black jeeps packed with SWAT teams, their Uzi submachine guns at the ready. I even spotted a heavy machine gun in one of the jeeps.

At the White House Diplomatic Entrance, I followed Shevardnadze out of the car, and we immediately found ourselves in the midst of a throng of people. The first U.S. official to greet Shevardnadze was Vice President Bush. I had not seen him for some fifteen years, since early in 1972 when he, as the U.S. permrep (permanent representative) to the United Nations, once sauntered into the interpreters' booths in Addis Ababa, where the U.N. Security Council was meeting for its first ever visiting session, to express his appreciation to us, the interpreters, for lending our "skill" and to slap us on the back in his signature gesture of friendship. As he greeted us now, I was struck by how little he had physically changed since then. He was the same easygoing and likable man with the same engaging smile and outgoing and friendly manners.

Next to greet Shevardnadze were Secretary Shultz and his wife, Helena. Then, two gentlemen, who introduced themselves to Shevardnadze as Jimmy Baker and Howard Baker. The former was secretary of the treasury and the latter a former senator who was now White House chief of staff. I observed that in contrast to Soviet high-ranking officials, Americans in prominent positions usually introduced themselves by name, not by rank, when they met you for the first time.

The ubiquitous Mrs. Roosevelt was always hovering nearby, making the introductions. Her main job as the administration's chief of proto-col was to ensure contact between the hosts and their guests, to help the latter feel at ease, to prompt them at the right moment, without seem-ing inopportune, to do what was expected of them by protocol. And she did it admirably. Now, after the first round of introductions, she gently guided Shevardnadze to a spot on the green lawn with his nameplate. It was to the right of the dais from which Reagan and Gorbachev would make their speeches. More nameplates fanned out on the grass: "Vice President and Mrs. Bush," "Secretary of State and Mrs. Shultz," and so on. A spot was also reserved for me between and slightly behind She-vardnadze and Bush. On the other side of the dais, across the green space of the lawn, I could see a group of senators and congressmen, among them the familiar faces of Bob Dole, Daniel Patrick Moynihan, Jim Wright, Alan Simpson, and Sam Nunn. There were more, of course, but their faces were not as familiar.

Among the Soviet guests farther down the line, I was greatly aston-ished to see Gen. Vladimir Kryuchkov, head of the KGB's First Chief Directorate, responsible for conducting KGB operations abroad. His presence here certainly did not go unnoticed by the Americans and raised a lot of eyebrows. It must have been the first time in the history of Soviet-American relations that somebody like this was officially present in the White House. Did Gorbachev have a special message to send by bringing him here?

At 9:59, President and Mrs. Reagan appeared in the doorway of the Diplomatic Entrance, he in an elegant black overcoat, she in a fur coat, even though it was sunny and warm. They were ready, along with some two thousand guests, to welcome "The General Secretary of the Com-munist Party of the Soviet Union and Mrs. Gorbachev," as was stated in the official program. At ten o'clock sharp, a long black bulletproof Zil, bedecked with Soviet and American flags, pulled up in front of the South Entrance, and the Gorbachevs emerged from the limousine. As always, he was followed closely on his heels by Medvedev, his chief bodyguard and personal aide-de-camp—a tall, lanky man with the rank of a KGB general.

When they were out of the car, Mrs. Roosevelt, who now stood next to the Reagans, formally presented the Gorbachevs to the president and his wife. In a brief but solemn moment, they exchanged their first hand-shakes on American soil. Then the dapper president began formally to introduce the Gorbachevs, first to Vice President and Barbara Bush, then to Secretary of State and Mrs. Shultz, and finally, to Chairman of Joint Chiefs of Staff Admiral and Mrs. Crowe. After the introductions,

Reagan invited Gorbacheva to mount the dais. In the meantime, Mrs. Reagan motioned Raisa Gorbacheva to join her at a designated spot at the side of the dais. The formal arrival ceremony on the South Lawn of the White House began. And the first full-scale Soviet-U.S. summit in fourteen years on American soil was on.

The first drama of the day was sharpened at its outset by the chemistry displayed between Reagan and Gorbachev. Looking at the two of them standing next to each other, I could not help recalling a bizarre episode in 1984 when President Reagan had made an offhand joke about bombing Russia. The remark, accidentally picked up by a microphone, reverberated loudly in the Soviet Union, where it was seized upon as more proof that the United States was led by "a madman bent on war." In those days Ronald Reagan was seen by the Soviets as a Hollywood cowboy stuck in the "procrustean bed of ossified anticommunism," a man whose speeches were "shameless lies from beginning to end," and whose "imperial" policies were likened to Hitler's. For average Soviets, the bombing joke was troubling: either it meant Reagan really was as aggressively hostile to the Soviet Union and as virulently anti-Soviet as Soviet propaganda had been saying, or it meant that the American president was irresponsible or none too clever and, therefore, not fit to govern his country. But during the years that followed, as Soviet-U.S. relations gradually improved under Gorbachev, that image had faded almost completely, and now in the Soviet popular mind Reagan was just an aging president approaching the end of his second term, whose policies were merely reactive and whose thinking was old school compared to that of the much younger Gorbachev, the new, dynamic leader in the Kremlin.

Now the two leaders stood next to each other before the whole world, ushering in a new era. They quickly established eye contact and what seemed to be a good rapport. As Reagan spoke from the dais, Gorbachev looked on, nodding slightly in acknowledgment, as though he understood English, which he didn't. Reagan for his part smiled through most of Gorbachev's remarks, although he, too, relied on interpretation. They stood shoulder to shoulder as the U.S. Army Band, the Third U.S. Infantry Fife and Drum Corps, and the U.S. Army Herald Trumpets— arrayed on the White House steps—provided a spirited full-honors arrival ceremony. "Ruffles and Flourishes" and the national anthems of both countries were played by a special military unit, Pershing's Own. Gorbachev was honored with a special twenty-one-gun salute.

The tableau on the South Lawn was extraordinary. Never before in the Reagan presidency had American soldiers been seen carrying Soviet flags, as well as American ones, along the driveway to welcome a foreign visitor. And the tiny, bright red Soviet flags were hoisted along with the Stars and Stripes by guests cheering the arrival of the Soviet leader, while outside the White House a larger Hammer and Sickle flew next to the Stars and Stripes—a sight that must have caused even normally blasé natives, to say nothing of the audiences back home, to marvel.

Despite the good chemistry between them in the first few minutes of his welcoming speech, Reagan made a point that Gorbachev's visit represented "a coming together not of allies, but of adversaries." But the word *adversaries* was translated into Russian as "competitors." Obviously aware of the potential fallout the direct translation of the word would have had on the Soviet audience, and perhaps wishing to play it safe, the American translator chose the fourth variant for translation of *adversary* as contained in the Galperin two-volume *Bolshoi English-Russian Dictionary*, i.e., *soperniki*. I whispered for Shevardnadze the correct translation of *adversaries* (*protivniki*, i.e., "adversaries" or "foes") and immediately regretted it, because I saw him wince as if in pain and become tense. After all, he, together with Gorbachev, Yakovlev, and a few other proponents of *perestroika*, was trying to demolish the "enemy" image, which was one of the legacies of the Cold War. I remembered very well how elated Shevardnadze was when he announced at his press conference at the end of the September Washington ministerial that final agreement had just been reached to go ahead with signing the INF treaty. His emotional voice then expressed great satisfaction, joy, and pride in the work that had finally yielded a tangible result after so many years of futile attempts.

Bush overheard my whispering to Shevardnadze and shifted from one foot to another, darting an embarrassed look at the two of us. It must have crossed his mind that the word *adversaries* did not sound endearing to the Soviet foreign minister. Then he exchanged meaningful glances with Shultz, who stood on Shevardnadze's right.

In the next phrase, though, to soften the impact of the previous sentence, Reagan added forcefully that the visit provided "an opportunity to move from confrontation to cooperation." Known as a lover of Russian sayings, Reagan did not disappoint his audience: "A poor peace is better than a bad quarrel," he remarked, calling for hard work and realism "to change that poor peace . . . and make it into a good one." "*Mir na nas smotrit*," said Reagan (the world is watching us). After Shevardnadze heard these words in Russian, he visibly relaxed, and Bush, too, looked relieved. Once more, Reagan proved, if proof was necessary, that he wasn't called the Great Communicator for nothing.

As expected, the translation of *adversaries* as "competitors" was used subsequently in Soviet official publications in an obvious attempt to soften the harsher impact of the word.

Gorbachev responded to Reagan's call by declaring that the Soviet people were prepared "to go all the way down . . . the road [to peace] with the sincerity and responsibility that befit a great and peaceful power."

At 10:20, after the exchange of speeches ended and the band struck up "The Stars and Stripes Forever," President and Mrs. Reagan invited General Secretary and Mrs. Gorbachev inside the White House through the Diplomatic Reception Room under the South Portico. Bush for his part invited Shevardnadze to ascend the outside staircase leading to the State Floor. When we got to the second floor, Bush explained, turning to me, that we were now in the Cross Hall and pointed to the marble floor. Chased in it were the major construction and renovation dates of the house. The indomitable Mrs. Roosevelt was already here, now directing people down the receiving line, which was beginning to form along the hall.

The president escorted Gorbachev into the Oval Office in the West Wing of the White House for their first meeting. We followed them inside this sanctum. My first impression was, how small, compared to Gorbachev's huge and cavernous Kremlin office! It struck me as being even smaller than it appeared when shown on television. Yet this room had been the president's locus of power since 1909 when it was built. The first thing Gorbachev did was to sign the guest book on the president's desk. Then Reagan presented him with a highly symbolic gift—a set of two solid gold cuff links emblazoned with the image of the prophet Isaiah beating swords into plowshares. Reagan said that the gift was a symbol of his hopes for arms control. Then the two leaders sat down on two white chairs by the fireplace for a photo opportunity, after which everyone else was ushered out, and they remained alone, with their interpreters. They talked together for nearly an hour.

As Gorbachev would later tell it to Shevardnadze at the Embassy, things were less friendly in that first private session in the Oval Office. Reagan confronted him with the issue of human rights and freedom of religion. He strongly urged him to allow not only increased Jewish emigration from the Soviet Union but religious freedom for those who remained behind. Gorbachev did not take well to the lecture, and according to him, at one point he told Reagan heatedly that they were not in a courtroom, that the president was not a prosecutor and that he himself was not a defendant: "I'm not on trial and you are not here to judge me." When Reagan criticized the Soviet restrictive emigration policies, Gorbachev responded by saying that the American authorities blocked would-be immigrants from Mexico. Retorted Reagan, "There's a big difference between wanting in and wanting out."

When the meeting was expanded to include Shevardnadze, Shultz, and others, and we joined the leaders later in the Oval Office, Gorbachev seemed highly displeased, if not downright angry. But he quickly cooled down and got control of himself. Reagan's cheeks were a bit flushed, but he kept his cool and even gave us a fleeting smile. Yet that little episode served to reveal Gorbachev's other side—a tough and doctrinaire power politician, ready to "give a rebuff," *dat'otpor,* to use the worn-out Soviet cliché, when he thought he was provoked. Obviously he could be forceful, combative, emotional, and tough, and he had apparently just demonstrated these attributes behind closed doors. He lived up to Gromyko's famous remark about his having "iron teeth." For all his sophistication and polish, he had not yet learned to react less explosively to criticism. That would come later.

After the morning meeting was over, Gorbachev, accompanied by Reagan, came outside to the lawn through a door in the Oval Office to get into his limousine. That afternoon he would return to the White House for the historic INF signing ceremony.

On arrival at the Embassy, Gorbachev had a private lunch with his closest top advisers—Shevardnadze, Yakovlev, Dobrynin, and Akhromeyev—and exchanged views on the first meeting with Reagan. I learned that Gorbachev and Reagan had agreed that two principal working groups would be formed to deal with major issues at the summit. One, to deal with arms control and strategic missiles, was to be cochaired by Amb. Paul Nitze, the chief U.S. arms control negotiator, and Marshal Akhromeyev. The other working group, on human rights and regional issues, was to be cochaired by Rozanne Ridgway, U.S. assistant secretary of state for European affairs, and Alexandr Bessmertnykh, Soviet deputy foreign minister.

After lunch, a bad dream that every interpreter dreads occurred: I missed my principal, and as a result I also nearly missed the historic INF treaty signing ceremony in the White House.

By mutual agreement with Shevardnadze, I was to join him after lunch on the fifteenth floor in his suite at the Madison to go together to the White House. Fifteen minutes before the agreed time, I was waiting for the elevator to take me to the fifteenth floor. I waited and waited and waited, but there was no elevator. When it finally arrived and I got out on the fifteenth floor, I was dismayed to learn from the security men that I had missed Shevardnadze by just a few seconds: he and his party were already down in the garage. Now I knew why the elevator took so long to arrive—it had been reserved for the principals. It was too late, however, to go down to the garage—the motorcade from the hotel had surely left by now. I rushed to the Embassy to join Gorbachev's motorcade, which, I knew, was to leave at 1:35 P.M. At 1:30, I was outside the Embassy gate where I found the motorcade of dozens of cars with their engines already revved up, ready to leave. They were waiting only for Gorbachev, who would appear any moment now. I had about three minutes in which to find a car to get a ride to the White House. To my consternation, however, I did not see a single familiar face to ask for a lift. I rushed around, scurrying from one car to another, but all the cars, both Soviet and American, were full.

I was still frantically looking for a car when Gorbachev came out from the Embassy and got into his limousine. Suddenly I spotted a gleaming black Mercedes with only the driver inside. It turned out to be Kamentsev's car (Kamentsev was Soviet deputy prime minister and a member of Gorbachev's entourage). He had failed to show up, and I decided to commandeer it. No sooner had I got inside than the caravan of cars was off, with sirens blaring and a motorcycle escort flanking the motorcade. I wiped the sweat off my brow.

When the motorcade stopped in front of the Diplomatic Entrance, I got out of the car and made a beeline for the entrance to catch up with Shevardnadze, who, I was told, was already inside. I could see the security getting mighty nervous at the sight of me rushing forward. Their reaction was to be expected: their hands instantly reached inside the bulging pockets of their coats. At that moment, in my mind's eye, I saw screaming headlines in tomorrow's papers, if I lived that long, that is: "Soviet Interpreter Mistakenly Gunned Down in the White House." God Almighty was merciful, however. Vladimir Chernishev, Gorbachev's chief of protocol, and an American protocol officer came to my rescue, like deus ex machina. They told the nervous security agents that I was all right, *"On nash"* ("he's one of ours," "he's our guy").

The two protocol men quickly whisked me off to the East Room on the second floor, which was already full of people invited to witness the historic signing of the INF treaty. As I walked in, I saw Shevardnadze sitting in the middle of the front row in front of the dais, with Raisa Gorbacheva, Nancy Reagan, George and Barbara Bush, George Shultz, and Jim Baker seated, in that order, on his right. Seated to his left were Dobrynin, Kamentsev (how he got there, I don't know), Akhromeyev, and Boldin (head of the General Department in the Central Committee), in that order. Luckily, a seat was reserved for me in the second row, behind and between Raisa Maximovna Gorbacheva and Shevardnadze. Shevardnadze turned to say he had missed me, and I explained what had happened. Imagine my surprise when he said he was sorry that he couldn't wait for me at the hotel and blamed the protocol. What a contrast with his predecessor!

Now I could relax. I paused for breath and shifted my gaze around the room. I recognized many people instantly: some of them I had met in person, the faces of others were familiar from the mass media. Behind me sat Paul Nitze, Kenneth Adelman, Max Kampelman, and Maynard Glitman—the principal U.S. arms control negotiators in Geneva who had actually crafted the treaty together with their Soviet counterparts, Viktor Karpov and Alexei Obukhov, who were also in attendance. Then there were Colin Powell, William Rodgers, and Alexander Haig, the two former secretaries of state, Sen. John Tower, and Reagan's daughter, Maureen. Across the aisle and to the right were a group of prominent senators and congressmen: Bob Dole, Jim Wright, Alan Simpson, and others—the people who would eventually be called upon to ratify the treaty about to be signed. Altogether, in my eyeball estimate, some 200–250 guests were gathered in the East Room.

The East Room, which is on the State Floor, is the largest in the White House. It is used for receptions, ceremonies such as the one on this day, presidential press conferences, and other events. It has been the scene of several weddings, including that of Lynda Bird Johnson. The bodies of seven presidents have lain in state here. Now this room was the scene of yet another historic event.

Those in the room remembered well how close nuclear Armageddon had seemed when the Soviets stormed out of the Geneva arms control talks in the fall of 1983. I for one certainly remembered well that 1983 was the most dangerous year in the second half of the Cold War, which I had the dubious pleasure of witnessing almost first-hand, working on the front lines of diplomacy, as it were, since 1968. The incredibly high level of stress and tension in the Soviet-U.S. relationship in 1983 and the risk of the two sides misreading or miscalculating each other's intentions were very real. They were the direct result of the confluence of circumstances such as Reagan's famous "Star Wars" speech in March (which did nothing to allay Soviet concerns and fears about U.S. intentions), the Soviets' shooting down of the KAL-007 in September (which made the world shudder with revulsion at this act of wanton brutality), the deployment of American INF missiles in Europe in November (in response to the earlier Soviet deployment of SS-20s), and the large-scale NATO nuclear military exercise conducted at about the same time. All those factors, coupled with the extreme nervousness in Moscow over presumed U.S. intention to launch a pre-emptive nuclear strike against the USSR, conspired to make nuclear war a real and distinct possibility in the fall of that year. Soviet personnel working in the United States, at least there in New York, were secretly told to be ready to be evacuated back home within twenty-four hours. The Soviet leadership appeared to believe that the United States had every intention of attacking the Soviet Union with nuclear weapons as soon as their deployment in Europe was completed and that nuclear war was now inevitable. With Gorbachev coming to office as the top leader of the Soviet Union, the two countries had entered a new phase of their relationship. But mistrust between them had not yet disappeared.

Interviewing Reagan on the eve of Gorbachev's visit to Washington, the CBS anchorman Dan Rather put it this way: "Winston Churchill once said that trying to maintain a good relationship with the Communists was not unlike trying to woo a crocodile, and when it opened its mouth, you could never be quite certain whether it was trying to smile or eat you up. . . . Now, Americans respect you, love you, and are pulling for you, but they are concerned that perhaps you are going to or already have allowed Gorbachev to eat you and us up. . . . Forty-five percent [of Americans] are convinced that you make too many compromises to Gorbachev. Now the question is, what assurance can you give, how can you convince Americans that you have the command of the kind of complex information that's necessary here not to have this young, energetic, intelligent Marxist-Leninist eat you and us up?"

Responding to this provocative question, Reagan summed up his position by reciting a well-known Russian proverb, *"Doveryai, no proveryai"* (Trust, but verify). He seemed to imply that the superpower relationship was now characterized by guarded trust, rather than naked mistrust. Indeed, since Reykjavík, it was only through political will at the top level on both sides, the patient work of Shultz and Shevardnadze, and the thousands of hours of meetings and talks by the two negotiating teams in Geneva to remove mutual concerns about trust and verification of compliance with future arms control agreements that there was now a treaty to be signed in the next few minutes to eliminate nuclear missiles from Europe.

All in all, 859 American missiles, both deployed and nondeployed, and 1,752 Soviet missiles, also deployed and nondeployed, were to be eliminated under that treaty within the next three years. All those missiles were to be either cut up, burned, crushed, flattened, or exploded. Their nuclear material and guidance systems were to be removed and retained by the owner country. The INF treaty defined in exhaustive detail just how, when, and under whose watchful eyes the missiles would be banished from the planet. For example, to ensure that medium-range missiles were not being hidden at bases for mobile long-range missiles, each side, within six hours of a request from the other, had to open garage roofs and take missiles from their launchers to expose them to the scrutiny of "national technical means" of surveillance—in other words, spy satellites passing overhead.

In addition to "national technical means" of verification, Soviet inspectors would be stationed at a U.S. weapons plant in Magna, Utah, and would be permitted short-notice visits to a plant in California. U.S. inspectors would be stationed at a plant in Votkinsk in the central region of the USSR and could make the same sort of visits. On-site inspections would also be conducted by both sides in the territories of their respective allies, where such missiles were located, namely in East Germany and Czechoslovakia on the one hand, and in West Germany, Britain, Italy, Belgium, and the Netherlands on the other. Inspections could continue for up to thirteen years, ten years after the missiles had been eliminated.

Such was the gist of the *Doveryai, no proveryai* program.

But the fact remained that only 4 percent of the two countries' total nuclear arsenal was involved. The further 50 percent reduction of big nukes was the subject Gorbachev and Reagan would tackle next in this summit. The 160-page text of the INF treaty itself, which had been completed in Geneva only on Monday (with the signing day being Tuesday), had arrived in Washington from Geneva by a U.S. Air Force plane forty minutes after Gorbachev had landed at Andrews Air Force Base. The treaty was brought to Washington in the briefcases of its two chief negotiators: Maynard Glitman and Alexei Obukhov. Before the signing, Obukhov told Shevardnadze that he and Glitman had spent much of the flight writing their initials on the margin of the final treaty text—a diplomatic procedure known as initialing.

1:45 P.M. The hour and the minute that would go down in history. The announcer's baritone intoned through the loudspeakers, "Ladies and gentlemen! The president of the United States and the general secretary of the Communist Party of the Soviet Union!" Out of the Cross Hall, to the accompaniment of a Marine band that played American and Soviet marches and the roll of a drum, appeared Reagan escorting Gorbachev down the red-carpeted hallway into the East Room. They were greeted by a standing ovation from the audience. Gorbachev and Reagan came up to the microphones set up for the occasion. As host, Reagan spoke first. This time around, he was interpreted into Russian by Peter Afanasenko.

As a well-coached actor, the seventy-six-year-old president spoke in short paragraphs, pausing for the interpreter to translate. He clearly disliked monologues—the Great Communicator wanted a rapport with his audience. He appeared good-humored and relaxed, seeming to relish this moment on the world stage together with Gorbachev.

"This ceremony and the treaty we are signing today are both excellent examples of the rewards of patience," the president began. "It was over six years ago, November eighteenth, 1981, that I first proposed what would come to be called the zero option. It was a simple proposal—one might say disarmingly simple." He then gave a brief recitation of the history of the INF treaty and told the famous tale from Ivan Krylov's fables about the swan, the crawfish, and the pike to illustrate the often futile efforts and the frustration the two sides had experienced in trying to hammer out this remarkable treaty. "It seems that once upon a time," he continued, "these three were trying to move a wagonload together. They hitched and harnessed themselves to the wagon. It wasn't very heavy, but no matter how hard they worked, the wagon just wouldn't move. You see, the swan was flying upward, the crawfish kept crawling backward, the pike kept making for the water. The end result was that they got nowhere, and the wagon is still there to this day. . . . Strong and fundamental moral differences continue to exist between our nations, but today, on this vital issue at least, we've seen what can be accomplished when we pull together."

And then, in the middle of his speech, Reagan surprised the audience by repeating his favorite Russian proverb: "We have listened to the wisdom in an old Russian maxim. And I am sure you are familiar with it, Mr. General Secretary, though my pronunciation may give you difficulty. The maxim is *doveryai, no proveryai*—trust but verify."

The audience broke into laughter. Gorbachev grinned and, without waiting for interpretation of the president's remarks, instantly interjected, "You repeat that at every meeting." Another burst of laughter followed. Gorbachev's remark, however, did not end this interesting exchange. Reagan came up with a repartee, combined with a disarming smile: "I like it." Another round of laughter and applause followed.

Reagan ended the speech by quoting another Russian proverb, this time in English: "The harvest comes more from sweat than from the dew." Sadly, I thought, that proverb had long been forgotten in the

Soviet Union. Under socialism people only pretended to work, and that was because the government only pretended to pay. Anyway, Reagan's proverb summed up nicely the incredibly complex and protracted work of the six long, hard years it had taken to prepare the treaty. Reagan then lightheartedly suggested that the negotiators of the treaty "get some well-deserved rest," but Gorbachev took the remark to mean that the Soviets should get some rest and again shot back, "We're not going to do that," prompting more laughter.

The spirited public banter and the trading of jokes between these two most powerful leaders in the world reinforced the mood of cooperation and goodwill between them. That day, December 8, 1987, would certainly be remembered in history as "a day of fame."

Now it was Gorbachev's turn at the microphone. Unlike Reagan, he did not use jokes, but he, too, resorted to a metaphor to make the point that this was "a chance to move toward a nuclear-free world that holds out . . . the promise of a . . . life without fear." "We can be proud," he said, "of planting this sapling that may one day grow into a mighty tree of peace." And he quoted the great American poet and philosopher Ralph Waldo Emerson: "The reward of a thing well done is to have done it."

Then, with eight strokes of a pen, Ronald Reagan and Mikhail Gorbachev signed the world's first historic treaty eliminating an entire class of nuclear-armed missiles. They sat side by side, with Soviet and American flags behind them, at a table once used by Abraham Lincoln, and signed the pages of the accord to do away with medium- and shorter-range nuclear-tipped missiles. Hundreds of bulb flashes lit up the dais, capturing forever the two leaders signing the treaty.

When they were done signing, Gorbachev said to Reagan, "Mr. President, I suggest we have these pens for a keepsake." Reagan gave him a puzzled look of incomprehension—the remark was not translated for him because the two interpreters doing this portion of the summit, Peter Afanasenko and Pavel Palazchenko, were at a considerable distance from where the two leaders were seated. After a moment, Pavel approached them from behind and translated Gorbachev's remark for Reagan's benefit. Reagan responded by exchanging with Gorbachev the copies of the treaty, handshakes, and the pens.

"We have made history," Reagan said.

"What has been accomplished is only the beginning," Gorbachev responded.

The audience rose to its feet and erupted into long spontaneous applause. I looked around and saw tears glistening on the cheeks of some of the most famous faces in the room, but those faces were mainly American, not Soviet. Most of the Soviets I saw remained silent, as if trying to understand exactly what was taking place. They were contemplative, serious. It was all very moving. My eyes swept the exquisite room. I looked at the magnificent chandelier. For a moment it seemed a symbol of the bright hopes for a peaceful future.

Raisa Maximovna turned to Shevardnadze. "*Pozdravliayou!*" she said (congratulations), her face flushed with emotion. Shevardnadze beamed and responded in kind. It was an emotional moment for him personally as it was for Shultz, who also received his well-deserved share of congratulations. Nancy Reagan, who stood next to Raisa, clapped her hands, looking at her husband with affection in her misty eyes. He looked back at her with his incomparable charm, nodding. An overwhelming sense of accomplishment and fellowship and triumph pervaded the East Room. I had witnessed many important ceremonies in my professional life, but never anything like this, either before or after. It was one of the greatest moments in my life. I felt a lump in my throat. December 8, 1987, had just become the date that separated the era of nuclear brinkmanship from the era of the demilitarization of human life. A real and tangible step for peace was taken on that day.

When all is said and done, however, it boiled down to the question of trust. Could the Americans and the Soviets really trust each other? While the treaty was being signed inside the White House, a white truck lumbered past Lafayette Park, a wooden horse's head protruding from the rear. It was the same truck I had seen the day before, warning, "TROJAN HORSE—INF Treaty Is Appeasement." The coming of Gorbachev to America had churned up the American national psyche. From what I had read and heard, Americans liked him, hated the system he represented, longed for peace, feared the peacemaker. But having lived in the United States for some time, I knew that for Americans there was only one question: Could they trust Gorbachev?

The Soviet spin doctors, or spinmeisters, dubbed by the American press "the *glasnost* brigade," that Gorbachev had brought with him to Washington—academicians, lawyers, scientists, politicians, economists, journalists—were all harping on one message: "We have changed. We are into 'new thinking.' *Doveryaite nam*—trust us!"

But what the spin doctors neglected to mention during their numerous press conferences in Washington was that while Gorbachev was meeting with Reagan to improve relations between the United States and the Soviet Union, back home in Moscow some top Politburo members, such as the KGB chairman Viktor Chebrikov, were making common cause with Kremlin number two and chief ideologist Yegor Ligachev to block Gorbachev's *glasnost* and *perestroika* reforms and stop rapprochement with the West. For example, on September 10, 1987, Chebrikov gave a hard-line speech in which he berated *perestroika*. Among other things, he claimed that unrest that was beginning to appear throughout the Soviet Union under the *glasnost* policy was caused by the "virus of nationalism" planted by Western "special [i.e., intelligence] services." He said too many public demonstrations were going on and communicated a sense that things were getting out of hand. Gorbachev knew he needed KGB support in maintaining and consolidating his power, and he tried to court it. The KGB was the only Soviet institution he had not publicly criticized, and from the beginning of Gorbachev's rule, General Chebrikov had enjoyed unprecedentedly high visibility. Now, by allying with Ligachev, Chebrikov was showing Gorbachev that he no longer enjoyed the crucial support of the Communist Party mainstream.

Could the Soviet Union be trusted under those circumstances? was the question on the minds of the Americans assembled in that historic room where the INF treaty had just been signed. Reagan clearly did not think so, and he showed his mistrust openly by quoting the Russian proverb "Trust but verify." But at the same time, Reagan regarded Gorbachev as a new type of leader and must have decided to give him the benefit of the doubt and continue working with him. A new and important element in the superpower dialogue was an instinctive understanding between the two leaders and a mutual sympathy that the two seemed to have developed in their meetings in Geneva, Reykjavík and now here in Washington. To be sure, Reagan, like Gorbachev, had his share of critics. But Reagan had a vision of the Soviet leader as one who genuinely wanted to avoid war. He was way ahead of many of his critics in discerning that Gorbachev really was trustworthy.

On the other hand, the legitimate question many Soviets asked themselves was, Could the *United States* be trusted? Gorbachev, for one, had the following to say on the question of trust in his book *Perestroika*, which he had recently completed: "When I hear that we must first take care of trust and the basic problems will be solved later, I cannot understand it. It rather sounds like a lame excuse. Is trust really a divine gift? Or will it emerge by itself if the Soviet Union and the United States both repeat that they support trust? No, it will not. Building trust is a long process. The extent of it always depends on actual relations and on cooperation in many areas."

Gorbachev recalled that in his meeting with Shultz in Moscow earlier in the spring of 1987, he kept bringing him round to the same idea: "Let us now try and live in a real world, let us take the interests of both our nations into account." Recalling further his conversation with Nixon in Moscow the year before, he said he had told him that if trust was to be created, people had to talk to one another to understand one another, and that was just what political leaders failed to do enough. His idea of building trust was for Soviet and American people at the grassroots level to meet more often so that they could form their own impressions of each other. He thought that "without full communication and mutual understanding between peoples, political leaders can do little." And so he called for normalizing Soviet-American relations and to that end to identify and enlarge the areas of common ground so as eventually to arrive at a friendly and trustworthy relationship between the two nations.

Following the signing, Reagan and Gorbachev made separate, tele-vised statements about the treaty for a worldwide audience; then they and their advisers headed for the Cabinet Room where the two leaders were scheduled to continue talks.

After everyone took their seat on both sides of the table, leaving two opposite chairs in the middle unoccupied, I eased myself into a seat behind the chair reserved for Gorbachev, ready to take notes and to interpret consecutively, if need be. To my surprise, I discovered two more Soviet officials in the room, who sat to my right, closer to the door, trying to keep a low profile. I had seen them in passing several times before within the Kremlin walls and at Staraya Ploschad—the head-quarters of the Central Committee of the Soviet Communist Party and the seat of real power in the Soviet Union. One of them was Nikolai Kruchina, the head of the so-called Upravleniye Delami or the Central Committee's Department for the Administration of Affairs. The other one, Valery Boldin, was the chief of Obschiy Otdel or the General Department in the Central Committee. That Department was respon-sible for day-to-day affairs in the office of the general secretary and of the Politburo, handling for them incoming and outgoing mail, etc.—a rather obscure function. To put it simply, it was a kind of paperwork mill, but obviously an important one because it placed Boldin in a position to influence some of Gorbachev's decisions by controlling some of the information that went to him. The department run by Kruchina had an entirely different function, being in charge of Party finances and pur-veying all kinds of goods and privileges for the top Party elite. An impor-tant function, no doubt. But what were those two men, both obsequious apparatchiks, doing *here*, in *this* place? Neither of them was Gorbachev's adviser or expert on any of the matters to be discussed. Yet they stayed on. I found it strange and vaguely and inexplicably disturbing even then.

At the time, neither Gorbachev nor anybody else in that room for that matter had any inkling of the role these two would play three and a half years later in the abortive coup against Gorbachev in August 1991. Kruchina would commit suicide in the wake of the failed attempt by jumping out of his apartment window. Boldin would land behind bars in Matrosskaya Tishina, a prison in Moscow. Clearly, they were at this meeting on somebody's instructions—perhaps to gather information on Gorbachev's dealings with Reagan and report it to somebody else. But who could that be? Could it be, perchance, KGB general Kryuchkov, whose visage I had glimpsed earlier that morning on the South Lawn and whose presence at the summit also seemed inexplicable? In August 1991 he would be one of the chief coup plotters, if not the principal mastermind.

As I sat there musing about the two strange neighbors on my right, the door from the Oval Office opened, and Reagan and Gorbachev walked briskly into the Cabinet Room and sat down. Gorbachev was flanked by Shevardnadze and Yakovlev, Reagan by Bush and Shultz. The meeting was opened by Reagan, who seemed to be vigorous, energetic, and in high spirits—at least in the beginning. He immediately turned the floor over to Gorbachev. "What would you like to begin with? You are the guest." His voice, with its familiar husky rasp, sounded confident.

Gorbachev wanted to begin with regional issues, and right away he shifted the focus of his remarks to Nicaragua. He was ad-libbing. He had prepared himself well by studying a lot of briefing material before coming to Washington. Now he only referred rather infrequently to one of several small green spiral notebooks in front of him on the table, which I could see from behind was filled with handwritten notes on both sides of each page. I must say he was full of information and a formidable opponent. He was strikingly attentive when Reagan or others spoke, working to process the information given him. He seemed to know exactly what he wanted, and at that meeting he was as tough and doctrinaire as any Soviet leader I had met before him. He could have been Gromyko in those minutes. He was firing off his points one after another, almost without pause. He kept up this electrifying oratorical onslaught for a full twenty minutes.

The gist of his discourse was that the Soviet Union would reduce its supplies of military equipment to Nicaragua and even stop them altogether, except for small or police arms, if the United States stopped supporting the contras and gave an appropriate guarantee of noninterference. He was clearly hinting that the U.S. administration was having difficulty in providing financial and material support to the contras because of growing opposition from Congress, which had already cut back appropriations for the Nicaraguan resistance. One could read between the lines the poorly disguised idea that all the attempts by the contras to overthrow Ortega's government were doomed to failure, whatever amount of aid the current administration might provide, and therefore Gorbachev was proposing an honorable solution for it "to save face."

But Reagan was not about to fall into this trap that Gorbachev was setting for him. He knew, of course, that the Soviet Union had, by now, supplied Ortega with more heavy weapons and military hardware than was needed to repel contra attacks for a long time, thus creating an enormous military imbalance that promoted tension in the region. The excess supplies could be used to pursue subversion in neighboring countries to expand the zone of Marxist influence in Central America. Reagan replied that the United States had committed itself to supporting the freedom fighters in Nicaragua and the institutionalization of democracy in Central America and had no moral right to deny that aid now. "Why hasn't Ortega kept his promise to the people of Nicaragua to give them civil liberties in that long-suffering country?" he asked. "Why doesn't he comply fully with the peace proposals of the Contadora group, the Arias peace plan?"

Like Gorbachev, Reagan, too, spoke seemingly impromptu, without looking into the briefing book that had been prepared for him by the State Department. Originally, the book was said to be a hundred-page document, but then supposedly it was boiled down to fifty pages of more digestible one-page summaries on the issues. The compressed book was also said to contain "talking points," giving the president a choice of three alternative responses to each comment Gorbachev was expected to make on any given issue.

By now, a certain sense of irritation was in the air, arising from that exchange; Reagan felt it and tried to lighten the atmosphere by resorting to his favorite method—telling a joke. "Mr. General Secretary," he said, "I heard this story the other day, and I think you may like it." Gorbachev nodded.

"An American professor was invited to Moscow one day to give a course of lectures," Reagan began in his smooth actor's voice. "So he bought a plane ticket and took a taxi from his home to get to the airport. The taxi driver was a young man, and they fell into a conversation as they drove along. Seeing a textbook on the young man's knees, the professor asked if he was a student. The driver said yes, he was. Then the professor asked him what he intended to do with his life once he finished studies, what were his plans? The young man replied that he was attending the local university's evening courses and would soon graduate, but hadn't decided yet what to do after he finished studying. Next thing you know, the professor arrived in Moscow and took a taxi to get to the hotel he reserved in downtown. The driver, a Russian this time, also turned out to be a young man roughly the same age as the American driver. He, too, had a textbook on his knees—he, too, was a student earning money by driving a taxi to support himself. As the professor could speak Russian, he asked the young man what he would like to do after he finished his education. Replied the young man, 'I don't know. They haven't told me yet.' "

I could see that the joke fell embarrassingly flat: Gorbachev didn't like it one bit. At first he gave the gag a polite laugh, but then remarked dryly, "Tell Ambassador Matlock to stop collecting such jokes; otherwise he won't have time left to improve relations between our countries."

Reagan was somewhat startled by this outburst, and his good disposition began to evaporate. He switched the subject and began to accuse the Soviet Union of expansionism. Throughout its entire history, especially recent history, he said, the Soviet Union had always pursued aggressive and expansionist aims. This was the principal factor, these were the "facts of history," that led to the distrust between "our two countries, between East and West." This forced the West, he continued, to take steps to strengthen its security. True, Reagan went on, with the advent of Gorbachev, so far he, unlike his predecessors, had not made statements to the effect that ultimately communism would triumph around the world. "We want to believe that you have now truly renounced the goal of expansionism," concluded Reagan. His good humor had worn off completely. It was now vintage Reagan speaking, the one who had denounced the Soviet Union as "an evil empire" and "a focus of evil" and consigned communism to "the ash heap of history."

Gorbachev frowned and his visage darkened. He turned halfway first to Shevardnadze, then to Yakovlev, as if looking for support. And then, he reacted explosively. Turning the tables on Reagan, he charged that "all the U.S. administrations without exception" had been bent on aggression and expansion. It was not the Soviet Union but the United States with its powerful military-industrial complex, he said, wildly gesticulating as he spoke, that had "earned the reputation as aggressor and expansionist bent on world domination."

Reagan parried this counteraccusation by saying that the United

States did not hold a single inch of foreign territory, while the Soviet Union had a strong military presence in Afghanistan where its troops were butchering innocent men, women, and children. The United States, he stressed, did not dominate a single country, while the Soviet Union had an iron grip on the East European countries. "Thus, it is clear who is the actual aggressor and expansionist," he said. In saying this, however, Reagan managed to keep his cool. He did not sound spiteful or angry. He spoke these words quietly and persuasively, as if he were a parent trying to reason with a child who had said something terribly wrong. He was quite a contrast with Gorbachev. Clearly, he won on points. Gorbachev had lost the round and he knew it. It appeared that Reagan's logic and reasoning were a hard act for him to follow.

The episode highlighted the difference in the debating styles of Reagan and Gorbachev when out of the public eye. When Gorbachev spoke in public, he turned on all his charm and charisma to win over the public, and in this he succeeded admirably. But in private sessions such as this one, when he encountered an argument he did not find to his liking, he was prone to quick anger. Apparently he didn't care much, at least in those early years of *perestroika*, about making a good impression on his opponents in private meetings. Assertiveness, not reasonableness, was his other face. I suppose it was due to the difficult legacy of his Party background, which he was still unable to shake off. Yet, in contrast to his predecessors as general secretary of the Soviet Communist Party, Gorbachev showed greater flexibility in negotiating and consequently was able to achieve better results. He had already proved that many times by his decisions and actions. Most importantly, he was a quick learner who analyzed his performance and how it could be improved; I knew he would do better at the next summit in Moscow. I sensed he had a quality few other Soviet leaders had: he was willing to listen and learn from his mistakes. He was *capable of evolving* and taking into account the views of others.

As to Reagan, he clearly had his own problems, too. For one thing his attention span was not long; no wonder—he was seventy-six years old. He did not try to go deep into details as Gorbachev did; he relegated this to advisers such as Secretary Shultz. Some thirty to forty-five minutes into the meeting he grew noticeably tired and drooped. He began to say something and wanted to quote yet another Russian proverb, but having made a couple of unsuccessful attempts to recall it, he gave up and turned the floor over to Shultz, who suggested switching the discussion to arms control and summoned his "heavy guns": Ambs. Paul Nitze and Max Kampelman, Gen. Edward Rowny, and Mark Parris (head of the Soviet desk at the State Department). Gorbachev, however, was still going strong and his intellectual agility was very much in evidence. Although he, too, had just summoned Bessmertnykh, Karpov, and Obukhov—his top arms control experts, who had been waiting in the anteroom to be called in—he did not turn either to Shevardnadze or anyone else in his entourage to ask for advice or guidance, not even during the exchange that followed.

With the reinforcements now in place, Gorbachev turned to arms control. He first discussed conventional arms, and then Reagan commented. Both agreed that it was essential to reach agreement, as soon as possible, on the mandate for the conventional arms reduction talks to start. On chemical weapons, they agreed on the need to speed up the completion of the convention banning them, but Reagan cautioned that one had to be realistic about it. Basically, Secretary Shultz spoke for the U.S. side when it came to discussing details of arms control. Reagan prudently avoided doing so.

At one point, Gorbachev raised the subject of future ratification of the INF treaty. He expressed the hope that the treaty would be ratified by the U.S. Senate "as soon as possible." But having said that, he expressed concern that, in his opinion, and in the opinion of his "colleagues," as he put it, a growing opposition to the treaty was coming from ultraright conservative circles, the military-industrial complex, and some rightist senators such as Jessie Helms, who were going to "give battle" to the treaty on the Senate floor. "Don't think, however, that this time the process of ratification in our country will be smooth or without hitches," he stated, as if forestalling the question from Reagan or Shultz. "This time we have many people, common people, not only among Supreme Soviet deputies, who are increasingly asking themselves if the Soviet leadership has done the right thing by deciding to agree to eliminate a greater number of missiles than the United States; they are wondering if such a decision will not lead to weakening our security. Those are legitimate questions. It won't be easy for us to convince our public opinion that the decision we made is the right one. So this time around the treaty ratification procedure will not be automatic at all. There is a lot of hard work to be done in the Foreign Affairs Commissions of the Supreme Soviet and in both its houses—the Soviet of the Union and the Soviet of Nationalities—to ensure its ratification. In this sense, a great deal will depend on how ratification will go off in your Senate. . . . We, too, are in for a major fight over the treaty."

As he spoke these words, I saw incredulous smiles and disbelief on the faces of Reagan, Bush, Shultz, and Carlucci. They obviously found it hard to believe that Supreme Soviet deputies would act at cross-purposes with the Soviet leadership, and Gorbachev in particular, as if they were really independent members of an independent parliament, not of the "rubber-stamp" body. Clearly, the American leadership viewed that extraordinary statement as a bluff to put pressure on the administration. In reply to Gorbachev, Reagan remarked that he and his administration believed the treaty *would* eventually be ratified by the Senate unless some extraordinary events occurred. "The best guarantee of this is my reputation as a hard-line anticommunist," he quipped.

Before the meeting adjourned, Reagan tried another joke on Gorbachev. "Would you like me to tell you a joke about Gorbachev?" he asked. Gorbachev shrugged and nodded. "Well," began Reagan, "the Soviet traffic police received strict orders to give tickets to speeders, no matter who they were. One day Gorbachev is late leaving home for the Kremlin, and he hurries to his car and tells the driver that he will drive himself to save time. So the driver sits in the backseat, and Gorbachev takes off lickety-split down the road and passes two cops on the side. One of the officers gives chase, but in a short time returns to his partner, who asked if he gave the speeder a ticket. 'No,' the cop answers. 'Well, who in the world was it?' asks the other cop. 'I don't know,' replies the first cop, but his driver was Gorbachev.' "

Gorbachev loved this joke and just roared with laughter. Some of the personal rapport between him and Reagan seemed to have been reestablished. The anecdotes and jokes seemed somehow to humanize the discussion of such momentous issues. Despite the jokes and the generally good atmosphere, however, I had the impression at the end of the meeting that the much vaunted "personal chemistry" between Gorbachev and Reagan did not completely work this time. The meeting laid bare the fascinating psychological battle of wills between the two leaders, who were separated not only by an age gap (Gorbachev was fifty-seven and Reagan seventy-six), but also by a chasm in their world outlook and philosophy.

Late that afternoon Gorbachev was to meet at the Soviet Embassy with *Amerikanskaya obschestvennost* or American public figures—artists, intellectuals, and scientists. The event was outside Gorbachev's official summit schedule and was arranged on his own initiative. It was a PR activity, at which Gorbachev excelled.

The guests began to arrive well before the appointed time of 5 P.M. Rented round tables adorned with bouquets of flowers, to seat five or six people each, had been set up in the Golden Room on the second floor. While waiting for my principal, who had gone to the hotel to change, I went around the room looking for table #2, which I was told was reserved for the minister and his table companions. The nameplates on each table read like a who's who in the world of politics, arts, and entertainment in America and the Soviet Union. I was thrilled to see that one of our table companions would be George Kennan, the U.S. ambassador to the Soviet Union under Stalin and the author of the celebrated 1947 article expounding his philosophy of containing Soviet communism, which he signed "Mr. X." The other guests at our table would be Mrs. Pamela Harriman, the wife of another ambassador to Moscow in Stalin's times, the late Averell Harriman; Cyrus Vance, the former secretary of state; and Robert McNamara, the former secretary of defense under President Kennedy. Table #1 was reserved for Raisa Maximovna Gorbacheva, Alexandr Yakovlev, and a few notable members of the American intellectual and artistic community.

The Americans at other tables included an eclectic constellation of former political heavyweights and present Sovietologists, and scientists: Henry Kissinger; William Fulbright, former chairman of the Senate Foreign Relations Committee; retired rear admiral Gene La Rocque of the leftist Center for Defense Information; Stephen Cohen, the Sovietologist from Princeton; Marshal Shulman, professor of economics and Sovietologist at Columbia University; Susie Eisenhower, granddaughter of the late president Dwight Eisenhower; Robert Adams, president of the Smithsonian Institution; Carl Sagan, the famed astrophysicist; the Kennedy administration stalwart McGeorge Bundy; Richard Garwin, the nuclear weapons scientist; and Brent Scowcroft, the former national security adviser to President Gerald Ford. Celebrities from the world of arts and entertainment included Hollywood actors Robert De Niro and Paul Newman; John Denver; Yoko Ono; the novelists Norman Mailer, William Styron, and Joyce Carol Oates. Altogether, some seventy to eighty famous names were on the guest list.

The list of Soviet guests, or I should perhaps say hosts, included Marshal Sergei Akhromeyev; Anatoly Chernyaev; Roald Sagdeyev, director of the Space Research Institute in Moscow; Academician Aganbegyan, Gorbachev's chief economic adviser; Sergei Zalygin, the editor in chief of the prestigious and popular monthly literary journal *Novy Mir*; actor Mikhail Ulyanov, best known in the Soviet Union as "Ulyanov-Lenin," because he had once played Lenin in a film; Vitaly Korotich, the editor of the increasingly popular *Ogonyok* magazine; and a few others.

As the invited guests began to arrive, they were shepherded by Embassy officials into the reception room with burgundy wall-coverings and oak strip panels across the foyer from the Golden Room, for cocktails. This room was called informally the Oak Room. While Shevard-nadze was conferring with Gorbachev, I mingled with other people.

A few moments later, as I stood near one of the numerous paintings on the wall, a small, thin woman with an oriental face, half of which was covered by huge dark sunglasses, came up closer to where I stood to examine the painting, which depicted Moscow of the last century. Despite the sunglasses, the face was easily recognizable as that of Yoko Ono, the wife of the late Beatle, John Lennon. As she scrutinized the painting, she asked me in a soft voice, "Do you know what city is that?" I explained what I knew of it, and we struck up a conversation. She introduced herself as "Yoko," and I asked her if this was her first time in the Soviet Embassy. "Oh, yes," she said, again very softly, almost whispering, with a noticeable accent. For some reason, she mistook me for an American at first, but after I told her who I was, she was curious. "Where did you learn your English?" she marveled. I told her I had lived in New York for many years when I worked for the United Nations, starting in 1968. When she learned I was a Beatles fan in those distant days, she came alive. "Oh, yes, those were the times when John and me and others were doing everything for peace. We fasted, gave concerts, took part in peace marches. We were the flower children then," she said smiling.

The conversation had apparently awakened in her reminiscences of her younger days—I judged her to be now about fifty years old. When she mentioned fasting, the famous poster of the late sixties, on which she was shown together with John Lennon in bed in their birthday suits, fasting for peace, came to mind. "And now you see," she said, "our dream of peace is coming true thanks to Gorbachev. Do you remember this?" she asked, making the peace sign.

At this point, Henry Kissinger walked into the room with a springy gait. He looked somewhat thinner than when I had met him earlier, in February of that year, in the Kremlin where I interpreted his talk with Gromyko. Like all major political figures I have met, he had a good visual memory. As he passed by me, he paused, gave me a close look, and nodded in acknowledgment. "Where did I see you?" he asked. I reminded him that we had met in the Kremlin. Now he came up closer and, with a sphinxlike smile, extended his hand for a handshake. "Yes, I remember you now," he said. "I remember that conversation very well—Gromyko is an interesting man." Kissinger was not in high favor with Soviet authorities in those days. They disapproved of his public statements, which they regarded as having an anti-Soviet slant. So, he was assigned a seat at a table in the back of the room, not up front near Gorbachev's table.

Gradually, the room filled with more people until no space was left. The din of conversation grew so loud that it was no longer possible to hear what was being said. When Shevardnadze appeared from behind the drape drawn across the narrow passage leading to the ambassador's office, I joined him, and we instantly found ourselves surrounded by a throng. A cheerful man, bubbling with energy despite his rather senior age, pushed his way through the crowd and spoke to Shevardnadze as though they had long known each other. He was saying something so fast, without letting me interject a word of interpretation, that I couldn't get his drift at first, and this unnerved me. Shevardnadze looked at me with a question mark in his eyes. "Who is he?" he whispered into my ear. "And what does he want to say?" I didn't have a clue. I asked the man to tell me his name so that I could introduce him properly to the minister.

Apparently rather taken aback by my frontal approach, or perhaps startled by my ignorance, he said he was Robert Altman. He said he was an American film director who was currently shooting a movie somewhere in the north of the country. And then, without pause, in his rapid-fire American English, he explained that he and his entire crew were "terribly busy" because they had to stick to the schedule. "A day of delay costs a lot of money." But when he received an invitation for a meeting with Gorbachev, he consulted his aides and decided to suspend the filming just for one day to come to Washington to see and, he hoped, to meet Gorbachev in person and to convey to him warm regards from his entire crew. It was so important in this day and age for people to speak to one another directly, he said. He and his group fervently hoped that Gorbachev's visit to the United States would help improve relations between the Americans and the Soviets; it would make a good contribution to a stronger peace and better understanding. Mr. Altman was a veritable cornucopia of words. But as a speaker, he was not at all easy to understand, perhaps because he had so many ideas in his head that he wanted to express at the same time.

I translated the gist of what he said, and Shevardnadze nodded in agreement. He said it would be a good idea if Mr. Altman could say all this to Mr. Gorbachev himself. Other people came up to congratulate Shevardnadze on the historic event of the day—the signing of the INF treaty. Some said it had become possible because of *perestroika* in the Soviet Union. Others thought it was due to Gorbachev's and Reagan's personal efforts and, of course, to people such as Shultz and Shevardnadze.

At 4:55, Gorbachev emerged from behind the same drape. Some welcomed him warmly, going so far as to give him a bear hug; others were awed to see him so close. In a brief exchange of remarks with Stephen Cohen, he said he had read "with serious interest" his biography of Nikolai Bukharin, a Bolshevik leader and an associate of Lenin's who was shot during Stalin's purges in the late 1930s. In response, Cohen said, in good Russian, that he was personally impressed by Gorbachev as a man "with a great belief in his own power of persuasion."

A few minutes later, the guests were invited into the Golden Room. Shevardnadze wondered if I knew where we were supposed to sit, and since I had already reconnoitered the place, I led him straight to table #2. But it was no longer where it had been just a few minutes before. It had been moved closer up front, to the spot that had been occupied by table #1 for Raisa Gorbacheva when I made my rounds. Her table, in turn, had been moved to the side and safely out of range of the TV cameras. It must have been a last-minute move to prevent any possible undesirable gossip about Raisa, who would otherwise have been seen in the spotlight in the television report that would be beamed live back home. Was Raisa Maximovna herself behind it? It could very well be, for she was acutely aware of the allergic reaction she caused among her compatriots and tried to avoid it as much as she could. Later on, upon my return to Moscow, I would learn from my friends that she had hardly been shown on Soviet television at that particular meeting at the Soviet Embassy.

The nameplates on our table had been changed, too. Gone was George Kennan and the others, and of the previous names I saw only that of Cyrus Vance, already seated at the table. The new nameplates included the Reverend Billy Graham, the celebrated evangelist, and Robert Adams, the president of the famous Smithsonian Institution. Another new name was Sergei Zalygin, the editor of *Novy Mir*. I had never met Billy Graham in person before now. He was tall, lean, and apparently in good physical shape. He wore an outlandish black spangled suit, a white shirt, and glasses. He sat to the left of me, with Shevardnadze between us. As I studied him furtively out of the corner of my eye, I noticed that, ahem, his fly was undone, with the hem of the white shirt sticking out. He was clearly unaware of the potentially embarrassing situation and was looking around the room, acknowledging the people he knew by nodding and waving. After some hesitation, I decided to alert him. I leaned closer to him across the table and said quietly, "Excuse me, sir, but I think your fly is open." He gave me a strange look and said nothing. His thoughts seemed elsewhere.

At this moment Gorbachev walked in and sat down at the head table in front of the fireplace. Almost immediately, he began to speak, and one of the TV cameras was pointed at Mr. Graham. Only now did the meaning of my words sink in, and as the cameraman tried to zoom in on him, he quickly put his hands down and did what he had to do. I could see he was grateful to me. He looked at me, now with an understanding smile, and said, "Thank you." The cameraman pointed the camera away.

Meanwhile, Gorbachev was making a speech.

Although the gathering was billed as a free-swinging discussion, Gorbachev went on for twenty minutes, emphasizing to the guests, many of whom had been longtime "peace activists," that there was a "new thinking" in the Soviet Union and if the politicians didn't understand it, the people would. "I feel something very serious is happening, something very profound . . . an awareness among the people both in the United States and in the Soviet Union that we cannot leave our relations as they are. . . . [There is] a ferment in the minds of people that always begins with the ferment in the minds of intellectuals. . . . They are the yeast of any society, as it were, the yeast that triggers new processes." At one point, he said for the first time publicly what he would increasingly emphasize in his subsequent speeches, and especially in his address before the United Nations a year later: "We are different . . . but we are all part of one and the same civilization . . . we are interconnected."

Before he finished, he made the case for *perestroika*, defended "socialist values," extolled Lenin for his thinking on the "country's [socialist] future," and called for tapping "socialism's potential." He spoke about passions running high in the Soviet Union in all spheres of society: political, economic, social, spiritual, and moral. To illustrate the point, he gestured toward Zalygin at our table and said that this man could tell all about it better than he could, from his experience of working at *Novy Mir*. He stressed that the conservatives at home were to blame for many troubles of society and they had to be put in their place. He spoke with refreshing candor and vitality about the Soviet Union's economic stagnation and the failure in the past of the two countries to create a new relationship.

As I heard him speak and watched his gesticulation and body language, I decided that Gorbachev was definitely a man of many faces. In front of this audience, he showed a different face from the one he had revealed barely two hours before in his meeting with Reagan. He was at times intensely serious and businesslike, at times playing to the audience and cameras, and at times he seemed almost to overflow with words and gestures in an extemporaneous appeal to what he called *"Amerikanskaya intelligentsia"* to bury the attitudes and images of the past and turn a new eye to a changing future. Curiously, he was appealing to these influential people, and to the American public via CNN, over the head of Ronald Reagan, as it were.

The audience generally seemed to be well disposed toward Gorbachev, and no one asked him any contentious questions, not even Dr. Kissinger, who sat with a skeptical expression on his face throughout the affair. Only Stephen Cohen, the well-known Sovietologist, struck a somewhat unusual note when he made a bold proposal to hold a joint seminar of Soviet Americanologists and American Sovietologists and Kremlinologists. Cohen said he believed that American Sovietology was far ahead of Soviet Americanology, which was rife with anti-Americanism and almost devoid of objective facts and analysis. Gorbachev promised to give it a thought. There were a couple more speakers: Mr. Fulbright, Mr. Galbraith, and Ms. Montandon among the invited guests. The latter called for wider exchanges among students of the two countries because it was an "important factor in promoting understanding between people." Gorbachev agreed: "We must start planting the seeds now, and they will bring in a harvest."

When it was over and as the guests began to leave, I asked Mr. Vance what he thought of Gorbachev's performance. He said it wasn't bad, he was impressed, but he thought that Gorbachev did not understand the United States well, especially on the issue of human rights, which was important if he really wanted to succeed in turning things around, both at home and in relations with the United States. Many others were left so impressed by Gorbachev's performance that they said if he were an American, he could very well run for president. All in all, he would spend more than seven hours meeting unofficial Americans such as these or members of Congress during the three days of the summit.

After the meeting with *Amerikanskaya obschestvennost* (public figures), which finished forty minutes later than scheduled, Shevardnadze and I went back to the hotel to change, and then we were off to what would be an unforgettable evening at the White House.

The first day of the summit ended with a glittering banquet at the White House for the Gorbachevs and their closest entourage and an impressive array of American guests, who included political dignitaries, military brass, business leaders, intellectuals, celebrities, and stars from the world of movies and sports. I knew that dinner at the White House, especially a state dinner, was always regarded as a premier social occasion to which everyone who was anyone dreamed of being invited at least once in a lifetime. But I never thought that one fine day, or perhaps I should say one fine night, I would be one of those lucky few with the coveted card:

The President and Mrs. Reagan request the pleasure of the company of

So-and-So at dinner on Tuesday, December 8, 1987, at 6:45 o'clock, said the invitation card. And in the bottom left corner, in small print: *Black tie.* A smaller separate card was attached, saying, *On the occasion of the visit of His Excellency The General Secretary of the Central Committee of the Communist Party of the Soviet Union and Mrs. Gorbachev. Please respond to the Social Secretary, the White House, at your earliest convenience.*

On the way to the White House, Mrs. Roosevelt told Shevardnadze that until now she had never even suspected she had so many friends all over America, and in other countries as well—perhaps as many as several thousand. They all begged her to help them get invited to this dinner. Everybody wanted to see Gorbachev firsthand. By all accounts, she said, the selection process was difficult. Status is difficult to define, but in this case, it seemed, it was determined according to standards ranging from strict merit (it didn't hurt to speak fluent Russian, for example) to careful calculations and/or personal whims (people might have been approved by the State Department, the National Security Council, and the White House chief of protocol, i.e. Mrs. Roosevelt, but lost out, say, to a retired baseball player such as Joe DiMaggio once the list reached the first lady's secretarial office, the final arbiter). Before Mrs. Reagan's office finished the winnowing, however, the list was touched, judged, and refined by more people than would sit down to dinner that night. It sounded almost the same as the guest selection for Kremlin gala dinners on the other side of the planet.

When Minister Shevardnadze and I got to the East Room, it was already crowded with guests. There were high society women wearing long evening gowns and men in black tie. During protocol meetings before the summit the Americans insisted that all men should wear black tie and women evening dresses, as was customary in this country on such occasions. But the Soviets objected that such a rigid dress code was not part of their culture and they had no black tie to bring. The Americans said that black tie could be rented, but the Soviets still balked. Finally, a diplomatic compromise was reached: the Americans would wear black tie and the Soviets dark business suits and regular ties. Well, in the Soviet Union in the 1920s, even regular ties were considered socially unacceptable as a bourgeois relic—so much so that in numerous incidents ties were torn by revolutionary zealots in leather jackets from the necks of hapless passersby and burned publicly.

Before walking into the East Room where most of the guests were mingling, we had to go past a majordomo who announced through a

loudspeaker the names of the incoming guests. I whispered Shevardnadze's name into the majordomo's ear, but apparently the poor fellow
was not blessed with a good ear for names, and so he made it sound like
"Foreign Minister Chevvy Nassau." My name did not fare any better: it,
too, came out in two parts as "Mr. Korchi Love." I took in the scene in
the room in which the INF treaty had been signed just a few hours earlier. In the crowd, not far from where we stood, I spotted a tall, elegant
elderly man in black tie and glasses. He was in the company of a woman
of middle age who wore a long, sparkling turquoise dress. Although I had
never seen them in person until now, they were easily recognizable: the
famous cellist Mstislav Rostropovich and his wife, Galina Vishnevskaya.

While my attention was riveted on the celebrated Russian couple, a
man whose face I instantly recognized from newspaper pictures came
up to us. Shultz, who stood nearby, introduced the man: "Richard
Helms. The former director of CIA. Who would've thought that you'd
meet like this?" he said with a slight smile.

Shevardnadze smiled back and said simply, "Shevardnadze. Foreign
minister."

"He knows a lot about you," remarked Shultz.

"Well, isn't it what his profession is all about?" retorted Shevardnadze.

Helms, who had been CIA chief from 1966 to 1973, smiled crypti-
cally, shrugged, but did not say anything and moved farther down the
room. It was the night of the peacemakers, as the press would describe
the event. Perceptions of one another as enemies were already beginning to change, albeit still so slowly and imperceptibly.

About me was a veritable kaleidoscope of famous faces. Almost everybody who was anybody walked past us or stood nearby, some stopping to
be introduced to the Soviet foreign minister, others not even giving him
the time of day. At one point another familiar figure with a dour face,
drooping eyelids, and bushy eyebrows slowly walked by without looking
at anyone. Absorbed in his thoughts was the famous nuclear physicist
Edward Teller, the father of the American H-bomb and the original pro-
ponent of SDI. I pointed him out to Shevardnadze. He looked at Teller
and said, "He looks very old." He did look old, indeed. Jeane Kirkpatrick,
the former U.S. ambassador to the United Nations, nodded politely in
our direction as she walked by at a distance, but did not stop. Then
there were such eclectic guests as Saul Bellow, the author and Nobel
Prize winner for literature; James Baker; Dave Brubeck, the celebrated
jazz musician; and Billy Graham. This time Billy Graham looked
comme il faut. He acknowledged our presence with a friendly wave of

the hand. Other guests included Jack Matlock and his wife, Rebecca; Max Kampelman; Paul Nitze; Zubin Mehta, the director of the New York Philarmonic Orchestra; Henry Kissinger, who waved in our direction from a distance—he was busy talking with Kathleen Sullivan, the pretty anchorwoman for the CBS early-morning show. Probably he found her more engaging than the Soviet foreign minister. Sen. Ted Stevens of Alaska stopped by to chat with the minister. Democratic Senate majority leader Robert Byrd paused as he walked by to let Shevardnadze know that the Soviets were right about the black ties after all, and to prove his point he tugged at his neckwear.

The slightly stooping figure of Caspar Weinberger, the now former secretary of defense, who had resigned not long before the summit, could be seen several feet away. He was pushing a wheelchair in front of him with his wife in it. She was said to be suffering from cancer, yet she courageously overcame the pain and attended the grand reception. Weinberger seemed to be shorter and smaller than on television, and a bit older. The indomitable and invariably ebullient Charles Wick, director of USIA (United States Information Agency) and a personal friend of the Reagans, came up to say "hi." The stern face of George Will, the political columnist, appeared for a moment in the crowd. I knew many others in that room either personally from previous meetings or from television and the press. All those people were now mingling in the room waiting for the Gorbachevs and the Reagans to appear so they could go through the receiving line and finally sit down to dinner. Gorbachev was late.

He and Raisa Maximovna arrived ten minutes after seven and were greeted by President and Mrs. Reagan on a thirty-foot-long red carpet at the south entrance to the White House. The carpet had been given one last sweep with a vacuum cleaner just before their limousine pulled up. Mikhail Sergeyevich wore a new dark blue, Italian-made three-piece suit and plain striped tie. Ties were not his strong point, but the suit looked good on him. Raisa Maximovna wore an ankle-length, black, form-fitting brocade gown with a bodice and a flared hemline. She had a long double strand of pearls around her neck and a pearl bracelet.

Mrs. Reagan was also dressed in black, but her gown was of glittering beads and accented with red and white beaded flowers, a jeweled neckline, and a big bow at the waist. Reagan, too, wore black, accented by a snow-white shirt and wide black bow tie. As they exchanged words of welcome, the two leaders and their wives shook hands and proceeded upstairs.

Prior to appearing before the guests, the two couples exchanged a number of gifts. The Reagans gave the Gorbachevs a personally inscribed photograph of themselves, a sterling silver Tiffany bowl, and Steuben crystal candlesticks. The Gorbachevs reciprocated with an embroidered leather saddle and a case of black caviar for "Ronald," and a crystal serving set and a box of assorted Russian chocolates for Nancy. The exchange of gifts, like everything else, had been a subject of arduous presummit protocol negotiation between the two sides. Also, no doubt to the great delight of the executives of Parker Pen, both leaders received through the protocol office the sterling silver pens engraved with their signatures that they had used earlier in the day to sign the INF treaty.

When the two first couples emerged on the State Floor, they formed a receiving line at the entrance to the State Dining Room, and the guests started to file by them. The State Dining Room is the second-largest room in the White House after the East Room. It is simple and elegant in the classical style. Its English-oak paneling painted light yellow dates from the 1902 White House renovation. The paneling is matched by yellow curtains of a darker shade. Carved into the fireplace mantel is a quotation from a letter by John Adams: "I Pray Heaven to Bestow the Best of Blessings on THIS HOUSE and All that shall hereafter inhabit it. May none but Honest and Wise Men ever rule under this roof." With its huge chandelier and numerous sconces, it looked light and airy, but when the lights were dimmed and candles lit, it became homey and cozy.

An usher led us to table #2 where the nameplates of our dinner partners read: Vice President Bush; Foreign Minister Shevardnadze; Mrs. Leslie Perle (wife of Richard Perle, former assistant secretary of defense); Robert Kaiser (managing editor of the *Washington Post*); Chris Evert (world tennis champion); James Stewart (Hollywood actor and a longtime friend of the Reagans); and Kenneth Bialkin (attorney and Jewish leader, a former chairman of the national Anti-Defamation League).

As I was looking at the nameplates and telling Shevardnadze what little I knew about our table companions, Armand Hammer materialized out of nowhere. As usual, he was in a jovial mood, and as usual, he wanted to practice his Russian on the minister. His Russian was very basic, and when he wanted to discuss serious business, he preferred to speak English and use an interpreter. But he always attempted small talk in Russian. "I gave Gorbachev a bear hug and he hugged me back," he said. "He told me he would sit with me, but he had to sit with the president." Hammer was the picture of happiness and good health. But then, I had never seen him gloomy, either before or after this occasion. "May I introduce to you Jimmy Stewart. He's an actor," said Hammer, pointing to the tall, elegant-looking, white-haired man who was to be one of our dinner companions. The man extended his hand. "Jimmy Stewart," he said. Shevardnadze reciprocated by introducing himself simply as "Shevardnadze." Then, in an attempt to engage the man in small talk, he said, "It seems we share the same table." But Stewart confined his answer to a monosyllabic "Yes." He clearly was not disposed to small talk, and there was something haughty about him. Shevardnadze was a proud man, and he instantly sensed that the two of them were not on the same wavelength.

The awkward pause that followed was filled in by Chris Evert. Until then, I had no idea who the lively young blond lady was, and when she introduced herself as our table guest without mentioning her name or who she was and I translated it for the minister, he seemed just as puzzled as I was. At this moment, Bush came up to us and clarified the mystery: "She's our best tennis player, Chris Evert. She can beat anybody, including me. And here's Robert Kaiser," he continued, switching his attention to another companion at the table, but Shevardnadze interrupted him, "I know. He used to work in Moscow." Shevardnadze had a tenacious memory. With a slight bow of the head, Kaiser said in fluent Russian, "Yes, indeed, I worked there for some time as a correspondent."

Then Amb. Max Kampelman and Admiral Crowe, chairman of the Joint Chiefs of Staff, came up to us simultaneously to congratulate the minister and the vice president on the INF treaty. "My name is Kenneth Bialkin, and this is Mary Lou Retton"—the soft voice came from behind me. It belonged to a man whom I didn't recognize. Shevardnadze asked me who the man was, but I didn't know. In the world of diplomacy it is not customary to ask people who they are unless they volunteer the information. Fortunately, the man must have realized that his name probably meant nothing to the Soviet foreign minister and added, "I was chairman of the Anti-Defamation League and now I am an attorney. And she is our favorite gymnast." He pointed to the diminutive girl standing nearby. "She has an Olympic champion medal." "You, too, have good gymnasts," Mary Lou Retton said, addressing the minister. "Olga Korbut, for example." She seemed even tinier standing next to Bush. She was so small in fact that when she later sat at her table to the left of ours, I could see her feet did not touch the floor. One more table companion introduced herself as Mrs. Leslie Perle. "And where's your famous husband?" Shevardnadze inquired. Mrs. Perle explained seriously that he shared the table with Mr. Gorbachev, to which Shevardnadze remarked, "They make an interesting pair of neighbors."

By now the room had filled with guests who only waited for the two first couples to appear. At about 8:30 P.M. Reagan finally sat down at a table to the left of the fireplace, and Gorbachev at a table on the right of the fireplace. Now that the Reagans and the Gorbachevs were seated, the guests could finally sit down, too. Only now I became aware that there was no chair for me. Since Bush and Shevardnadze were seated next to each other, I took my case to Bush directly: "Excuse me, Sir, perhaps Mr. Kaiser here could act as an interpreter for you and the minister. Unfortunately, there's no chair for me at this table, and apparently I will have to go." "No, no, no!" Bush protested emphatically. "Without you, the minister and I can't speak to each other. I don't speak Russian and he doesn't speak English. Wait a sec, I'll arrange it," and he motioned to an usher to bring a chair for me "right away."

The usher brought me a chair, and Bush moved his to the left so I could squeeze myself in between him and Shevardnadze. My seat afforded a good view of the two head tables just a few feet away. At one, President Reagan was flanked by two ladies—Raisa Maximovna on his right and Jeane Kirkpatrick on his left—with Bill Hopkins, the American interpreter, seated between him and Raisa. Also at the president's table I recognized Amb. Vernon Walters, himself a onetime English-Spanish interpreter. He had interpreted for President Eisenhower and General Franco of Spain at their summit meeting in the 1950s. Now he was the U.S. permanent representative to the United Nations, having replaced Jeane Kirkpatrick in that job. Walters was a polyglot: he also spoke Russian. At the same table there were Edward Teller and Mrs. Ruth Bunche, widow of the late U.N. undersecretary-general and Nobel Peace Prize winner, and two more people whom I didn't know. The honorable guests at the other head table occupied by First Lady Nancy Reagan, besides Mikhail Sergeyevich, who sat on her left, included Richard Perle, Republican congressman Dick Cheney, and the librarian of Congress and Sovietologist James Billington, who spoke fluent Russian. Carolyn Smith, the State Department interpreter for the first lady, was seated strategically between her and Gorbachev. A couple of the other guests I didn't know.

In the meantime, back at our table, Bush and Shevardnadze struck up what turned out to be a lively conversation and not just idle table talk. It was rather like a round of informal talks. They both were in a serious mood. Bush apparently was anxious to size up and get a closer look at the Soviet foreign minister with whom he would have to do a lot of business if elected president. Shevardnadze for his part wanted to sound out Bush about his views on some of the issues of the day to get an idea of what his foreign policy might be if he became the next president. He also wanted to take advantage of the opportunity to establish a personal rapport with him. The Soviets, of course, carefully monitored the political scene in the United States, and such think tanks as Arbatov's Institute for USA and Canada Studies, for example, to say nothing of Shevardnadze's own ministry, provided the Soviet leadership with relevant updated analysis and prognoses, according to which Bush was practically a shoo-in for president, even though the election was still eleven months away.

Trying to make his words sound as convincing and weighty as he could, Shevardnadze began the conversation as soon as we were all finally seated. He said the Soviet leadership, Gorbachev, and he personally had growing confidence that Bush would be the next president of the United States. And they all wished Bush every success in his "election struggle." Bush responded that he, too, was confident of victory, he had no doubt about it. But then he paused and added that the outcome would ultimately depend on the economic state of the country. If the economy was in good shape next fall, his chances of becoming president would be very good indeed. But if there was a recession, his chances would sharply decline.

Shevardnadze switched the subject to arms control. Bush made the point that he was the only Republican candidate who fully and unreservedly supported the INF treaty. Furthermore, he considered it but a first step toward more significant reductions in strategic arms, which were even more formidable and threatening, especially reductions in heavy intercontinental missiles. Shevardnadze interrupted him to say that the Soviet Union did not "yield the palm in this area to anybody" because it was seeking not only to reduce but also to eliminate nuclear weapons of all kinds. He then linked such reductions to the need to prevent testing of SDI system components in outer space. Bush replied he saw no sense in such linkage because "it would lead them nowhere." "But we could think together on what could be done about it," he said. Both a promise and a steely edge were in his voice.

The next issue concerned the Iran-Iraq war. Bush impressed me with his determination and conviction when he said emphatically that the Soviet Union ought to support the imposition of sanctions against Iran as the persistent violator of U.N. Security Council resolution 598. "What do you expect to gain by supporting Iran?" he questioned Shevardnadze. But Shevardnadze remained unfazed. He replied that the Soviet Union was trying to maintain even relations with both sides in the conflict because it didn't make sense to take sides. "But recently

we've been inclined to consider sanctions with a view of possibly imposing them, because we see that Iran has been intransigent, and we think
it's time the war was ended." This definitely suggested a new element in
the Soviet position. "We seem to see eye to eye on this," he went on.

Bush pressed ahead, saying Iran's intransigence caused deep concern
in the United States, for Iranian fundamentalism was a dangerous phe-
nomenon that threatened to spread to other countries. As long as
Khomeini was alive, there could be no hope that the war against Iraq
would stop unless the world community took emergency action such as
imposing arms sanctions against Iran. It was time to take concrete
action, and the sooner, the better, Bush concluded. Shevardnadze gave
the suggestion deep thought. True, he said upon reflection, the war had
already caused immense suffering and probably irreparable damage to
both countries. On top of everything else, with each passing day the
threat grew that it would cross its current boundaries and embroil other
countries. That would have unforeseen consequences. And then, his
mind apparently made up on the spot, he said, "We agree to think about
it once again and, together with you through our representatives in the
United Nations, to decide what should be done next. Perhaps the time
has indeed come to pass another resolution in the Council."

The table talk between the vice president and the foreign minister
had produced its first result. For until now there had been no agreement
between the Soviet Union and the United States in the U.N. Security
Council on how to act to put an end to the long-lasting war between
these two major powers in the Middle East.

The two men then turned to the subject of chemical weapons. Shevardnadze said that the adoption of a convention eliminating such
weapons could no longer be delayed, all the more so since its text was
almost agreed upon. What remained to be done was to negotiate some
details and clarify certain verification aspects having to do with compliance. Bush agreed that it was imperative to destroy chemical weapons
and recalled that way back in 1968 the United States had ceased the
production of these weapons, although some countries, "including
yours," he said, still continued to produce them. But the problem was
how compliance could be ensured. Any plant that manufactured chemicals for civilian purposes could easily be converted to produce chemical
weapons, and it was impossible to distinguish military production from
civilian. Bush was ready to do his best to advance the goal of 100 percent
verification, and if he became president, he would make it a top priority.

On Afghanistan, Bush stated flatly that the Soviet Union should
leave that country, and that the twelve-month withdrawal proposed by

the Soviets was too long; it had to be reduced. Besides, when exactly the USSR would actually begin the withdrawal of its troops was unknown. He hoped it would begin as soon as possible. Shevardnadze countered that the date for beginning the withdrawal depended on when outside interference stopped (a reference to the arms supplies for the muja-hedeen by the United States and Pakistan). Still, he thought some changes were in the offing. Next February there would be another round of talks between Pakistan and Afghanistan through the U.N. secretary-general's mediator, and he hoped they would produce a solution to the problem of outside interference. The important thing was that the Soviet leadership had made the political decision to pull out its troops, and now the other side had to stop outside interference and settle the situation *around* Afghanistan. So it appeared that the next year would be decisive in this respect, he said. Bush replied that all references to outside interference were nothing but a pretext to shore up and main-tain in power the regime that did not have any support from the people and that had been imposed upon them by force of foreign arms. There-fore, it was only fair to demand that the Soviet Union leave that country as soon as possible and let the people themselves decide their future. "If there is an outside interference," he stressed, "it comes only from you." Bush did not mince words.

The table talk went on almost nonstop for an hour and a half, occa-sionally interrupted by waiters, who brought new dishes and took plates away. Only once was the attention of the two diverted, by Mrs. Perle, who insisted that I ask the minister, "Did you enjoy the lobster?" She said this with a sweet smile and concluded, "I think it's delicious." I had no doubt that all she wanted was to share her enthusiasm about the tal-ents of the White House chef, but it's easy to imagine my reaction to this question. I didn't get to eat anything at all during the entire dinner. And now I was supposed to translate her remarks in the first person sin-gular—according to unwritten rules of interpretation. If I did, it would make it appear as if I myself had enjoyed the lobster. So after a momen-tary hesitation over how best to handle the dilemma, I decided to break the cardinal rule of interpretation and translated her remarks in the third person singular instead of the first. I said, "Mrs. Perle wondered if you enjoyed the lobster. She said *she* did." The minister looked at me with sympathy and confined his answer to a monosyllabic "*Da.*"

Many times before in similar circumstances, he had expressed bewil-derment and an acute sense of discomfort that interpreters were often bypassed at dinner parties such as this, and he even offered to share his food with me. And then it was my turn to feel embarrassed. After all, I was not there to eat, but to work. I was only an interpreter. But then I wondered what would happen if interpreters went on strike over such shabby treatment. Would the INF treaty, for example, have been possible? Would the START treaty ever be possible without them?

In the meantime, across the aisle at his table, Gorbachev took a leaf out of President Reagan's book and told a couple of jokes. One was about the "theory of a woman's evolution," as he put it. "First, there's a young girl, then there's a young woman, a young woman, a young woman . . . and finally a dead grandmother." On a more serious note, he, Cheney, and Perle talked about *perestroika, glasnost,* the Soviet economy, and defense spending. According to a "reliable source" of mine, Perle, whose hawkish views on defense were anathema to Soviet officials, asked Gorbachev point-blank whether anyone, even in the Kremlin leadership, really knew how much the Soviet Union spent on its defense. Gorbachev replied that he knew, but wouldn't tell—it was a secret. Perle persisted, "Are you sure you know?"

"I know everything," said Gorbachev. "I am chairman of the Defense Council, so you're talking to a military man."

"Well," replied Perle, "let me give you my estimate of Soviet defense spending: twenty-five percent of your GNP."

Gorbachev made no response. The figure Perle quoted was 9 percent higher than the usual U.S. estimate, but lower by at least 5 percent than the presumed actual figure for Soviet military spending.

During a pause in the conversation at our table I studied the menu in front of me: *Columbia River salmon and lobster medallions en gelée, caviar sauce, fennel seed twists; Loin of veal with wild mushrooms, champagne sauce, tarragon tomatoes, corn turban; A medley of garden greens, Brie cheese with crushed walnuts, vinegar and avocado dressing.* For dessert: *tea sorbet in honey ice cream. Jordan Chardonnay, 1984, Stags' Leap Cabernet Lot 2, 1978,* and *Iron Horse Brut Summit Cuvée, 1984,* were the wines. No vodka was on the menu.

The guests partook of the delicacies amid white orchids and tulips placed in the center of every table. Everything looked elegant and unexpectedly romantic.

At one point, while the minister was talking to Robert Kaiser and I didn't have to interpret, Bush said to me he was sorry I didn't get to eat anything but the space in the room was at such a premium that he and the president must have made hundreds of enemies that day because they couldn't possibly accommodate everyone. I said it was no problem, it went with the job (although not necessarily always), and gently reminded him that we had actually known each other for more than six-teen years now. "How so?" he asked. I said I had often interpreted his speeches in the "glass palace" on the East River when he was the per-manent representative to the United Nations starting way back in March 1971. Furthermore, I interpreted at some of his meetings with Mr. Yakov Malik, the famous Soviet ambassador to the United Nations, for whom Bush had had an apt nickname, the Stone Wall. I also reminded him that we had met in 1972, in Addis Ababa, Ethiopia, dur-ing the first ever Security Council session held outside of New York. "What d'ya know, it's a small world," Bush said cheerfully in response to my reminiscences and for some reason grabbed my hand over the table and shook it. "I'm surprised you still remember me. Welcome to the White House! Do you like it here?" I liked his sense of humor. I said I was thrilled to be here. "Oh, I just love it," he confessed with a misty look in his eyes. "It's full of history."

After the main course President Reagan mounted a small lectern with a microphone set up between the two head tables. He made a toast in which he said that both the United States and the Soviet Union had a respon-sibility "to settle our differences in peace." He spoke of being involved "in a dramatic march of events that has captured the attention of our two peo-ples and the entire world." He called for "hard and honest debate" in bilat-eral matters and on human rights issues. And, he quoted from "the brilliant French Tocqueville, who foresaw, a century and a half ago, that [America and Russia] would be the major countries of the world [because] history, geography, the blessings of resources, and the hard work of our peo-ples have made it so." He paid tribute to both sides' negotiators and said, "But we cannot afford to rest. There's more work to be done, and time and history are marching on." True to himself, he concluded the toast saying, "Za vashe zdorovie" (to your health), spoken in Russian, a gesture that met with applause and laughter from the Soviet party.

In response, Gorbachev spoke of the "winter of our discontent" being on the wane and of the need to "rethink the realities of the nuclear and space age." He said that "in our quest for a nuclear-free world we cannot be content with conquering just one or two islands called MRM-SRM" (the two acronyms that in Soviet terminology stood for medium-range missiles and shorter-range missiles and were covered by just one U.S.-NATO term, *INF*, i.e., intermediate-range nuclear forces; the difference in terminology was a major headache for the interpreters and translators who had been involved in the arms control negotiations). What Gorbachev was referring to, of course, was the next stage in this quest—reaching agreement on a START treaty. He, too, raised his glass to the "good health of President and Mrs. Reagan." Like Reagan, he said it in Russian.

With this the two leaders rose from their tables and moved toward each other until they symbolically met halfway in the middle, clinking their glasses. Before the toasts were made, Bush had beckoned a waiter and told him to bring a glass of champagne for me. I had dropped a hint that after this long, nonstop conversation interpreting both ways "my throat feels kind of parched." Besides, I said, I wanted to join in the toasts and drink to the health of the president. So now I, too, was enjoying a glass of bubbly.

After coffee and dessert, Reagan rose to invite the Gorbachevs to the Red Room next door "for a chat," while the other guests proceeded to the East Room where Van Cliburn was giving a piano recital. I noticed that before leaving the State Dining Room almost all of the honored guests carried away with them some little souvenir such as matchbooks with the presidential seal and menus with their dinner partners' signatures. The souvenirs were provided "so the guests won't take the silver," joked one White House official. It was quite thoughtful of the hosts.

Upon our return to the East Room I was surprised to see that it had been converted into a small concert hall with several rows of chairs placed in a semicircle around the dais on which the INF treaty had been signed earlier in the day. The bigger part of the dais was taken up by a grand piano. Van Cliburn was a child prodigy who had been taught to play the piano at age three by his mother, an accomplished pianist herself. He played his first public performance at age four. At the first Tchaikovsky Competition in Moscow way back in 1958, he won the hearts of the Soviet people and the praise of critics from around the world. Van Cliburn went on to play several more concerts in the USSR, each one to sold-out houses and tremendous acclaim. He was welcomed back to the United States with a ticker tape parade and rave reviews. After going on sabbatical in 1978, Van Cliburn had not appeared in public until now. This concert in the White House was his first after almost ten years. The special program included *Intermezzo* by Brahms, *Étude-Tableau* by Rachmaninoff, *Widmung* by Schumann-Liszt, and *L'isle Joyeuse* by Debussy.

After all the guests were seated, Van Cliburn appeared on the dais in elegant black tails. He made three deep bows, sat down on the edge of the stool, and sat still with his eyes closed. Then he began to play *Intermezzo*. When he finished, he assumed a picturesque pose by throwing his head back and remaining still until the applause died away. He did this every time he finished playing a piece. When the recital was over, he rose from the stool, made another three deep bows before the exalted audience, then stepped up to the edge of the dais. Suddenly, amid the stormy applause, I heard the voice of Raisa Maximovna six feet away: "Would you play for us Tchaikovsky's *First Piano Concerto?*" Cliburn understood her request without translation and replied that unfortunately he could not fulfill it because the piece could not be done without an orchestra. "But wait," he said, "I'll play something else for you." And he struck up a tune familiar to every Russian, the old, sentimental Russian drinking song "Podmoskovnie Vechera" ("Moscow Nights"), so dear to the heart of every Russian. He had picked it up while in Moscow in 1958.

As he played and sang along, verse after verse, first Raisa Maximovna and then Mikhail Sergeyevich joined in the singing, at first softly and then louder and louder. They were beaming. Soon, they were joined by Dobrynin, then Yakovlev, an uncomfortable Shevardnadze, and then the rest of the Soviet delegation followed—a veritable singing mini-Politburo. When the sing-along was over, Gorbachev and Raisa Maximovna burst into applause. Cliburn, who was a cult figure in the Soviet Union, ran down the dais, moved toward the Gorbachevs and planted three rounds of kisses on his cheeks and then on hers. The Americans were amazed at this display of emotions. "I'll tell him to stay around," said Reagan to Gorbachev, speaking of Cliburn, "I can get him some bookings." "I've never seen anything like it in this house," said Bush.

On this unusual note, the banquet came to a picture-perfect end. It was ten-thirty when we left the White House. On the way to the Embassy, Shevardnadze shared with me his impressions of the evening. "No wonder it was entertaining," he said, what with so many "representatives of the entertainment industry and so few politicians being present to discuss serious affairs of state," but he was speaking tongue in cheek. When we arrived at the Embassy, Gorbachev lingered to say to Shevardnadze, "Well, then, the first day has gone by well." He looked pleased. The minister nodded his agreement with this assessment.

Before going to bed that night, I called room service and ordered a hero ham sandwich and a bottle of ice-cold beer. To me, it tasted much better than all those lobster medallions en gelée with caviar sauce and what not. Only now did I realize how ravenously hungry I was.

December 9, Wednesday. Day Three.

I awoke early in the morning to banner headlines in the newspapers that were placed at the room door every morning, courtesy of the Madison management. "Reagan, Gorbachev Sign Nuclear Missile Treaty," said the *Washington Post*. And below that, in smaller letters, "Leaders Pledge Progress on Cutting Strategic Arms." Hints of progress would become more tangible later in the morning when Gorbachev would meet again with Reagan in the White House.

First, however, he had a breakfast meeting with American senators and congressmen at the Soviet Embassy. The freewheeling debate with the congressional leaders, including House Speaker Jim Wright, Sen. Bob Dole, Robert Byrd, Alan Cranston, Alan Simpson, and Democratic House Majority Leader Thomas Foley, ran the gamut from Afghanistan to the conservative resistance Gorbachev faced at home to human rights. Gorbachev defended Soviet policies. With a mix of candor and charm he urged patience while some of them were being reexamined and suggested Congress—which he believed often tried to dictate policy to the Soviet Union—subject its own policies toward his country to a similar reevaluation. The reaction of the group was generally positive. On the surface, at least, the most notable evidence of change as a result of this meeting was a shift in the positions and attitudes of some key lawmakers on the INF treaty. For instance, Senate Republican minority leader Bob Dole, who had previously avoided taking a position, said after the meeting that now he supported the INF treaty "in principle." He admitted, however, that he didn't trust Gorbachev yet. "I don't buy everything he said," he said.

The treaty would eventually be ratified, a few months later, both by Congress and by the Supreme Soviet. It would be the first congressional endorsement of an arms control agreement since the ABM (antiballistic missile) treaty of 1972.

The meeting was one more confirmation that Gorbachev had mastered the art of playing skillfully on his adversary's turf.

The most important substantive event of this third day of the summit was the meeting in the Oval Office. First, Reagan took Gorbachev aside and spent a few minutes with him in his small study off the Oval Office. Reagan produced a baseball and asked Gorbachev to autograph it for his "good friend Joe DiMaggio." The celebrated former Yankee star had brought the baseball to the White House banquet the night before, but had not dared then to ask Gorbachev to sign. Reagan also tried to assure Gorbachev that he was eager to get down to serious business. After that, the meeting went into a vigorous exchange on the subject of strategic arms talks and a "very frank" discussion of Afghanistan and other regional issues.

Gorbachev laid out the Soviet position on arms control. He wanted an agreement on START, preferably in time for the Moscow summit, which he thought could be held in the first half of the following year. He repeated his objections to SDI and asked the United States to join in a moratorium on nuclear testing. He then went on at length about the need to reduce conventional forces in Europe and to ban chemical weapons. Reagan repeated his determination to proceed with SDI and reminded Gorbachev that he was ready to make a limited commitment not to withdraw from the 1972 ABM treaty for the purpose of deploying strategic defenses not permitted by the treaty. The treaty, signed by Brezhnev and Nixon, covered antiballistic missile systems that were designed to destroy strategic ballistic missiles or their elements in flight. The treaty stated in Article V: "Each Party undertakes not to develop, test, or deploy ABM systems or components which are sea-based, air-based, *space-based* [my italics], or mobile land-based."

The ABM treaty is of unlimited duration, but contains an escape clause that allows either party to withdraw from it if it decides that extraordinary events related to the subject matter of the treaty have jeopardized its supreme national interests. Gorbachev wanted a ten-year period of nonwithdrawal. Reagan offered seven years. A hint of a compromise was in the air. In fact, at one point Gorbachev even startled Reagan and his advisers when he told him more or less casually that the Soviet Union would no longer object, as a matter of treaty law or principle, to eventual U.S. deployment of SDI and that Reagan was free to "go ahead" with it. But Gorbachev also implied that in such case Moscow might seek the ability to overwhelm any U.S. space-based defense by building more and better missiles. Reagan did not react, but perked up his head when he heard the translation and exchanged glances with Shultz.

On Afghanistan, Gorbachev repeated that the Soviet Union was willing to withdraw its troops over a twelve-month period but refused to set a date for the pullout to begin. Gorbachev refused to set a specific date while on American soil for it could be seen back home as a concession to Washington that could have a devastating impact on the Soviet-sponsored regime in Kabul. He also reiterated his condition for Soviet withdrawal, namely that the United States cut off its aid to the Afghan resistance fighters, or the mujahedeen, beforehand. Basically, Reagan said he could not do it because it would leave the "freedom fighters" at a disadvantage. In short, the discussion on Afghanistan did not produce a breakthrough, although Gorbachev confirmed to Reagan privately that the Soviet Union wanted to get out. Afghanistan was seen to be of particular importance at the summit because such regional disputes had the potential to undermine arms control accords, as the Soviet invasion of Afghanistan in 1979 had with respect to the unratified 1979 SALT II treaty. Nor did the meeting produce fundamental progress on any of the other major issues, although working groups of Soviet and U.S. officials continued to work late into the night.

In the meantime, while their husbands were trying to do away with the real Cold War, the story around Washington was that a new one was brewing between Nancy Reagan and Raisa Maximovna Gorbacheva. Reports said that the only thing they had in common was their mutual dislike. The American first lady gave the Soviet first lady a personal tour of the White House, including the Red, Blue, Green, and East Rooms, plus the State Dining Room, without the tables and people of the night before. Asked what she thought of her twenty-minute tour of the executive mansion, Raisa Maximovna was said to be something less than diplomatic. "It's an official house," she said through Oleg Krokholev, her interpreter. "A human being would like to live in a regular house. This is a museum." She didn't realize how offensive it sounded to her hostess. When the two first ladies emerged from their private meeting for coffee—running behind schedule for a trip to the State Department for a formal lunch—Gorbachev and Reagan were waiting for them in the White House Diplomatic Reception Room. When the women finally came through the door, Ronald Reagan, ever the Great Communicator, suggested, in a universal sign language, that he and Gorbachev simultaneously tap their watches to show mock irritation at their wives' tardiness. They got a good laugh out of the scene. While American newspapers wrote the two men were "teasing their wives about running late for lunch," Soviet papers presented their readers back home with something entirely different. The captions under the photo in question said "the two leaders are synchronizing their watches before their meeting," thus investing the mildly humorous scene with political content and robbing it of the human element.

Raisa Maximovna Gorbacheva and Nancy Reagan truly did not have much in common. Their paths in life were as different as could be. Nancy Reagan was from the world of Hollywood, Raisa Maximovna from the world of Marxism-Leninism. She was a professor with a Ph.D. in philosophical sciences, and her doctoral dissertation had a typically Soviet convoluted title: "Formation of New Features in Everyday Life of Kolkhoz [collective farm] Peasantry." As part of the work she did on her doctoral thesis, she reportedly delivered lectures and led discussions among propagandists at seminars conducted by the Regional Communist Party Committee in Stavropol. And she did a lot of walking around the villages to talk to people. Though all that was in the past, to Americans she still came across in her manner of speaking and in her public conduct, perhaps involuntarily, as the moralizing and sermonizing doctrinaire teacher that she had once been and the strong-willed woman that she was.

If Raisa Maximovna was a strong-willed woman, Nancy was positively iron-willed. On that Wednesday, it was Mrs. Reagan's day to play host to Raisa Maximovna as the gracious guest. But Raisa Maximovna seemed determined to upstage Nancy. During the tour of the White House, while Nancy was trying to point out the portrait of Pat Nixon, she assumed a teacher's tone and asked, turning to the portrait of the Lady Bird Johnson, "This picture that we face, to what century does it belong?" She answered herself, without waiting for Nancy, "I would say it's a typical picture of the twentieth century." Undaunted, Mrs. Reagan took Raisa Maximovna back to the portrait of Mrs. Nixon and patiently explained who painted it. But no matter what she said, Raisa's replies seemed to have an edge. Forgetting her role as guest, she peppered Nancy with questions as if she were a graduate student facing an oral examination, as if testing Mrs. Reagan's composure. Asked when the White House was built, Nancy could not give a clear answer, leaving it to a White House assistant to tell Raisa the dates.

And when Raisa Maximovna spoke at length about Soviet education after a reporter asked whether she had studied American history and English before the trip to Washington, Mrs. Reagan interjected, "Regrettably, we have to move on." Raisa Maximovna, however, didn't budge. She was known even among her compatriots as a forceful personality who liked to dominate every conversation. It was understandable though, for in the United States the first lady has an established position, while in the Soviet Union there was still no comparable image. Right or wrong, Raisa Maximovna was trying to carve out a position for herself as the first lady of the Soviet Union. As to the White House hostess—first lady of the United States—she did not appreciate the knowledge of history that the Soviet first lady was trying to demonstrate. According to some eyewitnesses, Nancy was clearly annoyed at her guest for her talkativeness, although she didn't show it. She described Raisa as "very nice, bright and intelligent." Also, throughout the summit, for some strange reason that she never explained, Mrs. Reagan wore anything but red, which was said to be her favorite color and, according to the same eyewitnesses, was determined not to wear her favorite color until the departure ceremony.

But when they later appeared before a group of reporters, they both denied reports that they didn't get along. Mrs. Reagan said the whole idea of competition between them was "so silly." Mrs. Gorbacheva officially agreed.

The lunch Secretary of State Shultz was hosting for the Gorbachevs was the first time in the history of Soviet-U.S. relations that a Soviet head of state was invited to the Department of State—a fact that Shultz mentioned in his toast.

The lunch was in the Benjamin Franklin Room, a beautiful reception room indeed, what with its glittering crystal chandeliers, sconces, portraits, and paintings on the walls. Shevardnadze looked around and remarked softly and, it seemed, wistfully, "Unfortunately we have nothing like this in our MFA" (Soviet Foreign Ministry). And added, "But we are going to put up a new building next to the old one, and we plan to have a restaurant there." Wherever we went, Shevardnadze, ever a popular figure, was immediately surrounded by people who wished to say something to him. They included "Capitalist Tool" Malcolm Forbes, then presidential hopeful Albert Gore, Sen. Ted Kennedy, and Donald and Ivana Trump, with the latter greeting Shevardnadze in Russian: "*Zdravstvuyite. Menya zovoot Ivana Tramp*" (Hello, my name is Ivana Trump). She explained that she spoke a little Russian because her mother was Czech and taught her to speak Russian in childhood. Shevardnadze was so pleased to hear Russian spoken by this ravishing woman that he made a joke for the first time that day, at my expense. "Well, it seems we have another man out of a job," he said, and pointed at me, with a broad smile. "Don't worry," said Donald, addressing me, "I hope we'll be able to get you a job." All levity was put aside when the minister and I sat down at our table and he turned to his neighbor, Secretary of Defense Frank Carlucci.

No sooner were we in our seats than he and Carlucci plunged into a discussion of serious issues such as strategic offensive arms, SDI, and the like. This was their third meeting, but the first one since Carlucci had been appointed secretary of defense to replace Caspar Weinberger.

Shevardnadze first raised the subject of SDI. "We must still clarify the issue of SDI and take a position," he told Carlucci without any preliminaries, and went on to explain the Soviet leadership's thinking. Although it was an internal affair of the United States, he said, in the event of a successful test of space-based elements of an SDI system, the United States would have a strong temptation to deploy the system in outer space. That would mean that the arms race would be transferred to outer space and would involve vast additional expenses that would be beyond even the U.S. capacity to sustain. Given such a turn of events, the ABM treaty would cease to exist with all the ensuing consequences.

Of course, he went on, the Soviet Union did not believe such a system could be developed at all or, even if it were developed, that it would be fully reliable. But work to that end would require enormous resources. "For that reason we propose that we agree on a list of items or objects the launching of which into space for the purpose of testing would be banned." The Soviet leadership was willing to agree to some research on the ground, in laboratory conditions, but not to testing in space. Such an understanding would preserve the ABM treaty and facilitate achievement of an agreement on 50 percent reductions in strategic offensive arms. Should matters reach the point of deployment of a space-based SDI system, however, "we will always be able to find an effective response to such a threat. And, our response will be much less costly than your spending for the development of a system in the SDI framework."

Carlucci said in response that the purpose of all work related to the development of a space-based SDI system was to find out whether such a system, designed for defensive purposes, not offensive, would be possible. If it was to be limited to testing on the ground only, then all this work would be meaningless. The United States was not going to abandon the task of creating reliable defenses in space, all the more so since the Soviet Union had considerably surpassed the United States in developing such a system for itself. "You've been doing this work for some twenty years now," he noted. And, while the Soviet Union had until recently gone out of its way to deny it, he continued, Gorbachev had admitted it just the other day. Carlucci was alluding to the interview Gorbachev had given to NBC earlier in December before coming to Washington.

As to the Soviet proposal for nonwithdrawal from the ABM treaty for ten years, Carlucci said, the United States was ready to discuss it more thoroughly, but on the understanding that the United States would adhere to the broader interpretation of the treaty, which would enable it to continue testing SDI components not only on the ground but also in space. The Soviets, of course, favored the "narrow" interpretation of the ABM treaty, which would have the effect of crippling SDI by denying the United States the possibility of space testing. But there was the working group on all those issues (chaired by Amb. Paul Nitze and Marshal Sergei Akhromeyev), "so let's wait for the results of its work," concluded Carlucci. Shevardnadze said that the group was working very hard indeed, even until late at night, and its members on both sides seemed to have their minds firmly set on work. Akhromeyev kept him posted all the time, and "today or tomorrow the group should present a progress report on its work. So we must wait a little," he counseled.

This conversation was in continuation of the bitter wrangling between the Soviets and Americans over SDI, which had started in the wake of Reagan's famous "Star Wars" speech in March 1983. At the D&S (defense and space) talks, which had been going on since 1985 in Geneva, the United States had been endeavoring to discuss how, if effective defenses proved feasible, the United States and the Soviet Union could jointly manage a stable transition to a deterrence based increasingly on defense rather than on the threat of retaliation by offensive nuclear weapons. On the other hand, the Soviet objective in the D&S talks had been to kill or hobble the SDI program by placing restrictions on it because the Soviet Union perceived the program as a threat to its nuclear capability. Up to and during the time of the summit, many differences divided the two sides, including the length of the nonwithdrawal period from the ABM treaty and the types of activities allowed during that time. All those issues and many more had to be resolved for a joint statement to be adopted before the end of the summit.

Earlier, at their September meeting in Washington, Shevardnadze and Shultz had spent a good deal of time on defense and space issues. But even before then the Soviets had proposed reaching agreement on which devices could not be put into space if they exceeded certain parameters. The Soviet list would impose limitations beyond those actually agreed to in the 1972 ABM treaty. Alternatively, the Soviet Union proposed agreeing to strict compliance with the ABM treaty as "signed and ratified in 1972," because the ratification record had been interpreted by Congress as barring realistic space tests. The U.S. position was that it would not accept anything that could undermine SDI. Shevardnadze stressed that he did not want to debate about SDI or ABM treaty interpretation. Rather, he indicated that both sides should tackle the issue in terms of "strategic stability." Shultz welcomed this kind of conceptual approach. In that sense, Soviet-U.S. discussions about defense and space were now more positive, resulting in a constructive exchange about how to proceed. Since then the Soviet position linking SDI and 50 percent reductions in strategic offensive weapons had begun to change, albeit slowly and almost imperceptibly. Some Soviet leaders, including Gorbachev and Shevardnadze, seemed to have realized that they could not kill the American SDI program by playing on public emotions. But they were not yet talking publicly about the change, and whether they would make any concessions on the issue before the end of the summit remained to be seen.

On this third day of the summit, neither side knew what would happen on this issue before the end of the summit. The Akhromeyev-Nitze arms control group continued to meet almost round the clock, but with no meeting of minds. And now at the luncheon table at the State Department the two top representatives of the two sides, Foreign Minister Shevardnadze and Secretary of Defense Carlucci, went at it hammer and tongs to see if they could narrow down their differences. But so far there was no progress. The issue of START and Star Wars would prove to be a real cliffhanger.

When toast time came—part and parcel of all such diplomatic events—Shultz, as the host, spoke first. He began by invoking Benjamin Franklin, "the father of American diplomacy, who exchanged correspondence with Catherine the Great. . . . [He] would be fascinated to be with us today, for this is the first time the leader of the Soviet Union has visited the Department of State." I must say I had never heard Shultz sound so emotional. He seemed genuinely moved by the occasion. He rightfully regarded it as the celebration of a diplomatic triumph of which he and Shevardnadze were the principal protagonists. As I observed him at close quarters at the next table, he seemed euphoric all afternoon, especially when he shook hands with Shevardnadze. Yet, in his speech, he called for realism and cautioned against "extremes of hostility or euphoria through the ups and downs of our relations." "The best approach to dealing with one another," he emphasized, "is one Ben Franklin might have suggested: be down-to-earth, pragmatic, and businesslike in seeking to solve concrete problems."

Fortunately, both Shevardnadze and Shultz had those qualities in abundance.

Shultz then listed six points that he said were the key to a more open, predictable, stable, and constructive relationship between the United States and the Soviet Union. Among them was the need to "look into the future without neglecting the lessons of the past. . . . *In five to ten years, our world would be vastly different from the one we know today* [my italics]. . . . Franklin—and Lomonosov, his contemporary—were ready, and eager, for the future. So should we be." When he finished his speech, Shultz came to our table and grasped Shevardnadze's hand. Shevardnadze stood up and moved toward him to reciprocate. They briefly stood there together in the spotlight, like two good old friends. It was one of the most emotional and memorable moments at lunch, provoking a long round of enthusiastic applause.

In his return speech, at one point Gorbachev departed from the text to pay a glowing tribute to "Comrade Eduard and Mister George Shultz" for their part in making possible the historic event—the signing of the INF treaty. He said that mankind had been forced to put up for too long with "a bad peace," and "this can no longer be tolerated." As he said it, he paused and looked at Shevardnadze. For the second time during that lunch, everyone in the room turned toward our table and applauded.

After the lunch Shultz and Shevardnadze signed an important joint statement on nuclear testing. A joint verification experiment was to be conducted for the first time ever at each other's nuclear test sites, in Semipalatinsk and in Nevada. The agreement, the first of this kind, broke new ground in the arms control field in terms of building mutual trust. The maxim *"doveryai, no proveryai*—trust but verify" would now be put to the test.

Then the foreign minister and the secretary of state were back at work on the nitty-gritty of the joint summit statement that had to be ready by the following day for signature by their leaders. It was now their top priority. They met with the working groups in a spacious office adjacent to the secretary of state's private study on the seventh floor of the State Department. In front of a cozy fireplace sat two chairs for the principals, separated by a small low table with two built-in microphones. More chairs were placed around the perimeter of the room in a double row for members of the working groups. The Soviet component of the human rights working group included Alexandr Bessmertnykh and a few other lower-ranking experts such as Yuri Rybakov, chief of the Legal Division at MFA, and Yuri Glukhov, an MFA expert on human rights and a former French-speaking interpreter. The U.S. component was represented by Rozanne Ridgway, Jack Matlock, and Richard Shifter, the State Department's top expert on human rights.

The small table for interpreters opposite the fireplace was positioned at some distance from the principals, and we quickly discovered that the portable equipment for simultaneous interpretation did not work. The meeting was about to begin, the fellow interpreter Bill Hopkins didn't know what the problem was, and, strangely enough, the sound equipment engineer was not around to help. Shultz spread his arms in a gesture of helplessness. He looked embarrassed. I felt like asking, "Why can America send men to the moon and probably build a high-tech Star

Wars system, but seems unable to provide simple low-tech interpretation equipment that works?" I didn't, of course. The technician was sent for and appeared soon after the meeting started. He pressed a single button from among more than a dozen on the equipment panel, and Bill and I were now in business.

The group leaders presented their reports, Shifter much more skillfully and persuasively than Rybakov, I thought. Several important human rights developments had occurred in the Soviet Union during the previous year. In December of 1986, for example, Soviet authorities permitted Andrei Sakharov, on direct orders from Gorbachev, to return to Moscow after seven years of internal exile. In February of 1987 they announced that they were releasing 140 political prisoners and reviewing the cases of 140 more. The Soviet authorities were also considering repealing laws on "anti-Soviet agitation" and revising laws on "anti-Soviet slander" used to convict most political prisoners. Jewish emigration figures began to rise in early 1987. Soviet German and Soviet Armenian emigration had also increased significantly that year. The Soviet Union continued to resolve family reunification cases from the U.S. government's so-called representation lists. Since Gorbachev's first meeting with Reagan in Geneva in 1985, Soviet authorities had resolved more than half of all the cases from the lists.

Those moves could be seen as part of Gorbachev's overall campaign for *glasnost* or openness. Still, many problems remained. To give just one example, "knowledge of state secrets" was now used more frequently by the Soviet authorities than before to deny exit permission, even when the applicant had no access to sensitive information or the access had occurred so long ago that anything learned was no longer important. Estimates of the total number of political prisoners still languishing in Soviet prisons ranged from one thousand to ten thousand. The jamming of the Voice of America and the BBC had ceased, but heavy jamming of Radio Liberty continued. In sum, Soviet human rights policy remained in flux. The situation had undoubtedly improved over the previous year, but the legal underpinnings needed to assure long-term government respect for human rights and fundamental freedoms remained inadequate.

In his presummit interview with Tom Brokaw, Gorbachev defended the Soviet human rights record and asserted that in terms of social guarantees, Soviet society was much better off than American society. The people's right to economic and social protection, he said, was guaranteed in the Soviet Union, but not in the United States. As to the right to leave one's country freely and return to it, Gorbachev stated flatly that all the U.S. side was concerned about was how to solve many of its own problems by organizing a brain drain from the Soviet Union, and they (the Soviets) would never allow their people to be lured out of their country. To make his point, he concluded defiantly by quoting a Russian saying: "V *chuzhoi monastir so svoim ustavom ne khodyat*" (Don't bring the rules of your old order when you join a new monastery). That statement puzzled and disappointed many people, to say nothing of Gorbachev's subsequent vehement declaration to Reagan, "You are not the prosecutor, and I am not an accused. I am not on trial here and it's high time you stopped interfering in the internal affairs of our country." Deep down, Gorbachev knew, of course, that Soviet human rights record was blemished, but he was not yet completely ready to admit that publicly. Still, he continued to evolve as a politician, and his views also evolved, including on human rights. In time he would make an about-face on what was a sensitive issue to Soviet officialdom.

After these human rights reports were presented, Shultz and Shevardnadze decided to take note of them in the joint statement to be published the following day. But when the statement was issued, it contained only a remarkably short and curiously toothless paragraph on the subject, as follows: "The leaders held a thorough and candid discussion of human rights and humanitarian questions and their place in the Soviet-U.S. dialogue." The Soviets preferred to avoid a detailed public discussion of a sensitive issue, and the Americans didn't want to press them in the belief that quiet diplomacy would be far more productive than a public expression of disagreement. Besides, Reagan, on Shultz's advice, did not want to darken the atmosphere of the summit by publicly castigating the Soviets for their continuing human rights abuses.

Shevardnadze and Shultz then heard the experts on regional conflicts. The rapporteur on the Soviet side was Evgeny Primakov, the director of the USSR Academy of Sciences Institute of World Economics and International Relations—one of the premier Soviet think tanks. He took a hard line as he presented the report. Several times during the presentation he charged that "in its ambition to bring the whole world under its domination, the U.S. stopped at nothing to instigate regional conflicts and exploit them for its own ends." In connection with Afghanistan, he used the standard Soviet phraseology to describe all of its problems as stemming from the situation "around" Afghanistan, not inside it. Undersecretary of State Michael Armacost, Primakov's counterpart in the working group, and then Shultz himself, took issue with him. They both stressed that the problem stemmed from the situation "in Afghanistan, not around it," and insisted on being told the specific dates for Soviet withdrawal. Afghanistan appeared to emerge as a central theme of the summit, and when all was said, the two sides remained far apart. The Soviets proposed a twelve-month timetable for the removal of their forces, and the offer was contingent on a halt in U.S. aid to the Afghan resistance. It was basically the same discussion Gorbachev and Reagan had had earlier in the day.

The two sides also discussed the Middle East, Kampuchea, Southern Africa, Central America, and the Iran-Iraq war. The gap in their positions remained wide after these discussions, and they agreed to "continue regular exchanges" on those regions. The arms control group did not present its report. Nitze and Akhromeyev agreed they needed more time to prepare it. Anyway, there was nothing to report as yet. The group had labored the whole previous day and almost all night long, but so far had little to show for it. The issues they grappled with were too complex and the stakes too high. So it was decided to hear them the following day—the last day of the summit. One could sense nervousness on both sides and uncertainty about whether there would be agreement in time for the leaders to unveil to the world.

Tonight, it was the turn of "His Excellency The General Secretary of the CC CPSU and Mrs. Gorbachev" to host a reciprocal dinner for "The Rt. Honorable President of the United States and Mrs. Reagan." It was a hearty welcome, Russian style, for the seventy guests, including many from Congress and the White House, held in the Golden Room on the second floor at the Soviet Embassy. In the Oak Room, all the delicacies on the menu were prominently displayed on the tables before they were taken to the guests in the Golden Room. The waiters in black suits and black bow ties, who were said to be young KGB officers, were shuttling between the Oak Room and the Golden Room with countless trays of food and wines. And what food! In the words of such a gourmet as Armand Hammer, who attended the lavish affair, "it was superb." Actually, it was flown all the way from Moscow, on express orders from Kruchina—the man in charge of the Soviet Party purse and party catering. And Reagan loved it.

Indeed, it was an extraordinary menu, as swell as anything served at 1600 Pennsylvania Avenue or even better. The guests were served mounds of moist *black Sevryuga caviar, Kulebyaka fish pie, Kamtchatka crab meat glacé,* and *cold suckling pig with creamy horseradish sauce* for *zakusski* or appetizers. The fare continued with *consommé and Solyanka fish soup, baked fish and Shashlik* or *lamb shish kebab à la Kars.* The feast finished off with *raspberry parfait, fruits, almonds, bilberry and almond pies, plum cake.*

Gorbachev used his formal ten-minute toast to signal that serious differences still remained on substantive issues in this third day of the summit. He said the talks were taking place "in a frank and businesslike atmosphere," using the Kremlin diplomatic code words for disagreement. Yet, he said, the Soviet people knew how to appreciate generosity and friendly words, adding, "Peace and cooperation are much wiser than confrontation and unfriendliness." Gorbachev also spoke, as he had all these days, of the young: "The kids are showing us how we should rid ourselves of prejudices, biased perceptions, and drab stereotypes." He closed with a direct gesture of friendship to the Reagans: *"Do vstrechi v Moskve"* (Until we meet in Moscow)—a reference to the hoped-for fourth Gorbachev-Reagan summit the following year in the Soviet capital.

Reagan, for his part, recalled the Soviet-American victory over Nazism at the close of Word War II, which he said united the people of both countries in "exultation and thanksgiving . . . forty-two years ago." As always, he lived up to his reputation as a storyteller: "As everyone in the United States knows, I have a weakness for anecdotes," he began with disarming frankness. And he told a story about one young American diplomat who was stationed during World War II at the U.S. Embassy in Moscow. When the news of victory, VE day, reached the city, he went to Red Square, which erupted in a spontaneous demonstration of thankfulness and joy. The young diplomat was moved to see the crowd lift the Americans from the nearby U.S. chancery, who were still in uniform, onto their shoulders and carry them on to Red Square. But he was even more moved by the words of one Red Army major standing near him in the crowd, words filled with newly found hope: "Now it's time to live."

This last phrase unexpectedly evoked bittersweet memories in me. Even though I had been only five years old at the time, I remembered well the great hopes my parents and all our friends and neighbors in Russia had had after the war ended. They sincerely believed that from then on it would be time to live. But their hopes were dashed as years went by, and then decades, without their lives improving in any way. It had gone on like that until now, when, thanks to Gorbachev and his reforms, the hopes of people for a better and freer life were rekindled again.

Before the dinner began, the arriving guests had been invited for cocktails in the Oak Room. When I walked into the room, Shevardnadze was not yet there. But Shultz was and asked if I could help him meet some of the prominent Russian cultural figures who had, as he had heard, come with Gorbachev to Washington. I looked around and saw a bunch of people huddled in a corner in an animated conversation. Among them I recognized Elena Obraztsova, the celebrated singer of old Russian romances, Mikhail Ulyanov, the eminent theater actor, and Sergei Zalygin, the notable editor of the *Novy Mir* literary magazine. I suggested to Secretary Shultz that he might find it interesting to speak to some of those people. I said that one of them, Mr. Ulyanov, was well known for playing the part of Lenin in *Peace at Brest*, a new play on the cutting edge of *glasnost* that had opened in Moscow the previous month. Shultz nodded and said he wanted to speak to "Mr. Lenin." And with those words he approached the group and introduced himself simply as "George Shultz." Obraztsova curtsied and said nothing; Ulyanov and Zalygin exchanged handshakes with him and also said nothing. They seemed awed, not knowing what to say to the U.S. secretary of state, who had singled them out among all the guests for special attention. It was up to me now to take the initiative and make the introductions.

Shultz expressed the regret that he did not have time to follow trends in the arts or literature. Still, he had heard that Zalygin's *Novy Mir* was going to publish *Doctor Zhivago* for the first time ever. It was a positive development, he said, which was in the spirit of the times. Turning to Ulyanov, he asked how he managed to perform in the theater so as to keep the constant attention of the audience, for he knew from his own experience that it was not easy. "I want to seek your advice," continued Shultz, keeping a straight face. "Sometimes when I speak before an audience I notice that some people, especially those in the front row, begin to nod from drowsiness. Apparently, I lull them to sleep with my monotonous voice. Could you advise me so that people would not fall asleep at my public appearances?" At first, Ulyanov seemed puzzled. Then, on reflection, he said it was all very simple. "When you see someone falling into a doze and his head beginning to roll to one side, you must lower your voice to a whisper, as if helping to lull him into sleep, and then suddenly raise it, so as to make the dozer almost jump out of his seat." He, Ulyanov, often resorted to this method, and it worked every time. He laughed. "Thank you for your advice," deadpanned Shultz. "Next time I'll be sure to use it."

At this moment Shevardnadze came up and Shultz told him about Ulyanov's advice and recommended using it whenever he had to speak before an inattentive audience. Shevardnadze replied that he always chose to speak before attentive audiences.

DECEMBER 10, THURSDAY. DAY FOUR AND FINAL.

The day began with an early-morning meeting between Shultz and Shevardnadze. Before parting after dinner the previous night, they had agreed to meet the next day at 8:15 A.M., at the Soviet Embassy, to grapple with some of the remaining issues, including strategic arms reductions (START) and observance of the ABM treaty. No progress had been made until then on this most important issue before the summiteers, although the Nitze-Akhromeyev working group had labored again late into the night, until four o'clock in the morning.

Gorbachev's schedule was as tight and heavy as ever. At 9 A.M. he was to host a breakfast in honor of Vice President Bush. He wanted personally to take a closer measure of the would-be president with whom he was likely to deal in the next four years. At 10:15 he was to leave for the White House for the concluding meeting with Reagan. Between 12 noon and 1:55 P.M. he was to have a private lunch with the Reagans in their family quarters in the White House. And following the lunch, he was to bid a formal good-bye at a farewell ceremony on the South Lawn at 2 P.M. Then in the afternoon he was to meet with U.S. businessmen and young people at the Embassy, and finally, at 5 P.M., he was to speak at a press conference. Afterward he was to go home—back to the USSR. But the whole schedule would be rearranged due to some unforeseen developments.

At 5:30 A.M., I was already out of bed so I could prepare myself for the long and difficult day that lay ahead. I took a shower, alternating hot and cold water to wake up (they say it also helps to look younger), got dressed, had a solid breakfast at the "oasis of communism"—the Mount Vernon Room at the Madison—and at eight on the nose I was at the Embassy, "armed," as usual, with a few notepads—the mandatory tools of my trade. Shultz arrived at 8:10 A.M., accompanied by Paul Nitze. Bill Hopkins was the third person in the group. Shevardnadze and I met them downstairs at the entrance, and then we all went up to the second floor. There, Shultz and Nitze were greeted by Akhromeyev, Karpov, and Dubinin. No time was wasted, and the meeting got under way as soon as we took our seats at the table set up overnight in the Oak Room.

Shultz spread his papers on the table and turned to the main issue of the day: the U.S.-Soviet joint statement to be released at the end of the summit—specifically the part that dealt with strategic arms reductions and observance of the ABM treaty. The text of the joint statement would be a guide, a set of instructions, to the arms negotiating teams in Geneva, and so a statement that would enable the negotiators to make substantive progress on START was crucial.

As is customary in bilateral diplomatic negotiations, the parties had agreed on much of the text for the joint statement but had bracketed phrases and sentences still in dispute. This useful device of bracketing allows the parties to talk to proceed and narrow down differences and leave aside until later contentious phrases. In further negotiations the draft gradually sheds the brackets as the language is finalized. For the joint summit text, the English version had two sections with brackets that Shultz wanted to remove. One of these read:

"Taking into account the preparation of the treaty on strategic offensive arms, the leaders of the two countries also instructed their delegations in Geneva to work out an agreement that would commit both sides to observe the ABM treaty [as signed and ratified in 1972] while conducting their research, development, [and testing for the purposes of deploying ABM components in space], which are permitted by the ABM treaty."

Now, in this section, the brackets around the Soviet-proposed words *as signed and ratified* were American, and the brackets around the phrase *for the purposes of deploying ABM components in space*, which was the original U.S. proposal, were Soviet. The bracketed words were the main bones of contention between the two sides because they spelled the crucial difference between the possibility of testing ABM components in space or prohibition of any such testing.

Shultz pulled out the notes he had taken the day before during the meeting between Reagan and Gorbachev and quoted from them. According to Shultz, Gorbachev said the following: "If it is decided to deploy [U.S. territorial defenses], it is a matter for the United States to decide, but only after an agreed period of nonwithdrawal." And then, in Shultz's words, Gorbachev added, "After the end of this period, if the U.S. decides to do it, the Soviet Union will accept that." Shultz continued, "Consequently, given the mutual desire to consider questions of strategic stability and the general secretary's statement of yesterday, all this could be combined in one phrase which could be incorporated into the bracketed text at the end of the first long sentence. I will read it first and then give it to you. It corresponds fully to yesterday's statement of the general secretary. Of course, there is a difference of view on this paragraph, which we will try to narrow down. So I propose including in the first phrase, after the word *testing*, two words, *as required*, in place of *for the purposes of deploying ABM components in space*."

The words *as required*, in the Soviet interpretation, meant that testing (of space-based components of an ABM system) would have to be done on the ground only, in laboratory conditions—at least until the end of the nonwithdrawal period, the exact length of which was yet to be agreed upon. Testing *as required* limited the scope of testing and therefore suited the Soviet side. Shultz's proposal was a concession. What it accomplished for Shultz was a different matter, however. He knew that the Soviets would never accept a phrase like *testing for the purposes of deploying ABM components in space* in the text of the joint summit statement, to say nothing of the START treaty itself. And so, rather than continue to wrangle over it, Shultz decided to drop the phrase. But he kept the words *and testing*. This way the statement did not shut the door on eventual testing in space, but only postponed it, by mutual agreement, until after the end of the nonwithdrawal period. He was a man of unusual common sense and an able negotiator. A bird in the hand was worth two in the bush. This decision also made further progress possible.

Shevardnadze welcomed Shultz's proposal as a step in the right direction.

Thus, little by little the outline of an agreement on the complex issue that had been an apple of discord until then began to emerge at this early-morning working session between the two principal foreign-policy makers of both sides. The meeting was efficient and businesslike, with no bickering or arguing. Again, this reminded me of the sharp contrast between the approaches of Shevardnadze and Gromyko when it came to negotiating with their foreign counterparts.

Shultz summed up the discussion by suggesting that military experts of both sides report to them as soon as possible. Later that day, the outline would take on a more concrete shape that would include some specific numbers of missiles and warheads and important language on ABM.

The last hours of the Washington summit were shrouded in a touch of mystery and marked by some suspense, with last-minute negotiations and consultations that had not been planned. According to some eyewitnesses, it resembled the last few hours at Reykjavík.

While the talks between Shevardnadze and Shultz were in progress, another meeting was going on simultaneously in the Red Room nearby where Gorbachev was receiving Vice President Bush. To paraphrase Humphrey Bogart's line from *Casablanca*, it was the beginning of a beautiful friendship, a friendship that would grow and become stronger over time. At this meeting they talked about Afghanistan, the Persian Gulf, and arms control. Then they moved to the Golden Room for breakfast.

At 9:15, Shultz looked at his watch and said the vice president was already waiting for him. This discussion, he said, could be continued in the White House at the meeting with the president at 10:30.

When we joined Gorbachev and Bush in the Golden Room, we

found Gorbachev in high spirits. He greeted us saying, "We've been waiting for you. We thought you should have resolved all the problems by now. Sit down, or else the blinis will get cold." Blinis are thin Russian buckwheat pancakes, and they were served for breakfast that morning. The Soviet and American guests were seated alternately on both sides of a long table in the middle of the room with the curtains drawn—for security reasons. Bush sat opposite Gorbachev.

After we sat down, reporters were let in for a few minutes to photograph the scene for history and to ask a few questions. Then they were ushered out of the room, and mounds of blinis with fresh black caviar and sour cream were served. The breakfast ended at 10:20 A.M., with only ten minutes remaining before the last scheduled meeting in the White House. From this point on, events took an unexpected turn.

Before breaking up their intense discussion to join Gorbachev and Bush, Shevardnadze and Shultz had agreed that they would report back to their leaders after the breakfast to inform them about progress made and the remaining stumbling blocks. Gorbachev was anxious to hear about the results of the Shultz-Shevardnadze meeting. He escorted Bush to the staircase landing on the second floor and told him that he wanted to confer with his experts before meeting Reagan. It should take no more than fifteen to twenty minutes, he said. Would the vice president kindly convey his apologies to the President for this delay and tell him "we will be there at ten forty-five instead of ten-thirty"? He said this in the presence of Shultz, who wanted to go to the White House immediately. The secretary of state was aware that Bush wanted to stay and wait for Gorbachev and offered to convey this message to President Reagan. Bush nodded in agreement.

Gorbachev then asked me to escort Bush and Shultz downstairs to their cars—"in the interest of saving time," as he put it. I did as requested. Shultz and Nitze got into their respective cars and drove away to confer with Reagan and other U.S. top officials, and Bush lingered. He asked me where he could while away the time, and I showed him to the waiting room on the ground floor. The tiny room was made available for the use of U.S. Secret Service agents and protocol people for the duration of the summit. When I got back to the second floor, Gorbachev asked me urgently to find Karpov and Akhromeyev, who had not attended breakfast, and bring them to the Oak Room. I found them both in the Red Room, conveyed Gorbachev's message, and they immediately went to the Oak Room. Gorbachev asked Yakovlev and Dobrynin to stay on. This group was the core of Gorbachev's brain trust on arms control issues. He wouldn't make any final decisions on arms control without consulting them. He convened the group now to decide what to do next about the contentious language of the joint statement, which Reagan and Gorbachev were supposed to approve at their last meeting, in light of the latest suggestions made by Shultz to Shevardnadze.

From that minute on, the program for the day, which had taken so much effort and time for both sides to agree upon, was hopelessly out of kilter. But everyone realized that something significant was going on—Gorbachev was about to make a momentous decision on how much to accommodate the Americans with regard to the interrelated issues of SDI, START, and the ABM treaty. Twenty minutes passed, then another thirty, but the doors of the room where the conference was going on remained closed. I decided to go downstairs to inform the vice president that the meeting was still in progress. The door to the waiting room was open, and from the threshold I could see him talking on the phone. "Cool your engines, Ron," I heard him say. "They've gone into a long huddle."

I liked the colorful expression, and when Bush finished talking, I asked him if it had a touch of Texas. He laughed. No, he said. He explained that "to go into a huddle" was an expression borrowed from American football, then anxiously asked me when Gorbachev would be ready to go to the White House—the President was concerned, he said. I only shrugged and spread my hands to indicate that no one knew. It was getting close to eleven o'clock. In the meantime, Reagan, too, was in a huddle with Shultz and other advisers on the same issues—the linkage between START and ABM.

Mrs. Roosevelt and her protocol assistant, whom both the Americans and Soviets called simply Bunny, were downstairs, too, waiting for Gorbachev. By now we had become rather friendly, and to while away the time we exchanged anecdotes. An increasing nervousness was apparent among the Americans in the lobby, and every now and then Bush would step out of the waiting room to ask if Gorbachev was coming down, and each time I shook my head. Mrs. Roosevelt was pacing the lobby. Bunny could not sit still. She would begin to rise from the chair only to sit down again. Only Yuri Plekhanov, chief of Gorbachev's security detail, remained sitting stolidly in the corner, immobile and imperturbable, surveying the scene with his hooded eyes half-closed, watching us. He resembled not so much an owl as a bird of prey.

My watch read 11:30. It was exactly one hour later than the time originally set for the meeting in the White House. Suddenly, Plekhanov jumped to his feet. Gorbachev, Shevardnadze, and their team were coming down the stairs. The long huddle was over. Everyone in the group wore an impassive, solemn expression. Gorbachev went straight to his Zil, and as he was passing by the room where Bush was waiting for him all this time, Bush stepped out and joined him. Gorbachev looked genuinely surprised, as if he didn't know that the vice president had been there waiting for him. He told Bush if he had known it, he would have come down sooner. He apologized and offered the vice president a ride in his Zil. As usual, I joined Shevardnadze in his Zil, together with Mrs. Roosevelt, and the motorcade began to move. Sirens wailed, blinkers flashed, and the helmeted, leather-clad policemen rode on their huge motorcycles flanking the general secretary's Zil just ahead of us. The motorcade departed from the Embassy at 11:35 A.M. and should have arrived at the White House some five or even three minutes later. But Gorbachev had something else in mind.

As the motorcade reached the intersection of Connecticut Avenue and L Street, Mrs. Roosevelt was saying something about Washingtonians being jaded and fairly blasé about foreign dignitaries and not paying enough attention when the motorcades sped by. No sooner had she said those words than our driver suddenly hit the brakes, bringing the car to a halt so sharply I nearly fell off the jump seat. The Zil almost slammed into the rear fender of the security car in front. Shevardnadze instantly reacted, "What happened? Are they shooting!" He thought something had gone terribly wrong. Ignoring all the security rules, he pushed open the heavy right-side door, jumped out of the car, and ran forward toward where Gorbachev was. I, too, jumped out and ran after him.

What we saw, about a hundred feet ahead on the sidewalk, was a crowd of people gesticulating excitedly and saying something. From a distance, it fleetingly resembled the scenes that the whole world had witnessed on television when attempts had been made on the lives of President Reagan, the pope, and other notable figures. Fortunately, it seemed so only at a distance. It turned out that Gorbachev's car had suddenly come to a stop at his own request. The security agents in the front had kept driving until they discovered, obviously in a panic, that they had lost the Soviet general secretary. Then, in a remarkable scene that looked like a movie being run backward, the lead cars threw themselves into reverse and drove quickly back to where they had lost Gorbachev's car. I took in this scene as I was running toward the crowd, without knowing yet what had happened. When I plunged into the crowd after Shevardnadze, I saw Gorbachev standing in the middle of onlookers, talking to them and pressing the flesh, as it were; those tall and burly security men, who surrounded Gorbachev in a tight ring, nervously looking around and clutching at their holsters. Some even had their guns drawn and Uzis out and ready to fire. Only the previous night a telephone threat on Gorbachev's life had been made to police headquarters.

Several security agents asked me who I was. I said I was an interpreter, and they let me through. Of course, they would never have let me come any closer if some of them didn't know my face or hadn't seen the coveted button prominently displayed on my lapel. By now I was in the midst of the crowd where Gorbachev was, and I could see and hear the supposedly blasé Washingtonians scream with delight and surprise. In fact, there was a nearly hysterical buzzing around where he stood. It was a nightmare for the horrified security agents, some of whom were yelling to the crowd, "Keep your hands out of your pockets! Keep your hands up!" Agents were everywhere. They fanned out in a protective shield around Gorbachev. They leaped on a row of newspaper vending machines, looking around, to and fro. This was not part of the agreed game plan. The passersby seemed enthralled at the scene. George Bush stood nearby at the edge of the crowd, watching. He waved at people on the sidewalk, but few people seemed to notice him. A helicopter was whirring overhead. Shevardnadze, now visibly relieved and smiling, also stepped to the side.

Gorbachev's sudden plunge into a lunchtime crowd was like a classic American-style whistle-stop of the kind I had seen so many times on television and on the streets of New York during election campaigns. Years later, in his meeting with Ronald Reagan when the latter was already an ex-president, Gorbachev would tell him that the decision to stop the car to greet common people was unplanned and came to him on the spur of the moment. When he was asked about it by people from his entourage after they returned to the Embassy later that day, he would shrug off their concern for his safety, saying he didn't feel it was dangerous because would-be malefactors could not possibly know that he would stop his car at that particular time and place. This remarkable event of Gorbachev's final day in Washington was in keeping with the supercharged atmosphere his visit had created. The *New York Times* wrote: "If a spaceship had landed in the middle of Washington, it could not have caused more commotion. Pedestrians quivered with excitement. The Secret Service looked terrified. The KGB looked stunned. 'The door [of the car] opened, he got out and took my hand,' said one young woman, looking at her hand as though it were a foreign object. 'I'm still shaking. It was like the coming of the second Messiah or something.' "

Surrounded by nervous security agents in dark suits, Gorbachev spent about five minutes at the curb, waving, chatting, and shaking hands. And people responded. Some were hesitant at first. I heard one woman shout, "May I shake your hand?" Gorbachev saw her hand and, without waiting for translation, reached over and grabbed her hand. "Come on up for lunch! We have borscht!" I heard someone else shout from somewhere above. I looked up and saw an old man shouting the invitation. He stood amid a group of people leaning over the terrace on the second floor above a marquee with a sign "Washington Square." He was the owner of a popular restaurant. When I translated the invitation to borscht, Gorbachev shouted back in Russian, "Next time. They are waiting for me." By now he was an hour and a half late for his appointment with President Reagan. As he turned to go back to his car, the applause grew louder and he could not resist lingering at the door. He and Bush stood together, their arms now linked, smiling and waving back at the crowd, one of the more compelling and thrilling images of this Soviet-U.S. summit.

Before I turned to go back to the car with Shevardnadze, I heard Gorbachev say with a smile to the people, "Nudge your president. Pressure him, just as Soviet people are pressuring us." It was as if he were trying to tell this crowd of common people, "It's them, the leaders. They're the ones who ruin everything. But you and I, we understand. We're in this together. We're the ones who really matter and we know what must be done." *Gorby, Gorbachic, Gorbomania,* or even *Gorbasm,* as Secretary of Education William Bennett put it, whatever the epithet the inventive press chose to describe Gorbachev's popularity, you had to hand it to him: Mikhail Sergeyevich Gorbachev was a real PR genius.

When he finally got to the White House, Reagan wryly remarked: "I thought you'd gone home." Mikhail Sergeyevich replied, "You see, I had a little chat with a group of Americans who stopped our car." It was 11:45 A.M.—almost high noon.

For all his eagerness to be accepted by Western leaders, Gorbachev was a formidable negotiator, as I had seen for myself by now. In closed meetings, he was alternately menacing and charming. There was no telling which style he was going to adopt from moment to moment. No doubt, the Americans viewed this as a downside in doing business with him. They could never be sure, especially since Reykjavík, that he would not throw them a curve, or a knuckleball, or a spitter if he could get away with them, as Richard Nixon once remarked. Sure enough, on this final day of the summit his conduct and closed-door conferences were keeping the Americans guessing and on edge.

After greeting Gorbachev on the South Lawn, Reagan took him up the path leading to the Oval Office, while the rest of his entourage—Shevardnadze, Dobrynin, Akhromeyev, and Karpov—headed straight to the Cabinet Room using the same path. As usual, I was to be with Shevardnadze. No sooner had we entered the Cabinet Room, however, than Shevardnadze and Dobrynin were invited to join the principals in the Oval Office. I followed.

In our presence, Gorbachev and Reagan announced that they were tasking the arms control working group to make a last-ditch attempt at finalizing the part of the text of the joint statement that still remained bracketed and therefore contentious. The sticky problem was still the linkage between 50 percent reductions in strategic offensive arms and observance of the ABM treaty. The group was to try to remove the brackets around some portions of the text, while the president and the general secretary would be having a working lunch in the family quarters two floors above. Gorbachev personally instructed Akhromeyev to get down to brass tacks, together with Paul Nitze, without further delay. Akhromeyev nodded.

At this moment the Nitze-Akhromeyev arms control group was without interpreters—the decision to convene it had just been made by the top leaders on the spur of the moment here in the Oval Office. Akhromeyev and Karpov turned to me to ask if I could stay on to help them. Thus I became an eyewitness to and a direct participant in what turned out to be a crucial no-holds-barred bargaining session in the Cabinet Room of the White House, which lasted two hours and fifteen minutes and delayed the farewell ceremony on the South Lawn.

The three main points of contention concerned START, SDI, and ABM. The Soviet Union wanted adherence to a strict, or narrow, interpretation of the ABM treaty, which would severely limit the scope of testing for a space-based missile defense—hence the insistence on observing the ABM treaty "as signed and ratified." The Soviet Union wanted each side to promise not to withdraw from the treaty for ten years. The United States had offered a pledge of nonwithdrawal for seven years, through 1994. Once the pledge of nonwithdrawal expired, the United States wanted to be free to immediately deploy a space-based missile defense system on the assumption that it would be ready by then and the treaty would no longer be in force. The Soviet Union wanted the treaty to remain in force, with current restrictions on withdrawal applying. These required six months' notice and the justification that supreme national interests were involved. In addition, while Gorbachev and Reagan had agreed at Reykjavík to 50 percent reductions in strategic nuclear arms, the two sides were still far apart on the caps on various types of weapons. All those points were discussed at this meeting, but I will describe here only a small bit of the final negotiations to give the reader a taste of what high-level talks about the so-called nuclear chips are like.

The members of the group took their seats at the long table, with Akhromeyev and Karpov facing Nitze, Kampelman, and Linhard. The group had held eight meetings so far during the summit, working almost round the clock, but the experts were still deadlocked.

The Soviet team leader, Marshal Sergei Fyodorovich Akhromeyev, was a wiry sixty-four-year-old. He had represented the Soviet military's interests at the Reykjavík summit the year before, where he was said to have played a conciliatory role. But the man was certainly no dove and was hardly a true Gorbachev loyalist. He had expressed, for example, repeated uneasiness with Gorbachev's eighteen-month moratorium on nuclear testing, which had ended in February 1987. He was also associated with the old, hard-line military leadership of the late defense minister Dmitry Ustinov, who died in 1984, and Marshal Nikolai Ogarkov, the former chief of the Soviet Armed Forces General Staff, whom he replaced.

The marshal was an interesting personality. He had joined the military when he was seventeen years old, on the eve of World War II, and was wounded during the nine-hundred-day siege of Leningrad. He was seen by Western analysts as part of a passing generation whose views of world affairs were shaped largely by their wartime experience. He proudly called himself "the last of the Mohicans." The Americans called him "very much a soldier's soldier" and had respect for him. He had authority to work out compromises on the spot, as he would prove in the meeting in question. "When Akhromeyev says something, it sticks," said one U.S. official. He was regarded by the Americans as highly intelligent, well-informed, and a pretty savvy pragmatist, and one who had Gorbachev's ear. Only two weeks before, in the crucial presummit negotiations in Geneva, he had informally suggested that a limit of 5,100 might be set on the total number of land-based and sea-based ballistic-missile warheads on each side. It was a step toward the American demand for a ceiling of 4,800.

Viktor Karpov was chief of UPOVR or Upravleniye po Problemam Ogranicheniya Vooruzheniyi i Razoruzheniya (Department on Arms Control and Disarmament Problems) at the Ministry of Foreign Affairs. He was an old hand at dealing with arms control, with more than twenty years of experience. He was Shevardnadze's number one civilian expert when it came to arms control and was said to have Gorbachev's respect. Another important member of the Soviet negotiating team was Alexei Obukhov, the head of the Soviet delegation at the Geneva talks on nuclear and space arms. Oddly, he was absent from this meeting. It was no secret that he and Karpov did not get along well, and consequently, Karpov kept him on the sidelines.

Akhromeyev's opposite number, Paul Nitze, was the urbane, silver-haired grand old man of American policy who was a special presidential adviser on arms control and strategic planning and had held key posts at the Pentagon and State Department almost continuously since 1944. He took part in negotiations for the first strategic arms treaty in 1972 (SALT I). Like Akhromeyev, he was no dove. In fact, in October of 1962, during the Cuban missile crisis, he was one of the men present in this very room at the meeting with President Kennedy and was said to have strongly recommended an air strike against the Soviet missile sites in Cuba. He was now eighty years old, but he still looked tough and sinewy.

The second member of the group on the U.S. side, Amb. Max Kampelman, had been head of the U.S. negotiating team at Geneva the previous three years. He was one of Reagan's "core" advisers and was said to have detailed knowledge of Soviet negotiating tactics. And the third member of the U.S. team was Col. Robert Linhard, a military expert from the Pentagon whom I hadn't met before and who was presumably a top arms control specialist.

As everyone took his seat at the oval-shaped table, I wondered if I would have to interpret both ways single-handedly, because there was no interpreter on the U.S. side. I knew it would be hard to do technically, because the portable equipment for simultaneous interpretation, set up at the top of the table near the fireplace, was designed for two interpreters, with one going into Russian and another into English. Professionally, I could manage, of course, but technically it would be a breach of the protocol. At the last moment, when Nitze had already begun to speak, a breathless Peter Afanasenko, the State Department interpreter, rushed into the room and took a seat next to me. He had been sent for and found somewhere in the depths of the White House. Since he was supposed to interpret into Russian, and I into English, I was seated on the U.S. side of the table, and Peter on the Soviet side.

After a preliminary exchange of views, Akhromeyev came straight to the point and proposed a trade-off: the Soviet side would remove its brackets around the words *and testing* if the U.S. side agreed to add the words *as signed and ratified in 1972* after the words *to work out an agreement that would commit both sides to observe the ABM treaty.* As to retaining the words *for the purpose of deploying ABM components in space*, it was out of the question, he said. A heated debate followed, after which Nitze and Kampelman agreed to add the proposed phrase, but without the words *and ratified*.

As at the Shultz-Shevardnadze meeting earlier that morning, neither Peter nor I were given the text to work with. In the haste with which the meeting was arranged, not enough copies were made, and we had to rely on what we heard through the earphones. It did not make our job any easier. Later in the meeting, however, when the U.S. team was reinforced by Colin Powell and Frank Carlucci, I asked Powell if he could get a copy of the text for us, the interpreters, and he handed me his own copy, in English. It was a nice gesture, although everyone around the negotiating table should have realized it was in their own interest for the interpreters to have a text to work with. Drafting work of this delicate and sensitive nature can hardly be done with any degree of accuracy if the interpreters do not have the relevant text.

Here is just one small example to illustrate the point: a simple combination of words in Russian such as *v tselyakh*, which was used in the text, could be translated into English in at least five different ways. It could be translated as *for the purpose of, with a view to, with the aim of, with the object of*, or simply *in order to*. The last version turned out to be the one used in the text. So, how could the interpreter be expected to guess what version was correct if he didn't have the text in front of him? Of course, it was not vital if I said *with a view to* instead of *in order to*, but it would not quite correspond to the original and could therefore be perceived by the other side as a change in the Soviet position, which it wasn't.

Peter was less fortunate. He didn't get a copy in Russian. Akhromeyev and Karpov had only one copy between the two of them. Throughout the meeting, Peter kept looking over my shoulder at the English copy. Amazingly, it did not occur to anyone to make a copy of the text, most likely because time was of the essence.

With one phrase thus settled upon, Akhromeyev unexpectedly made a last-ditch attempt to delete the words *and testing* after the phrase *while conducting their research, development*. Although the words in question had been proposed earlier in the day by Shultz and accepted by Shevardnadze and just now by Akhromeyev, he simply could not resist the temptation to try to wring this concession from the Americans. That was part of his nature. As was to be expected, Nitze strongly objected: the words *and testing* were, of course, the key words for the U.S. side.

But he said he would make a counterproposal to accommodate Akhromeyev. The proposal was to add the words *as required* after the words *and testing* in the English text and to delete the phrase *for the purposes of deploying ABM components in space.*

The proposal provoked a dispute between Nitze and Akhromeyev about the philosophical concept of security. Akhromeyev charged that the United States was seeking to continue its military buildup to strengthen its security. Nitze retorted that so far he hadn't heard that the Soviet Union was seeking to diminish its own security. They agreed to disagree about the differences as to what constituted real security.

At one point, the negotiations nearly broke down—over a comma. But it was a critical comma. Depending on where the punctuation went, the ABM treaty would or would not permit testing in space for SDI. After Nitze proposed adding the words *as required* after *testing,* Akhromeyev accepted it, but on second thought suggested inserting a comma before *and testing.* That way, he reasoned, testing would be separated from *research* and *development,* which are permitted by the ABM treaty, and could not be claimed to be an integral part of research and development. That comma was a fig leaf, of course, and Akhromeyev was perfectly aware of this. But if the United States ever started testing in space for SDI purposes, the Soviets would then feel justified in accusing it of violating the spirit, if not the letter, of the treaty. Really, arms control can be and is an arcane business. Following a brief huddle in whispers with Colin Powell, who had joined the meeting in progress, and Max Kampelman, Nitze nodded acceptance of the comma.

This little wrangle over punctuation reminded me of the story about a telegram that went from Lenin in Moscow to a province in Russia soon after the revolution of 1917. It contained just three words: *KAZNIT' NELZYA POMILOVAT'* (EXECUTE IMPOSSIBLE PARDON), which were not separated by any punctuation. The absence of the punctuation could be fateful to the individual concerned. A comma or a period could spell the difference between life and death. If the recipients of the telegram decided the punctuation went after EXECUTE, the individual would die. If it went before PARDON, he or she would live.

As I listened to this discussion, I couldn't help wondering why the two venerable negotiators were still fighting over what had basically been agreed upon earlier in the morning by Shultz and Shevardnadze. But, of course, this was the way any sensitive diplomatic negotiations were conducted, with each side trying, until the very last moment, to get the other guy to "blink" first and make a concession. What I didn't realize at the time was that the tough going at those negotiations in the Cabinet Room, on the Soviet side at least, was due to Akhromeyev himself.

Although he was more flexible and reasonable than most other Soviet generals, he still represented the interests of the Soviet military as a whole. A rift between the Soviet diplomatic apparat, as represented by "new thinkers" and by Shevardnadze in particular, and the Soviet military (and industrial complex) was beginning to widen as more progress was being made in arms control talks and in improving relations with the United States. The rift was discernible even at the early stages of *perestroika*. Now Akhromeyev might have been deliberately stonewalling at the last minute despite Gorbachev's instructions to the contrary. The marshal did not even bother to hide what was at first his bewilderment at and then later rejection of Gorbachev's and Shevardnadze's innovative arms control ideas and policies, to the extent that he would become implicated in the coup against Gorbachev in 1991.

The atmosphere in the working group, however, would change remarkably with the appearance of Shevardnadze, who, at Gorbachev's urging, would leave the lunch with Reagan to give a push to the stalled negotiations in the Cabinet Room.

At one point in the text where it said "intensive discussions of strategic stability shall begin not later than three years *before the end* of the specified period" (of nonwithdrawal), Akhromeyev repeated several times the phrase *"before the beginning* of the specified period" as in the Russian version of the text he had before him. The error was quickly discovered by the U.S. negotiators thanks to my correct "mistranslation." It goes without saying that I translated the marshal's words exactly as he spoke them, in the belief that the Americans would detect the illogicality of it. And they did. At first Nitze was baffled by Akhromeyev's reference to the *beginning* rather than the *end* of the specified period of nonwithdrawal and questioned him about it. Akhromeyev scrutinized the Russian text and admitted it was an error. A deliberate mistranslation is sometimes the right thing to do. In other words, the interpreter should translate only what he hears, even if he knows it's wrong or a slip of the tongue, not what he thinks is right. Oddly enough, it helps avoid possible misunderstanding later, and then the burden of responsibility rests with the speaker, not the interpreter.

The two sides then took up the second-biggest problem of the day, dealing with the additional steps necessary to ensure that the START reductions enhanced strategic stability. Akhromeyev surprised the U.S. team when he proposed adding the number "forty-eight hundred or fifty hundred" as he put it, in the text that dealt with establishing a ceiling on the aggregate number of ICBM plus SLBM warheads. The proposal was now much closer to the U.S. proposed number of 4,800. He then clarified himself by saying that "the number, let's say forty-nine hundred" [warheads], could be included after the word *ceiling*. The relevant portion of the final statement now read:

"As priority tasks they [i.e., Soviet and U.S. negotiators in Geneva] should focus on the following issues: (a) The additional steps necessary to ensure that the reductions [in long-range nuclear arms] enhance strategic stability. This will include a ceiling of 4,900 on the aggregate number of ICBM plus SLBM warheads within the 6,000 total."

Now, to go down from 5,100, which was Ahkromeyev's previous proposal, to 4,900 warheads, was a remarkable concession by any standard. The destructive power of any one of the two hundred nuclear warheads that Marshal Akhromeyev had just agreed to eliminate was enough to obliterate a city the size of New York or Moscow. In making this proposal, Akhromeyev said he was doing it on his own authority, thereby "putting [his] own head on the block" (*"kladu svoyou golovu na plakhu"*). Of course, the marshal spoke tongue in cheek. He made it seem as though he were acting on his own authority, but in fact he was operating within the parameters that Gorbachev had given him earlier in the huddle at the Embassy. Akhromeyev simply stuck to his guns until the last minute in an attempt to concede as little as possible. He fully lived up to his reputation as a down-to-the-wire negotiator.

At 1:55 P.M., as the participants in the official farewell ceremony were already waiting for Gorbachev and Reagan on the South Lawn, the negotiators in the Cabinet Room appeared all but deadlocked over some last details until Reagan and Gorbachev sent Shultz and Shevardnadze downstairs to see what was preventing an agreement. Their intervention was absolutely imperative at this point if the intense bargaining was to be crowned with at least a modicum of success. Only five minutes remained before the official farewell ceremony, by which time the statement had to be agreed upon.

After Shultz and Shevardnadze sat down at the negotiating table, facing each other, Shultz asked Nitze to make a progress report for the U.S. side. Nitze reported that Akhromeyev had initially proposed the aggregate number of ICBM and SLBM warheads "at a level of between forty-eight hundred and fifty hundred, settling finally on forty-nine hundred" which was acceptable to the United States. It was far better than the number 5,100, which had been floated before the summit as the maximum extent to which the Soviet side was prepared to go.

Shultz and Shevardnadze then asked the chief negotiators to read aloud the parts of the joint statement that were the subject of this extraordinary last-minute bargaining. Shultz and Shevardnadze carefully listened to the reports and, then, like a deus ex machina, quickly found a solution to the points at issue. They simply told the negotiators to agree to what they had disagreed on. For example, with regard to the contentious period of nonwithdrawal from the ABM treaty, they proposed inserting just one word, *specified*, before *period*, which suited both sides. And so, after four days of fighting, the two top diplomats put their imprimatur on the text, which was a masterpiece of obfuscation and compromise. Now the relevant part of the final text, intended as a guide for Soviet-U.S. negotiators in Geneva, read as follows:

I. . . . As priority tasks, they should focus on the following issues:

(a) The additional steps necessary to ensure that the reductions [in long-range nuclear arms] enhance strategic stability. This will include a ceiling of 4,900 on the aggregate number of ICBM plus SLBM warheads within the 6,000 total. . . .

(e) Taking into account the preparation of the treaty on strategic offensive arms, the leaders of the two countries also instructed their delegations in Geneva to work out an agreement that would commit both sides to observe the ABM Treaty, *as signed in 1972*, while conducting their research, development, *and testing as required*, for a *specified* period of time. Intensive discussion of strategic stability shall begin not later than three years before the end of the specified period, after which, in the event the sides have not agreed otherwise, *each side will be free to decide its own course of action.* [My italics]

As to what would happen after the period of nonwithdrawal from the ABM treaty ended (which was one of the points to be settled), Shevardnadze accepted U.S. language acknowledging the fact that "each side will be free to decide its own course of action." The phrase in the summit statement actually meant that either party to the would-be START treaty would be free to proceed with deployment of SDI, if it so chose, after the period of nonwithdrawal ended. The phrasing of the joint summit statement papered over the continuing lack of agreement on Star Wars. It allowed each side to claim some victory. For instance, a week later, in an article in *Pravda* of December 16, 1987, Akhromeyev presented his view of what transpired at the meetings of the arms control working group. He wrote:

The task of the group was to negotiate instructions to accelerate the preparation of a draft treaty on 50 percent reductions in strategic offensive arms, or a START treaty, as it is called in English. The negotiations were strenuous, difficult, and had been going on for three days. . . . Especially complex were the negotiations on the relationship between a future treaty on strategic offensive arms and the existing ABM treaty, which had been signed by the two sides as far back as in 1972. The struggle was over how to interpret this treaty. The American experts proposed to us the development of an antimissile system (ABM defense) for a defense of the territory of a country. We strongly opposed it. That is to say, the USA was seeking to break or weaken the relationship between the ABM treaty and a future START treaty. To prevent this, we made sure that the following was recorded in the joint statement: "the sides are obliged to observe the ABM treaty, as signed in 1972."

Reagan portrayed the summit statement as a U.S. victory. He said it resolved the SDI issue, allowing the United States to "go forward with our research and development, and added, "And then, after a certain point . . . we will deploy." He assumed that the Soviets were finally giving in on SDI. Gorbachev, however, didn't see it that way. He said again, publicly, that the Soviets would accept the deployment of weapons in space. "But if the U.S. administration does not heed our voice," he stressed, "if it decides to go ahead with the development of SDI . . . if the Americans have too much money—let them spend it on SDI. We will respond in a different, asymmetrical direction, which will be a hundred times cheaper, and maybe even more than a hundred times." This statement could be taken as a threat to reescalate the arms race if the Soviets judged that the U.S. tests in space went beyond what was permitted by the ABM treaty, i.e., beyond "as required." Gorbachev was calculating, however, that the SDI momentum might die at the hands of Congress or a new administration and he would not have to make good on his threat.

Still, the START agreement looked like an attractive firebird that the two leaders now held by the tail. The bottom line was that Reagan and Gorbachev had just put off the day of reckoning on Star Wars. But the joint statement did allow the negotiating teams in Geneva to get their instructions for the important arms reduction work that lay ahead. And, of course, both leaders knew that without the last-minute appearance of agreement on START, the summit would have looked like a failure or even a setback, and they both wanted to avoid that at all costs.

All in all, the summit *was* a success because both Gorbachev and Reagan wanted it to succeed. They appeared to have come to the same conclusion—that the time was ripe to improve Soviet-American relations, even if their specific differences could not be resolved at this point. After years of angry rhetoric in which Reagan had predicted the demise of communism in the "dustbin of history" and the Soviets had depicted Reagan as a "nuclear-crazed cowboy," the two leaders found themselves talking in virtually the same language of hope and optimism. Ronald Reagan and Mikhail Sergeyevich Gorbachev may have accomplished something even more significant than signing an arms-reduction treaty and agreeing, however vaguely, on an outline for another, even bigger one. They demonstrated that they and their two nations could put aside lingering hostilities and act responsibly in pursuit of a more secure world.

At 2:15 P.M., twenty minutes after they had come to the rescue, the foreign minister and the secretary of state were in agreement on the language and were ready to report back to their leaders on their results. They rose to leave, and everyone followed. I took off my earphones and joined Shultz and Shevardnadze, who wanted to see Gorbachev to show him the text. Protocol people took us to the Map Room, which is between the Library and the Diplomatic Reception Room on the ground floor. Shultz explained that the room was so named because during World War II President Roosevelt set up his information center here, keeping the maps in this room, and, together with his chiefs of staff, developed the tactics and strategy for fighting Germany. Ever since, the maps have remained here. As we passed through the corridors leading toward the Map Room, the military honor guards were already assembled for the departure ceremony outside.

When we reached the room and walked inside, we found Gorbachev and Reagan standing by the wall between the two windows facing the South Lawn. Taking turns, Shevardnadze and Shultz briefed Gorbachev and Reagan on what had transpired in the Cabinet Room. Then Gorbachev turned to Reagan: "Mr. President, could you leave us alone? We want to confer among ourselves." Reagan spread his arms in a gesture of understanding. He did not seem to be surprised at this request and, together with Shultz, left the room. Before he went, he told Gorbachev the room was at his disposal as long as he needed, but would he please remember that the people outside had already been waiting for him for some time now, probably wondering if Gorbachev had gone out the back door. Even at a moment like this Reagan could not resist a joke.

Gorbachev then asked me to find Dobrynin and Akhromeyev and bring them in. It was the crucial moment of decision-making for him, and before committing himself he wanted to hear what his other advisers had to say. I didn't have to go far to find them. Akhromeyev,

Dobrynin, and Yakovlev were standing just outside, near the door. I conveyed Gorbachev's request, and we all went inside the Map Room. The door closed behind us. Gorbachev was still standing by the window, impatiently tapping his fingers on the windowsill.

"Well, what do you think?" he began. Then, turning to his bodyguard, who never left him unattended, he said in a peremptory tone, which I had never heard him use before or since, "Give me the folder, Medvedev!" Medvedev handed him the folder in silence and stepped back. It was like a mini-meeting of the mini-Politburo, held in the White House, since one-quarter of the voting members of that top policy-making body were here in this room: Gorbachev, Shevardnadze, and Yakovlev.

Dobrynin spoke most of all, gesticulating as he did so. Akhromeyev was trying to make his points calmly, dispassionately. He counseled against making haste. Yakovlev only nodded. Shevardnadze and Gorbachev listened. Gorbachev had a pensive look on his face. When Dobrynin and Akhromeyev finished presenting their arguments, Gorbachev's mind was made up. He shook off his pensiveness and said in a loud voice, "Well, then, let it be so!" Eight or ten minutes after it began, the private conference was over. Gorbachev gave his unqualified approval to the text of the joint draft statement, as it had just been agreed upon in the Cabinet Room by the arms control working group in the presence of Shevardnadze and Shultz. Now that the decision had been made, it only remained for him to inform Reagan.

At this moment, Reagan, who had been in the Library Room while Gorbachev was huddling over the text with his advisers, stepped out into the hall, bumping into Gorbachev, as if accidentally. Gorbachev said tersely, "We agree." Reagan gave him a broad smile and shook his hand. With this the business part of the summit was over. But the Cold War wasn't. Not yet.

By now, all the members of the Soviet delegation had been arrayed in a line along the left wall of the Diplomatic Reception Room. Here President Roosevelt had given his famous "fireside chats" over the radio during World War II. President and Mrs. Reagan began to move down the line, shaking hands with each and every one, bidding good-bye. I stood close to the exit, next to Shevardnadze and the Gorbachevs, and as a result I was the last person to whom President and Mrs. Reagan bid farewell. Nancy's handshake was unexpectedly firm, coming from a woman of her stature and health (she had recently had an operation for cancer). As Reagan gripped my hand in his, he said, "Good luck to you!"

He had that kindly avuncular look on his face. "Thank you, Mr. President," I responded, "I could use that."

Outside, it was beginning to drizzle. As we walked out of the White House, a protocol officer or an usher thrust an umbrella in my hand, saying that unfortunately there were not enough umbrellas for everybody, but would I please share it with the foreign minister? It was a huge, "family-type" umbrella. When I opened it, Shevardnadze was grateful. Now it was raining steadily. Yakovlev, who stood nearby, did not have an umbrella, only a gray fedora to cover his head. Soviet chief of protocol Chernishev saw this and asked me to share the umbrella also with Yakovlev. "We can't leave him like this, he is a Politburo member, after all," he whispered in my ear. Fortunately, the umbrella was big enough to easily shield three people. Bush and his wife, Barbara, stood next to us. In his right hand he held an umbrella high over their heads. Shevardnadze told him that, according to old Russian folklore, "It's a good omen when it rains at parting." Bush replied that he knew it. "You call it the mushroom rain," he said. "*Da, da* [Yes, indeed], we call it *gribnoi dozhdik*," echoed Shevardnadze. The other 2,300 guests, gathered for the ceremony, were not so lucky. Some of them covered their heads with newspapers and even handkerchiefs.

"Ladies and gentlemen! The president of the United States and the general secretary of the Communist Party of the Soviet Union!" intoned the announcer's sonorous voice, amplified through the speakers. The Marine band struck up the Soviet national anthem and the Gorbachevs and the Reagans mounted the dais. Nancy looked dramatic in a red coat, high-heeled red shoes, and black gloves. So did the president. He wore an elegant black camel coat with a white scarf and a red tie, and no hat. The Gorbachevs looked a little less dramatic. Raisa Maximovna wore the same karakul coat as at the welcoming ceremony and no gloves. Gorbachev, too, wore the same dark gray coat with a plaid scarf.

The two leaders made the obligatory departure remarks. Reagan spoke of "a sense of accomplishment" and singled out the INF treaty as "the greatest accomplishment of the summit." He quoted President Calvin Coolidge, "History is made only by action," and said this was a "treaty that does indeed make history," but it "should be viewed as a beginning, not an end." He called for more progress in arms reductions. He stressed that his goal was "a more constructive relationship between the two governments, long-lasting, rather than transitory, improvements." He concluded with an appeal for peace and freedom and did it in his own inimitable way by telling a story: "During World War Two, when so many young Russians served at the front, the poem 'Wait for

Me' became a prayer spoken on the lips of Russian families who dreamed one day of the happiness that their reunion would bring. The cause of world peace and world freedom is still waiting, Mr. General Secretary. It has waited long enough."

Gorbachev for his part described the INF treaty as "an unprecedented step in the history of the nuclear age," expressing the hope that it "has set in motion the process of disarmament." He spoke of some headway having been made in his talks with Reagan on the central issue of achieving substantial reductions in strategic offensive arms. He got a standing ovation when he said that he was looking forward to a new encounter with America in the hope that he would then be able not only to see its capital, but to "meet face-to-face its great people, to chat and have some lively exchanges with ordinary Americans."

At 2:45 P.M.—twenty-five minutes later than planned—they finally bid their public good-byes "until next year in Moscow" by exchanging handshakes and applauding each other under umbrellas that protected them from the downpour, in front of the cameras and reporters on the South Lawn. Then, the Gorbachevs got into their limousine. The Reagans waved as the Zil picked up speed. I couldn't get rid of the impression that the two of them looked like the proverbial good neighbors or a particularly benign pair of in-laws—they looked so friendly. It could have been any parting of hosts and houseguests, except that the two men had spent part of the week tossing around the future of the world and helping to ensure that there would be one. Shevardnadze and I followed in the next car. The last scene that etched itself in my memory, as our car started to move, was that of a young girl sitting on her daddy's shoulders, munching away at an apple and waving at us with a combination Soviet-American flag. I remember thinking, maybe she and other kids of her age, Soviet, American, and all others, would be the ones who would no longer live in fear of a nuclear holocaust. I called Shevardnadze's attention to the scene, and we both waved back at her.

Late in the afternoon Gorbachev had a meeting at the Embassy with U.S. business leaders to discuss Soviet-American economic cooperation, followed by a marathon press conference, which lasted two hours and ten minutes. Then, before leaving for the airport, he wanted to brief senior Embassy diplomats on what had really been accomplished at the just-concluded summit, to give them his inside view of things. The briefing was held in the Oak Room.

He began with an evaluation of the results of his visit. His private assessment in this restricted group of his own people contrasted somewhat with the public assessment he had shared with the large American, actually worldwide, audience a short while before. He intimated that at the press conference from which he had just returned he had intentionally put higher marks on the outcome of his meetings with the president than they deserved. He said the results of his visit had to be portrayed in upbeat tones, although there were no grounds for such a positive assessment. It was necessary above all to bolster "our image" in the eyes of the American public. "We had to impress it upon them that we are doing everything to strengthen peace and make progress. This will only benefit us all. The public is a mighty force. It has to be cultivated, and its opinion channeled into a direction suitable for us. So from this point of view, the visit has been successful indeed.

"In actual fact," he continued, "there has been almost no success. On the central issue—strategic arms reductions in linkage with observance of the ABM treaty—it was important for us to preserve at least an outward appearance of a momentum. We were obliged to go along with the idea of establishing a ceiling on ICBMs and SLBMs at the level of forty-nine hundred warheads, although it is not to our advantage to go below the level of five thousand. Nor were we successful in persuading them to give their consent to the limitation of testing in the framework of what they call 'defense in space' and what we call 'preparation for space wars.' True, even here, to preserve the semblance of progress, we had to resort to a kind of trick in the language of the relevant provision in the joint statement, which speaks about 'observing the ABM treaty, as signed in 1972.' Speaking of human rights, here the president attempted once more to interfere in our internal affairs. We had to give him a rebuff. I told him bluntly that he was not a prosecutor and I was not an accused, and that here we should talk on an equal footing—otherwise there would be no talking at all. The president also tried to bring pressure to bear upon us with regard to regional conflicts, especially on Afghanistan.

"In a word, not everything was as we would have liked. But I say once again that it was more important for us to win the public over to our side, and not only the American public. For the entire world public has been following the course of the visit and its results. Therefore, we should never forget it. We cannot afford to lose the battle over public minds. A great deal for us will depend on how they will be shaped and in whose favor.

"I want to assure you that we, in the Center [i.e. in Moscow], read and follow very carefully what you report to us from here. On the whole, we understand that you work here in difficult conditions. You send a lot of material to us. But when one starts to look for answers to some particular questions, one often fails to find them in these materials. You do not submit enough suggestions, proposals, or express new ideas and thoughts. Perhaps there is something here for you, comrades, to work on. We expect practical and realistic cables with your proposals, not just statements of facts. Be bolder in developing and submitting new and innovative ideas and proposals. We have a right to count on this. One more thing. Study the host country more carefully and thoroughly. Do not disperse your attention. Concentrate it on those aspects that have the greatest importance for us. Know this country well. Make broader contacts not only with representatives of the administration and Congress, but with the public at large as well, especially with those who are in sympathy with us. In short, *perestraivaites'* [restructure or change yourselves]. Use the new thinking in your practical work. We will support you. But then we will demand more of you. . . .

"The president and I agreed that he would pay us a visit late in May—early in June of next year. We must see to it that by then some weighty documents are prepared for signing. That visit will not be ours, of course, but we must try to turn it to our benefit."

With those words the briefing was concluded. Suddenly Gorbachev looked tired. He now had bags under his eyes. He admitted that he was indeed exhausted—he was working on his "second wind"; but he would recover, he said, when he got back home. It was just due to the grueling pace of work.

The departure from Andrews Air Force Base had been delayed three times. Instead of 7:30 P.M., as originally planned, we left the Embassy at 8:30, in the same long motorcade as when Gorbachev had arrived. Bush and Shultz came to the Embassy to escort Gorbachev and Shevardnadze respectively to the airport. I was waiting in the lobby for the minister to come down. He appeared together with Gorbachev, who shook everybody's hand and bid farewell to all, and then he joined Bush, who was already in the limousine. I followed Shevardnadze into the second Zil, where Shultz joined us.

As the motorcade started to roll, both men turned serious. With the car windows fogged, we couldn't see anything outside, and it was just as well because nothing distracted their attention now. Ever a pragmatist, Shultz began to discuss the just-completed summit. The president viewed it as a clear success, he said. Later tonight, he said, after Gorbachev left, the president would appear on national television to tell about it in greater detail.

"But," said Shultz, "you and I still have our work cut out for us.

Unfortunately, we were unable to make progress in such an important matter as Afghanistan. But I think some positive developments are beginning to emerge in this direction. It seems it would be a good idea for you and me to meet several times before the next meeting in Moscow. I think we should hold at least three such meetings." Shevardnadze nodded his assent: "Yes, indeed, there's a lot of work for us ahead, so much so that we cannot afford to rest."

We were now approaching Andrews Air Force Base. The limousine was hot and humid now, its windows completely fogged—the air conditioner did not work properly. Soon the motorcade passed through the open gate and pulled up at the edge of a red carpet leading to Gorbachev's aircraft. He and Raisa Maximovna were already here, shaking hands with the members of the farewell committee, who were lined up on both sides of the carpet.

As we got out of the car, gunshots rang out. Shultz hastened to reassure Shevardnadze: "Have no fear, they're not firing at your plane, but into the sky. It is a salute in honor of the end of your visit. Twenty-one salvos." I did not see Shultz smile frequently, but now he broke into a wide grin. "I have no fear," replied Shevardnadze. "I know you are a peaceable people."

The rain had stopped by now. The Gorbachevs lingered at the top of the ramp to wave at the officials below on the ground, with the tall figure of Bush in the front. At exactly 9 P.M. the door was closed, and the plane began to taxi down the runway. Gorbachev, Shevardnadze, Yakovlev, Dobrynin, Akhromeyev, and their closest aides headed first for Berlin to inform the Warsaw Pact allies on the summit's results. And I took another plane to Moscow.

A few words about the real results of the summit. Despite the lack of dramatic progress on key arms control and regional issues such as Afghanistan, Gorbachev had reason to be pleased with the visit overall, his qualified priavte assessment notwithstanding. The centerpiece of the summit—the signing of the INF treaty eliminating a whole class of medium-range and shorter-range nuclear weapons—was viewed more of a milestone in the Soviet Union than in the United States because it removed weapons based in Western Europe that directly threatened the Soviet Union. In a country where memories of World War II were still fresh in the minds of the people and shaped the national psychology, and where the threat of American aggression had been drummed into the heads of citizens for four decades, any step that promised to reduce the threat of war carried a special significance that was hard for Americans to appreciate.

The Kremlin had mobilized its opinion-shaping machinery to make sure that no Soviet citizen failed to see the treaty as a triumph of Soviet diplomacy under Gorbachev. He returned home on Friday, after the brief stopover in Berlin to meet with his Warsaw Pact allies, declaring that his domestic and foreign initiatives, which had until then produced few tangible results, could lead to real benefits, in this case a treaty that eliminated the dire threat of a nuclear missile attack on short notice.

No less important to the Soviet leader was that his performance in the United States, most of which was broadcast live on television in the Soviet Union, had generally played well at home because he managed to be both charming and firm. His unyielding stance on human rights policies, for example, was intended in part to demonstrate to his other Kremlin colleagues and to the Soviet people at large that he could not be pushed around on a sensitive issue. Gorbachev left Washington with his political fate linked more closely with President Reagan, a man who had entered the White House as an implacable foe of the Soviet Union as the "Evil Empire." On his return to Moscow, Gorbachev was in a position to say that he and Reagan now trusted each other more. That, too, was a significant accomplishment soon to be followed with more.

Finally, the summit marked a happy political coincidence for both leaders. Gorbachev, eager to show concrete achievements at a time when his domestic reforms had yet to produce them, wanted to show he could maneuver the most stridently anti-Soviet U.S. president into a more cooperative posture.

All in all, it was a successful summit, and a major milestone in bringing the Cold War to an end.

CHAPTER THREE

SLAYING-A-FEW-DRAGONS SUMMIT

Gorbachev-Reagan Moscow Summit, 1988

As spring gave way to summer in late May 1988, almost six months had passed since the Washington summit. Over this period the ferment of *glasnost* in the Soviet Union had become real. Change was evident in the political and spiritual spheres. In fact, change operated on many levels and in different directions. The gradual weakening of censorship of the press, literature, theater, music, movies; the increasing criticism of the Soviet past, the present, and even the Soviet leadership, which was not only tolerated but actually encouraged; the emergence of so-called cooperative food stores, cafés, and restaurants, including the first McDonald's in Moscow—all this and much more were the unmistakable signs of a transformation in Soviet society.

In May, far-reaching proposals had been completed under the supervision of Alexandr Yakovlev, whom Gorbachev had put in charge of ideology, and issued as "theses" for discussion at the all-important 19th Party Conference scheduled to be held after the upcoming summit, in June. When I read them, I couldn't believe my eyes. The "theses" included provisions on the freedom of speech, press, and assembly, multiple-choice elections and secret ballots, the rights of citizens, the separation of powers, independence of the judicial branch, etc. In other words, they contained the seeds of real democracy, the beginning of the long-awaited liberation of people from the suffocating embrace of the monopolistic Party rule. If put into practice, this would spell the end of the Communist Party's legal monopoly on political power enshrined in the notorious Article 6 of the Soviet Constitution. Much later, I learned that Gorbachev had even more radical plans for instituting a multiparty system, but they had been rejected by the entire Politburo—with the exception of Yakovlev and Shevardnadze, who sided with Gorbachev. At this point in time I began to change my view of Gorbachev's real intentions. Things had finally started to move. In his assault on the Soviet power structure and the stultifying effects of the ideological conservatism of the Communist Party, Gorbachev continued, with Yakovlev's help, to reach out to form a political alliance with the intelligentsia. He needed ways to summon the pressure of public opinion to help him break the power of the Party apparat, and *glasnost,* or the process of eliminating the Big Lie, was his strategy for arousing the people of the Soviet Union to action in favor of reforms. Although *glasnost* did not yet mean complete freedom of speech and freedom of the press, it is clear in retrospect that Gorbachev's reforms would not have been possible without them.

In the central streets of Moscow, and especially in the Old Arbat area, one could daily observe this unusual sight: the sidewalks jammed with people craning their necks to see over one another's shoulder to read the latest editions of newspapers that were displayed on billboards. *Moskovskiye Novosti (Moscow News),* which had until now been a boring propaganda sheet for foreign tourists—and a badly translated one, I might add,—suddenly became one of the city's most exciting newspapers. It was now full of formerly taboo items—such as exposés about crime, corruption involving high-level Party officials, political abuses of power, and even prostitution—and was sold out as soon as it hit the newsstands. So were the newspapers *Izvestiya* and *Literaturnaya Gazeta,* the weekly magazine *Ogonyok,* and the monthly journal *Yunost,* and many other publications. Some of them were making a specialty, as it were, of exposing Stalin's and Beria's crimes.

In yet another sign of *glasnost,* to the great joy of those Soviet citizens who spoke foreign languages, it was now possible to buy at major newsstands in Moscow *The New York Times, The Washington Post, Time, Newsweek, Le Monde, Figaro, Der Spiegel,* and so on. Until now all foreign periodicals had been banned and unavailable to common people. At the same time, it was still ill-advised for common citizens to discuss controversial items in public. I remember I once called a friend to ask if he had managed to buy the latest edition of *Ogonyok,* which I had missed, and he said, yes, he had. But when I asked him to tell me what was worthy of attention in it, he paused and then said, "I'm sorry, I'll tell you when I see you. I can't talk about it on the phone." The fear of the KGB was still very much alive in the hearts of people. In a joke then making the rounds in Moscow, one dog asks another how things are different under Gorbachev, and the other dog replies that the leash is still too short and the food dish is still too far away to reach, but they let you bark now as loud as you want. However, one still had to be careful even about the barking.

Despite this and the bleak economic news, the spring of 1988 in Moscow was pregnant with expectations. Gorbachev, true to his word to Reagan, had begun preparations for withdrawing from Afghanistan. On the night of February 8, I had sat watching the TV news program *Vremya* and heard the anchorman read a long statement on behalf of Gorbachev, announcing May 15 as the date for the start of the withdrawal, and declaring that all Soviet troops would be out of Afghanistan by the following March 15. It had been long-awaited, welcome news and brought vividly to my mind the adamant insistence with which the Soviet delegation at the summit in Washington had proposed a twelve-month schedule for the removal of Soviet forces from Afghanistan. Gorbachev was obviously in a hurry to turn over a new leaf. Elsewhere on the international front, Gorbachev's policy of new thinking continued to gain ground, and for me it was a busier time than ever—I was heavily involved in interpreting and translating work both in the MFA and in the Kremlin.

On January 15, Gorbachev had met with the founding members of the just established International Foundation for the Survival and Development of Mankind, which included some of the most prominent personalities in the fields of science and technology, culture, and business from different countries. Among them was Andrei Sakharov. The very fact that he was invited to this high-level gathering in the Kremlin was a remarkable sign of the ongoing change inside the country. At the meeting, Gorbachev told his audience that no radical change for the better had yet occurred in the world situation, although positive trends had indeed emerged in all major areas, especially in the field of disarmament. He called for further intensive efforts to restructure international relations and thus achieve a genuine breakthrough.

Less than two weeks after the announcement of the Soviet withdrawal from Afghanistan, Shultz flew into Moscow, on February 21, for the previously scheduled round in a series of talks with Shevardnadze and Gorbachev, to begin planning the Moscow summit. On that first day, Shultz and Shevardnadze talked well past midnight, covering a wide range of issues, including the START treaty, but focusing mainly on regional issues, especially on the remaining differences on Afghanistan. The Americans were determined to continue their military aid to the Afghan resistance fighters even after the last Soviet soldier had left Afghanistan unless the Soviets terminated theirs to the Kabul regime. Shevardnadze pointed out that providing aid to a legitimate government, recognized by the United Nations, was not the same thing as helping rebel forces seeking its overthrow. The two top diplomats went round and round the same points, but no compromise was in sight. The next day, Shultz met with Gorbachev in the Kremlin. The upshot of their long conversation was that Gorbachev had only one request of Shultz, namely that the United States work for the early signing of the U.N.-negotiated Geneva Agreements and for their implementation, so that there could be "a neutral, nonaligned, and independent Afghanistan."

On March 11, Gorbachev met with U.S. senators Sam Nunn, Alan Cranston, Alan K. Simpson, and Carl Levin and some leading American scientists. In the three-hour meeting he reaffirmed the Soviet position linking strategic arms reductions to the observance of the 1972 ABM treaty, expressed confidence that a START treaty would be ready in time for Reagan's visit, and outlined some ideas about further improving Soviet-U.S. relations.

Then, on March 21–23, Shevardnadze went to Washington for the second round of ministerials with Shultz and a meeting with Reagan, and I, together with a fellow interpreter, Pavel Palazchenko, accompanied him. Shevardnadze was all business, and the business at the top of the list was again Afghanistan. He personally had played a key role in the Kremlin's decision to withdraw, believing, as he would admit later, that it was an "unjust war." Shevardnadze pleaded, often in emotional terms, for the United States to stop its arms supplies to the mujahedeen, arguing that Moscow had done almost everything possible to accommodate Washington. During the six-and-a-half-hour nonstop marathon session at the State Department on March 22, Shultz proposed only a three-month moratorium on arms transfers to either side. Shevardnadze did not accept the offer. He said Moscow could not abandon its friends just like that. On the last day of the ministerial, March 23, the two sides finally announced the dates for the Moscow summit: May 29–June 2.

The Geneva Agreements—the primary parties to which were Afghanistan and Pakistan, with the Soviet Union and United States as "guarantors"—were finally signed on April 14, in Geneva, by Shevardnadze and Shultz, along with the Afghan and Pakistani foreign ministers. In this face-saving document, Moscow "front-loaded" its pullout from Afghanistan, as Washington had asked. *Front-loading* was one of those arcane words in the military lexicon that always gave us, the interpreters, a big headache. What it actually meant, as used by Shultz and his experts, was withdrawal of as many as half of all the Soviet troops from Afghanistan in the first three months. The accords provided for a political settlement "around Afghanistan," but not among its warring factions inside. It contained Soviet and U.S. pledges of "noninterference" in its internal affairs and called for national reconciliation in that country. Pakistan and Afghanistan for their part pledged not to carry out any hostile acts against each other and to help the Afghan refugees return home. The question of Soviet and U.S. arms supplies to the opposing parties in Afghanistan was not covered in the Geneva accords.

On April 21, one week after signing the Geneva accords, Shultz arrived in Moscow again, for yet another round of meetings to prepare for Reagan's forthcoming trip to the Soviet Union. Once again, I was busy interpreting every day from early morning until almost midnight at the MFA Guest House on Tolstoy Street. For the first time, Afghanistan did not dominate the discussions—arms control and START did. On April 29, in another sign of improving relations between the Soviet Union and the United States, there was an unprecedented meeting in Bern, Switzerland, between Soviet defense minister Dmitryi Yazov and U.S. secretary of defense Frank Carlucci. Meantime, the delegations of the two sides in Geneva continued the START and CTBT (comprehensive nuclear test ban treaty) talks, which had resumed earlier in the year, in an attempt to finish the preparation of the respective treaties in time for the summit.

As the summit drew closer, I became heavily involved in translating numerous documents for it: a program of Reagan's visit, speeches, statements, texts of agreements and protocol events, and even the menu for the dinner to be hosted by Gorbachev for Reagan in the Kremlin.

MOSCOW. MAY 29, SUNDAY. DAY ONE.

One day before Reagan's arrival in Moscow, which was already dressed up in new spring foliage, the streets near Spaso House, the traditional residence of American ambassadors, where the Reagans would be staying for the duration of the summit, had been repaved, while the two nearby dilapidated houses on the Sadovoye Koltso (the outer Garden Ring road) were repaired and whitewashed. Buildings opposite the Kremlin had been repainted in an assortment of pastel colors. Even the grassy strip on a boulevard in front of a school in Kropotkinskaya Street that Nancy Reagan was to visit had been replanted. Like a latter-day Potemkin village, Moscow was being spruced up for the forthcoming summit meeting between General Secretary Gorbachev and President Reagan—the first such meeting in the Soviet capital between Soviet and U.S. leaders since Nixon's visit in 1974. Like in 1980, on the eve of the XXII Olympic Games in Moscow, the city authorities had begun nightly raids to flush out *valyutniye prostitutki* (prostitutes who worked for hard currency only) from the downtown tourist hotels where Reagan's entourage of about 800 and 3,300 visiting journalists would be staying. Parked cars had been banned from all the routes of the presidential motorcade for the duration of the summit. Last but not least, the city authorities boasted on television that they had even arranged for the lilacs to be in bloom and for the sun to shine on the president— two predictions that surprisingly came true.

Muscovites were ecstatic. They still remembered with fondness how the city had been beautified on the eve of Nixon's visit fourteen years before, with houses repainted, potholes patched, and all roads leading to the Kremlin repaved. Moscow took on the appearance of "a model communist city," "the capital of the world," the two titles to which the communist authorities in those distant days laid a serious claim. Now the people of Moscow expected more of the same and they were not disappointed. The Communist system did not like to reveal its flaws to any distinguished foreign visitors, particularly the president of the United States, and especially such a one as Ronald Reagan. That attitude had not changed even under Gorbachev. "We wish American presidents would come to visit us more often" was the general sentiment on the streets.

But the Kremlin leadership was also intent on polishing other parts of its image. Far more important than sprucing up the city was the fact that, on May 15, two weeks before the summit, the Soviet army had indeed begun a scheduled retreat from the eight-and-a-half-year war in Afghanistan. Gorbachev had kept his word, although doubts persisted until the last moment whether it would come to pass.

And on May 28, just one day before Ronald Reagan's arrival when he was already in Helsinki, the Presidium of the Supreme Soviet of the USSR unanimously ratified the INF treaty between the Soviet Union and the United States. This ratification followed the U.S. Senate's by one day. The action by the Supreme Soviet and the Senate now made it possible for the Soviet and U.S. leaders to exchange the instruments of ratification, thus putting the treaty officially into force. The dual ratification was of great importance because the previous three Soviet-U.S. treaties—the TTBTs (Threshold Test Ban Treaty) of 1974 and 1976, and the SALT II Treaty of 1979, signed by Brezhnev and Nixon, Ford, and Carter, respectively—had been stopped in the Senate and never ratified by the United States.

As to what was hoped to be the centerpiece of this summit—the signing of a groundbreaking treaty mandating deep, 50 percent cuts in both sides' long-range or strategic nuclear weapons—it now seemed clear that it would not be ready for signing. Despite the instructions issued five and a half months before by Reagan and Gorbachev to the delegations in Geneva, the START talks had proved so complex that an accord anytime soon seemed unlikely. Even though the treaty was about 90 percent complete, the remaining 10 percent was most troublesome. Although Reagan clearly wanted to crown his successful presidency with a START treaty, the Soviet leadership was divided on the matter. Gorbachev had now become a man in a hurry and, like Reagan, wanted to strike while the iron was hot. Soviet hard-liners, however, did not want to hand to the American president what they considered another victory for the United States, and the Soviet military was still reluctant to give up its advantage in strategic arms and resorted to all kinds of tricks at the Geneva talks to slow them down and buy time. Gorbachev was intent on not antagonizing anti-American hard-liners because he would rather spend his energy on reforms at home. Soviet leaders were now preoccupied with what was to them an even more crucial "domestic summit," an extraordinary conference of the Communist Party of the Soviet Union scheduled to be held soon after the Soviet-U.S. summit. At issue would be the future pace of *perestroika* and *glasnost*, the twin pillars of Gorbachev's program of internal reform.

In the meantime, his policies both at home and abroad came publicly under attack. On March 14, as I opened *Sovetskaya Rossiya*, the newspaper of the government of the Russian Republic, I was startled to read, on page three, a ringing antireform and anti-Gorbachev article. The piece, which amounted to an anti-*perestroika* manifesto, was titled "I Cannot Forgo My Principles," and it was signed by some obscure Leningrad teacher of chemistry, Nina Andreyeva. The article was clearly published with the blessing of a conservative member of the Politburo, Yegor Ligachev, who considered himself number two, while Gorbachev was away on a visit to Yugoslavia. The article extolled Stalin as the leading "trailblazer" of socialism and clearly bore Ligachev's imprint.

It wasn't a putsch per se, but it was the greatest challenge to Gorbachev's leadership yet, and it took him three weeks to strike back through his friend and ally Alexandr Yakovlev. A full-page article rebutting Andreyeva appeared in the Communist Party's *Pravda* only on April 5. All the while Gorbachev's credibility and authority had hung in the balance. The incident was actually the first alarming sign that the conservative forces in Soviet society were no longer willing to take the diminution of their power lying down. The heretofore hidden resistance to Gorbachev and his policies had come into the open. The first salvo against him had been fired.

On this last Sunday of the month, May 29, at 12:55 P.M., one hour before Reagan's arrival, I was already at Vnukovo-2 airport, which is somewhat equivalent to Andrews Air Force Base in Washington and is used for ceremonial visits of heads of state and for official travel by top Soviet VIPs. The day was gorgeous, warm but not too hot, with the sun shining from the blue skies. The fresh green foliage had not yet collected dust and dirt as it would by the middle of summer, for Moscow, alas, is one of the most heavily polluted cities in the world. It was one of the best days in the city I remember.

On the tarmac side of the terminal, a bright red streamer with white lettering proclaimed in English, "Welcome, Mr. President." The pleasant breeze rippled the Soviet and American flags flying over the terminal. On the left of the exit facing the tarmac was a platform for reporters and cameramen, among whom I glimpsed Sam Donaldson, the controversial American reporter from ABC-TV. He was bickering with someone over the best spot on the platform. A guard of honor was being lined up on the right. A long red runner carpet was rolled out from the terminal building to a microphone stand near where Reagan's plane would come to a stop. Soon, more familiar faces appeared on the tarmac. Selwa Roosevelt, White House chief of protocol, greeted me like an old friend. She was delighted to be here, she said. Until the last moment she wasn't sure she would come. Another familiar face, Carolyn Smith, was also there. She said she was assigned again to be Nancy Reagan's interpreter, as she had been at the last summit in Washington. As we stood there chatting, Igor Scherbakov, the MFA deputy chief of protocol, came out of the terminal looking for me. He said it was time for me to get back inside the terminal to meet Andrei Andreyevich (Gromyko), who was due any minute now. As titular head of state Gromyko was to greet the Reagans officially here at the airport.

Gromyko, the "old Kremlin wolf," as some wicked tongues dubbed him, had been "kicked upstairs" in the summer of 1985 when Gorbachev made him chairman of the Presidium of the Supreme Soviet of the USSR, a position formally equal to that of a head of state, but largely ceremonial. Gromyko was said to be one of the men in the Politburo who had voted against Gorbachev following Andropov's death, although the second time around, after Chernenko died, Gromyko did nominate him for the job of general secretary. Gorbachev was not a vengeful man, but he was a realist and knew that the veteran foreign minister would not be the right man for conducting the new foreign policy that he, Gorbachev, had in mind. So he replaced Gromyko with Shevardnadze and gave him what was basically a protocol function.

For Reagan's arrival, Gorbachev decided to stay in the Kremlin and send Gromyko to Vnukovo to meet him. But he didn't know what to do with Gromyko after he greeted Reagan at the airport. Gorbachev clearly didn't want him around for fear he might be a spoiler. Initially, the plan was for Gromyko to take Reagan from the airport first to Spaso House where Reagan would spend some twenty minutes—to "wash his hands" after the journey. This would enable him to graciously accompany Reagan in his limousine to his residence and there take leave of him and quietly drop from public view for the remainder of the day. But the Americans upset the plan by insisting that the president wanted to go straight to the Kremlin with Nancy alone, without Gromyko. The Soviets balked because the idea raised too many problems for them. Where, for example, would Gromyko go after the welcoming ceremony for Reagan at Vnukovo? He had no role in the Kremlin at this summit. But this Soviet dilemma was apparently of no concern to the Americans. Despite all the pleading by the Soviets, they were adamant. "Do what you think you have to do under the circumstances. That is your problem. The president is not going to change his mind. This is his first visit to your country and he wants to do it his own way," they said. Eventually, the Soviets gave up. They accepted the American plan for President and Mrs. Reagan to go straight to the Kremlin. Gromyko would meet the American president at the ramp of his plane, review the guard of honor with him, introduce the president to the diplomatic corps, have a brief conversation with him in the airport terminal, then take him to the presidential limousine where he would bid farewell. Thereafter Gromyko would quietly go home.

When Gromyko was told about this plan, understandably he got upset. According to some of his close aides, his greatest secret desire was to be seen escorting President Reagan along Moscow streets in a motorcade so the people would see them together, in the hope, perhaps, that this would be perceived as a symbol of reconciliation in the spirit of the new times. But, as usual, he was "loyal and obedient to authority" to the very end. "Tell him to drop down his pants and sit with his derriere on a block of ice and he will sit there until told to rise" was how Khrushchev characterized, with his typical flamboyance and peasant straightforwardness, Gromyko's sense of duty and loyalty.

When I returned inside the terminal vestibule, Shevardnadze and Dobrynin were already there, with their wives. This was in sharp contrast to pre-Gorbachevian times when Soviet leaders never appeared with their wives in public. The world didn't even know that Andropov, for example, had a wife. She was seen in public for the first time only at his funeral. Until then, he was believed to be a bachelor. Shevardnadze was in high spirits. When he exchanged greetings with Ambassador Matlock, he said in reference to the fine day, "We have specially ordered good weather today for the president." "Thank you, we appreciate this," answered the ambassador in Russian. Apart from his affability and professional competence and demeanor, the fact that Ambassador Matlock spoke excellent Russian was one of the reasons why he was popular with ordinary Russians.

The vestibule was now full of people. Soon Vladimir Chernishev, chief of Soviet state protocol, gave me a sign to follow him. Through the double glass doors on the other side I saw a long black Zil limousine pull up at the entrance and then Gromyko step out—with his wife. All the officials in the lobby, especially the MFA people, pulled themselves up straight at the sight of Gromyko. They were still in awe of this man who had been their boss for twenty-eight years, even though he had left the Ministry almost three years before. He wore his favorite nondescript diplomatic gray wool pinstripe, made in the MFA tailoring and dressmaking establishment. Despite the fine summer weather, he held a gray homburg in his hands—the invariable accessory of any Soviet leader. It was a symbol of power for them, I suppose, although wearing hats in public did not become the in thing with Soviet leaders until after Stalin's death in 1953.

With his closely cropped hair, Gromyko looked strong and robust in spite of his seventy-nine years. His wife, Lydia Dmitriyevna, a heavyset woman of about her husband's age, wore a flowery gathered dress with a short dark blue jacket over it. She seemed to have gained a few more pounds since I had last seen her. With five minutes remaining before the arrival of Reagan, Gromyko and his spouse went across the hall, dignifying with nods the people assembled there, and stopping to shake hands with two or three officials. That in itself was a remarkable change in Gromyko's public demeanor. In the fourteen years I had known him, he had seldom, if ever, condescended to such "fraternizing" with people "less equal" than himself. The times were really "a-changing." I was assigned to act as his interpreter at this welcoming ceremony for Reagan, although Gromyko could speak English well enough to make himself understood, and of course, he understood everything said to him in English. But he always liked to have an interpreter around because he was entitled to one.

He and his wife led the welcoming committee, which included Shevardnadze, Dobrynin, Ambassador Matlock, and a few other officials, who were also with their wives. As we walked down the long red carpet, the blue-and-white jet, with "United States of America" written on its sides and the large presidential seal below the front door, had landed and taxied toward us. At two o'clock on the nose, it came to a stop at the designated area near the red carpet. A few minutes later President and Mrs. Reagan emerged from the doorway and stepped onto the ramp, squinting against the bright sunlight. They both waved in a friendly fashion in our direction. Hand in hand, they slowly descended the ramp. At precisely 2:05 P.M. they stepped on the soil of the "Evil Empire." It was a thrilling, historic moment.

Exuding a dazzling Hollywood smile, President Reagan was the first to extend his hand to Chairman Gromyko. "Velkom to Moscow," said Gromyko in his accented English, his lips pursed in a typical fashion with the left side of the lower lip sagging, as if he were displeased with something. Then, bending slightly at the waist, Reagan turned to me next and said, while extending his hand and looking me straight in the eye, "It's good to see you again." He said it simply and sincerely as if he really remembered me and was glad to see me. Suddenly I knew why he was the Great Communicator. It was the way he conducted himself toward other people, whatever their station in life. It was his warmth, friendliness, and affability, it was the way he looked you straight in the eye, it was his firm and lingering handshake. I must say that face-to-face he was tremendously likable, as Gorbachev was. No wonder they had hit it off, almost at first sight.

Nancy Reagan was chicly dressed in a two-piece suit with "power shoulders." She impressed a lot of Russian people with how svelte she was and how youthful she looked. In general, the American first couple made a great impression on the Soviets.

After Reagan and Gromyko reviewed the guard of honor and the Reagans were introduced to all members of both the U.S. and Soviet welcoming committee, the entire party proceeded to the air terminal. There, everyone else was *otsechen* (cut off) by burly Soviet security men, and only President and Mrs. Reagan, Chairman and Mrs. Gromyko, Reagan's American interpreter, Peter Afanasenko, and myself were allowed to go inside the lounge especially reserved for Politburo members. Without a word, Gromyko motioned for the Reagans to sit down on a dark brown leather sofa, and he and his wife each took a chair, thus flanking the American first couple. According to the protocol arrangements, the Reagans and the Gromykos were supposed to make "small talk."

All this time Reagan had not said a word either. He waited for his host to take the initiative. But before Gromyko could open his mouth, his wife, Lydia Dmitriyevna, suddenly lurched forward and startled the Reagans by making a welcoming speech herself. Mixing up English and Russian words, she said, "Vait, Andryusha [Wait, my dear Andrei], I vill say." And, turning to the Reagans, who sat next to each other on the sofa holding hands, she continued in half-English, half-Russian, "Misterr Prezident [accenting the last syllable, the Russian way]. *Ya khochu velcome vas na zemle ov Moskva. Ve live v Amerike* eight years *i* I learn English *tam*" (I want to welcome you on Moscow soil. We lived eight years in America and I learned my English there). "Ve vish you plezant," and here she stopped short—she had forgotten the English word *stay* and turned to me for help. After I prompted her with the right word, she finished, "Plezant stei in our country."

Laudable as her attempt to welcome the American president in his own language may have been, her English was hopeless. To add insult to injury, Gromyko turned to me at one point and stunned me by asking me bluntly who I was. "*Vi nash ili ikh?*" (Are you ours or theirs?) he demanded. And this after I had been interpreting for him for so many years, sometimes as often as several times a month, to say nothing of our last meeting in the Kremlin barely two weeks before! Piqued, I replied evasively that I was "the missing link in the communication chain." He looked at me with bewilderment and drawled, "Aaa . . ." The Reagans looked mystified. They didn't quite grasp the welcoming speech and I didn't translate it because Lydia Dmitriyevna had told me not to, apparently believing that she said the whole thing in perfect English.

Still holding hands with Nancy, Reagan responded, "Mr. Chairman," addressing Gromyko by his Soviet title. "I am thrilled to be here in Moscow for the first time ever. Nancy and I have been looking forward to this moment, and here we are." Gromyko clearly felt ill at ease and didn't know what to say. Then lapsing into Russian, he mumbled something about having seen the president for the last time a few years before. Indeed, he and Reagan had not met since September 1984 when Gromyko visited him for the first and last time in the White House at the height of the Cold War. Reagan, too, seemed to be at a loss for words, but he responded that "those were different times." With this, Gromyko rose, hat still in hand, giving us to understand that the official welcoming ceremony was over. Reagan and Nancy exchanged glances and, escorted by the Gromykos, walked outside, to their limousine. The presidential Lincoln, which had been flown in from Washington ahead of Reagan, was waiting at the entrance. They bid formal good-byes, and then, escorted by fifteen helmeted Soviet motorcyclists, the Reagans' motorcade drove toward the Kremlin along Lenin Prospekt and the city streets bedecked with Soviet and American flags. And I went to the Kremlin for another welcoming ceremony for the Reagans.

On the eve of Reagan's arrival in Moscow, Gorbachev had publicly paid him an unusual tribute. "I would like to say that realism is an important quality in President Reagan as a politician," he said to Katharine Graham of the *Washington Post* and editors of *Newsweek*. "Who would have thought in the early eighties that it would be President Reagan who would sign with us the first nuclear-arms reduction agreement in history?" Indeed, that the most conservative and anticommunist of all postwar U.S. presidents should be ending his White House tenure with a visit to Moscow, this "focus of evil in the modern world," seemed to confirm the correctness of Gorbachev's course in Western eyes. If nothing else, the visit was an intermission in the Cold War. It was also an important moment in the evolution of Reagan from a hard-line anticommunist to a man who referred to the Soviet leader as "a friend." But while regarding Gorbachev as a friend, he still considered the Soviet system per se as evil. As to Gorbachev, the previous year in Washington he had had to be on the offensive, making sure that the folks back home saw him as a forceful defender of Soviet interests. Now here in Moscow he could afford to relax. The process he had set in motion as a means of gaining international acceptance for himself as a major world leader had worked, and he could now reap some of the benefits.

It was clear from the beginning that this would be mostly a symbolical rather than substantive summit. But while no major breakthroughs toward a new strategic arms treaty were expected, Reagan considered another issue just as important: human rights. Before coming to Moscow, Reagan said he intended to make it the number one item on the summit agenda. He pointed out that one reason for the emphasis on human rights in the Soviet Union was the large number of Americans who traced their ancestry to it and watched events there carefully. "Government is influenced by public opinion," he said in one interview with Soviet reporters, adding that one of eight Americans had roots "in your area." "And so we can get along and make treaties much better with each other as governments," he said, "if human rights are respected."

But while he wanted to encourage greater change in Soviet life, many observers asked the question, Would he succeed in spreading Western-style values without embarrassing Gorbachev?

The motorcade carrying President and Mrs. Reagan entered the Kremlin grounds through the Borovitsky Gate and proceeded to the

Grand Kremlin Palace building (or BKD for short, in Russian, pronounced *BeKaDe*). When the motorcade stopped and the Reagans alighted, they were greeted at the entrance, bedecked with Soviet and U.S. flags, by the commandant of the Kremlin with the rank of a KGB general. Then, escorted by the Soviet chief of protocol, Vladimir Chernishev, they negotiated the sixty steps of the Grand State Staircase on both sides of which stood members of an Officer Honor Team, and, lo and behold, at the very top of the stairs Reagan was greeted by none other than . . . Lenin himself!

It was a fifteen-foot canvas of the founder of the Soviet state, shown declaiming to a crowd of members of Komsomol, or the Communist Youth League, in 1920. He seemed put there on purpose to test Reagan's self-possession. But Reagan didn't miss a step: "I sort of expected him to be there. I knew I was going to see a lot of Lenin." It was no secret that Reagan had a thing about Lenin. He frequently quoted him when he spoke about the "expansionist aims of Soviet Communists." When Valerian Zorin, the infamous Soviet TV commentator who had interviewed Reagan on the eve of his trip to Moscow, asked him to list the works of Lenin he had read, Reagan said, "Oh, my! I don't think I could recall and specify here and there," and went on to describe how he had read Karl Marx in college, saying that Marx had argued that "communism could only succeed when the whole world had become communist. And so the goal had to be the one-world communist state." Reagan said the American government at the time knew that Lenin had "a plan that involved Latin America and so forth." "And the one line that sounded very ominous to us," he concluded, "was when he said that 'the last bastion of capitalism, the United States, would not have to be taken; it would fall into their outstretched hand like overripe fruit.' "

After they had had enough of Lenin, President and Mrs. Reagan proceeded to St. George's Hall. As the Reagans entered at one end of the vaulted, resplendent room, the largest ceremonial chamber in the Kremlin, embellished by the insignia of thousands of celebrated soldiers and military units of czarist Russia, Gorbachev and his wife walked toward them from the opposite end. The two first couples met on the red carpet in the center of the hall.

After exchanging handshakes, Gorbachev and Reagan added to their summit anthology of Russian folk wisdom. Referring to Reagan's first ever visit to the Soviet Union, Gorbachev said in his welcoming remarks, "Aware of your interest in Russian proverbs, I would like to add another one to your collection: 'It's better to see it once than to hear about it a hundred times.' " Reagan rejoined, "In the past, Mr. General

Secretary, you noted that I like Russian sayings. In order not to disappoint anyone on this visit, I thought I would mention a literary saying from your past, another example of your people's succinct wisdom." And alluding to the benefits of an evolutionary, step-by-step improvement in superpower relations, Reagan then said in Russian, or to be more precise, meant to say, "*Rodilsya, ne toropilsya.*"

Some of his listeners, both American and Russian, were bemused by Reagan's mispronunciation. Neither Mikhail Sergeyevich nor Raisa Maximovna seemed to understand what he was trying to say until Dimitry Zarechnyak, one of Reagan's interpreters from the State Department who interpreted into Russian, unscrambled the adage. "He was born, he was not rushed," he said in unaccented Russian. Thus enlightened, Gorbachev responded on the spur of the moment that he was always for avoiding haste and for moving with consistency and confidence. I myself was grateful to Reagan for adding to my knowledge of Russian sayings: like all of my colleagues, I had never heard this one before.

In their official remarks, both leaders stressed the positive and spoke of cordiality and cooperation. Both called for more hard work to improve relations between the two countries.

The welcoming ceremony concluded with Reagan's traditional "Thank you and God bless you," which sounded to the ears of some of the Soviet officials present almost like a blasphemy in the Kremlin. Many of them made wry faces. The heretofore impregnable edifice of Communist atheism was being assaulted before their very eyes by a man who had made his name as a hard-line anticommunist.

Gorbachev led Reagan through the White Corridor and several richly decorated chambers to St. Catherine's Hall for their one-on-one meeting. Raisa and Nancy walked down the Grand Staircase and left through the Annunciation Entrance for a tour of the Kremlin. On the way to St. Catherine's Hall, Gorbachev queried Reagan on his first impressions of the Kremlin. "I like everything that is older than me," quipped Reagan. Gorbachev flattered Reagan by telling him that a man's age was not determined by the number of years he had lived but by the condition of his blood vessels, and that despite the long trip the president had just made, he looked more robust and ready to work than many young men of thirty. Reagan asked if it was possible to see Red Square, of whose beauty he had heard a lot from George Shultz. Gorbachev was all for it. "When you find the time to do it, we'll go together," he assured him. "George Shultz recommended you as a great guide," said Reagan. Gorbachev was pleased. He said he wouldn't let Shultz down and would try to live up to his expectations. The first deal of the summit was made.

Then, before they sat down to begin their first negotiations in St. Catherine's Hall, they were pelted with questions from reporters, who waylaid them in this opulent chamber, hung with pink silk and adorned with malachite pilasters, that once served as Catherine the Great's throne room. When Reagan was asked how he felt being in the "Evil Empire," he shrugged off the question with a smile: "Just fine."

Despite this public display of bonhomie, once Gorbachev and Reagan found themselves alone together, tensions began to emerge when Reagan quickly engaged Gorbachev in a discussion of human rights. The discussion ranged over such issues as freedom of religion and the right to emigrate. Gorbachev was irritated by Reagan's insistence on discussing these issues and did not bother to hide it. He accused Reagan of lecturing him on something he did not clearly understand as an outsider and bristled as he considered it an intrusion into the internal affairs of the Soviet Union, just as the previous Soviet leaders had.

Reagan handed Gorbachev a list of fourteen cases of families seeking to emigrate and political prisoners that he wanted to see resolved. He explained that American citizens placed a high value on this issue and were pressuring the administration to raise it with Gorbachev during the summit talks. Gorbachev rejoined that it was a "two-way street" and that the issue was not well served in a propagandist spirit. He proposed setting up a regular seminar on human rights issues between the two countries at the parliamentary level. Reagan said he would "consider it." Reagan also suggested to Gorbachev that the Berlin Wall be torn down—another theme that he would repeat in one of his major speeches. Gorbachev said he could not agree with the president's view, and before they broke up, he pulled out of his pocket a paper containing the Soviet version of language for the closing joint communiqué and handed it to Reagan. The one-paragraph statement, that we, Soviet interpreters, had translated into English the day before, read:

> Proceeding from their understanding of the realities that have taken shape in the world today, the two leaders believe that no problem in dispute can be resolved, nor should it be resolved, by military means. They regard peaceful coexistence as a universal principle of international relations. Equality of all states, noninterference in internal affairs, and freedom of sociopolitical choice must be recognized as the inalienable and mandatory standards of international relations.

Reagan looked at it perfunctorily and said agreeably that it looked all right to him, but he wanted to confer with his advisers before committing himself. It would turn out to be more problematic than either leader anticipated.

By some strange coincidence, I happened to see Reagan once again that day, but in a different, informal setting. After the welcoming ceremony in the Kremlin I had a few hours to kill before returning to St. Catherine's Hall to check the equipment for simultaneous interpretation for the scheduled formal meeting the following day. So I decided to walk back to my home in the Arbat not far from Spaso House. I strolled down Old Arbat Street, and as I passed Staropeskovsky Pereulok, which leads to Spaso House, I saw a large crowd of onlookers in front of a photo studio. I heard people in the crowd exclaiming excitedly, "Reagan, Reagan!" I stood on my tiptoes to peer over their heads, and indeed, right in the middle of the crowd, there was Reagan holding hands with Nancy. After the meeting in the Kremlin the Reagans had decided to take an unscheduled stroll along the Old Arbat, Moscow's only pedestrian mall and liveliest thoroughfare. The unannounced ten-minute walk was obviously Reagan's answer to Gorbachev's impromptu curbside chat during the Washington summit the previous December.

The Arbat had been completely renovated not long before, and now it was crowded with new cafés and boutiques, quick-sketch artists and kitsch dealers, especially those selling *matreshki* (Russian wooden dolls). Frequently, one could see here a Russian Dixieland band performing, an impromptu guitar serenade, an accordion concert, and even displays of break dancing by Soviet youngsters imitating Western-style "depravity." The Arbat, an ancient highway leading out of Moscow to the west and for at least the last century a busy shopping street, is first mentioned in a document of 1493. The name is said to be derived from an Arabic word meaning "suburbs," since the city proper was for long restricted to the Kremlin, which stands about a mile east, and the relatively small area beyond that is circled by the inner Boulevard Ring, itself once a fortification.

As I stood there at some distance, balancing on my tiptoes, the crowd applauded. I saw Ronny and Nancy make their way to a painted carriage set up by the studio photographer as a prop for souvenir photos. The Reagans climbed aboard and waved, clearly savoring their first close encounter with the Soviet public. Soon enough, however, the Reagans' smiles gave way to looks of apprehension as the crowd surged forward and the Soviet *devyatchiki* (KGB security agents), evidently panicked by the spontaneous conduct of the people, plunged into the crowd, elbowing and punching, to clear a path to the Reagan limousine a hundred feet away. They were roughing up everyone in their way. The American

Secret Service agents got alarmed and, surrounding the Reagans, formed a protective cocoon around them.

I turned back to go home. As Reagan would tell it to Gorbachev the following day, he was stunned by how shabbily the KGB security men treated their own people. Gorbachev winced, but said nothing.

MAY 30, MONDAY. DAY TWO.

The work of the second day of the Moscow summit began with Reagan's arrival at the glittering Grand Kremlin Palace. With its seven hundred rooms and great halls, it was once used by Russian czars as their Moscow residence and, until recently, by the Communists for their imitation of a parliament, the Supreme Soviet of the USSR. It was built in 1849 by Nicholas I, the most austere and reactionary of the czars. It was rarely used, however, until the arrival in 1918 of the Bolsheviks, who made Moscow the capital of the new Soviet state and the new government. Its main facade faces the Moskva River. The ground floor of the palace still contains the luxurious private suites where the czar and the czarina lived with their family. On the second, principal floor there are ceremonial halls and chambers, such as St. George's Hall, St. Vladimir's Hall, and St. Catherine's Hall, dedicated to the old Russian orders of St. George, St. Vladimir and St. Catherine. The Grand Kremlin Palace is closed to the public.

At this morning's plenary meeting in St. Catherine's Hall, Reagan would be backed by the same eight-member team as the previous year in Washington: George Shultz, Frank Carlucci, Howard Baker, Colin Powell, Paul Nitze, Edward Rowny, Jack Matlock, and Rozanne Ridgway. Gorbachev's team included Eduard Shevardnadze, Alexandr Yakovlev, and Anatoly Dobrynin among others, and in place of Marshal Akhromeyev was Dmitryi Yazov, the new minister of defense, whose star was definitely rising. There was also Andrei Gromyko, who had insisted on attending the talks. It would have been odd indeed if he were absent.

Before the plenary meeting got under way, Gorbachev was asked by reporters what he thought of human rights as a subject for discussion at the summit. His reaction to this question was mild. But when pressed to respond to whether he was going to discuss with Reagan the list of fourteen human rights cases, he was evasive. "There are too many lists floating around," he replied, showing his irritation over Reagan's concentration on human rights. When he was asked what he thought of Mr. Reagan's plan to meet later in the day with Soviet dissidents, Gor-

bachev said curtly, "I don't know. We are now meeting in this room."
Gorbachev knew he could come under fire from some of his more orthodox Kremlin colleagues if he gave Reagan a domestic stage from which
to criticize Soviet policies on human rights. So he hastened to usher the
reporters out.

A little after 10 A.M., the doors were closed and the participants on
both sides took their seats at the table, with Reagan and his party facing
the windows. Gorbachev once again proved he could be a congenial
interlocutor. He said since Reagan was the guest of honor, he should
speak first. Reagan began by proposing expanding what he called "peo-
ple-to-people" exchanges between Soviet and American citizens. Gorbachev readily agreed. But when Reagan brought up what the United
States considered to be a Soviet violation of the ABM treaty at the Krasnoyarsk radar station, Gorbachev once again expressed Soviet opposition to SDI:

"I would like to give you a piece of advice—for free. Kissinger would
charge you millions for such advice! I believe the president has been
misled through Weinberger, and now through Carlucci. Someone
thinks there is an opportunity in outer space for the United States to
achieve superiority again. First, it runs counter to the declaration that
'we will not seek superiority.' And second, during the next eight and a
half years [i.e., until 1996, when presumably the United States would
begin to deploy antimissile defenses], while your SDI plans will be
floundering in research, throughout all this period a lot of positive
things will occur in the world. Don't meddle with space—we shall find
the right response. But once again, there will be no trust. Again there
will be trammels in the way. So I think Carlucci is pushing you in the
wrong direction. Where are they pulling us?"

Reagan patiently explained his rationale for pursuing SDI:

"Let me give you some background on the SDI idea. I came to office
believing that instability in the world was based on missiles we have.
The average person can see and shoot a plane or defend himself. But
here you just push the button and a whole city blows up. It is destabiliz-
ing. When I came to the White House, I convened the Joint Chiefs of
Staff and asked them if it was possible to develop a weapon to intercept
missiles before they are out of their silos, in order to make them obsolete. They didn't answer right away. But later they said, 'We think it's
possible to do it, but it will take a lot of time.' So I said, 'Let's do it.' It is
purely a defensive weapon. . . . Why is such a defense necessary? We all
know how to make nuclear weapons again—once invented they cannot
be disinvented. There can be some madman who can blackmail the

world should he get hold of nuclear weapons. So everybody should keep their gas masks ready. This is the theory."

Reagan became so emotional, gesticulating with both his hands as he spoke, that he knocked down the carafe in front of him, spilling water on the sleeve of his jacket.

Gorbachev was unconvinced, however, and continued to maintain that SDI "is not only a defense but a way for developing space weapons to strike against targets on earth." He relented enough, however, to say the experts in Geneva should continue their work on a START treaty. Gorbachev next complained about what the Soviets deemed to be U.S. resistance to verification measures proposed by the Soviets to monitor mobile missiles, areas of their deployment, aircraft, and specifically verification of ships capable of carrying nuclear weapons, and of American private chemical companies whose facilities could be used to manufacture chemical weapons. In frustration, he exclaimed, "You said you were ready for verification, but now we are trying to persuade you to accept verification. What was it then, a bluff? Is it not necessary now to verify ships? Just like [it is not necessary to verify] private chemical industries! What then is to be verified? The White House and the Kremlin?"

At one point, in a heated exchange with Carlucci on the matter, he said: "It seems I am better informed about what is going on around the president than he is himself." Finally, Gorbachev raised the issue of conventional arms in Europe. Reagan claimed that the Soviet Union had superiority in conventional arms, but Gorbachev disagreed and accused the United States of using the purported asymmetry as a propaganda tactic.

Soon after a vigorous exchange on this matter the inconclusive meeting came to an end. As at their Washington summit, Gorbachev clearly had a better grasp of detail than Reagan. He never even opened the folder with talking points that he had in front of him. But he was clearly at odds with the Russian language when he spoke off the cuff. Sometimes he would impart to some words a meaning they did not have. Or he would use words out of place or stop suddenly in the middle of a sentence, leaving it in abeyance as it were—this invariably created problems for us, his interpreters, who had to finish saying it for him at our own risk. Also, he would often accent the wrong syllables. His speech was abundantly interspersed with regional words and phrases of the kind I mentioned in one of the earlier chapters, whose meaning was not always immediately clear.

But despite all this, he was expressive, managing to get across his thoughts and ideas in a way that was understandable if somewhat convoluted. Those of us who had worked with him for some time were familiar with all these linguistic idiosyncracies, and we did our best to smooth over the rough spots and inaccuracies in his colloquial speech. The most important thing was to get across his thoughts and ideas without distorting them. Gorbachev's foreign interlocutors were, of course, unaware of all these language problems.

As to Gorbachev's demeanor during the meeting, my impression this time was that he still could not shake off entirely the habits and manners typical of most Soviet Party bosses. Occasionally, he could not control his outbursts if he found something disagreeable in his counterpart's views. Frequently, he would not hear out his interlocutor to the end and would interrupt him in the middle of a phrase. He would often raise his voice and even bang his fist on the table to drive a point home. At one point during the plenary, he even suggested that the two of them, he and Reagan, bang their fists together. Reagan politely declined. On the other hand, if he found it necessary, Gorbachev could instantly turn on his famous charm and do a volte-face. Then he would smile, lean back in his chair, throw his hands up as if to show he was now ready to reconcile himself with his interlocutor and accept his arguments, or, conversely, to have it understood that he would not buy them. Like Reagan, he was a good actor and even a better tactician. And he demonstrated these qualities amply in the first meeting that morning.

What I found most interesting was that despite his previous year's visit to Washington, Gorbachev's view of the United States remained colored in many ways by his Party background and training, which were imbued with a Marxist analysis of the West. Judging from his remarks, his attitude toward the United States was still grounded in distrust. Thus, he remained convinced, as most Soviets did, that real power in the United States flowed from Wall Street rather than from the White House and Congress and that the military-industrial complex dominated the American political process, although he had admitted in a recent interview that he now realized that it was not the only force shaping American policy.

But just as he had seen beyond the conventional wisdom of Soviet society as he sought to change it, Gorbachev was also fashioning a sober-minded and realistic approach to relations with the outside world. He was above all a realist capable of adapting his views to the changing situation, while remaining faithful to his convictions. And, for all the talk about "new thinking" in foreign policy, a code word for Gorbachev's appeal to do away with Cold War attitudes, the primary reason for the rapprochement with the West in general and with the United States in particular was, of course, self-interest, both national and his own, as it should be. If the Soviet Union was to overcome its economic backwardness and devote resources to the reconstruction of its economy, international tranquillity and a lower level of defense spending were a must.

After the morning talks with Gorbachev, Reagan visited Danilovsky Monastir, the St. Daniil Monastery, founded in 1282 by Alexandr Nevsky's son Prince Daniil, who had been canonized. Alexandr Nevsky was one of Russia's greatest national heroes, known for his victories over Russia's enemies. Reagan took advantage of the visit to call on the Soviet Union to reopen churches and to end the oppression of religious groups. The message was played down, however, in the nightly TV news program *Vremya*. His remarks were not reported either on TV or in the mass media. In the eyes of the Soviet authorities they did not constitute news that was "fit to print." They found it irksome. But the coverage of Reagan's official comings and goings was generally upbeat.

If the American president's visit to the monastery was officially viewed as an irritation, his unprecedented meeting with Soviet dissidents and refuseniks later in the day at Spaso House was perceived as positively anti-Soviet, and accordingly it was reported negatively in the Soviet press. That was a clear sign of annoyance on the part of Reagan's official hosts. This notwithstanding, I did not hear any reports of dissidents who attended that meeting having been harassed by Soviet police or the KGB, although they were derided in the official press. And that in itself was a sign of change. A small step for the dissidents, it was a giant leap for Soviet society under Gorbachev.

The day culminated with a grand dinner hosted by General Secretary and Mrs. Gorbachev in honor of President and Mrs. Reagan in the Kremlin's Granovitaya Palata or Faceted Chamber, that "holy of holies," as Gorbachev intended to describe it in the original version of his toast speech, but didn't—the words were later scrapped because, on second thought, it was decided that they did not exactly fit the socialist notion of that locus of power.

I arrived at the BKD about an hour and a half before the gala event, scheduled for 7 P.M. Guests, both Soviet and American, were already beginning to arrive in St. George's Hall where, in accordance with Gorbachev's prohibition on alcohol, they were offered juices and soft drinks but no hard liquor—not even wine, to say nothing of vodka. Among the more notable guests I spotted the Patriarch of All Russia Alexi, a tall man with dignified manners and a long white beard, who wore a long, white ceremonial robe. This was yet another departure from the Kremlin traditions of the hard-line era, when no priests had been invited to participate in such functions as this.

As the guests mingled, I was approached by the ubiquitous Armand Hammer, who now greeted me like an old friend. Only a few days before, on May 21, he had turned ninety. When I wished him "many, many happy returns of the day" and told him that he looked like a man in his early sixties, he protested, "I don't know how young I look, but I know I feel like a man half my age. Recently I've had a complete physical and the doctors told me my internal organs are those of a man twice younger than me." Hammer looked pleased with himself. He told me he was determined to celebrate his centenary here in Moscow and even invited me to attend the occasion ten years from now. That would be 1998.

Whenever I saw this uncommon man, I could not help wondering to myself where his loyalties ultimately lay, with the United States or with the Soviet Union? I had heard it through the Moscow grapevine that he was classified as an "agent of influence," and that he had delivered funds in the 1920s to help the American Communist Party at the behest of Lenin and the Komintern (the Communist International). But perhaps Hammer's fascination with the Soviet Union had more to do with his craving for recognition than with any fixed purpose, financial, political, or otherwise. He clearly had a tremendous ego. And I suspect his egocentricity allowed no room for wider motives.

All those invited to the Kremlin dinner were supposed to arrive not later than fifteen minutes before dinnertime. But an exception was made for members of the Politburo as well as for top-ranking secretaries of the CPSU Central Committee. These so-called "servants of the people" did not wish to be seen mixing with people who sat below the the salt, so to speak, in the socialist social hierarchy, however unproletarian this may have been. (The exceptions to the rule were Gorbachev, Shevardnadze, and Yakovlev.) They gathered in the Winter Garden instead, where the Gorbachevs met the Reagans upon their arrival. Reagan wore his dark, well-tailored pinstripe suit with a plain regimental-striped rep tie. Nancy wore a flower-patterned, knee-length, scarlet dress with a heavy gold chain around the neck. Gorbachev wore a black pinstripe and his nondescript polka-dot tie. Raisa Maximovna sported a plain black skirt, also knee-length, and a glittering blouse with big colorful diamond shapes. She wore nothing around her neck, not even a strand of pearls—only small diamond earrings. Every time I saw her, her wardrobe became less and less glamorous. It must have been due to the criticism leveled at her by her compatriots.

After the obligatory receiving line and introductory ceremony, the Gorbachevs and the Reagans proceeded to the Faceted Chamber to take their seats at separate tables for eight persons each. It was another remarkable departure from the Kremlin tradition, in which "The Master Himself," i.e., the general secretary, would sit in the middle of a long U-shaped table with other guests seated at the same table on both sides. The change in seating was made at Raisa Maximovna's personal behest because she liked the seating arrangements in the White House and at the State Department, which she found cozier and more conducive to conversation.

Granovitaya Palata or the Faceted Chamber in the ancient Palace of Facets, so called because of its walls of stone facings in the form of diamond facets, used to be the audience hall for the czars before Peter the Great's time. It was built in 1491 and is the oldest public building in Moscow. The Faceted Chamber is one large, almost square, room with a massive pillar in the center. Its painted vaulted ceiling is nine meters or twenty-seven feet at its highest point. Here, Ivan Grozny, better known in the West as Ivan the Terrible, celebrated his victory over the Tartars at Kazan and the end of three centuries under the Tartar-Mongolian yoke. Here, too, he received ambassadors from his throne, with his boyars in tall sable hats ranged along the walls on benches. In this chamber in 1653 the Zemskoi sobor, or the Assembly of the Land, voted for the reunification of Russia and Ukraine. In 1812, Napoleon threw lavish parties here after he invaded Moscow and until the Great Fire forced him to flee.

Throughout the years, whenever I found myself in this airy chamber, I invariably experienced a sense of trepidation. It was the focus of history itself. It was not hard to imagine state occasions or formal dinners with the czar sitting alone at a raised table on a high-backed throne. Below him, *boyari* or gentlemen of the court sat in order of rank and favor while servants busied themselves carrying dish after gold dish of various meats, of which roast swan was the highlight. Dinner would begin with the czar, in the Russian tradition, proffering bread and salt to the most important guests while the czarina watched from an upper-level secret chamber, which can still be glimpsed through a small window located on the upper level to the right of the entrance. In those days, not even czarinas were allowed to share formal dinners with their husbands. It was a man's world. Today, while the sense of tradition lives on in the Faceted Chamber, roast swan is no longer served, and the Soviet (now Russian) head of state no longer sits alone at table. Most importantly, the wife of the Kremlin host no longer has to watch from a secret room—she now occupied a place of honor at one of the two head tables.

As soon as the guests were seated, speeches were exchanged between Gorbachev, who spoke first, and Reagan. Translations of the speeches in English and Russian, on which I had labored together with Sergei Berezhkov, were placed on each table in front of every guest. In yet another, rare departure from the established tradition in this hallowed chamber, four or five representatives of the mass media from each side were admitted inside and the toasts were nationally televised. Another first!

In his speech and in a clear response to his guest's remarks on human rights at Spaso House, Gorbachev said that contacts between Americans and Soviet citizens should be improved without lecturing one another. Standing before a wall of painted figures of Russian saints, Gorbachev said that the Soviet Union favored widening exchanges but that "this should be done without interfering in domestic affairs, without sermonizing or imposing one's views and ways." From where I sat, Reagan appeared to be drowsy with his eyes half-closed.

And then, after Gorbachev finished, Reagan surprised the guests and startled Gorbachev with a long toast of his own in which he described the plot of *Friendly Persuasion*, an old, 1956 American film starring Gary Cooper, a copy of which he presented to Gorbachev as one of his gifts. Reagan described it as "an American classic." In his highly unusual toast Reagan said the movie showed "not just the tragedy of [civil] war, but the problems of pacifism, the nobility of patriotism, as well as the love of peace."

And then, as the guests looked on, rather baffled, the president plunged into a complicated discussion of a key scene in which a Quaker's barn is burned down by the Confederate Army, and the Quaker debates with his neighbors about whether to join in the fighting. Reagan raised his glass for "the art of friendly persuasion" in superpower negotiations and expressed the hope that all disputes would be settled peacefully. And he startled his Soviet hosts once again when he concluded the toast with his traditional "God bless you."

At his table, Reagan bantered and joked, told stories, and asked all kinds of questions about the Faceted Chamber. As he had admitted, he liked everything that was older than himself.

As I watched and listened to him, I found it hard to believe that it was happening right here in this "focus of the Evil Empire," which he had castigated so often. That the former sworn enemies were now sharing almost the same table in the Kremlin and exchanging not only formal speeches, but also private jokes and anecdotes, was hard to believe. I could have pinched myself to make sure it was not a dream. Reagan carried on a lively conversation with Raisa Maximovna, and Mikhail Sergeyevich exchanged remarks with Nancy. The other guests talked with one another. I had never before witnessed a livelier atmosphere in this holy of holies. To be sure, enemies did not behave like this. The tired image of "the enemy" was visibly crumbling before my eyes, being replaced with the image of "the friend."

The ice of the Cold War seemed to be melting right before my eyes.

MAY 31, TUESDAY. DAY THREE.

Reagan arrived in the Kremlin shortly before 10 A.M. and was immediately taken to see Gorbachev. After an inconclusive discussion about the need for economic cooperation and the imperatives of the domestic program of *perestroika*, Gorbachev pulled out of his folder several cables and handed them to Reagan. The cables, he said, had arrived from all over the country, and many were addressed to the president of the United States. Some senders informed him that they had named their newborn babies Ronald or Nancy after him and his wife and asked the president to be their godfather. On a serious note, Gorbachev expressed exasperation with the absence of progress in removing key obstacles in the negotiation of a treaty to reduce long-range strategic nuclear weapons. "Maybe now is the time to bang our fists on the table again," he said again, in a reference to their joint effort in Geneva in 1985 to clear the hurdles in the way of agreement. And he clenched his fist as if intending to bring it down on the table.

Clearly, there was not much of substance to discuss at this tête-à-tête, and this summit in general revolved largely around ceremonial events. And what better public ceremonial event than taking a stroll together around the nation's premier square, which Reagan wanted to see so much. So the two leaders cut short their meeting at 11:10 A.M. to walk to Red Square. As they emerged from the Spassky Gate to the Kremlin clock-tower, chimes were striking a quarter of an hour. Gorbachev gave Reagan a brief lesson in the Russian language, explaining that *krasnaya* (red) in Russian means also *krasivaya* (beautiful), and for the first time in four decades there was no American rebuttal. "Red and beautiful are the same word," declared Gorbachev as he and Reagan strolled in Red Square. It sounded as if he wanted to say that the Cold War was some frightening, forty-year misunderstanding.

When I heard him say that, I remembered the phrase that I had heard so often in America in the late sixties and chuckled. "Better dead than beautiful" would never have had the same ring in the old Cold War debate in the United States. Nor would the "Beautiful Army" have helped the Pentagon much in its weapons appropriation requests.

Red Square is really an immense rectangle of cobbled pavement. On one side of it, opposite the Kremlin, stands the huge GUM, the State Department Store that was Mecca to shoppers from all over the Soviet Union, although it had never held a candle to its Western counterparts. Between the Spassky Gate, which is the main Kremlin tower, and GUM is St. Basil's Cathedral with its nine onion domes, each different in color and design. That morning Red Square was especially *krasivaya*, with the evergreens gleaming outside the wine red Kremlin walls (more rosé than burgundy) and a giant red flag (more scarlet than red) snapping in cloudless blue skies over the cupola of the "Senate" building where Gorbachev had his office. As stunned tourists hurried over to get a better look at the spectacle of the leaders of the two superpowers peacefully talking to each other, Gorbachev savored the word from three centuries before that has survived as both the archaic form of "beautiful" and as the modern word for "red," a color favored for its beauty in all the seasons of this ancient square. *Krasivaya. Krasnaya.*

Reagan was a quick study. It took him only a couple of times to learn the word. "*Krasivaya,*" he said with an American accent, looking at some flowers past Lenin's Tomb. Gorbachev attempted to steer him gently toward the tomb, but Reagan realized what was about to happen and made an about-face to go back. "Before we go too far," he said to Gorbachev when they were dangerously close to Lenin's Tomb, "let's better stand this way." And he put his arm around Gorbachev, turning away from the loathsome structure that must have had the same effect on him as a silver cross would on Count Dracula. Later Reagan was asked by reporters why he didn't go to see the body of Lenin—he was so close. "The tomb is only open four days," Reagan replied diplomatically. "And the line was so long we did not want to interrupt it." But the line he had in mind was an ideological limit to photo opportunities that he apparently was not willing to cross.

On the other hand, that Reagan believed that Gorbachev himself was far removed from Lenin was plain. He admitted that his friendship with Gorbachev was real. "There is good chemistry between us," he said. "I think progress has been made by us. I think that through this succession of summits there is a much better understanding. I think we made gains this time." This summit was something personal, Reagan went on. Systems might be brutish, bureaucrats might fail. But men could sometimes transcend all that, transcend even the forces of history that seemed destined to keep them apart. Reagan admitted he had never expected to be here—in the very heart of the "Evil Empire." The idea that he would ever come to Moscow was only a dim possibility until he met Gorbachev in Geneva.

Reagan was born to campaign. I had watched his act on television as he conducted his campaigns in 1980 and 1984. He obviously loved it and did it well. This time, in 1988, he did it amid the onion domes of the Kremlin. Strolling around Red Square, he was unmistakably campaigning in the twilight of his presidency. Oddly enough, he seemed to be campaigning on behalf of his onetime adversary, the general secretary of the Communist Party of the Soviet Union. He praised Gorbachev and his reforms. Mikhail Sergeyevich, on the other hand, had never had to run for office, which I think was a mistake on his part, but he, too, was a natural campaigner and a great PR man. At one point during the Red Square walkabout he picked up a child and told him to shake hands with *Dedushka Reigan* (Grandfather Reagan). Reagan and Gorbachev stopped to talk with several more groups of people. It was, perhaps, the most lasting image of this summit. For Ronald Reagan was now a costar with his fellow showman Mikhail Gorbachev in Red Square. While there may have been some "missed opportunities," as Gorbachev would complain later at his press conference, there were certainly no missed photo opportunities at this summit, except, perhaps, for one near Lenin's tomb.

During the walk Reagan replenished his collection of Russian proverbs. Reacting to Gorbachev's soliloquy about the need to live "in peace and friendship," a Russian tourist interjected, "Here's another saying for the president: V *sporakh rozhdaetsya istina*" (Truth is born out of arguments). Gorbachev promptly picked up where the tourist left off. "Mr. President," he said, turning to a mystified Reagan, "they want to add to your collection of proverbs. The truth is this saying has a sequel: *Yesli spor nakalyaetsya, istina isparyaetsya*" (If the argument gets heated, the truth evaporates). During their stroll Gorbachev took Reagan aback when he broached the subject of a joint flight to Mars. Reagan replied he did not know when this idea could be implemented because he was not a scientist. At another point Reagan turned to Gorbachev and told a group of people, "We decided to talk to each other instead of about each other. And it's working just fine. . . . We want friendship between our countries." "*Da, da,*" confirmed Mikhail Sergeyevich after he heard the translation.

While Reagan toured Red Square and then the Kremlin, a tall man in a U.S. Air Force major's uniform followed him everywhere close on his heels. He attracted attention because his left wrist was manacled to the "football," a black briefcase that contained the codes to be used by the president in ordering a nuclear attack on the Soviet Union in case of war. Those who guessed what was in the suitcase could heave a sign of relief, though: they knew that right now the safest place on earth was here in Red Square. I have to admit it was an amazing sight: the Soviet general secretary and the American president walking together through the symbol of all things Soviet, Krasnaya Ploschad, or Red Square, accompanied by their interpreters, aides, and bodyguards. It was cause for shaking the head in wonder. Some twenty minutes later it was all over when the two leaders returned to the Kremlin through the Spassky Gate. Before they got to the BKD, however, they were waylaid by a horde of reporters. And here came the question of questions: "Mr. President, do you still believe that the Soviet Union is an evil empire?"

Reagan confined himself to a monosyllabic "No." That was perhaps the biggest news of the day.

On the way to the BKD, Gorbachev made a little detour to the right to show a surprised Reagan what he described as his "secret weapon"— the giant Czar Cannon. Lest Reagan think that it could be used as a bargaining chip in the Star Wars argument, Gorbachev hastened to reassure him that it never fired, it was only a "monument." There was no getting away from Lenin for Reagan that day, however. When they reached the BKD and mounted the grand marble staircase to the second floor, Gorbachev couldn't resist the temptation. Pointing to the giant painting that Reagan had already seen on his first day in the Kremlin, he said, "Lenin. It would be interesting to talk with him. He was a man of a very strong intellect. A great pragmatist and a realistic politician." Gorbachev said it with a twinkle in his eye—he knew, of course, how Reagan felt about Lenin. Reagan said nothing. But that was not all. Before the day was over, he would encounter Lenin once again.

Later in the day after witnessing the signing of some minor accords, Reagan lunched at the Central House of Writers with Soviet *tvorcheskaya intelligentsiya* or cultural figures such as writers, artists, filmmakers, architects, actors, and so forth. Unfortunately, I did not get to accompany him as he took with him only his interpreter, Bill Hopkins. The meeting with the Soviet cultural elite was at Reagan's own initiative and was not part of the summit's official agenda, just like Gorbachev's meetings with American public figures and businessmen when he was in Washington. I do not wish to appear presumptuous by discussing events that I did not personally attend or witness, so I will only mention some of the more colorful incidents on the language front, which reached me from reliable sources.

Reagan was said to have picked up several more Russian sayings for his collection. *Khorosheye nachalo poldela otkachalo* was one of them, supplied courtesy of Vladimir Karpov, secretary of the Board of Writers, meaning "A good beginning is half the battle" or "Well begun, half done." Not to be outdone, the vintage actor Ronald Reagan responded, "Well, as Henry the Eighth said to each of his six wives, 'I won't keep you long,' " and went on, in an eloquent speech, to impress his audience with frequent allusions to Russian literature and quotes from Boris Pasternak, Anna Akhmatova, and Nikolai Gumilev and Aleksandr Solzhenitsyn. Those names and allusions were appropriate in that setting, but, alas, they were mispronounced in Russian. They did reflect an intellectual depth and literacy that Reagan had not previously been known for, and his performance got rave reviews from some of those present. It was all scripted, of course, but the identity of his brilliant ghostwriter was a mystery. And like Henry VIII, Reagan kept his promise—he didn't keep them long, indeed. At 1:25 P.M. he was back at his residence, Spaso House.

When they had met beneath the gilded bronze chandeliers in St. George's Hall on the first day of the summit, they had smiled with brittle cordiality. When they had listened to their husbands' duel in proverbs, their stolid expressions had melted into laughter. By the time they emerged from the tour of the Kremlin, Raisa Maximovna Gorbacheva and Nancy Reagan were even holding hands.

Six months before, in Washington, everyone heard the rumors of their mutual dislike and even disdain. Now, from all accounts by people who were close to both first ladies, it appeared that they were making a concerted effort to get along. After the exchange of greetings in the Kremlin, while their husbands were having their first meeting of the summit, Raisa Maximovna escorted Nancy toward the Assumption Cathedral. As usual, she talked to her guest through her interpreter, Oleg Krokholev of the MFA, in brisk and instructive tones explaining the sights around them. She also talked about "peace and friendship." When they were persistently questioned by reporters about their feud, they both got annoyed. When Mrs. Reagan was asked how she felt about being in the Soviet Union, she said it was exciting and a little overwhelming.

But while an atmosphere of determined harmony prevailed, a moment of tension inside the cathedral made headlines in foreign newspapers the next day. Raisa Maximovna had just finished a discourse on a copy of an icon of the Madonna and Child when Mrs. Reagan hurriedly put in a question: "This cathedral now, is it mainly used as just a museum or for religious activities also?" Raisa Maximovna's reply was brief: "*Nyet.*" "Oh, yes, the word *nyet*—that I understand," said Nancy. That was her retribution to Raisa for Washington. Nancy remembered how Raisa Maximovna had referred to the White House as a museum not fit for living, and now she had turned the tables on her.

In fact, when the program for the leaders' wives was being drawn up, it was decided, at the suggestion of Raisa Maximovna, to divide the job of playing hostess to Mrs. Reagan among several Politburo wives. Nanuli Rozhdestvenna Shevardnadze would greet her at a school, and Lydia Dmitriyevna Gromyko had welcomed her at the airport and would also serve as hostess for the American first lady's trip to Leningrad. But when Nancy would visit Peredelkino, the Soviet writers' colony outside Moscow where Pasternak is buried, no one would accompany her officially. Raisa Maximovna would resume her duties as chief hostess only when Nancy returned to Moscow from Russia's old imperial capital, taking her to the Tretyakov Gallery. She would also accompany Mrs. Reagan to the Bolshoi for ballet. She obviously wanted to limit her exposure to Nancy as much as possible because, while they both felt duty-bound to show affection for each other in public, no love was lost between them.

Everything went according to plan and the first ladies seemed to get along when they were together. Yet the temptation to snipe was too strong. In a ceremony where Raisa Maximovna accepted a sculpture as an official gift from Greece, she said, in impromptu remarks, and in obvious reference to Mrs. Reagan's well-known passion for astrology, "I don't believe in astrology. I believe in facts and practical things."

In the afternoon I decided to get back to the MFA to watch Reagan's address at MGU or Moscow State University—the alma mater of both Mikhail and Raisa Gorbachev. I knew in advance that his speech would not be broadcast live or in full on Soviet television or radio. However, starting earlier that year, in another sign of *glasnost* at work, the MFA had been wired to receive CNN English-language programs, something that was of great value for us interpreters.

Whatever else may have lain in store for President Reagan in his first-ever visit to Moscow, he thought he would finally realize one dream: a full-dress solo performance on Soviet television, in a setting of his own choosing. I could well imagine his disappointment when only snippets of his speech were shown later in the evening on the main news program *Vremya* (Time). Still, only one American president before him had been permitted even this much exposure—Richard Nixon, in 1972, during the summit meeting with Brezhnev. Reagan's desire to address the Soviet people was long-standing. In 1982, addressing the British Parliament, Reagan said he was prepared to offer Brezhnev an opportunity to speak to the American people on American television if Reagan was allowed the same opportunity with the Soviet people. The idea of a TV duel, judged subversive, was ignored by Brezhnev, then by Andropov and Chernenko. When Reagan met with Gorbachev in Geneva in 1985, he resurrected the idea, but nothing happened, except for an exchange of brief New Year's greetings on TV in 1986 and in 1988. But even that caused a stir among the Soviet people who watched. So when Shultz negotiated with Shevardnadze before the Moscow summit, he emphasized that a speech on Soviet TV was at the top of the president's wish list. Gorbachev agreed, although reluctantly. Even so he changed his mind at the last moment, deciding to show on television only excerpts of Reagan's speech. Perhaps it wasn't his own doing. Perhaps this was done without his knowledge. Three years into *perestroika* the Soviets still suspected that Reagan would preach American values and virtues, something they thought Soviet people were not yet ready to hear, *glasnost* notwithstanding.

For President Reagan this opportunity to speak to the Soviet people on TV was a climactic moment, a chance to convey directly to hundreds of millions of Soviet citizens his vision of a peaceful future, and to plant a few seeds of democracy. So, with this knowledge in mind, I made myself comfortable in a chair in front of a TV set in my boss's office, ready to watch. I wasn't disappointed. It was a real tour de force by the president-turned-professor.

Like a real professor, Reagan gave an impressive lesson in American civics, in which he emphasized concepts of freedom—freedom of thought, freedom of speech, freedom of information, freedom of communication, and the virtues of democracy. I think it may have been his finest oratorical hour. He reached out to the Soviet people and encouraged the forces of change that Gorbachev had unleashed. But Reagan , prudently or imprudently, avoided direct criticism of the Soviet system and instead cited detailed examples from the American experience. As he spoke to an audience of students and faculty, he stood in front of a vast mosaic filled with surging red flags of revolution, and a huge, larger-than-life, white marble bust of who else but Lenin on a tall yellow pedestal who looked down sternly from above the president's head. Perhaps, this was what Lenin had had in mind when he spoke about "peaceful cohabitation between countries with different social and political systems."

In fact, the bust had been the subject of negotiations between the Americans and the Soviets long before the summit. After surveying the scene at MGU, an American advance group, invoking Reagan's organic incompatibility with Lenin, asked the Soviets to remove the bust. The request was denied. So Reagan had to agree to the silent presence of Lenin behind his back, if he wanted to make his address at MGU, a place he had chosen. But it was a field day for photographers—Reagan at the rostrum, dwarfed by the giant bust of Lenin.

As a linguist, I found Reagan's attempt at Russian in the beginning of the speech somewhat amusing but certainly welcome. To the students, who were to take their exams that week, he said, "*Zhelayu vam uspekha*" (I wish you success). He pronounced it well, although that was not what he'd wanted to say originally. Originally, he'd asked his aides and inter-preters to find an appropriate Russian expression to fit the occasion, and they came up with just the right one, *Ni pookha, ni pera*, a well-known and popular Russian saying used to wish someone, especially students before their exams, good luck or success. It means literally "Neither fluff nor feather to you" and had originally been used to wish luck to a hunter setting out after wildfowl. The use of the negative was based on the superstition that openly wishing success would jinx the hunt. The tradi-tional response to this expression is *K chertu!* (Go to the devil!) The expression was just perfect for the occasion, except that after rehearsing it in Russian several times, the president had to give it up, on his inter-preters' strong advice. It all boiled down to his pronunciation. No mat-ter how hard he tried, it came out like *Ni pooka ni pera*—an expression that could not be permitted to escape the presidential lips, since its off-color connotation has to do with various degrees of flatulence. After some debate, the difficult-to-pronounce saying was replaced with the more manageable *Zhelayu vam uspekha*.

Even though Reagan was playing the role of a professor, he remained faithful to himself as an actor and told a few anecdotes. Criticizing bureaucracy, which, he said, was a problem around the world, he told a story about "a town—it could be anywhere—with a bureaucrat who is known to be a good-for-nothing, but he somehow had always hung on to power. So one day, in a town meeting, an old woman got up and said to him, 'There is a folk legend here, where I come from, that when a baby is born, an angel comes down from heaven and kisses it on one part of its body. If the angel kisses him on his hand, he becomes a handyman. If he kisses him on his forehead, he becomes bright and clever. And I've been trying to figure out where the angel kissed you so that you should sit there for so long and do nothing.' "

He spoke of faith, and in drawing a comparison between Gorbachev's campaign for economic renewal and a scene from the popular cowboy movie *Butch Cassidy and the Sundance Kid,* he clearly puzzled the audience not only in the MGU lecture hall, but at the MFA, too. He called for removing that "sad reminder of a divided world: the Berlin Wall." He quoted from Pasternak and Lomonosov. And in the end, speaking of "the most exciting and hopeful times" of *perestroika* in which the younger Soviet generation was living, he effectively concluded by reciting a passage from Gogol's *Dead Souls,* which is required reading in Soviet schools and in which the Russian nation is compared to a speeding troika. "Gogol asks," Reagan exclaimed, " 'What will be the destination?' But there was no answer, save the bell pouring forth a marvelous sound. . . . We do not know what will be the conclusion of this journey, but we are hopeful that the promise of reform will be fulfilled." Concluded Reagan, "In this Moscow spring, this May 1988, we may be allowed to hope that freedom, like the fresh green sapling planted over Tolstoy's grave, will blossom forth at last in the rich, fertile soil of your people and culture. We may be allowed to hope that the marvelous sound of a new openness will keep rising through, leading to a new world of reconciliation, friendship, and peace. Thank you and God bless you." When he finished his stirring speech, he was greeted with wild applause, and when he finished answering questions from the audience, in another sign of change, he, an American president, was given a standing ovation.

It was one of the finest examples of oratory I had ever heard. The words he said may have been his speechwriter's, but the emotion with which he said them was definitely his own. In retrospect, many of the things he said in that speech would become a reality only a little more than three years later. And the Berlin Wall would fall in less than a year and a half.

The dinner at Spaso House that the Reagans gave for the Gorbachevs later that night was a low-key, candlelit affair enlivened by the famous Dave Brubeck. I arrived there a little late, in the company of Gromyko, but before Gorbachev appeared. Soviet senior officials, Ligachev, Yazov, Yakovlev, and others—many with their wives—and a group of Americans, mostly White House and State Department officials, were already mingling in the columned main room with Soviet artists, poets, athletes, and scientists. Among the Soviet guests was even one woman cosmonaut, Valentina Tereshkova, who was on Moscow's A-list of invitees to social occasions of this kind. Most of the Soviet guests from outside the diplomatic and military spheres were artists and athletes. The U.S. Congress was represented by Senators Robert Byrd and Bob Dole.

But the person who attracted my attention most that night was Andrei Sakharov, who had been freed from internal exile by Gorbachev in December 1986. When Gromyko and I entered the spacious room, Sakharov and his wife, Elena Bonner, were conversing, in Russian, with Ambassador Matlock. Gromyko pretended not to see Sakharov and went to the opposite side of the room to avoid meeting him. I had to follow, but I noted that Secretary Shultz spent extra time with the Sakharovs, greeting them effusively. I had met Sakharov in the Kremlin soon after his return from exile in Gorky, at a meeting in St. Catherine's Hall in January 1988 chaired by Gorbachev, who made it a point to warmly welcome him and talk briefly with him. True to himself, on that occasion Andrei Dmitriyevich raised with Gorbachev the question of human rights and political prisoners. Generally speaking, for Gorbachev and most members of the Politburo to sit down now at a dinner with Andrei Sakharov was a powerful symbol, and one quite unimaginable before the Gorbachev era. It was evidence that Gorbachev and his associates, at least some of them, had accepted the issue of human rights as a legitimate concern, despite Gorbachev's public protestations to the contrary.

When the Gorbachevs arrived, they were met by the Reagans at the entrance to Spaso House. Reagan looked well rested and in high spirits after his tour de force at the university; Nancy looked somewhat tired after her lightning trip to Leningrad. Mikhail Sergeyevich was bubbling with energy, as always, and Raisa Maximovna looked very dignified. Reagan shared his table with her, Alexandr Yakovlev, Senator Robert Byrd, and a few other people. Gorbachev's dinner companions were Nancy Reagan, Senator Bob Dole, Yegor Yakovlev, chief editor of *Moscow News*, and a few other officials.

In his toast speech Reagan waxed lyrical. He paid a glowing tribute to the beauty of Moscow, and for the second time that day he quoted from Boris Pasternak's poem "The Garden of Gethsemane": "You cannot decide a dispute with weapons. That's the voice . . . that is the imperative, the command," declaimed Reagan with a quivering in his own voice, like the thespian that he had been. "Put your sword in its place, O man. . . . And so we will work together, that we might forever keep our swords at our sides." The dinner ended with President Reagan bantering with Dave Brubeck, the idol of Soviet jazz lovers, as Gorbachev and other members of the Politburo looked on with broad grins. "Who is that man?" I heard Defense Minister Yazov ask Gromyko when we got up from the table, and Gromyko replied with an air of sophistication and, I thought, barely disguised condescension, "He is a well-known American jazz musician."

After the dinner was over that night, on the way home I bought a couple of plain Russian *pirozhki* in Arbat Street, for twenty kopecks (about fifteen cents at the time) each, to assuage the pangs of hunger I had felt the whole day. The lone but daring entrepreneur from some cooperative was doing a brisk business. Hot stuffed pastries, or *pirozhki*, in the Soviet Union were the equivalent of hot dogs in America. *Perestroika* was beginning to bear tangible fruit.

JUNE 1, WEDNESDAY. DAY FOUR.

On the fourth day of the summit Gorbachev and Reagan held their final formal session. Like the meeting the day before, it was to be a "nine-by-nine" or "wall-on-wall" session, i.e, a meeting with the members of both delegations—nine on each side—seated opposite one another across the negotiating table, in St. Catherine's Hall. As in the previous days, I was assigned to do the simultaneous interpreting.

When the two leaders appeared in the conference room shortly after ten, accompanied by Gromyko and Shultz, who were then joined by the other members of both teams, they were pelted with questions by reporters. After a good two minutes of handshaking for the benefit of the cameras, Gorbachev and Reagan took up the questions. Before answering one on START, Reagan first consulted with Shultz, then replied, "As the general secretary and I told you in the beginning of the talks, START is a complex area. It is not so easy to answer your question. We are still working." To the question on SDI, he replied that there was no major breakthrough, but they continued to discuss this problem. Then Gorbachev told the reporters to save their questions for the press conference and guided Reagan to his seat. The minibriefing was over, but before the reporters were shooed out, Reagan and Gorbachev exchanged another handshake for their benefit, as if to confirm that this was truly a summit of photo opportunities. When the reporters finally left, without wasting a moment, Gorbachev turned the floor over to Shevardnadze to present a progress report on all the issues covered by the groups that had been working throughout the summit. Then Shultz presented his own report, noting some progress on START, though clearly not enough to ensure the treaty would be ready while Reagan was still in office. Some minor progress had also been made on regional issues such as Southern Africa and the Middle East. As to human rights, Shultz stressed that significant progress had been made compared to where the two sides had been when they started. "It's a completely different world now," Shultz concluded emphatically.

Gorbachev and Reagan approved the reports, but then Gorbachev brought up a sticky point in the joint communiqué to be issued at the summit's end. It was the passage he had quickly shown Reagan on the first day of the summit.

Gorbachev said, "I ask you to discuss one point. I attach great importance to it. Everything that has been [achieved] since Geneva shows that war is unacceptable. We are now engaged in a broad political dialogue through which we have achieved the gains that are reflected in these reports. I've got a Russian copy of your speeches. We must learn to live in peace, respect one another's choice and that of others and recognize the political realities. We have both seen that even acute problems such as regional conflicts do not have military solutions either. And here solutions may be found only through a political settlement. I have this question: What is it that compels the colleagues of the president to reject this point in the final document [the joint statement], that is to say that 'a political approach must become the only means of settling conflicts'?

"Second, the universal principle of international relations is to live in peace. You are not against it, are you? Why then should it not be reflected in the final document? . . . In Geneva we said that nuclear war is inadmissible and cannot be won. This had a tremendous response all over the world. As a matter of fact, this has influenced our practical activities. Since Geneva we have satisfied ourselves that all problems should be solved on the basis of a political approach. Both you and we can say this separately. But if we say this together, it would be quite another matter. It would raise the status of our joint document and offer better prospects both for us and for the whole world. The president read our version of it in English and said [at the first private meeting], 'I understand it; it's all right,' thinking that he read it in Russian."

Gorbachev was trying his best to persuade Reagan to accept the Soviet-inspired language that contained the words *peaceful coexistence*.

"I think," Gorbachev continued, "if we included such a preamble to the effect that our experience of cooperation over the recent years shows that we must rely on political means and respect the choice of the peoples, then it would have a different ring to it. After all, you and I came to an understanding about this, didn't we! And now you are balking. Why, there must be some kind of revisionist in your ranks! [Laughter on both sides of the table] I have read this [joint] document. It's a good statement. But we can make it even stronger. Do you admit that we must live in peace? Why, you yourself were the first to say in Geneva that 'nuclear war must not be fought.' Why don't you want then to record it here? You said you were for peaceful coexistence. Why then not include these words in the communiqué? You are misled by your aides, Mr. President!" (*Vas vvodyat v zabluzhdeniye Vashi pomoshniki, gospodin Prezident*)

The very last phrase used by Gorbachev in his tirade was mistranslated into English as "You are deceived by your aides" by a colleague of mine whose turn it was to interpret at this particular moment, as we alternated every twenty minutes. After the meeting I went up to Colin Powell to prevent a potential misunderstanding due to the mistranslation. Did the U.S. side notice the blunder? I asked. Yes, he said, they had noticed Gorbachev's "strong language," but decided against making it an issue to avoid unnecessary aggravation. I translated what Gorbachev had really said and Powell said he would make it a point to bring this to the president's attention.

In response to Gorbachev's passionate appeal, Reagan only spread his arms and turned to Shultz, who flanked him on his right.

Shultz objected, "We resist the words *peaceful coexistence*."

Gorbachev responded, "Then we'll drop this word, too. [A long pause] The president finds it difficult to say what is not good here. [Looking at Shultz] And what will Mr. Secretary of State, George, say? [Shifting his gaze to Ridgway] Mrs. Ridgway, don't forget what Engels said: 'Work is the second civilization.' What isn't right for you here? The president was agreeable, after all. [Turning now to Carlucci] Well, Frank, pitch in! [Carlucci smiles, but says nothing.] Well, then, things are looking real bad!"

Shultz noted, "We'd like to have a caucus."

"There's no bomb there," said Gorbachev. "It's the question of a political approach, not military. We are saying life shows that reliance must be placed on political methods, not on military ones. That is the thrust. After all, this idea belongs to your president. If we drop *peaceful coexistence*—it is our term—then all the rest is acceptable? This is a political guideline. It doesn't mean that everything will fall by the way-side already tomorrow. I would be happy if we had such a strong political statement. It worked in Geneva. And then the document could be con-sidered ready. . . ."

"I feel uncomfortable with this language," Shultz stressed. "But I work for *him* [points to Reagan]. We'd like a caucus."

"It's up to you," Gorbachev allowed.

At this point, at 11:49 A.M., the meeting was suspended, and Reagan, Shultz, Carlucci, Powell, and the rest of the U.S. delegation went into a huddle in the adjoining room. Sixteen minutes later they returned to St. Catherine's Hall, and the meeting ended without resuming formally. Reagan walked over to Gorbachev and, standing face-to-face, toe-to-toe with him, said that the U.S. side was not ready to accept the language as proposed by him. "I am sorry," Reagan said softly, "this language is not acceptable."

"Why not, Mr. President?" asked Gorbachev.

"We can't accept it."

"All right, I see I can't change your mind." With these words Gor-bachev put his arms around Reagan and turned him gently to walk him to St. Vladimir's Hall, where they were to formally exchange the letters of ratification of the INF treaty.

The problem was the words *peaceful coexistence*, as originally pro-posed by Gorbachev. Although the proposal was a call for the renuncia-tion of military force to settle disputes and praised "peaceful coexistence," Gorbachev did not seem to realize that for many Ameri-cans, especially the conservatives, these words were anathema and evoked Khrushchev's missile-rattling over Cuba, the invasion of Hun-gary and Czechoslovakia, and President Kennedy's classic comment after the Vienna summit meeting in 1961: "For Khrushchev it means what's mine is mine and what's yours is negotiable." Gorbachev didn't seem aware of all the intricacies behind the inevitable American responses to his pet proposals. A psychological gap remained between him and Reagan.

At their first tête-à-tête three days before, when Gorbachev showed Reagan the language for the final communiqué, he'd scanned it per-functorily and said that at first glance it looked all right, but added that he wanted to discuss it with his aides. When Shultz and Carlucci looked at the language later on, they reportedly decided it had too many Soviet code words such as *peaceful coexistence, no use of force,* etc., which could be interpreted, or so they thought, as preventing the United States from insisting that the Soviet Union respect human rights and stop supporting Communist rebels in the third world. After that, the experts on both sides, mainly Bessmertnykh and Ridgway, went over the language once again and submitted to Gorbachev and Reagan a more neutral version.

In the exchange over the text, Gorbachev was alternately friendly and bullying. Reagan appeared soft and malleable—no doubt due to jet lag and exhaustion. I had the distinct impression that if it had not been for Shultz and Carlucci, Reagan would have knuckled under to a more vigorous, energetic, and assertive Gorbachev.

While this last formal meeting of the summit was still going on in St. Catherine's Hall, the guests for the ratification ceremony for the INF treaty had already arrived in St. Vladimir's Hall. All the Politburo members were there except for Viktor Nikonov and Nikolai Slyunkov. Among the guests in the audience I spotted Armand Hammer and Dwayne Andreas, chairman of the giant U.S. agricultural conglomerate Archer-Daniels Midland Company. According to Hammer, he was here in Moscow at his own invitation because he couldn't miss this "historic event," meaning the summit, although his ostensible motive for coming to Moscow was to "help the Russian people raise their living standards" by building a golf course outside the city. Hammer, of course, was no stranger within the Kremlin walls and had secured the go-ahead for a golf course way back when Brezhnev was still alive.

The ceremony was not unlike the one in Washington at the previous summit when the INF treaty was signed. The signing table was set up on the steps leading from the Winter Garden. The national flags of the Soviet Union and United States were placed upright on the floor at both sides of the table and slightly behind it. The guests, including those who had just arrived from the meeting with Gorbachev and Reagan, were now seated in the hall, flanking the two first ladies, who occupied the front-row chairs in the center. During the signing, the president and the general secretary sat side by side.

Gorbachev and Reagan briskly signed the two protocols, in English and Russian, and stood up to exchange the leather-bound folders containing the just signed instruments of ratification, i.e., the formal documents confirming the approval of the treaty by the top legislative bodies of both countries—the Supreme Soviet of the USSR and the U.S. Congress. From this minute the INF treaty was in force. Then they made brief statements that were translated, or to be more exact, read simultaneously. Gorbachev spoke of ushering in "an era of nuclear disarmament" and promised to "continue to work honestly and with perseverance . . . to fulfill the historic mandate" given to them by the

Soviet and American peoples. After the similar but more emotional ceremony of signing in the East Room of the White House of what had by now come to be known as the Washington Treaty, this ceremony was somewhat anticlimactic. After all, it was only a formal act giving effect to what had already been agreed upon and signed. Then Reagan took the rostrum.

Unfortunately, I could not stay until the end of the ceremony, as I had to rush to the MFA Press Center where I was to interpret Gorbachev's press conference scheduled for one o'clock. And so, as I left St. Vladimir's Hall in the middle of Reagan's speech, I heard him talking about the need to expand "the limits of trust . . . although we will verify, Mr. General Secretary, we will verify." His words were accompanied by general laughter.

By one o'clock I was in the MFA Press Center, which is located on Sadovoye Koltso about a mile from the MFA "wedding-cake" building itself. I had never seen this conference room so chock-full of people. It was crammed with reporters and dignitaries, both Soviet and American, "like herrings in a barrel," to use a Russian expression, with no standing room even. The previously dingy Press Center auditorium had been renovated especially for this occasion, with new, comfortable seats installed and a new simultaneous interpretation system built into the armrests. The interest in the press conference was enormous—it was Gorbachev's first press conference in Moscow, broadcast live on Soviet television. It began at 1:27 P.M. and lasted until 3:20 P.M. I think it was fifteen minutes shorter than the one he had given in Washington. In contrast, Reagan's press conference, which he would give later in the afternoon at Spaso House, would last only about thirty minutes.

When Gorbachev arrived in the press conference room, he took his seat at the center of the raised dais, with three high officials on each side of him: Shevardnadze, Yakovlev, and Dobrynin, and Chernyaev, Yazov, and Gerasimov. Guennady Gerasimov was the MFA's chief spokesman at the time. Gorbachev's opening "few words" about the results of the summit took up half of the almost two-hour news conference; the other half was a question-and-answer period. Twenty-three questions were asked and twenty-three answers given. In comparison, Reagan would speak for some ten minutes and take thirty questions. While Gorbachev's answers were long and repetitive, Reagan's were short and often humorous.

Basically, Gorbachev balanced his criticism of Reagan by calling the president's visit to Moscow a "major event" that moved relations "maybe one rung or two up the ladder." While he characterized their working relationship as warm and constructive, at times he portrayed Reagan in unfavorable terms, suggesting that he regarded the American president as a man with little command of detail and perhaps overly dependent on cautious underlings. The main result of the summit, Gorbachev went on, was the continuation of the dialogue between the two superpowers, which became possible due to a new realism in the leadership of both the United States and the Soviet Union. "Vse techet, vse izmenyaetsa," he said, quoting the Greek dictum to stress his point about the new sense of realism—"All is flux, nothing stays still." In his opening statement, Gorbachev referred to the reporter's question to Reagan during their tour of the Kremlin about whether he still considered the Soviet Union an "evil empire." Said Gorbachev, "He [Reagan] said, 'no.' And he said that at a [impromptu] press conference next to the Czar Cannon, in the Kremlin, in the very focus of the 'Evil Empire'! We take note of that."

With the important 19th Communist Party Conference just four weeks away, Moscow was alive with rumors about disagreements within the Politburo. The press conference was galvanized when a British journalist asked about Boris Yeltsin's charge in an interview he gave to the BBC and ABC that the archconservative Politburo member Yegor Ligachev was "putting on the brakes" to perestroika and should step down. What did Gorbachev think about Yeltsin's call for Ligachev's resignation? The question put Gorbachev on the spot, live and on camera. He had previously declined to comment on this sensitive issue, especially since Yeltsin had been dropped from the Politburo and was now a pariah in the Soviet political wilderness.

As I finished translating the question into Russian, I saw Gorbachev, who sat right in front of me below, slowly get red in the face. But to my surprise, Shevardnadze, who sat to Gorbachev's right, managed an amused smile. The other members of his team sat with impassive faces. Gorbachev took a long time to answer. After a bit of oratorical backing and filling, he said he hadn't read the interview, and then he went at Yeltsin with sudden ferocity. Gorbachev called on the BBC to provide an unedited tape of Yeltsin's interview so that the Central Committee could establish exactly what he had said and "demand that he explain his position." As to Ligachev's resignation, Gorbachev said simply that the problem in the Party Central Committee and the Politburo was "nonexistent."

The answer was revealing in that, for all the glasnost and talk of democratization and political reform, inside Kremlin politics still remained shrouded in secrecy.

*   *   *

After interpreting at Gorbachev's press conference I had enough time to get back to the MFA to watch Reagan's live on CNN and jot down some of the things he said. The seventy-seven-year-old president appeared fatigued. In his brief opening remarks he struck a different note from Gorbachev's, emphasizing that "a good deal of important work" had been accomplished in Moscow and stating that a great deal of the credit for the changes now taking place in the Soviet Union belonged to Gorbachev personally.

Reagan was asked if his views of the Soviet Union as an "evil empire" had changed and whether it was due to Gorbachev's being the general secretary or to his own changing views. "No, I think there is quite a difference today in the leadership and in the relationship between our two countries," Reagan replied. When another questioner wondered if the president's changing views had contributed to "this better atmosphere," and whether the Cold War was over and American people could now trust the Russians, Reagan replied, "I think now, yes, of course, as I already said: 'Trust but verify.' I think that a great deal of it is due to the general secretary, whom I have found different than previous Soviet leaders have been."

At the end of the press conference, a reporter asked him, "What have you learned in your first trip to Moscow?" Reagan's response left his audience rather mystified: "I am going to give this one answer because I've wanted to say this, and I say it every time I get a chance. I think that one of the most wonderful forces for stability and good that I have seen in the Soviet Union are the Russian . . . women."

Ironically, Russian women did not get to hear Reagan's last answer—his press conference was not broadcast live in the Soviet Union either on television or on the radio. However, later that night when the Reagans dined with the Gorbachevs at their country dacha after watching ballet at the Bolshoi and when the table conversation turned to *perestroika,* Raisa Maximovna, as representative of that wonderful force, enriched Reagan's treasure-house of Russian proverbs by contributing what I thought was a real gem with a nice twist: *"Kooi zhelezo poka Gorbachev"* (Strike iron while Gorbachev is hot).

JUNE 2, THURSDAY. DAY FIVE AND LAST.

On this warm, sunny day Reagan as president and Gorbachev as general secretary said good-bye to each other for the last time. In the following years they would see each other several more times, but informally. The official farewell ceremony in the Kremlin's St. George's Hall began at 10 and ended at 10:15 A.M. Gorbachev may have set a personal record for the shortest speech of his life—one and a half minutes.

In his speech of reply the president surprised the hosts by addressing Gorbachev's wife as "Raisa Maximovna," a highly unusual form of address for a foreigner, but the Russian way of addressing women in public. Whoever was Reagan's adviser on Russian customs, he or she was good. Reagan also tried out his Russian again for the last time, and just as on the previous Sunday, he puzzled both his hosts and the listeners with a proverb that sounded bizarre, at least within these Kremlin walls. "Mr. General Secretary," he said in the middle of his remarks, "if you will permit me just one more proverb. I think a very old and popular saying you have here about last Sunday, the day of our arrival, spoke to the promise we have seen fulfilled at this summit in this Moscow spring. Truly, then, *Troitsa—ves' les raskroyetsa*" (On Trinity Sunday, the whole forest bursts into blossom). The proverb may have been known to Russian believers, but hardly to the general secretary of the Communist Party of the Soviet Union or to the atheist officials attending the farewell ceremony.

Reagan concluded on a personal note, professing friendship for the Gorbachevs: "I think you understand we're not just grateful to you and Mrs. Gorbachev, but want you to know we think of you as friends." And in that context Reagan asked one favor of Gorbachev: "Tell the people of the Soviet Union of the deep feelings of friendship felt by us and by the people of our country toward them." And for the last time the hallowed Kremlin walls resounded with what had now become Reagan's trademark closing: "Thank you and God bless you."

After the ceremony the Gorbachevs escorted the Reagans, all walking arm in arm, down the central staircase to the exit from the Grand Kremlin Palace. Before getting into his car, Reagan showed Gorbachev a copy of the issue of *Time* magazine that named Gorbachev Man of the Year and asked for his autograph. With a broad grin, Gorbachev complied. "Well, you are now a popular man, Mikhail Sergeyevich," commented Raisa Maximovna. "The president of the United States himself asks you for an autograph. And that means something, doesn't it?"

With that they parted, like good friends, only to see each other again here in Moscow in two years, but under somewhat different circumstances.

The basic purpose of the Moscow summit was to move Soviet-U.S. relations onto a more regular footing and thereby, hopefully, bring an end to the Cold War nearer. Viewed from this angle, the summit was a success, despite the lack of practical agreements. On a personal level, the relationship between Gorbachev and Reagan got a further boost, especially from the U.S. president. But despite the assertion of friendship, vast psychological gaps remained between them. Perhaps Gorbachev had more intricate motives for leaning hard on Reagan at their last working session, but I was convinced that he simply was not fully aware of the inevitable American reaction to his pet proposals and was still guided by the "old thinking" in this case. After all, vague rhetorical pledges were bound to lead to conflicting interpretations and, as a result, to recrimination and bad faith.

As Reagan left Moscow for London to brief Thatcher and other top British officials on the summit's results, Gorbachev publicly characterized it as marked by "missed opportunities." However, privately he said it was "yet another milestone to better relations with Americans."

As to the linchpin of the Soviet-American relationship, arms control, no breakthrough had been achieved, although some modest progress had been made. Gorbachev and his team felt increasingly pessimistic that a treaty to cut long-range strategic arms by 50 percent could be completed during the Reagan administration. And Gorbachev was running into increasing resistance from his military, who thought they could get a better deal with the new administration and, accordingly, held back on some potential concessions they could have made. The mistrust was still there. Yet, slowly but surely, a more positive relationship between the two countries was emerging. In short, great advances were not made, but neither were great hopes dashed.

It was fitting that Reagan met a final time with Gorbachev in St. George's Hall where he first set foot on the previous Sunday. Referring to the legend of St. George, the famous dragon-slayer, the president said, "I would like to think that our efforts during these past few days have slain a few dragons and advanced the struggle against the evils that threaten mankind—threats to peace and to liberty." The president had slain a few dragons of his own—he no longer regarded the Soviet Union as an evil empire, and he gave Gorbachev the credit for this. The truth is, after meeting Reagan in person on their own turf, ordinary Russians found it difficult to see America as a threat. Much of the credit for the judicious selection of themes and the overall approach to the Soviets that made Reagan's day and made him popular with the common people should undoubtedly go to Jack Matlock, the American ambassador in Moscow. I think Matlock was not only a superb diplomat, but also a superb student of the Soviet Union and an excellent speaker of the

Russian language. As such, he must have seen the openings for Reagan to reach the ordinary people. I have no doubt that Matlock skillfully guided and coached Reagan to compliment Gorbachev in every speech on the liberalization already achieved, deliberately trying to give him a boost prior to the crucial nineteenth conference of the Communist Party, which would become a turning point in the life of the country and radically change the course of internal reforms.

That the most conservative and anticommunist of postwar American presidents should be ending his White House tenure with a visit to Moscow, describing the Kremlin leader, Gorbachev, as a "friend," was a confirmation of the correctness of Gorbachev's course. Reagan and Gorbachev ushered in an "era of nuclear disarmament" by exchanging ratification documents of the INF treaty. The Cold War was not over yet, but the two leaders had agreed to an important intermission.

One couldn't help noticing that Gorbachev treated Reagan like an equal, although they no longer called each other Ron and Mikhail, as they had tried to in Washington. In contrast, most foreign leaders, even old friends of Reagan's, such as Margaret Thatcher, tended to defer to him because of his age and stature. But Gorbachev hardly showed any deference or respect for Reagan's age or position as an elderly and senior statesman. This enabled Gorbachev and Reagan to speak with each other freely and frankly, stepping literally on each other's toes at their last meeting. If they had not become friends in the real sense of the word, they had become partners who held each other in genuine respect. That was no small achievement, which added solidity to Soviet-U.S. relations, which the two leaders sought to put on a steady, even sustainable basis.

CHAPTER FOUR

ROMANTIC SUMMIT

Gorbachev-Thatcher London Summit, 1989

By the spring of 1989 things began to move in earnest. As a direct result of Gorbachev's policies both at home and abroad, the Soviet Union and its relations with the rest of the world were definitely in flux. In late March, per Gorbachev's proposal, the USSR held its first free elections since 1917. The elections were for a new Congress of People's Deputies. Although Communist candidates had the power and the purse of the Communist establishment behind them, many were defeated. Boris Yeltsin, the former Politburo member and Moscow Party chief, was swept into the new Congress with 89 percent of the vote as Moscow's deputy on a platform opposing privilege and halfhearted attempts at reform.

Also on the home front, in a sign of further liberalization, after thirty-three years of official silence, the Kremlin published, for the first time, in the *Izvestia TseKa KaPeSS (CPSU Bulletin)* the full text of the secret speech delivered by Nikita Khrushchev to the 20th Communist Party Congress. That speech denouncing Stalin's crimes had long been regarded by the West as a landmark event in the history of the Soviet Union and communism. Release of the speech followed the publication of excerpts from Khrushchev's memoirs by *Argumenti i Facti*, a popular Soviet weekly newspaper. *Glasnost* was taking deeper root. But *perestroika* was not yet irreversible. Even senior government officials were not sure they could manage the process without a specific plan. The gap between the economic and political fronts was growing ominously wider. Living standards continued to decline even while freedoms increased. But one thing was patently clear: whatever the outcome, the world would never be the same.

Early in 1989, Europe was still divided by the Iron Curtain, but it was getting rusty. To the east of it, Poland, Hungary, Czechoslovakia, Bulgaria, and Romania were dominated by Communist Parties beholden to

Moscow. They had been kept in power for the past forty-four years by the threat of Soviet military intervention under the so-called Brezhnev Doctrine. It was becoming increasingly clear, however, that with Gorbachev as commander in chief Soviet military forces would not be used to prop them up. East Germany was ruled by the hard-line Honecker regime, and despite Reagan's appeals, the Berlin Wall was still standing. But the viability of the GDR's regime was increasingly being questioned. The stormy petrel of change heralded a new, hopefully peaceful revolution in what had until now been the "mighty socialist camp." By this time, too, Soviet troops were out of Afghanistan, as Gorbachev had promised. Moscow had placed on the negotiating table in Vienna proposals for drastically cutting conventional forces. Since January 20 the United States had had a new president, George Bush. And Britain's prime minister, Margaret Thatcher, was still a strong and charismatic leader whose views and positions commanded respect.

But the most amazing development since the previous year's Moscow summit was perhaps the renunciation, in July 1988, soon after Reagan left the Soviet Union, of the Marxist doctrine of the "class struggle" as a basis of Soviet foreign policy and promulgation of a policy based on "common human values" and "common interests of mankind." Until then the theory of "class struggle" had, in fact, been a justification for the conduct of the Cold War with the West. Also, from then on, peaceful coexistence, over which Gorbachev had argued with Reagan, was no longer to be seen as a form of the class struggle or identified with its concept. The struggle of the two opposing systems, communist versus capitalist, was no longer the "decisive tendency of the contemporary age."

Against this political backdrop, Gorbachev was to pay an official state visit to Great Britain at the invitation of Margaret Thatcher and her government. This visit had originally been planned for December 1988, but had been postponed because of the devastating earthquake in Armenia. It would be Gorbachev's third visit to the British Isles. In December 1984, Gorbachev had visited Britain at the head of a Supreme Soviet delegation. His talks with Prime Minister Thatcher and his meetings with parliamentarians and with representatives of the worlds of politics and business had started, after a long hiatus, a substantive political dialogue between the two countries, and between their two leaders. It was then that Mrs. Thatcher had taken Gorbachev's measure and returned her famous verdict: "I like Mr. Gorbachev. I think we can do business together." In December 1987, Gorbachev made a stopover at an airport at Brize Norton, England, on his way to the United States, during which the two leaders explored each other's views on the launching of real disarmament in Europe and searched for ways of reducing armed confrontation on the Continent and replacing it by collaboration between East and West. The trip to Britain would be Gorbachev's first visit to Western Europe as head of state. He had been elected chairman of the Presidium of the Supreme Soviet of the USSR by the Supreme Soviet barely six months before, in October 1988, in place of Gromyko, who had been sent into retirement. This position was a rough equivalent of a head of state. While gaining this largely ceremonial role, he, of course, retained his more important and powerful post as general secretary.

Gorbachev's host, the extraordinary lady who had become almost a friend, Mrs. Margaret Thatcher, was the Conservative member of Parliament for Barnet, Finchley, Britain's forty-ninth prime minister, and the first woman to hold the office. She had been appointed prime minister, first lord of the treasury, and minister for the civil service almost ten years before, on May 4, 1979. Mrs. Thatcher was the first British prime minister this century to have successfully weathered three consecutive general elections. She was reappointed prime minister in 1983 and in 1987. In 1989, she became the longest-serving British prime minister of this century. She was no longer the "Iron Lady" in the eyes of Soviet officialdom. Although the sobriquet coined by *Pravda* under Brezhnev had all but disappeared under Gorbachev, Soviet diplomats in London still relished the following joke: One day the elders of the Conservative Party, known as the men in the gray suits, would approach Margaret Thatcher with a gun and a bottle of whiskey and tell her the time had come for her to go. Thatcher drinks the whiskey and shoots the men in the gray suits, thus living up to her image as the Iron Lady.

For Gorbachev's official visit to London, I was assigned to interpret mainly for Alexandr Nikolaievich Yakovlev, member of the Politburo and secretary of the Central Committee, and Gorbachev's closest comrade-in-*perestroika*. I was also assigned to provide simultaneous interpretation of Gorbachev's speeches during his scheduled appearances at Lancaster House and at Guildhall—where it was believed he would make important statements—and elsewhere. I was to double in brass, so to speak.

LONDON. APRIL 5, WEDNESDAY.

Gorbachev was to arrive this evening. Throughout the day a cold sleet fell, there was heavy fog, and it was chilly—about forty-five degrees

Fahrenheit. They say the British like to banter about the weather. They themselves say that all they talk about, as a rule, is three subjects: weather, weather, and weather, although not necessarily in that order. But Gorbachev's impending arrival gave them a fourth topic to discuss—the political weather.

The evening of Gorbachev's arrival I went to the Soviet Embassy on Kensington Palace Gardens, where I had an interesting conversation with Lev Parshin, a political counselor. His responsibilities during the Gorbachev visit included briefing him and his entourage on the political situation in Britain, which he took the trouble to describe for me in great detail. He said that the previous night Thatcher had given an interview to Soviet television, in which she described Gorbachev as a man of "tremendous political courage." She likened his vision to "a searchlight into the future." Within Britain, however, Gorbachev had critics. On the eve of his visit, reports appeared in the press that the Soviet Union had sold Libya advanced SU-24 jet bombers with the ability to reach Israel with missiles. The British were disturbed by this. It was two years since President Reagan had ordered the bombing raid on Colonel Gadhafi's headquarters, carried out by aircraft from U.S. bases in Britain. The discovery of this sale apparently prompted Sir Geoffrey Howe, foreign secretary, to attack Gorbachev's arms control policy proclaimed in January 1986. The overriding objective of that policy was to achieve a world free of nuclear weapons by the year 2000. Sir Geoffrey described Gorbachev's call for the elimination of all nuclear weapons as an attempt to "beguile public opinion" in the West. "The thing that still looms large over the European continent is this huge bear of a Russian army, a tremendously well-armed, massive army well stocked with tanks and artillery," he said in an interview for the BBC.

To be sure, *Pravda* also attacked Thatcher's nuclear policies. It wrote on the eve of Gorbachev's visit: "We consider the way to ensure stable security in Europe is not through modernization of nuclear weapons [the course Thatcher advocated], but through modernization of the whole system of interstate relations on our continent." While arms control would be a major topic at the summit, Soviet ambassador Leonid Zamyatin suggested Gorbachev wanted to raise an even larger theme and hinted that he would make an important speech at the Guildhall. "The Anglo-Soviet dialogue is gaining momentum," Zamyatin said, "but it is only a part of the efforts to create a common European home." The main purpose of the visit, according to Zamyatin, was to sound out Thatcher on Britain's willingness to participate in overcoming the divisions in Europe and laying a foundation for a meaningful dialogue on building such a "home." Gorbachev would also attempt to step up the Soviet Union's puny volume of trade with Britain, aiming for a 40 percent increase to 2.5 billion rubles (roughly U.S. $2 billion) by 1990, and expanding the number of joint Anglo-Soviet ventures.

The British press speculated that Margaret Thatcher would not fail to tell Gorbachev that the USSR must cut down on its spying. Back in January, Sir Geoffrey Howe had expressed his concern, in a speech in Munich, Germany, over what he described as "increasing Soviet intelligence activities" worldwide and in Britain in particular. In the past, several batches of Soviet diplomats and trade mission representatives had been expelled from Britain "for activities incompatible with their diplomatic status." In September 1985, six months after Gorbachev had taken office, Britain expelled twenty-five Soviet diplomats whom it accused of spying. Moscow retaliated by ordering six British diplomats to leave, and Britain replied by increasing the number of Soviets expelled to thirty-one. The relationship between the two countries had recovered since then, especially since Thatcher's visit to Moscow in March 1987. But Sir Geoffrey Howe had constantly been calling for vigilance.

Raising the political temperature in the House of Commons, Margaret Thatcher, too, had stated only the day before that no reduction in the KGB activity around the world had occurred since "Mr. Gorbachev became general secretary in 1985."

Ironically, by prior agreement with the Soviets, armed KGB security agents were to be allowed on the streets of London to guard Gorbachev—the first time Britain had sanctioned such a thing. On the day Gorbachev arrived in London, a poll published in *The Times* revealed that in the British public's mind the threat posed by the Soviet Union had diminished significantly since he took over as Soviet leader. Only 17 percent thought that the Soviet Union's policies were harmful to Britain, compared with 42 percent in a similar poll in 1981. In the area of human rights, however, 212 MPs, in an advertisement in *The Times*, qualified their welcome to Gorbachev by criticizing the Soviet Union's "continued abuse of basic human rights." Nevertheless, in a goodwill gesture, the day before the visit Moscow had given permission for eighteen more refuseniks and nine prisoners of conscience to emigrate, including the mathematician Georgi Samoilovich, aged sixty-six, who had been the subject of a long campaign by the Foreign Office. Sir Geoffrey Howe said in a television interview, "Five years ago the Soviet Union had no respect for human rights whatsoever. Today it is a topic we can talk to Mr. Gorbachev about and make headway."

Despite areas of tension, there had certainly been major improvement in relations. British government sources were describing Anglo-Soviet relations as the best since the Second World War and expected that Thatcher would extend and deepen her remarkable personal relationship with Gorbachev. The British press emphasized that Gorbachev and Thatcher would be meeting as friends with conflicting minds and that this would be the first full-scale important visit to Britain of a Soviet leader since Khrushchev and Bulganin in 1956.

At 11 P.M., the Il-62 carrying Gorbachev and his party touched down at Heathrow. Earlier that day the Soviet leader had wound up a four-day visit to balmy Cuba. Now he and Raisa Maximovna stepped out of the plane to the sleet and Siberian-like cold. Prime Minister and Mr. Thatcher, Secretary for Foreign and Commonwealth Affairs Sir Geoffrey Howe, Soviet ambassador Leonid Zamyatin, and other shivering Soviet and British officials were on hand to greet them. Her Royal Majesty's Chamberlain Lord Strathclyde represented the Crown. Her Majesty herself never goes out to the airport to meet foreign leaders. Gorbachev was accompanied by Shevardnadze, Yakovlev, and Kamentsev, the Soviet first deputy prime minister responsible for trade. The delegation comprised twenty officials, including Sergei Akhromeyev, Evgeny Primakov, Valentin Falin, Valery Boldin, and Nikolai Kruchina.

Wearing a gray trilby (or was it a fedora?—I could never figure out the difference, but the former seems to be an English word and the latter American), scarf, and overcoat, Gorbachev looked impervious to the bitter wind, sleet and snow, and dank air. He shrugged off the drizzle. "This is a natural massage. It's good for the skin of the face. I can understand why the English people are so hardy," he said to Margaret Thatcher with a big grin. Raisa Maximovna, wearing a mauve leather coat, spent several minutes in animated discussion with Denis Thatcher at the aircraft steps. Her hair was dyed blond, not red, and appeared now to be the same color as that of Mrs. Thatcher, who wore a red coat with a collar of black sable. She stood behind her guests as the Soviet national anthem was played by the Queen's Color Band of the Royal Air Force. Amid tight security and also protected by a large umbrella, Thatcher accompanied Gorbachev to his Zil limousine, which whisked them away to the Soviet Embassy where he would stay for the next forty hours or so.

When the Gorbachevs and the Thatchers arrived at the Embassy at 11:45 P.M., they went to the Golden Salon for their first informal meeting, which lasted until well after midnight. The true-blue lady Mrs. Thatcher was dressed appropriately for the occasion: a bright red dress with a pink silk scarf around the neck. I noticed that the color red was well represented at summits—in Washington (mainly in the parting ceremony), in Moscow, and now here in London. After exchanging pleasantries, the two first couples clinked glasses in a welcoming toast and joked about . . . what else? The weather, of course! It looked almost like the good old family reunited for "a nightcap."

It is difficult to imagine that a U.S. president would go to the airport almost at midnight to welcome the leader of a country that was still in the opposite camp. But when it came to protocol, the British prime minister was second to none in lavishing attention on the man with whom she was about to do business.

There was not much to interpret that night, and I returned to my room at the Royal Gardens Hotel at two in the morning. The next day would be very busy.

April 6, Thursday. Day One.

Woke up at six in the morning. Outside the windows of the Royal Gardens Hotel, where the Soviet delegation was staying, I saw rain, sleet, and snow. The skies were gloomy. And the temperature was only five degrees Celsius or about forty Fahrenheit—unusual for London at this time of year.

Yakovlev was a stocky, slightly pudgy, bald man who walked with a limp, the result of a wound in his left leg in the Second World War. He wore thick, horn-rimmed spectacles that made him look like a wise owl. He was one of the troika of Soviet intellectuals who had been elevated by Gorbachev into what could be described as a kitchen cabinet on foreign policy. The other two members of the troika were Eduard Amvrosiyevich Shevardnadze and Anatoly Sergeyevich Chernyaev, appointed by Gorbachev in 1986 as his chief foreign policy adviser. Apart from Shevardnadze, the most powerful was Yakovlev, a member of the Politburo and the head of the Central Committee's newly established international commission.

Yakovlev had studied at Columbia University in New York in the 1950s and written several books on American capitalism—most of them quite unfavorable. In the early 1970s, Yakovlev had been deputy head of a Central Committee department until his strong criticism of Russian nationalism offended Brezhnev and Suslov (the latter a loyal Stalinist and the self-appointed top watchdog of Communist ideology), who got rid of him by "exiling" him as ambassador to Canada, where he served for ten years. In Stalin's time those who fell afoul of "the supreme leader and father of all peoples" ended up in front of the firing squad; Khrushchev pensioned them off; while in Brezhnev's epoch of *zastoya* (stagnation) they were sent as ambassadors to faraway countries. Gorbachev brought him back from Canada where he had first met him during a visit in 1983 and where they were said to have seen eye to eye on many things that were wrong in the Soviet Union. Yakovlev's experience of the West and his broad outlook had bred in him the belief that the Soviet Union had much to learn from Western social democracy. He was Gorbachev's closest ally and the spiritual father of *perestroika*. Like Gorbachev, Yakovlev, too, evolved as *perestroika* progressed. When I had met him for the first time at the 1987 Washington summit, he did not impress me. He seemed gloomy and too conservative in his appearance to be a true reformer. He spoke some English, mostly on social occasions, but when he wanted to convey finer nuances to his interlocutors and listeners, he preferred to use an interpreter.

As Yakovlev emerged from his suite at the Royal Gardens Hotel that morning, escorted by his bodyguard, I introduced myself as the interpreter assigned to work with him. Yakovlev gave me an inquisitive look, shook my hand and said that my face was familiar, but could I please remind him where he had seen me? "In Moscow and in Washington," I said. He exclaimed, "But of course; now I remember!" As we walked down the corridor to the elevator, he asked me some more questions. In contrast to the summit in Washington, he was now congenial to the point of being jovial. He asked me if I was ready for some "serious work" in Parliament where he was scheduled to speak before the special foreign affairs committee later in the day. I showed him my legal pads. "You are well armed," he said. "So everything should be all right," he added in English with a big smile on his face. His affability put me at ease, for until now I didn't know what to expect of him. This was my first real introduction to him, and my second impression of him, which was quite favorable.

That impression was reinforced later when he invited me to sit next to him in his Zil limousine. "Let them think I am being accompanied by someone important," he joked. "Let them wonder who it is." As we walked, at his suggestion, all the way from the hotel to Gorbachev's residence in the Embassy, he questioned me about my job and about London, saying at one point that Moscow still had a long way to go to catch up with London as a clean and beautiful city. I couldn't agree more.

After a meeting with David Owen, the leader of the Social Democratic Party, we headed to the House of Commons for Yakovlev's meeting with MPs. I was excited to get to see this "mother of all parliaments" from the inside.

While we were being driven along Kensington High Street on the way to the Parliament on the Thames, Yakovlev did some window-shopping through the car's window. The store windows were well stocked with all kinds of goods. As we passed yet another store display, Yakovlev showed his sense of humor by pointing to the window and saying, "I am really disappointed. I thought I would find England to be different from Russia, but it's just the same here as in our country. In our country, especially in the provinces, whenever *nachalstvo* [the bosses] come to town, the local authorities fill the normally empty store shelves with goods overnight to show how well they take care of their people and make a good impression on the bosses. The English must have taken the leaf out of our book."

I was amazed to hear him say this. Yakovlev continued, "It was quite different in Cuba, though. Yesterday, while driving around Havana, we saw that all the store shelves and windows were completely empty. Although Cuba is socialist, they are not at all like us. They don't care what the bosses might say. So it would seem that we have a lot more in common with the British than with the Cubans."

I decided that Yakovlev was definitely a man after my own heart. It was encouraging at last to meet a top Soviet leader who was obviously very much aware of some of the most glaring shortcomings in Soviet society and who felt sufficiently free to speak openly about them to his interpreter. Although he was not young—he was sixty-four, I think—he seemed to be more open-minded and forthcoming than all the other Soviet leaders of the past with whom I had worked. I could not imagine Gromyko or any other old-guard leader saying a thing like this, even to his closest friends.

At 11:15 A.M. our motorcade pulled up at the private entrance, reserved for MPs, to the House of Commons, in the inner courtyard of the Houses of Parliament. The chairman of the House of Commons Select Committee on Foreign Affairs, Mr. David Howell, and the leader of the British Group of the Inter-Parliamentary Union, Mr. Michael Marshall, met us at the entrance and took us through the long, meandering, maze-like corridors of this venerable building to the foreign affairs committee's room, which faced the Thames. Yakovlev brought with him Primakov, Falin, and Parshin. The British group consisted of some twenty MPs.

The MPs wanted to ask Yakovlev "ten thousand questions," but in the forty-five minutes that were allotted for the meeting Yakovlev had the time to answer about 9,990 fewer. The MPs were particularly anxious to know his answers to "the central question" regarding the new thinking in Soviet domestic and foreign policies, what it all meant in practical terms—in Eastern Europe, in the prospects for Soviet-European economic cooperation by 1992, and in whether the Soviet Union still posed a threat to Europe. His answers were more or less a repetition of relevant Soviet public statements, except for an interesting response to a question about Eastern Europe. He indicated that the old Soviet policy toward the socialist camp, the so-called Brezhnev doctrine, was apparently no longer in effect.

Gorbachev and his closest advisers, including Yakovlev, of course, had decided even then, in the early spring of 1989, to leave Eastern European countries alone and give them freedom of choice. "It is their own business to move in any direction they wish," said Yakovlev. "We are very serious about the freedom of choice. It is not just rhetoric. If it were, our troops would still be in Afghanistan. And we would have reacted by now to the emergence of a multiparty system in Eastern European countries. So it is a question of their own choice. . . . Let each nation make its own choice." The quickening pace of subsequent events in Eastern Europe, which would culminate in the tearing down of the Berlin Wall on November 9, 1989, showed that it really was not just posturing by the Soviet leadership. The new thinking in foreign policy was beginning to manifest itself in practice.

After the meeting with the MPs and a courtesy call on Speaker of the House of Commons Bernard Weatherill, we went on to 10 Downing Street to attend the signing ceremony of some Anglo-Soviet agreements. The prime minister's residence is a short distance from the Palace of Westminster and is located on a rather narrow and certainly one of the shortest streets in London. On the sidewalk in Whitehall at the entrance to Downing Street, which was restricted even then because of terrorist treats and bombings, stood a modest crowd braving the wind and a cold drizzle to wave at our passing motorcade. I caught a glimpse of "Gorbachev" and "Thatcher" in the crowd—the two grotesque masks were shouting something at us and waving the British and Soviet flags.

At 12:20, our motorcade pulled up at the door of the unpretentious dark-brick building with no sign other than a simple "10" made of brass. The world's most famous number ten. The prime ministers of Great

Britain and Northern Ireland have lived and worked in this building for over 250 years. The unprepossessing edifice and its rooms turned out to be far more modest than the Grand Kremlin Palace or even the White House. In front of it, across the street from the entrance, on a hastily erected platform, stood a crowd of shivering reporters and cameramen waiting for some tidbits of information.

As we got out of the car, we were first greeted by two hefty bobbies in black helmets who stood guard at the door, and then inside the house by three smiling young women, who took our raincoats and led us down the corridor through a room with claret-colored wallcoverings. On our left a portrait of Winston Churchill hung above a table on which stood a vase with flowers. A tall Englishman who was our escort explained that President Reagan liked to be photographed in front of this portrait when he came to visit. On our right, a narrow, rather steep wooden staircase led to the second floor. The entire wall on both sides, from floor to ceiling, was hung with portraits of Britain's former prime ministers, going as far back as 1732. The incumbent prime minister's portrait was conspicuous by its absence. To Gorbachev's question later as to why her portrait was not among the others, Thatcher would reply that it was because she was "still very much in office." If and when she quit, it would be a different matter. Her favorite portrait was that of Harold Macmillan.

Yakovlev had a problem climbing the stairs. Refusing offers of help, he dragged his lame leg as he held on to the banister. It was all right, he was used to it, he said. On the second floor we were ushered into an anteroom where we saw Shevardnadze and Howe engaged in an animated conversation. The room was already filled with invited Soviet guests and British hosts, with the exception of Thatcher and Gorbachev. A few minutes later the two leaders emerged from Thatcher's private office and joined us. Earlier in the morning, before the talks had begun, the entire staff of the prime minister's residence, some seventy-five people, had lined up and applauded the Soviet leader.

Both Gorbachev and especially Thatcher looked pleased. They came up to where we stood and Thatcher extended her hand. Her grip was strong, almost like a man's. She had intense blue eyes that looked directly at you with a serious and probing expression. She looked elegant in her two-piece, light gray, checkered suit with a raised collar. She wore a strand of pearls around her neck. Her light-colored hair was done in a typically Thatcheresque fashion—a "thatched" style. "Welcome, welcome!" she said to us. A Soviet cameraman later told us an amusing anecdote about earlier that morning when Mrs. Thatcher had indulged in a little housework just before Gorbachev's arrival. The prime minister was anxiously pacing inside Number Ten, he said, when she suddenly braked sharply and bent down to remove a piece of fluff from the hallway carpet. This vignette of domestic vigilance was recorded by a pool of photographers admitted inside to record the arrival of the Soviet leader. The cameraman said he automatically took a shot of her stooping, but then tore out the film of her backside and offered it to her to dispose of. She gallantly declined to take it.

Mikhail Sergeyevich came up to us. Jovial and cheerful, he began to tell us about his "interesting and productive meeting," but at this point the prime minister invited all the guests to proceed to another room for the signing ceremony. In the far end of the room, a small oval table was set up in front of a fireplace under the portraits of three British prime ministers.

Before the two foreign ministers, Shevardnadze and Howe, sat down at the table to sign the agreements, Raisa Maximovna, who had been at the side of Mikhail Sergeyevich from the minute he and Thatcher emerged from their talks in the prime minister's study, detached herself from him and came up to us to meet Dr. Irina Kirillova, a professor of Russian literature at Cambridge, who was one of Mrs. Thatcher's interpreters. Raisa Maximovna said she had heard an unfamiliar woman's voice speaking Russian nearby and wondered who it was. She complimented Kirillova on her "excellent literary Russian" and said she wanted to see Cambridge University, of which she had heard so much. She was so sorry that her schedule did not allow this. She had been at St. Paul's earlier in the day and said she had been struck especially by the painting *The Light of the World*, with its symbolism of the door to heaven without a handle.

In the afternoon, she would go to see the Museum of London, another outstanding landmark of this great city. The last time she had visited London in 1984, she was said to have gone to Cartier to buy jewelry, thereby incurring the wrath of her compatriots back home. Much of that part of the story was embellished and greatly exaggerated. This time, her "conspicuous consumption" had taken a decisively cultural turn. Later that day, at dinner, she told Margaret Thatcher she had enjoyed every minute of her tour, adding that as a historian she had been thrilled to see, in the Museum of London, the execution vest worn by King Charles I.

For this occasion—the signing ceremony and a working lunch—Raisa Maximovna was dressed in a dark gray two-piece suit with a large navy-blue bow in the front. It made her look much younger. Mikhail Sergeyevich was visibly proud of her, judging by the occasional adoring glances he cast in her direction. They made a very nice couple indeed.

Without much further ado, Shevardnadze and Howe affixed their signatures to three accords. The agreement on joint ventures was designed to safeguard investors against political, not commercial, risk and provided for the unrestricted transfer of capital and profits by joint ventures. A memorandum of understanding was intended to ease visa rules to make business and private travel between Britain and the Soviet Union simpler. And finally, there was a memorandum of understanding on building, furnishing, and equipping a school in Leninakan, Armenia, to replace the one destroyed in last December's earthquake. Lord Young, the trade and industry secretary, said these "exciting new initiatives" demonstrated the importance both sides attached to improving cooperation and trading links, noting that these formal protocols were "only the first step" in expanding Anglo-Soviet economic cooperation. These were the only accords produced by Lord Young and Kamentsev, chairman of the influential Soviet State Foreign Economic Commission and a deputy prime minister of the USSR.

Still, the agreements signed involved an estimated £200 million. As to joint ventures, Maxwell Communications, Robert Maxwell's publishing group, concluded an agreement with the Soviets, said to be worth about £20 million, for the exchange of nonclassified scientific and medical information with the Soviet Academy of Sciences and the All-Union Institute of Scientific and Technical Information.

Throughout the signing ceremony Raisa Maximovna kept stealing curious glances at Mrs. Thatcher, who stood behind her foreign secretary. Champagne was then served and the general secretary and the prime minister toasted the agreements. Curiously, Mrs. Thatcher's eyes, which were fixed on Gorbachev's, had a look of sheer rapture and adoration. In her toast remarks, she said her first reaction to that "horrible earthquake in Armenia, which killed twenty-five thousand people, including five thousand children," was how to help them. When she asked, through her ambassador, the people in Armenia what they would like as a gift, they said "they would like a new school." The earthquake-proof school would cost about £4 million to build and furnish, and the offer struck a responsive chord in the hearts of the Armenian people.

When the brief signing ceremony was over, Gorbachev and Thatcher went to the working lunch that had been scheduled here on the premises of Number Ten, and I went, together with Yakovlev, to another lunch, with George Younger, the secretary of defense.

The first round of Anglo-Soviet summit talks between Gorbachev and Thatcher showed their complete agreement on the need to preserve the

Namibia settlement—Namibia should and would become independent and no longer be a colony of South Africa—and then complete disagreement on the modernization of NATO's short-range nuclear missiles in Europe. Thatcher thought this was necessary to counterbalance the Soviet preponderance in conventional arms in Europe. Gorbachev was concerned that such modernization might slow the pace of disarmament, stressing that all nuclear weapons should be eliminated. The two leaders also discussed the apparent hiatus in American foreign policy. After seventy-five days of the new U.S. administration in office, Gorbachev was concerned that Bush was "dragging his feet," taking too long to come to grips with foreign policy, and he feared that the momentum in relations between the USSR and the U.S. gained during the later Reagan years could be lost. Gorbachev, of course, believed Thatcher carried weight with the new administration in Washington and thought that if she conveyed this message of concern to Bush, it would dispel his hesitation. Gorbachev told Thatcher with remarkable candor about the opposition to his reforms, and more than half their time was taken up with a discussion of *perestroika*. Thatcher was sympathetic. Other sensitive issues such as Soviet stocks of chemical weapons and human rights were referred to the foreign ministers to discuss.

The talks were characterized by a Downing Street spokesman as "extremely frank exchanges" involving "warm, passionate, animated, and solemn" discussions. Mrs. Thatcher said later the discussions with Gorbachev were "very, very deep, very wide-ranging, and very friendly." Gorbachev later described the talks, in his inside circle, as "frank and businesslike." They were able, he said, to get down to brass tacks without wasting time. He said he respected Thatcher for her "businesslike approach" to things. Before their morning session, Gorbachev had poked fun at Mrs. Thatcher's famous handbag, wondering about its contents. "I see you are well armed," he said, pointing to her handbag. She responded by showing him the contents—a batch of briefing cards.

Later in the evening in the Embassy there was a briefing on the results of the talks between the two foreign ministers. Howe and Shevardnadze, in contrast to their bosses, had had a sharp exchange. Sir Geoffrey expressed his government's concern over reports of the sale of Soviet planes to Libya. Shevardnadze parried with, "What about Britain's arms supplies to other countries in the Middle East? What about Britain's arms sale of the century?" (in a reference to a multimillion-pound deal with Saudi Arabia). According to Shevardnadze, Britain undeniably sold far more weapons to some of the Middle East countries than did the Soviet Union. He said it both privately and publicly. But the difference was that while Libya was totally unpredictable, Saudi Arabia, the main recipient of British arms, was a stable, pro-Western regime, which justified the sale in the eyes of the British.

There were also major disagreements on chemical weapons, the role of nuclear arms in the future defense of Europe, modernization of short-range nuclear missiles and the exclusion of such missiles from the CFE (conventional forces in Europe) talks in Vienna, Afghanistan, the Middle East, Southern Africa and Namibia, and Central America. Last but not least, they discussed human rights; only this time, said Shevardnadze, he turned the tables on Sir Geoffrey by raising the sensitive subject himself.

Officially, the tone of their talks was described as "civilized, very warm, and businesslike." On a personal level, Shevardnadze and Sir Geoffrey enjoyed a good relationship, which had been solidified through the memorable private dinner for Howe given by Shevardnadze at his Moscow apartment the year before—something that was very unusual for Soviet leaders even in the third year of *perestroika*. I remember that occasion well for I was there. But although by this time the two of them had met fourteen times, they were still on surname terms. Mrs. Thatcher, too, addressed Gorbachev formally as "Mr. President" rather than "Mr. General Secretary," and he addressed her formally as "Mrs. Prime Minister."

After lunch at the Savoy Hotel with George Younger, secretary of state for defense (which we ate "at the speed of a MIG-29," as Younger put it), Yakovlev and I went to Westminster Abbey for a wreath-laying ceremony. Yakovlev was in good spirits. As we passed Cleopatra's Needle, he wondered what it was. I explained. He asked me if I had ever worked in Britain. I said no, never, but I had been to London twice, I had read books about it, and I happened to like the city very much. "So do I," he said with sincerity. A dash through the rain, and we were at the Great West Door of the Abbey. Here, small knots of KGB men tried in vain to appear inconspicuous. With their crumpled leather coats and smoking cigarettes either in their hands or mouths, it was easy to spot them.

Just as we stepped out of the car, Gorbachev's motorcade arrived. He was accompanied by Margaret Thatcher, and Raisa Maximovna by Denis Thatcher. They were greeted loudly by cheering crowds braving the rain.

Westminster Abbey is a truly majestic monument to British culture and history. Here lie Shakespeare, Churchill, Newton, Darwin, and many other famous sons and daughters of England: kings and queens, statesmen and scientists, writers and poets.

Under the archway, Gorbachev and Thatcher were greeted by the Very Reverend Michael Mayne, the dean of Westminster. He introduced them to the members of the Abbey Chapter, whose scarlet cassocks and black gowns matched, as though by design, the red and black of the three layers of poppies that surrounded the Tomb of the Unknown Warrior. After his brief remarks, in which the dean paid tribute to Gorbachev's achievements in *perestroika*, Mikhail Sergeyevich stepped forward and laid a wreath on the black marble tomb of the Unknown Warrior. After a minute of silence, the dean said a quiet prayer for peace and for the Armenian earthquake victims. In this moment of introspection for Gorbachev and all of us, I could see Mikhail Sergeyevich was visibly moved. Afterward, in the Embassy, he would say in private, "To be honest, I did not expect it to be such a moving occasion."

Thatcher remarked that the unknown soldier was buried among kings. Gorbachev told the dean that he was deeply concerned that politics and morality should go hand in hand, and that religion had an important role to play in this. He and the dean discussed the symbolism of the tomb, with its coffin of English oak, its French soil, and its lettering of Belgian bullet metal. Gorbachev mentioned the recent millennium celebrations of the Russian Orthodox Church held in the Soviet Union, and the dean replied that the Abbey had marked the event with an oratorio by an English composer set to words by a Soviet priest who had suffered in a Siberian labor camp in the 1940s.

Then Mikhail Sergeyevich and Raisa Maximovna signed the visitors' book and were presented with an illustrated history of the Abbey and tape recordings of religious music by the choir. Away from the unrelenting blinding lights of television cameras, the leader of a superpower whose official policy was still institutionalized atheism spent twenty minutes inside this British sanctum. At the exit from the Abbey, the Gorbachevs took leave of the Thatchers: *"Do vechera"* (Till evening). The next destination was the Embassy. It was time to confer.

As the motorcade was pulling away from the curb, the lead car came to a sudden stop, and to the apparent consternation of the British security men, if not the Soviet, who were becoming inured to such forays, the Gorbachevs climbed out of their car, into the rain, and strode across the road to shake hands with a rain-soaked crowd on the opposite sidewalk. Spontaneous bursts of "pressing the flesh" had by now become Gorbachev's signature trademark. Someone in the crowd sang out to Raisa Maximovna, "You are beautiful!" Another shouted something about the "Red Little Star."

There was a lot of cheering, and a boo or two, with many placards welcoming Gorbachev and *perestroika*. There were shouts of "Gorbachev! Gorbachev!" An old woman held a placard high above her head reading, "We shall triumph over Red Army." This struck Yakovlev as incongruous. "And how does she think she will triumph over the Red Army if we ourselves don't know how?" he said in a yet another display of his peculiar sense of humor and candor. Later, at the Embassy, he would make a point to tell Gorbachev about the placard's message. They had a good laugh about it.

Still on the way to the Embassy, somewhat emboldened by his affability and friendly disposition, I asked Yakovlev how this visit to England compared with their just completed trip to Cuba. Yakovlev turned serious, paused, and said he was not happy about the Cuban trip. On the whole, ordinary Cubans seemed to be genuinely glad to welcome Gorbachev, he said. But Castro was unresponsive to the gentle prodding from Gorbachev about restructuring. He was as militant as ever and showed no signs of willingness to reform his regime or restructure his ailing economy. Outwardly and publicly, Castro was friendly toward Gorbachev, but he clearly had deep inner reservations. He even cracked a tactless joke about Stalin in the presence of Gorbachev, wittingly or unwittingly giving offense to his Soviet guests. However, Yakovlev did not elaborate.

After another pause, he suddenly spoke of the crimes Stalin had committed against the Soviet people. The subject troubled him deeply. "The time has come to expose those crimes fully," he said. "Otherwise, history would not forgive us, and *perestroika* cannot succeed unless we exorcise this demon." Stalinism was still firmly rooted in the minds of many people, he went on. What happened after Khrushchev had exposed the "personality cult" was a good illustration of this. Stalinism was an obstacle to reform that had to be removed. He was afraid that the new generation, which had not lived through the horrors of Stalin's rule, did not understand the dark side of Stalinism. If we were to make real progress, he said, and ensure genuine freedom and democracy, we had to confront our past squarely.

I couldn't agree more. Some months later, as a result of a decision by the newly founded Congress of People's Deputies, another brainchild of Gorbachev's, Yakovlev would be put at the head of a special commission to investigate and expose Stalin's crimes against the Soviet people. He was the right man for the job. As a result, he earned the hatred of the die-hard Party apparatchiks and the hard-core KGB Stalinists, who would launch a harassment campaign against him. He would receive threatening anonymous telephone calls and would even be accused by none other than Vladimir Kryuchkov—who was now the KGB chief—of being a CIA agent. They stopped at nothing to smear him. After the failure of the putsch in August 1991, Yakovlev would reveal, in an interview with *Izvestia*, that he had once been shown a paper that described him as the leader of some imaginary conspiratorial organization of democrats. Stalinism was still very much alive, indeed. So were the Stalinists. Yakovlev's star would begin to decline sometime in 1990. Under the growing pressure from the hard-liners he would be relegated to the background long before Shevardnadze's speech of resignation, in which he would sound a prophetic warning of imminent dictatorship.

After touring Case Communications, Inc., a computer factory near London, on the way to Lancaster House for his meeting with business leaders, Gorbachev asked Yakovlev to join him in his Zil. This was unusual. Something was up. But Gorbachev put his worries on hold and strove to appear optimistic for his audience at Lancaster House. The House is one of London's most beautiful buildings, situated off The Mall between Queen's Walk and St. James's Street, not far from Buckingham Palace. It was built in 1825 for the Duke of York and is so sumptuous, especially the interior, that Queen Victoria, who made her home in Buckingham Palace, is said to have remarked to her hostess on coming here, "I have come from my house to your palace." Here Gorbachev was to meet the captains of British trade and industry to make a big pitch for them to increase their trade links with the Soviet Union.

I did the simultaneous interpretation into English of Gorbachev's opening remarks and replies to numerous questions, and Dr. Kirillova, the British interpreter, interpreted the questions from the floor into Russian. We occupied a glass-enclosed booth set up in the Music Room, just behind the table that Gorbachev shared with Lord Young, Sir Trevor Holdsworth, and other officials. The meeting was meant to be informal. The Soviets and the British mingled freely with one another at round tables arranged in the meeting room on the second floor of Lancaster House. After a long opening statement by Gorbachev—true to form he discarded the prepared text of his remarks and spoke mostly off the cuff—he fielded a lot of questions.

I really enjoyed the interpreting. If the speaker knows his subject well and speaks while standing up, which Gorbachev did this time, without a prepared written text, he becomes a genuine speaker, not just another reader of a prepared text going at breakneck speed. Then it becomes a fair challenge and a sheer pleasure for the interpreter.

Gorbachev said that his country was slowly moving from a centrally planned economy to a more market-oriented one. He was keen to see the following areas of British-Soviet trade expanded: light industry and food, chemicals and electronics, agriculture and tourism. He cited Spain's as an example of a tourism-oriented economy that the Soviet Union wanted to emulate. He had cited this example earlier in the day in his talks with Thatcher. He said that while Spain received more than 50 million tourists a year, the figure for the Soviet Union was barely 2.5 million. He concluded his presentation with a linguistic challenge that I had to cope with in just a split second, if I wanted to preserve the original flavor of his colorful turn of phrase.

He appealed to the businessmen to act more boldly and courageously and promised them bigger returns—the more and the earlier they invested. He said, using a well-known Russian saying, "In short, I invite businessmen to act on the principle that 'none but the brave deserves the fair.'" The original Russian saying, *Smelost goroda beret*, translates literally as "Courage captures cities," which does not exist in English as a saying. My version was close to the original, though. Of course, that I was able to instantly come up with this appropriate English equivalent was not a sheer fluke. I had been fascinated with proverbs and sayings ever since my first, not entirely successful, experience of interpreting for Nikita Khrushchev many years before, when I was still a student at college, formally learning English. I remember that among other colorful sayings Khrushchev then used was the well-known Russian saying, *Pervyi blin vsegda komom* (The first pancake is always lumpy). Truth be told, my "first pancake" on that occasion left much to be desired. It could certainly have been much better had I done more studies on Russian and English sayings and proverbs. So ever since, I had been assiduously learning Russian adages and their English equivalents. I still am. I like proverbs. As to Khrushchev, that was his last impromptu public speech. Two weeks later, in mid-October 1964, he was ousted from office in a palace coup masterminded by Brezhnev.

Gorbachev wanted to convince the captains of British industry to invest in the Soviet economy more boldly, since they were hesitant for fear of political instability and the nonconvertibility of the Russian ruble. Gorbachev emerged from this one-hour meeting buoyant and cheerful. It was a well-rehearsed performance—he had already made a similar pitch to American businessmen sixteen months before, in Washington, but without much of a return on his verbal investment. The American business community was lukewarm toward the new investment prospects, citing the same reasons as their British counterparts. But Gorbachev was remarkable, at least in foreign policy, for his doggedness in pursuit of a goal in spite of temporary setbacks.

The meeting ended at seven, and I emerged from the interpreter's booth to rejoin Yakovlev for the last event of the day, a dinner for Gorbachev and his entourage hosted by Prime Minister and Mr. Thatcher on behalf of Her Majesty's government at 10 Downing Street.

Remembering the American experience of trying to persuade the Soviets to wear black tie to dinner in the White House in 1987, the British invitations to dinner at Number Ten were marked simply "lounge suit." I looked forward to this experience with great interest, to compare it with the one in the White House and especially with Kremlin banquets.

Sixty-five guests were in attendance, fifteen Soviet and fifty British. Besides the Gorbachevs, Shevardnadze (without his wife), Yakovlev, and Kamentsev, the Soviet guests included Valery Boldin, who was described in the guest list as head of the General Department of the Central Committee, and Nikolai Kruchina, head of the Administrative Department of the Central Committee. These two made a strange pair. As I have already mentioned, they had both appeared rather inexplicably, or so I thought, at the Washington summit and even sat in quietly on the meetings between Gorbachev and Reagan in the Cabinet Room of the White House. I could not understand then what their function was, for clearly they had no business in being present at those meetings. And now here they were again. There were also Academician Evgeny Primakov in his capacity as director of the Institute of World Economics and International Relations of the USSR Academy of Sciences, some lesser officials, and another "academician," Ivan Frolov, the new editor in chief of *Pravda* handpicked by Gorbachev to replace the conservative Viktor Afanasiev. Conspicuously absent from the guest list was Marshal Akhromeyev, although he accompanied Gorbachev on this visit, too, and had attended the lunch at the Savoy earlier in the day..

On the British side, besides Prime Minister and Mr. Denis Thatcher, there were His Royal Highness Prince Michael of Kent; Rt. Hon. Sir Geoffrey Howe, MP; Rt. Hon. Douglas Hurd, MP; Rt. Hon. George Younger, MP; and various lords. Here and there among the titled officialdom there was even the occasional plain "Mister So-and-So" and "Ambassador So-and-So." These people represented Her Majesty's government, the House of Lords, the business community, Parliament, the media, science, economics, the arts, farming—in a word, *la crème de la crème*, the upper crust of British society.

The British upper class and American high society are indefinably different. Something in the former's posture and manner of speaking makes them different. And I don't mean the difference in pronunciation or intonation. It goes much deeper. Where the Americans, as a rule, are open and friendly, the British tend to be stiff and reserved. There is much less display of charisma. Strangely enough, however, this did not apply to Margaret Thatcher. Despite her abrasiveness in public debates, she had plenty of charm and charisma. Even her speech was devoid of that peculiar enunciation so typical of the British upper class, and of her husband in particular. But then she was of rather humble origins.

Out of sixty-five people at the banquet only two were ladies: the British prime minister and the Soviet first lady. The latter arrived for the glittering banquet in a tight-fitting navy-blue pinstripe suit over a pearl gray satin blouse, fastened at the neck with a malachite brooch. Among her numerous assets emphasized by the Western press was that she was "the first Soviet leader's wife to weigh less than her husband." With a doctorate in sociology and expertise in the arts and science, she was "not really the sort of person Thatcher can leave to Denis to entertain," wrote the *Daily Mirror* in a brilliant example of British humor. "The only thing he knows about science is the chemical reaction you get when you add gin to tonic." Raisa Maximovna was indeed one of Gorbachev's most powerful diplomatic weapons because appearances do matter, whether the Soviet man or woman in the street liked it or not. They matter especially in international politics. "Her weakness for Dr. Zhivago–style coats and the penchant for changing her clothes frequently have achieved as much as her husband's new policies at summits in breaking down the barriers between 'them and us,' " wrote one newspaper. "By giving *glasnost* a bit of *glamornost* she has made us feel a bit safer. And proved that style doesn't have to be a substitute for substance," concluded an editorial in another.

When earlier that morning Raisa Maximovna had visited the London Museum, she met a group of schoolchildren and planted a kiss on the face of a little boy. It left him with red lipstick all over his cheek. "Ugh!" he yelled as he wiped it away. "I don't mind being kissed by women, but I'd rather they didn't leave any evidence." The boy then presented her with a bunch of flowers.

As soon as the Soviet first couple, accompanied by their British opposite number, entered the salon where the guests had congregated, a momentary hush ensued and all eyes were on them. The two couples formed a receiving line, and the small salon soon filled with even more people. In a few minutes a man dressed in black appeared; in his right hand he held what appeared to be a gavel, and he began slowly to approach where we stood. Abruptly, he knelt on the floor on his right knee and began to pound the gavel on a small round plate of polished brass, which protruded slightly from the floor in the middle of the salon. The man was a majordomo.

"My lord! Ladies and gentlemen! Pray silence! By the command of Her Majesty and on behalf of Her Majesty's government, I beg His Excellency the General Secretary of the Central Committee of the Communist Party of the Soviet Union, Chairman of the Presidium of the Supreme Soviet of the Union of Soviet Socialist Republics and Mrs. Gorbacheva to proceed to the dining room!" he intoned in English as he got up to his feet. That was quite a mouthful. I had never witnessed anything as quaint and striking as this either in the Kremlin or in the White House. The gentleman in black certainly deserved a commendation for his flawless mastery of what must have been one of the world's longest titles.

Then, the Right Honorable the Prime Minister and Mr. Denis Thatcher led the way to the dining room. She took the seat at the head of a U-shaped table, with Mikhail Sergeyevich on her right and Raisa Maximovna on her left. Seated next to Raisa Maximovna was Denis Thatcher, and I sat slightly behind, between him and Yakovlev. Space at the table was at a premium, for the dining room was not large and the guests had little elbow room. As soon as the guests had taken their assigned seats, Margaret Thatcher stood up to make a rather long but remarkable speech.

In her speech, she endorsed Gorbachev's reform policies in lavish terms and heaped effusive praise on him for his "peaceful revolution." "In barely more than four years since your first visit [in December 1984], we have seen changes in the Soviet Union which can only be described as a peaceful revolution. We admire, very much admire, the vision and boldness which inspired these changes." She described the recent "exciting" election of the Congress of People's Deputies as a watershed whose results had provided a firm endorsement of Mr. Gorbachev's "new thinking," and she wished him well. "With all our mind and strength we want you to succeed," she told him. She added, "People like to believe that the future is a promised land, which will arrive if you sit and wait for it. It has to be earned by *effort*" (my italics).

She went on, "Relations between Britain and the Soviet Union are better now than they have been at any time since the Second World War."

The prime minister reserved specific praise for seven points: the change of emphasis in Soviet policy to "sufficiency in defense"; the INF treaty; the withdrawal from Afghanistan; greater cooperation in the United Nations; progress on human rights; a switch from class to common human values; and the resolution of regional conflicts. She emphasized one essential point that Gorbachev had made to her in their talks earlier in the day, namely that economic change can only come about as a result of political change.

Having said this, she cautioned against unrealistic expectations, saying that policies could not be based on illusions, implying that the two countries were still divided on a range of issues, above all on arms control: "Both our countries know from bitter experience that conventional weapons do not deter war in Europe, whereas nuclear weapons *have* done so for over forty years. As a deterrent, there is no substitute for them."

While welcoming greater openness, she wanted it extended to military matters. She also expressed great concern over chemical weapons. The British suspected that Moscow was concealing the true size of its chemical weapons stocks. But she did not elaborate on the subject. Finally, she asked the guests "to raise your glasses in honor of the General Secretary of the Central Committee of the Communist Party of the Soviet Union and Chairman of the Presidium of the Supreme Soviet of the USSR!"—a title that she delivered with a touch more fluency than even the majordomo. The resounding and inimitably British cheer "Hear! Hear!" followed.

Continuing their duel over nuclear weapons, Gorbachev said in his speech of reply, "I am a staunch opponent of nuclear weapons and strongly advocate their total elimination . . . Mrs. Thatcher perceives a good measure of romanticism in this. I cannot accept that—my position reflects the harsh realities of our time . . . We firmly intend to move toward . . . a non-nuclear world." He pledged to resist attempts by some in the West to discredit *perestroika*: "The attempts in the West to provoke mistrust and sow suspicions about the goals and purposes of *perestroika* and to distort its progress are aimed at thwarting the efforts to improve international relations."

He praised Thatcher and said the British leadership was among the first in the West to discern the approaching major changes in the USSR. He spoke of his relations with her as "truly a dialogue, one that always addresses the overall philosophical subjects and general political problems." He spoke of the "new quality" of the Anglo-Soviet relationship. He concluded with a toast: "To the health of the Prime Minister of Great Britain Mrs. Margaret Thatcher and Denis Thatcher! To the development and deepening of relations between our peoples and countries!"

The speeches were not interpreted—they had been pretranslated and placed on the tables in front of the guests. As Thatcher read her speech in English, the Soviet guests followed the Russian text in front of them; when Gorbachev read his text in Russian, the British hosts followed the English text in front of them. Every minute was precious. This method saved at least thirty minutes.

Thatcher spoke with emotion in her voice, punctuating her speech with the typical Thatcheresque qualifier *very*: "We are *very, very* happy" "We *very* much admire," "We *very* much welcome," etc. The use of *we* in place of *I* was also typically Thatcheresque. Then, as Gorbachev was making his speech, she gazed at him intently. She was practically dewy-eyed. Mikhail Sergeyevich, by contrast, was more restrained. He showed every sign of respect toward his hostess, but his emotions were not so pronounced.

When they were done making speeches and clinking glasses, everybody around the table relaxed and started to eat. As the guests plunged into animated conversation with their immediate neighbors, the din of the table talk began to grow. Since I was seated between Mr. Thatcher and Yakovlev, I was able to observe these two men at close range. Unexpectedly for me, the "first gentleman," if I may be permitted to coin the expression, Denis Thatcher, proved a gifted raconteur after he imbibed a little wine. Jovial and outgoing, he came across as pretty much bored by his role as husband to the de facto ruler of the land. He noticed, when toasts were proposed and everyone raised their glass, that I did not have a glass and ordered the waiter to bring one for me and to fill it with champagne. "To the Queen!" he said, winking and clinking his glass with mine. I made a return toast, "To the Queen and to the Prime Minister!" "And to President Gorbachev!" he added. After these preliminaries, Denis Thatcher regaled Yakovlev and me with some great stories.

It seems that earlier that afternoon, just a few hours before the banquet, Mrs. Thatcher had not answered questions in the House of Commons, as she traditionally did every Thursday afternoon, pleading talks with Gorbachev. Explaining her absence, the leader of the House, who represented her in her absence, provoked considerable merriment among MPs when he told them that she couldn't be present because she "has made herself available to Mr. Gorbachev." One Labor MP shouted from his seat, "Does Denis know? Is this part of their special relationship?" As Mr. Thatcher told the story, which he said he had heard from the Speaker, he roared with laughter.

While Yakovlev was busy talking to Nigel Lawson, the secretary of the treasury, on his left, I asked Mr. Thatcher if he had seen the play *Anyone for Denis?* which had played at the Whitehall Theater, the home of

British farce. I was itching to ask him what he thought of the play, which I had seen way back in 1981 when I was in London in passing.

In a nutshell, the play was about Denis Thatcher, who runs the household while Mrs. Thatcher is attending to affairs of state. For some inexplicable reason, they have a butler named Boris, who, unbeknownst to Denis, is a KGB agent. Each time Denis steps out of the room, Boris dashes to a cupboard where he keeps a secret radio transmitter to broadcast to Moscow the bits information he picks up from Denis. One day Denis catches Boris red-handed, but the artful agent fobs him off with some yarn that seems totally plausible to Denis. The plot thickens and in the end the prime minister, Margaret Thatcher, gets wind of these strange goings-on and confronts them both to demand an explanation. It was very funny.

"Yes," Mr. Thatcher replied, he did see the play. "What nonsense!" he exclaimed in a manner that struck me as a typical example of British upper-class speech. It was difficult to tell whether he was mimicking the character in the play or vice versa. "But this is a free country," Mr. Thatcher said, "and they do whatever they like." I asked if it was true that he did the cooking, as the press claimed. Denis said that was "an exaggeration," although occasionally he and Margaret shared the pleasures of cooking. He did the dishes. Their living apartments were on the floor above, but he and Margaret preferred to spend their free time, if any, at Chequers, the prime minister's country residence, where they had received Gorbachev for the first time in 1984. He and Margaret were impressed by Gorbachev and his ideas. They would never forget that first meeting. They saw even then that he was an extraordinary man. They sincerely wished him every success.

Mr. Thatcher complained that Margaret was always busy with something or other. Even at home, her idea of relaxation was to read more official papers. He said he was not only a husband but a businessman. He often traveled to America where he sat on the boards of many companies as a consultant. Sometimes he would go to the States as often as twice a month. Few people knew about this aspect of his life, he said. For obvious reasons he shunned publicity.

At one point, seeing that Yakovlev was in conversation with someone else, and apparently glad to have me as a captive, albeit quite willing audience, he changed the subject and asked what, in my opinion, was the optimal term of office for a head of state. I said I thought it was four years or five at most. He declared that he agreed entirely. He and Margaret often debated the merits of the American system versus the French system and concluded that the American system was preferable, because a president cannot be elected for more than two terms, i.e., for more than eight years. And that was more than enough time to serve the country well. In the French system, where the term of office was seven years, if a president was reelected for another term, such as, Mitterrand, that meant fourteen years. Too long for anyone, even for a good leader, to be head of state or government. He said that as far as British prime ministers were concerned, four years was an optimal term to serve. But of course, if people insisted that the prime minister should stay for another term, he or she would bow to their will and run for reelection. In the case of Margaret, he said proudly, she was serving an unprecedented third term—ten years now since she was elected in 1979—and wasn't this a sign that she was doing the right thing if people wanted her to be their leader for so long? "She enjoys it very much," he said, then asked, "And what about Mr. Gorbachev? What is *his* term of office?"

I explained that as general secretary he was to serve five years nominally, if not for life, if one was to be guided by the previous Soviet practice, but it could be changed by the impending Congress of People's Deputies, which would be convened in a couple of months. He mulled it over for a while and said that if Gorbachev served two terms, ten years, that should be enough for him to carry out his reforms and establish himself as a leader who had made a quiet revolution for the good of his country and the world.

He discussed with me the advantages and disadvantages of living in London. He objected to my sincere praise of London as "a very clean city." He thought it was no longer what it used to be, but did not elaborate. I suggested that he go to Moscow and take a walk around its streets to compare it to London, and do so incognito, rather than as a VIP. He laughed and had the waiter pour me another glass of champagne.

In the meantime, leaning closer to me, Yakovlev whispered in my ear, "Do you see that gentleman over there, on Mikhail Sergeyevich's right? The one with the mustache and beard? Whom does he remind you of?" I did not have to turn my head to see the gentleman, as he sat opposite me across the table, just a few feet away. I said he resembled Nikolai II, the last Russian czar, but I didn't know who the gentleman was. Yakovlev chuckled, "This is His Royal Highness Prince Michael of Kent. He does indeed look like Nikolai. His uncle, the Duke of Kent, was Nikolai's cousin. So they are related by blood." And then, tongue in cheek, he said, "Perhaps we should invite him to our country as a new czar? What do you think? Do you think the people will accept him?"

Alexandr Nikolaievich was warming up. While Mr. Thatcher was playing a charming gentleman toward Raisa Maximovna, who was seated on his right, Yakovlev called my attention to the hostess herself, asking if I had noticed something unusual about the way she behaved toward Mikhail Sergeyevich. I had noticed, like probably everybody else in the room, that when Gorbachev was giving speech, she'd looked at him with such intense adoration in her eyes that this could only be interpreted as a manifestation of that "special personal chemistry" that was said to exist between these two extraordinary leaders. Later, when we returned to the Embassy after dinner, Yakovlev would attempt to tease Gorbachev about it, but Raisa Maximovna discouraged the insinuation by grasping him firmly by the arm and leading him away upstairs, saying, "Good night, everybody."

The dinner was so successful that it did not end until 10:50 P.M.—almost one hour later than planned. When everyone finally stood up to leave, Mrs. Thatcher led her guests of honor downstairs, past the portraits of British prime ministers, and out the front door. Raisa Maximovna was holding fast to Mikhail Sergeyevich.

My fellow interpreter Pavel Palazchenko and I stayed at the Embassy that night until well past midnight. Anatoly Sergeyevich Chernyaev, Gorbachev's senior aide, was still working on the latest amendments for tomorrow's Guildhall speech. Chernyaev came out of Gorbachev's suite to tell us we could go back to the hotel to rest because they were still working on the speech, and we'd better come early tomorrow morning. There might not be that many serious amendments after all, he added. That night Gorbachev and his closest advisers worked until after two in the morning.

The British press attached great importance to the Guildhall speech, speculating that Gorbachev had a few surprises up his sleeve, and that he might startle the world with some new arms control initiative. The domestic background against which he would be speaking had been continuously changing ever since the previous summer of 1988 and the Soviet Communist Party conference that had been held for the first time since the early 1940s. The conference was a major milestone, perhaps even a watershed in *perestroika*. Things began to happen fast soon thereafter. The growing loss of confidence in the Communist Party and the system it had created had three implications for the foreign policy of the Soviet Union. First, competition with capitalist countries was a losing game, so it was best not to compete, especially in the military sphere. Second, cooperation with capitalism made sense as a means of reviving the economy. Third, this required an escape from the antagonistic relationships inherited by Gorbachev from his predecessors. So the natural conclusion suggested itself: jettison the "old thinking" and completely embrace the "new thinking," which had been around for quite some time now. That was exactly what Gorbachev had been doing. Why carry on pretending to believe in a system of ideas that was no longer credible?

Curiously, the West took Leninist notions of international revolution more seriously than did the Soviet leaders themselves, who espoused these ideas even as they became steadily incompatible with their own developing interest in the established order. The key phrase among them now was *the normalization of relations*—with the United States, Western Europe, and China. That is to say, contact and communication with these countries should not be based on the presumption of an imminent confrontation. The other key phrase in the terminology of new thinking was *interdependence*, referring to the complex of relations that create a shared fate in the world, a common interest in avoiding nuclear war, and an understanding that disputes must be solved by political rather than military means.

Those who had doubts as to whether the new thinking had anything to do with Marxism-Leninism, which still remained the official ideology of the Soviet Union, resorted to ingenious ways to justify it. "No problem," said one Soviet academic. "Lenin's true views are wholly in line with *perestroika* and *glasnost*, but unfortunately they became obscured during the years of dogmatism and stagnation." "Well," said another, "one can find support for all sorts of views in Marx and Lenin, and so one is able to adapt their words to circumstances." "Actually," said a third, "Marx and Lenin were wrong because they failed to anticipate many of the key developments of recent history, in particular the advent of the nuclear age." Take your pick.

As the moment of the Big Speech drew closer, the excitement was mounting. What would Gorbachev say this time? What further bold steps would he announce?

APRIL 7, FRIDAY. DAY TWO AND LAST.

The morning promised a fine day. Overnight, the clouds had dissipated and a brilliant sun was shining in the unexpectedly clear blue skies. When I met Yakovlev in his room at the hotel to join him for an expected trip to see Gorbachev at his residence, he decided to walk. We left the Royal Gardens escorted by some twenty or so hefty and burly men from both the KGB and Scotland Yard and, after a twenty-minute walk up Kensington Palace Gardens, otherwise known as Embassy Row, arrived at the Soviet Embassy in the middle of the long tree-lined block.

Gorbachev and Yakovlev met with Gordon McLennan, the general secretary of the Communist Party of Great Britain, and assured him that the "special chemistry" with Margaret Thatcher was not all it was cracked up to be "in the capitalist press." If anything, they said, the "special relationship" was between *his* party and theirs. The idea was, of course, to soothe McLennan' ego and to reassure him as the leader of what, in the words of Moscow, was one of the most important Communist Parties in Europe (although it was in fact Europe's smallest Communist Party, devoid of any meaningful influence) that he could still count on Moscow for support. After all, Gorbachev was still the general secretary of the Soviet Communist Party.

Meantime, Pavel and I were putting the finishing touches on the Big Speech. The few amendments that had been introduced were mostly stylistic in nature. Then, at 10:25 A.M., Mikhail Sergeyevich with Raisa Maximovna, walking arm in arm, and Yakovlev came down to the Embassy lobby, ready to board the cars to go to Guildhall. Shortly, the motorcade departed from the Embassy gate, and when it entered the City, which is the financial center of London, much like Wall Street in New York, I saw from the car window the streets leading to the Guildhall lined with crowds on both sides. They were waving at the passing motorcade in a friendly way and, obeying Yakovlev's "direct orders," I waved back from my seat to the left of him. He even rolled down the window the better to see the people and be seen. I must admit I felt embarrassed. I decided Yakovlev was having a little fun at my expense when he told me to wave, but that was all right with me.

The head Zil limousine carrying the Gorbachevs turned into King Street, which is very short, and at the end of it pulled up at a striped canopy that for security reasons was stretched over the entrance to the Guildhall.

The first written reference to the Guildhall occurs in 1120, and for many centuries it has been the center of the city's administration. The ancient, magnificent town hall of London has witnessed numerous major events. It is one of the most prestigious national rostrums and is put at the disposal of the most distinguished foreign statesmen only in exceptional cases. Throughout the centuries it has seen and heard kings and queens, presidents and prime ministers. Her Majesty the Queen Elizabeth II spoke here two months before to mark the eight hundredth anniversary of the lord mayoralty. Less than a year before, on June 3, 1988, right after the Moscow summit, President Reagan delivered his keynote address here on the future of East-West relations.

Now the great honor of speaking from this rostrum had been bestowed on Gorbachev. For his benefit, Margaret Thatcher had chosen this splendid hall with nine hundred years of tradition, although the structure itself had in fact been designed in 1954 out of the shell of the previous building, which was bombed during the War. At the entrance, Mikhail Sergeyevich and Raisa Maximovna were met by the Right Honorable the Lord Mayor, Alderman Sir Christopher Collet, and his wife. Inside, taped music played by a Royal Air Force band floated over the assembly hall, while some men in pith helmets upholstered in feathers ushered in the audience between two rows of halberdiers. For once, instead of those rows of blank-faced Communist Party functionaries, dominating the Soviet (and British) guests was a group of elderly gentlemen in medieval-fancy, red, fur-lined cloaks. They were aldermen of the City of London. The men who wore more plain blue cloaks were ordinary councillors. There were also all sorts of marshals, sheriffs, aldermen, chief commoners, recorders, and other assorted personalities, all representing the Corporation of London. And, of course, there were also heads of many diplomatic missions, as is customary on such occasions.

As I looked over the audience, it seemed a sea of hats and white gloves. All the women, or I should say ladies, present wore their hats throughout the entire ceremony as a sign of special respect for the distinguished guest speaker. Such is the tradition here. The only two ladies who broke this hallowed custom were the British prime minister and the Soviet general secretary's wife. An exception was made for the Soviet first lady, who refused to wear a hat and gloves for fear of being misunderstood back home. So Mrs. Thatcher, out of deference to her wishes, apparently decided that she, too, would not wear one either.

As soon as I entered the hall, following in the footsteps of the exalted guests, I saw a gentleman, apparently from the Foreign Office, who held up a sign saying "Korchilov, Esq." I introduced myself, and the gentleman said his job was to show me to the interpreters' booth. He led me to the left and up the steps to a makeshift scaffold on which an interpreters' booth was set up. My booth colleague on the British side, Dr. Irina Kirillova, was already in place. All around us were journalists and reporters with their TV and photo cameras, ready to broadcast the proceedings live throughout the world. At 10:50 A.M. the taped music suddenly quickened and then ceased. Four heralds, in Tudor gold lamé, sounded a fanfare on their trumpets, everyone stood up, and the lord mayor conducted the Gorbachevs onto the dais of Great Hall. Prime Minister and Mr. Thatcher followed and took the seats reserved for them. Gorbachev wore his habitual dark gray pin-striped suit, and Raisa Maximovna a short red jacket, all buttoned up, and a plain black skirt. The ensemble was rather austere, but in good taste and befitting the occasion. It was a red-letter day after all. Red was in evidence every-where: between marble busts and under wooden rafters, in the red cloaks of the aldermen, and in the hammer and sickle flags draped from a balcony alongside a marble relief celebrating great naval victories.

Then, the Right Honorable the Lord Mayor of London, Head of the City Lieutenancy, Clerk of the Markets, and much else besides, Sir Christopher Collett, removed the doughlike, pasty wig he had been wearing and came up to the microphone to make a speech of welcome. But before that there was the now familiar announcement made by the toastmaster. "Pray silence for the General Secretary of the Communist Party of the Soviet Union!" rang out his stentorian voice. As the Soviet anthem was being played, everyone stood up. Instead of a customary bust of Lenin, a couple of policemen in Victorian-style dress stood impassively behind Gorbachev. Copies of his pretranslated speech had just been placed in the seats, and Margaret Thatcher began to read hers after the Soviet and British anthems were over, without waiting for Gor-bachev to pronounce it.

When everyone sat down, the lord mayor gave a short speech of wel-come. And then the Big Moment arrived. I was aware that my interpre-tation into English of Gorbachev's speech would be carried live around the world on CNN, BBC, and many other major domestic and foreign TV networks. Usually, I do not have the jitters in such cases, although I get into what I call "a state of enhanced readiness." After all, all I had to do this time was to read in English, into a microphone, the translation of Gorbachev's speech. I knew there would be little ad-libbing, if any. It is a different matter, of course, when one has to do real interpreting, something that gives jitters to many an interpreter. Still, I had to force myself to forget that perhaps half the English-speaking world would be listening and would judge Gorbachev's speech on the basis of my deliv-ery. I tricked myself into believing that there was only one listener—the prime minister, Mrs. Thatcher. It is helpful to focus on only one person when interpreting, and so I focused my full attention on her alone, watching her reaction as I went on interpreting. She put aside the copy of Gorbachev's speech, which she had been reading, and listened "very, very" attentively to my interpretation. That was just what I needed. Once I establish such "rapport" with my principal listener, whoever he or she is, I know I'll be up to the mark. Only I wondered fleetingly if all those ladies in hats could understand what Gorbachev was saying because the hats prevented them from putting on their headphones. At least one of them, though, solved the problem by wearing the headset like a bonnet strap, under her chin.

After the expectations built up by Gorbachev's officials and the British press, the Big Speech proved somewhat anticlimactic and left many Britons disappointed. Rather than putting forth bold new policies, the first half of the speech was a progress report on *perestroika*, which was "irreversible," "in earnest and for the long term," and "there [was] no turning back." And the second part was an appeal for a new international order based on interdependence rather than on the threat of nuclear force. Strangely enough, a major theme of Gorbachev's latest speeches, "a common European home," was totally absent from this speech. Perhaps not entirely accidentally, Gorbachev caused some embarrassment to Mrs. Thatcher by passing over in silence what had been expected to be the major theme of this address. Mrs. Thatcher had prepared a reply based on that assumption and made an unavoidable gaffe when, speaking after Gorbachev, she said, "You spoke, Mr. President, of 'a common European home.'" That Gorbachev did not mention the "common home" was due, at least in part, to his saving the announcement of his next initiatives on the subject for his important visit to West Germany on June 12—a little over two months from now.

Despite the embarrassing moment, in her effusive speech of thanks Mrs. Thatcher hailed Gorbachev as "one of those rare people who has the vision, the boldness, and the sheer power of personality to change the whole future of his country, and to have a profound effect on the wider world as well." She said, "We want you to succeed in your task!"

Gorbachev's speech did contain two points of special interest, though. First, he announced that the Soviet Union had decided to stop the production of enriched uranium and phase out the production of fissionable weapons-grade materials, and to shut down two industrial reactors for producing weapons-grade plutonium that year and the following year. He wanted it clearly understood that nothing would move him from his belief that a nuclear-weapons-free world was within the grasp of its leaders, even though he was well aware that Mrs. Thatcher remained unconvinced.

The other point of interest was his announcement that total Soviet military forces numbered 4,258,000—the first time he had given such a figure. He added that the total would drop to 3,760,000 by the end of 1990 in accord with cuts he had pledged the year before, in December, when he appeared at the United Nations General Assembly in New York. Some Western experts disagreed with these figures. For example, according to the International Institute for Strategic Studies, 5,096,000 troops were in the Soviet armed forces. The difference was that Gorbachev's figures included only an active duty roster, while excluding

500,000 armed KGB border troops and reserves. Gorbachev also said that the newly elected Soviet legislature would, for the first time, publish a full accounting of the Soviet military budget at the end of the year.

In their speeches and conversations Gorbachev and Thatcher, or "Mikhail and Maggie," as the British press referred to them, both called each other "romantic," but for diametrically opposite reasons. While Mikhail declared that Maggie was romantic because she passionately believed in nuclear weapons as a guarantor of peace, Maggie asserted he was romantic because he passionately wanted to eliminate them in the cause of peace. They differed tremendously on the philosophical plane. Thatcher saw Soviet reforms as recognition that socialism could never work and that capitalism was best. Gorbachev, however, vigorously defended socialism and did not accept capitalism. Yet, the special feature of their special relationship was their ability to disagree on much without rendering dialogue futile.

All in all, it was a morning of exciting ancient pageantry, if not trailblazing policy. Throughout his speech Gorbachev paused to sip some whitish liquid from a teacup, prepared for him by his bodyguard Medvedev. Gorbachev later said that when he spoke for long periods of time, his throat got dry, his vocal cords clogged up, and he lost his voice. Small wonder: I remember once at the 27th Party Congress he spoke for five-and-a-half hours. To avoid losing his voice, he moistened the cords every now and then by sipping regular tea with milk. He denied that his special tea contained any stimulants.

One hour later, the Big Moment was over. At 11:55 A.M., the remembrancer announced the order of procession to leave the hall: first the marshal, then the sword and mace, and only then the lord mayor and the general secretary. I thanked my British colleague for her cooperation, wished her the best of luck in her future endeavors, and hurried to rejoin Gorbachev and Yakovlev, so as not to be left behind. It would not have been the first time!

At noon, or 12:05 P.M. to be exact, everybody was back at the Embassy in Kensington Palace Gardens. We had only twenty minutes to freshen up before the next and last, but not least, event of the day and of the entire trip—a visit to Windsor Castle to lunch with the queen. Twenty minutes was not enough time to go back to the hotel, so I decided to stay at the Embassy, where I noticed at once that something was amiss. The powerful troika, Gorbachev, Shevardnadze, and Yakovlev, had worried looks on their faces. No one knew what had happened, but some people guessed it was developments back home, in Tbilisi, where troops had been sent to quell a possible nationalist rally in the capital of Georgia. Two days later the guess would, alas, be borne out.

When it rains, it pours. A few hours later, on the plane bound back for Moscow, I would learn what had been the real cause of concern to Gorbachev and his advisers that day. A Soviet nuclear-powered submarine had sunk in the Norwegian Sea after a fire on board, prompting fears of a serious release of radioactivity. There was also speculation that the sub had nuclear weapons on board. It was another terrible blow to Gorbachev.

Despite his burden of worries, Gorbachev gamely set out on his visit to the queen at her dacha—Windsor Castle, the royal family's "second home," which is located some twenty miles from London, in Berkshire, and is said to be the largest castle in England. It was founded by William the Conqueror way back in the eleventh century. Visits to the queen by Soviet leaders are not exactly common. It had been thirty-three years since Nikita Khrushchev and Bulganin dropped in for tea. The invitation to Gorbachev to lunch with the queen was, in fact, an extraordinary accolade for the leader of a country still considered Britain's main potential enemy.

Britain's Queen Elizabeth II had reigned for thirty-seven years almost to the day at the time of Gorbachev's visit, and she was giving clear signals that she had no intention of abdicating in favor of her son Charles, the Prince of Wales. She was said to be displeased with his conduct, which she considered to be often simply disgraceful. The queen still commanded a rare authority and an unparalleled degree of affection among her subjects. She was said to be professional, funny, friendly, and supremely competent. And she was also extremely rich. Philip Beresford, the appraiser who produced an annual review of the richest people in Britain, put her total wealth at £6.5 billion. Estimates of the value of the queen's jewelry, for example, were as high as £40 million. Incidentally, the queen's personal jewelry included the Romanoff jewels bought by Queen Mary from the Russian czar's relatives in the English exile, which were valued at £10 million in modern prices. But being royal she paid no taxes.

No one sat in her presence unless she gave the okay, and no one spoke to her unless she initiated the conversation. As first in the realm, she signed documents at the top of the page rather than the bottom. Yet, most of her subjects seemed to find her comfortably British, a lot, in fact, like themselves. Her clothes undoubtedly cost a bundle, yet anyone could easily match her wardrobe at Marks & Spencer—the famous department store, something like the American Macy's. Her favorite head covering, even in her Rolls, seemed to be a "babushka," which is a lot lighter than the crown, and she made no secret of the fact that, next to horses, her favorite pastime was watching the daytime soaps. She was said to be very much in the middle-class mold.

A few minutes before 1 P.M. London time, the Soviet motorcade of eight Zils, led by a Daimler and a Rolls-Royce with British security chiefs and protocol people, crossed the Thames, entered the small town of Windsor, with its picturesque streets and houses, and turned into a straight, narrow gravel road leading to the castle. I was riding with Yakovlev. As our car made the final turn, I saw a broad, open vista with a large gray castle in the background. The castle was said to be the largest inhabited residence in the world and was open to visitors even when the queen was in residence, such as on the day of Gorbachev's visit.

On both sides of the road lined with thick rows of trees, tourists were walking on the emerald green grass, taken aback by this unexpected long cavalcade of cars, which had forced them off the road. The castle sits in a large park, surrounded by meadows and trees, and dominates the Thames below. As we approached, I also caught a glimpse, above the Round Tower, of the Royal Standard and the Hammer and Sickle, flying opposite each other. The Soviet flag clearly was not a frequent sight here.

When we arrived at the castle's State Entrance, the queen and the duke of Edinburgh, her husband, Prince Philip, were waiting to greet their Russian guests under the portico along with the prime minister, Mr. Denis Thatcher alongside, and other British hosts and guests. By now the sky had become cloudy, and it began to drizzle. After the motorcade crunched up the gravel at the Grand Entrance of Windsor Castle, Gorbachev was the first to get out of the cars, together with Raisa Maximovna. A guard of honor, mounted by the First Battalion Coldstream Guards, with a State Color, the band of the regiment, and the Battalion Corps of Drums in decidedly unimperial gray greatcoats, was already in position inside the courtyard. At least they had those gorgeous black bearskins on their heads.

The long-awaited moment came. Gorbachev, wearing his favorite fedora-trilby, approached Her Majesty, who remained sheltered under the portico, and, smiling, shook her hand firmly, doffing his hat as he did so. The queen stepped forward slightly and warmly reciprocated. It was the highest mark of diplomatic esteem to be welcomed by Her Majesty.

Contrary to general expectations regarding her favorite color, which was said to be "royal blue," she wore a shocking pink wool suit with a black patent leather handbag over her arm. She looked plain and rather amiable indeed, like the proverbial kindly auntie from auld lang syne. She could very well step into a crowd and blend into it nicely, without being noticed or recognized, if unaccompanied by her retinue. She wore almost no jewelry, as if to belie all those rumors about her fabulous wealth. Somehow, I felt a little disappointed. I had expected Her Majesty to look regal and her demeanor to be that of the proverbial fairy-tale queen. Well, perhaps, if she had worn a crown on this occasion . . .

As Her Majesty exchanged handshakes with Gorbachev, Raisa Maximovna was greeted by the duke of Edinburgh. The queen and the duke then introduced their son Prince Edward, who was the only other member of the royal family present. Then the queen turned around and, in a welcoming gesture, extended her right hand to Yakovlev and then to me. Because we stood together and right behind her, she practically bumped into us when she turned round. She appeared unruffled, though, by this breach of royal protocol and gallantly greeted us with a royal "Welcome."

All stood stiffly at attention while the band of the Coldstream Guards played the Soviet national anthem ("The unbreakable Union of Free Republics has been bound forever by the Great Russia . . ."). It stirred echoes among the castle's walls. Then the captain of the guard invited Gorbachev—addressing him in Russian—to inspect the guard of honor, which he did with hat in hand and the towering duke of Edinburgh at his shoulder. Like the majordomo at 10 Downing Street the previous night and the toastmaster at Guildhall earlier that morning, the captain must have been practicing, learning to pronounce the unfamiliar, long, jaw-breaking title of the Soviet leader. But he did it marvelously. During the inspection, Gorbachev seemed dwarfed by the tall gray-coated soldiers, but the soldiers didn't flicker an eye at the guest. They were well trained. The famous British reserve . . . As they strolled back across the lawn, Gorbachev and Prince Philip appeared to share some private joke, for they were laughing. But the mutual comprehension was feigned, of course, since neither spoke the other's language, and at that moment we, the interpreters, were not with them.

Inside the castle, the Military Knights of Windsor lined the Grand Entrance. The party moved, with the queen in charge, up the grand staircase for a walk through the State Apartments. We walked past the armor, the swords, and the portraits of all those ancestors and relatives of the queen. In the Waterloo Chamber, dedicated to the memory of the First Duke of Wellington, also known as the "Iron Duke," and his great victory over Napoleon in 1815, the queen took the opportunity to explain to her guest that less than three months after he arrived in Moscow the cold

Russian winter had driven Napoleon from Russia. Gorbachev, never at a loss for words, remarked that Napoleon was driven out by "the Russian general named Winter." As we moved farther down the halls, Raisa Maximovna displayed her not inconsiderable knowledge of the paintings. In another room was a portrait of Emperor Alexander I of Russia. When the queen pointed at it, Mikhail Sergeyevich took a quick look at Raisa Maximovna, and she immediately identified the man in the portrait. Gorbachev beamed. To her credit, she habitually read up on works of culture before going to any country with her illustrious husband.

During the brief queen-guided tour, a vast green malachite vase in a side room caught Gorbachev's eye. That, the queen explained, had been given to her great-great-grandmother, Victoria, by Czar Nicholas I sometime in the last century. Mikhail Sergeyevich insisted on closer inspection, and he and the queen veered off into the side chamber for a few moments.

After they reemerged, Her Majesty finally led the way to the State Dining Room, located on the ground floor. The spacious room had a high ceiling and modern windows running almost its entire length. Through the windows was a broad panorama of meadows and receding forest amid gently sloping hills. The scene was bucolic and serene.

In the middle of the room stood a long and broad oval table. The luncheon seating chart contained thirty-four names, not counting the five interpreters. According to the list, "His Excellency Mr. Mikhail Sergeyevich Gorbachev" was seated to the right of the Queen, while "Mrs. Raisa M. Gorbacheva" had the Duke of Edinburgh Prince Philip on her left and Prince Edward on her right. The queen and the duke were seated in the center of the oval table, opposite each other. Descending below the salt, other British guests included members of the royal household; the archbishop of Canterbury, who was head of the Anglican church; the Lord Mayor of London Sir Christopher Collet; the chairman of Sotheby's, Lord Gowry; the president of the famous British trading house Mark and Spenser, the Lord Rayner; the president of British Industries Confederation, Sir Trevor Holdsworth. There were few politicians.

The guest list was pared down to the barest possible minimum. Apart from the Gorbachevs, it included only four people on the Soviet side: Shevardnadze, Yakovlev, Kamentsev, and Ambassador Zamyatin. Of the twenty-eight British guests, apart from Prime Minister and Mr. Denis Thatcher, I recognized the Right Honorable Sir Michael Heseltine; the British ambassador to Moscow, Sir Rodric Braithwaite; and of course, Secretary of State for Foreign and Commonwealth Affairs Sir Geoffrey Howe. The rest of the faces were unknown to me, but included such celebrities as Sir Isaiah Berlin, the venerable professor at Oxford Univer-

sity and specialist in Russian philology; Sir Peter Hall, the former director of the National Theater; Jeremy Isaak, the director of Royal Opera
House; and Lord Blake, the historian. Last but not least, besides the
queen, the prime minister, and the Soviet first lady, there was only one
other woman—Lady Elton, apparently from the royal household.

The waiters were so well-trained and efficient that they were virtually
invisible. Yakovlev was seated between Margaret Thatcher and Prince
Philip, and I was seated slightly behind and between Yakovlev and the
duke of Edinburgh. On my left, somewhat behind Mrs. Thatcher, was
Richard Pollock, the prime minister's interpreter. He and I didn't have
much to do except to observe and exchange impressions because
Yakovlev was trying his English both on the duke and on the prime minister and seemed to be doing all right. Only once, as he was telling
Thatcher something about Soviet Eskimos, did he turn to me for help.
He didn't know how to describe in English, or in Russian for that matter,
the houses in which Eskimos live. Something clicked in my "brain computer" and I instantly came up with *igloo.* Yakovlev said it was a strange
word, but Mrs. Thatcher came to my rescue, confirming it was just the
right one.

The queen treated her guests to *smoked salmon cornets filled with
crabmeat,* followed by *fillets of beef with duck pâté and artichoke baked in
pastry, with broccoli, carrot mousse and croquet potatoes (pommes Elizabeth),* accompanied by *an avocado salad.* To finish, *a fruit salad or
oranges and melons,* all accompanied by *a Gewürztraminer Dopff 1983, a
Château Beychevelle 1970 and a 1950 vintage port.* As for the interpreters, however, all we could do was to look on stoically as the guests
tucked away all those delicacies to the accompaniment of all those German and French wines. I couldn't help remembering the appropriate
Russian saying, *Po usam teklo, a v rot ne popalo* (literally: It flowed down
my mustache but missed my mouth). To put it differently, "The honey
was probably sweet, but there was many a slip twixt the cup and *my* lip."

Once again Mrs. Thatcher impressed me as a dynamic and forceful personality. She was seated on Yakovlev's left, and whenever Yakovlev
turned to the right to talk to the principal host, Prince Philip, she would
converse with me. She had so much energy she simply could not stay
silent even for a minute. She had to talk to someone. So, looking me
straight in the eye, she began by expressing her "*very, very* deep admiration for President Gorbachev." For some reason, she did not refer to him
as "general secretary" but as "president"—the title he would assume
one year later. She had thus anticipated, as it were, developments in

Moscow. The Kremlin. December 1975. The presentation of letters of credence. Seated left to right are: Supreme Soviet Secretary M. Gheorghadze, the ambassador of Somalia, Chairman Nikolai Podgorny, and Leonid Ilyichev. The author stands second from the right. Standing or sitting, almost at attention, at formal functions in the Kremlin was de rigueur in those days. (photo credit: official USSR Soviet Supreme photograph)

Moscow. The Kremlin. June 1976. At the negotiating table with the powers that be. From right to left: Foreign Minister Andrei Gromyko, the author, General Secretary Leonid Brezhnev, Prime Minister Alexei Kosygin, and other officials. Gromyko accused me of being an "aggressor" because I wedged myself between him and Brezhnev as the principal, for I had to be within hearing and thus be better able to catch his slurred remarks in a sea of words. (photo credit: TASS)

The Kremlin. June 11, 1979. A photo op before the talks. From right to left: Prime Minister Morarje Desai of India, the author, General Secretary cum Chairman Leonid Brezhnev, ambassador Yuli Vorontsov, and other officials. Brezhnev, the "star bearer," was distinguished for two rows of gold medals and orders that he enjoyed wearing on solemn occasions such as this. (photo credit: TASS)

Moscow. The Kremlin. June 27, 1987. General Secretary Mikhail Gorbachev in a one-on-one meeting with President Robert Mugabe of Zimbabwe in Room #3— the same office which Brezhnev had used to receive foreign visitors, with the same furnishings and the same long table, minus the famous cigarette dispenser. (photo credit: TASS)

Washington. The State Department. December 9, 1987. The author with Eduard Shevardnadze and George Shultz exchanging handshakes and pens, "two for one," upon signing the Soviet-U.S. documents on mutual verification of nuclear testing. (photo credit: TASS)

Washington. Soviet Embassy. December 9, 1987. Dinner hosted by General Secretary Gorbachev in honor of President and Mrs. Reagan. Seated from left to right: Raisa Maximovna Gorbacheva, the State Department interpreter Dimitry Zarechnyak, President Ronald Reagan, Mrs. Nancy Reagan, Foreign Minister Eduard Shevardnandze, and Mrs. Barbara Bush. Standing from left to right: Mikhail Gorbachev, the author, the Chief of Soviet State Protocol Vladimir Chernishev, and Pavel Palazchenko, my colleague and fellow interpreter. (photo credit: TASS)

Moscow. Vnukovo-2 Airport. May 29, 1988. The President and Mrs. Reagan arrive for their first-ever visit to the "evil empire." From left to right: Mrs. Gromyko, President Reagan, Chairman Andrei Gromyko, and Mrs. Reagan. The author stands behind Reagan and Gromyko. (photo credit: TASS)

Moscow. The Kremlin. On January 17, 1989, Dr. Henry Kissinger paid a farewell call upon Andrei Gromyko who had retired, or "dropped anchor," as he put it, on October 1, 1988. The author interpreted their conversation during which they revisited some of the salient points of the Cold War. Gromyko died on July 2, 1989, at the age of eighty. (photo credit: TASS)

Moscow. The Kremlin. March 26, 1990. The author with the First Lady, Raisa Maximovna Gorbacheva, in St. Vladimir's Hall with children from twelve countries who had brought with them 65,575 well-wishers' letters for President Gorbachev. (photo credit: TASS)

Zagorsk, near Moscow. May 17, 1990. The author touring the famous St. Sergius-Trinity Monastery with Secretary of State Jim Baker and Foreign Minister Eduard Shevardnadze. While there, Baker was urged to sit in Peter the Great's chair, and announced with a grin, "The longer I sit, the greater I feel." (photo credit: TASS)

Washington. In front of the White House. May 31, 1990. With Presidents Bush and Gorbachev during the welcoming ceremonies. The proverbial "unidentified man in the middle" behind the shades is actually the author, not a bodyguard.
(photo credit: Bush Presidential Library)

Washington. June 1, 1990. Gorby-mania. The author is next to Gorbachev helping him to communicate with an enthusiastic crowd of his admirers. It was as if he was a friendly Martian on a peace mission. (photo credit: TASS)

Washington. The White House. June 1, 1990. Presidents Bush and Gorbachev alone with the author in the Red Room. Bush is seen in a moment of deep reflection. At the last minute he decided to go ahead with signing an all-important trade accord, although his critics would "give [him] hell." (photo credit: Bush Presidential Library)

Camp David. June 2, 1990. Washington Summit II. An illustration to the joke about Gorbachev that Reagan told him at their meeting in 1987. The driver is President Gorbachev himself and, as in the joke, he was speeding. Next to him is President Bush, with Dimitry Zarechnyak and the author as "the backseat passengers." (photo credit: Bush Presidential Library)

Camp David. June 2, 1990. On the terrace of Aspen Lodge, the presidential retreat. The men and women "behind them" (in the Balzacian sense) who made the summit a success. From left to right: Jim Baker, Barbara Bush, George Bush, Raisa Gorbacheva, Mikhail Gorbachev, Eduard Shevardnadze, Brent Scowcroft, and Sergei Akhromeyev. (photo credit: White House photo by David Valdez)

Moscow. June 8, 1990. Prime Minister Margaret Thatcher and President Mikhail Gorbachev at their first joint press conference. The author looks like a zombie but is actually fighting off severe jet lag. (photo credit: TASS)

Moscow. The Kremlin. September 17, 1990. Reagan and Gorbachev exchange pleasantries and reminiscences about their first meeting in Geneva where the "ice of the Cold War began to melt." Reagan told Gorbachev: "We were then two in the room, with our interpreters. And I said to you, 'We may be the only two men in the world who together can bring about world peace.'" Replied Gorbachev: "Those were not mere words—they were followed by actual deeds." The author is seen here "in action" interpreting both ways and taking notes. (photo credit: TASS)

Moscow. The Russian "White House." September 18, 1990. Yeltsin presents Reagan with a drawing of an INF missile on a wooden wagon with a dejected soldier astride the missile. Cracked Reagan: "If this drawing had been made in my country, they would have depicted *me* on top of the missile!" The author is seen explaining the symbolism of the picture. (photo credit: TASS)

New York. October 26, 1996. The author with Mikhail Sergeyevich Gorbachev, six years later. (from the author's collection)

regard to the Communist Party of the Soviet Union and its leader. What he had started was "simply unprecedented in the difficult and troubled history of your country," she continued. She hoped very much that he would succeed in his "incredible" undertaking. The whole world stood "to benefit from his success."

She felt she was "second to none" in understanding what a difficult challenge it was to turn things around in so many ways in such a big country as the Soviet Union. After all, she said, she was in a position to say so because she herself had only recently completed what she described as "a mini-*perestroika*" in Britain, which took "many, many years" to carry out in "this country which is much smaller than yours." In her opinion, the key to economic success was unleashing people's initiative through privatization—something that she knew would be difficult to do. People were mostly passive and did not accept change easily. To succeed, Gorbachev had to be persevering. She knew it from her own experience. Where there was a will, there was a way. Then suddenly she "handbagged" me with a question: What did I think she could do as prime minister to help Gorbachev? I was rather startled that she cared to know what I thought.

This was really the sixty-four pound (and ruble) question. What could I say to her? Who was I, after all, to give advice to the prime minister of another country? I decided that her question was more in a rhetorical vein, one to which she did not really expect an answer. She knew, of course, that was I was just an interpreter, maybe a diplomat, but not a statesman, not even a political figure. Be that as it may, I felt I ought to say something in reply, as she turned to me again and looked at me inquiringly with her bright blue eyes. I knew that Mrs. Thatcher had a reputation for not tolerating empty and meaningless talk.

So, I began by noting that Gorbachev was appreciative of her support for him and said that, speaking strictly for myself, I thought that perhaps she could help him best by providing him with credits and arranging for more large-scale investments in the Soviet economy. A strong economy was by far the most crucial factor for his success. Along with welcome political freedoms that Gorbachev was promoting, I thought the Soviet government should be encouraged to grant our society broad economic freedoms and above all the freedom of individual enterprise based on private property and competition, which would be good for everyone. People would thereby be empowered to take their destiny in their own hands, and by developing economic initiative they could achieve material well-being.

She heard me out "very, very" carefully and said, "When we took over ten years ago [again using the typical Thatcheresque *we* instead of *I*], Britain, too, was in decline as an economy. It had its full share of strikes." But "we have turned this country" into one whose standards had improved, and inflation had been brought under control. The key to everything was competition, self-reliance, private initiative, and free enterprise, she emphasized. And, she said, it was "very, very important" to involve people in politics so that they would realize that freedom brings responsibility, although to change human psychology was the most difficult thing of all. It was as though she were talking to Gorbachev, not me. And, in hindsight, how right she was about human psychology!

Her convictions were strong. She had just demonstrated to me a small example of "Thatcherism"—the uncompromising doctrine of self-reliance and unfettered free enterprise. She pondered my answer for a while, then said with determination that as long as she was prime minister, she would give Gorbachev every kind of support and assistance. To conclude our conversation, she said half-seriously, half in jest, that she hoped she was not giving us, the interpreters, too much trouble, because she understood what a difficult job it was to interpret. I mumbled that I enjoyed doing it and so did my colleagues. This episode convinced me that she was sincere about "doing business with that man Gorbachev." I wished that she were the prime minister of the Soviet Union even for a short while. Maybe that would be the best way for her to help Gorbachev.

Somewhere between the Beychevelle and the port, Gorbachev extended his much anticipated invitation for Her Majesty to visit the Soviet Union. The tantalizing talk of the town that day and the day before, as reported in the press, was "Would he ask her?" "Would she accept?" It would be an unprecedented royal visit to postrevolutionary Russia and was not as simple as it might seem. This invitation, which Gorbachev issued in a seemingly casual manner, presented the Foreign Office with a whole range of problems and diplomatic niceties. If the queen came, where would she stay? In the Kremlin? Or in the British Embassy? Whom should she see? Where should she visit? Whom would it be politically unwise to invite to appear before her? What should she be advised against? And so forth.

The first big problem would be how to deal with the murder of her cousins of the imperial family of the last czar of All the Russias. A lingering embarrassment still remained over the wanton murder of the Russian imperial family. The queen would undoubtedly want to visit the graves of her relatives murdered in 1918, less than a year after the Bolshevik revolution. Reportedly, it was "widely felt among the queen's royal cousins that she should go." They believed she was the one to ask the four questions that had never been answered: Who killed the family? Who, if any, escaped? Where were they killed? Where exactly were they buried?

Although, as of this writing, the queen still has not visited what is now the former USSR, these questions have now been answered, more or less. Until recently, the fate of the Romanovs had been the subject of myth and whispers. Russians have been as troubled yet as tantalized by it as Americans have been by the assassination of President Kennedy. Numerous stories and theories had grown up around the killings, one of the most obstinate being that only the czar and czarina had been murdered, and that the executioners allowed other members of the House of Romanov to escape. Throughout the 1920s and 1930s, sightings of one of the czar's daughters, Grand Duchess Anastasia, had been reported but never confirmed. In July 1992 a forensic scientist reported that the remains of Anastasia and Alexei, the czar's fourteen-year-old heir, were not in the common grave where bones of the other members of the imperial family had been found. But that again was speculation.

The truth is, according to the chief executioner's report, which has recently been found, along with no fewer than six eyewitness accounts of the murders, Nicholas II and ten members of his family and entourage were brutally shot, stabbed, and clubbed to death with bayonets and sticks by the revolutionary Bolshevik soldiers who had kept them under house arrest in a house in Yekaterinburg in the foothills of the Central Urals. The names of the executioners of the czar, his family, and their retinue have now been established, too. In the early hours of July 17, 1918, amid the chaos that engulfed Russia after the Revolution, the entire imperial family was killed by local Bolshevik commissars on orders from Moscow that came from Sverdlov and Lenin. No one escaped execution, not even the small children. The imperial family, along with four servants, were first shot in the cellar of the house of Ipatiev in Yekaterinburg, then their bodies were taken to the mines nearby, hacked to pieces, doused with sulfuric acid, burned, and dumped into an abandoned mine. The Ipatiev house had since become a place of pilgrimage for Russians. In 1977, Boris Yeltsin, who was then the first Party secretary for the Sverdlovsk region, ordered the house destroyed, on the Kremlin's orders, to prevent the place from being turned into a national shrine.

But during that lunch in Windsor Castle, those answers were not yet known, and the queen was probably unaware of these grisly circumstances surrounding the murder of the Russian imperial family. Of course, a long consultation between Buckingham Palace, the Foreign Office, and the Kremlin would be necessary before a program for her visit to the Soviet Union was set. But the most important thing was that the invitation had now been issued.

With consummate discretion and concealing her own inclination, the queen neither accepted nor rejected the offer to make a state visit to the Soviet Union. She thanked Gorbachev, but explained that her visits were fixed years in advance. She added, however, that she hoped to visit the Soviet Union "in due course." The queen's response deflected the ball diplomatically to the court of 10 Downing Street, where Margaret Thatcher had rejected Soviet overtures for a royal visit in November 1988. The murder of the Russian czar and his family was the official explanation given at the time. The queen, who indicated even then that she was prepared to go and to let bygones be bygones, was said to have been distressed by the decision. The queen let it be known that she remained keen to see Moscow, the only major world capital she had not yet visited.

After the lunch, over coffee in the drawing room, the queen hinted she might visit the Soviet Union "perhaps two years from now." Several present members of the royal family had visited the Soviet Union for private purposes. The Duke of Edinburgh Prince Philip told Yakovlev during the table conversation that he and Princess Anne had attended the European three-day equestrian championships in Kiev in 1973, where the Princess Royal competed in the events, and that he had returned to Moscow in 1979 as president of the International Equestrian Federation for a planning meeting before the 1980 Moscow Olympics. On hearing his father say this, Prince Edward, who was a patron of the National Youth Theater, added that he was planning to make a private visit to Moscow the following year to see the young British actors perform there.

To all appearances, Prince Philip had an amiable disposition. He said he still remembered his first visit to Moscow in 1973 when he was shown the tombs of the early czars of the Romanov dynasty. His guide was none other than the then president (chairman of the Presidium of the Supreme Soviet of the USSR, to be exact), Nikolai Podgorny, who proved to be less than tactful. "We got rid of them, you know," he told his royal visitor. The prince pondered awhile, then said, "They were my relatives, you know." Podgorny said nothing.

As the duke was telling Yakovlev the story, he did not come across as an embittered man. He and the queen were in a relaxed mood. The atmosphere was not strained and conversation flowed smoothly. During the lunch, the queen, noticing Gorbachev's momentary distraction by the sound of an aircraft taking off in the vicinity, revealed the royal sense of humor: "Our visitors often ask us, why did we build our castle so near the airport?" (Heathrow is just a few miles away.) And she paused for effect. "Especially Americans," she added. Gorbachev laughed heartily. All in all, it was a friendly chat between the queen and the general secretary.

After the lunch the queen invited Gorbachev and his party to an adjacent drawing room "for port and coffee." Here, the same unobtrusive, silent, and efficient waiters served coffee and sherry from trays, and I helped myself to a cup of what seemed like espresso.

The queen led Mikhail Sergeyevich and Raisa Maximovna to a stand that contained an etching of the Kremlin, made in the last century, and explained that it had been given to her grandfather, George V, by the Russian czar Nicholas II. The Kremlin on the etching looked very much as it does today, minus those huge ruby stars on its towers that were put there by Stalin. The queen also showed us a couple of beautiful Fabergé eggs. Mikhail Sergeyevich apparently could not resist the temptation and delicately wondered who would be the next king. The queen said she had no plans to abdicate for the time being and, after some hesitation, added that her son Prince Charles was next in line of succession, but she was not absolutely sure she wanted to make him king at this time. She said she had not yet made her final decision and would stay on as long as she could, for she was only sixty-two years old and in good health. She spoke these words with a tinge of sadness in her eyes.

Finally the time came to leave. The lunch was running fifteen minutes behind schedule and the whole affair had lasted almost two hours, from 1 to 2:45 P.M., including the time for the pomp and circumstance and the tour of the castle. As the queen bade farewell, she and her guests stood talking for several minutes at the door, as though she was in no hurry to be rid of them.

Upon leaving Windsor Castle through the Frogmore Gate, with Gorbachev and Thatcher sharing his Zil, the motorcade went straight to the airport, where Gorbachev's plane was waiting to take him back to Moscow. We had been told to pack and turn in our bags the night before. So now it was straight to Heathrow, but without the usual fretting and anxiety of the average citizen, even though we were fifteen minutes late. When your host lives near the airport and your pilot is not about to take off without you no matter what, when you have a police escort and you bask in the glow of diplomatic success, you can afford to take your time and linger over the port and coffee.

The occasion was officially described as "relaxed, happy, and very successful." Speaking at a press conference later that day, Thatcher sounded positive, describing the queen's reply to Gorbachev's invitation as "a very definite yes," and said she was "very positive, very happy" that the queen had been invited. "There will be tremendous advantage. It will indicate the warmth of our relationship," Thatcher said. Speaking of Gorbachev, she said after his departure that she found him as "dynamic, determined, stimulating, and confident as ever in carrying out his reform program." And she added, "I think he is a man engaged on a historic mission, and he has our full support in pursuing *perestroika*. We want to make that support apparent, because it's good for the people of the Soviet Union in having their greater freedom, which eventually will lead to greater prosperity. We think it is also good for humanity as a whole. . . . He is a man with whom I look forward to doing more business in the future."

On the way to the airport Yakovlev commiserated with me on my having attended the royal feast and walked away hungry. But at least "we have invited a queen, if not a czar, to our country," he quipped. Then, switching the subject, he exclaimed, "What a woman! Mikhail Sergeyevich has a lot of respect for her." He was referring to Margaret Thatcher, of course. With every new meeting, he said, he came to appreciate her more and more as a talented and skillful politician. The feeling was obviously mutual. "Did you notice the dew in her eyes last night?" he asked. I said, "How could I fail not to?" At 3:15 P.M. we reached Heathrow. On the tarmac, Gorbachev asked Mrs. Thatcher, who had accompanied him to the airport to bid farewell, to make a second visit to Moscow. She said she would, and she did indeed come to see Gorbachev in Moscow later the same year, in September, but it was just a working visit, a stopover. In June 1990, she would visit Moscow again—this time it would be a full state visit.

And then Gorbachev's Ilyushin taxied off as Prime Minister and Mr. Thatcher and other British and Soviet officials waved from the tarmac. "Fare Thee well, England, and if for ever, still for ever, fare Thee well." Gorbachev would never come back here again as the leader of the Soviet Union. He was flying off into a maelstrom of domestic politics with growing nationalist unrest in Georgia and a host of other problems.

On April 7, 1989, Gorbachev, Shevardnadze and Yakovlev arrived at Vnukovo-2 late at night at about 11:30. The entire Politburo was there to greet them: Ryzhkov, Ligachev, Zaikov, Medvedev, Chebrikov, Nikonov, Slyunkov. Also, the alternate members of the Politburo: Yazov, Lukyanov, Biryukova, Vlasov, Razumovsky. And Oleg Baklanov—a Central Committee secretary in charge of the Soviet military-industrial complex. Like Yazov and Lukyanov, he, too, would join the August 1991 coup against Gorbachev.

Immediately after Gorbachev's arrival, all of them went to a room at the airport terminal reserved especially for Politburo members—the same room where Gromyko had received Reagan the year before—for what would later become known as one of the most controversial unofficial Politburo meetings. The subject was the alarming developments in Tbilisi, Georgia, where on Sunday morning of April 9, 1989, i.e., one day later, nineteen peacefully demonstrating Georgian girls and women would be brutally killed by soldiers on the orders from somebody "above." Subsequently, addressing a session of the Congress of People's Deputies—at which some Communist hard-liners, in an unscrupulous attempt to cover up their tracks implicating them in the murders, would try to blame Shevardnadze and Gorbachev for what had happened in the streets of the Georgian capital—Shevardnadze would describe what really happened at that meeting at Vnukovo-2 on the night of April 7, 1989.

That extraordinary informal Politburo meeting at the airport was a jarring epilogue to the otherwise glowing impressions of the visit of Gorbachev to Britain.

CHAPTER FIVE

END-OF-THE-COLD-WAR SUMMIT

Gorbachev-Bush Washington Summit, 1990

In May 1990, as Gorbachev prepared to visit Washington for a second time, he did so in a vastly changed world. The Cold War was over—or almost so. The Berlin Wall had collapsed in November 1989, and the Communist regimes in the former "fraternal" socialist countries had fallen like dominoes, helped by Gorbachev's policy of noninterference. Gorbachev was trying in earnest to regularize relations with the United States and China. He had advanced a more sophisticated approach to international affairs and created a climate in which he could encourage a reduction of the U.S. presence on the Soviet Union's flanks in Western Europe. After ending the Afghan adventure, he had shunned strategic responsibilities and engagements in the third world—in a stark contrast to the statement he had made some three years before in a meeting with Robert Mugabe. Moscow no longer fomented revolutions or sought to offer ideological inspiration to others.

Instead, Gorbachev sought to make the Soviet Union a full partner in the international community, starting with a "get-to-know-you" summit with George Bush in early December 1989 in Malta. Gorbachev held numerous meetings to build and improve relationships with important partners in the United States, Western Europe, and elsewhere. For example, in just one month in the spring of 1990 he received in his Kremlin office former U.S. chairman of the Joint Chiefs of Staff Adm. William Crowe, Sen. Edward Kennedy, British foreign secretary Douglas Hurd, Senate Democratic majority leader George Mitchell, and other prominent U.S. senators, to mention only a few. He also spoke on the phone with Prime Minister Thatcher and met with French president Mitterrand and many other foreign dignitaries. In all those meetings he expressed the desire for expansion of trade and economic cooperation. That desire was quite understandable: the Soviet economy was in dire straits and desperately needed foreign investments. While Gorbachev told his visitors that *perestroika* was designed to modify communism—"put a human face on it"—not abandon it, he stressed that a Communist USSR would not infringe on America's interests or those of other Western nations.

In short, by the summer of 1990, the world seemed poised on the threshold of a brave new era of economic growth and peace, though the issue of German reunification aroused many concerns and would dominate European politics for some time to come.

On the home front, however, Gorbachev faced mounting problems. The country had begun to disintegrate. On March 11, 1990, the Republic of Lithuania decided to secede from the Soviet Union. While Gorbachev feared a domino effect among many other republics, he was willing to grant Lithuania independence if it went through the process mandated by the constitution. But Lithuania wanted independence immediately and acted unilaterally. Gorbachev in turn imposed an economic blockade on the breakaway republic. The Soviet economy continued to deteriorate rapidly in spite of the steps taken to improve it. The social fabric of society was unraveling, and its moral underpinnings, which had begun to erode under Brezhnev, were practically nonexistent now. In short, at home disaster was staring Gorbachev squarely in the face.

But the Party, nostalgic for the pre-*perestroika* times, still retained its monopoly on power and resisted all reform. In a masterly tactical move at the Third Congress of People's Deputies on March 12, 1990, Gorbachev loosened the Party's deadly grip on power by maneuvering the Congress into eliminating the notorious Article 6 of the Soviet Constitution, which gave the CPSU the preeminent role in every sphere of national life. It had been introduced in 1977 by Brezhnev as a constitutional guarantee of the Communist Party's monopoly on political power. The Party was to be de jure, as it had been de facto all along, the supreme judge, a deity, as it were, in all matters pertaining to Soviet society at large. The removal of Article 6 meant that the Party had lost its monopoly. Instead, in another masterly stroke and a parliamentary sleight of hand—which I was privileged to observe (with some admiration) from the interpreters' booth perched high above the floor of the Kremlin Palace of Congresses (the proceedings were interpreted into English and other languages and carried live on television)—Gorbachev had created the post of president and had himself elected, on March 15, as the country's first president ever.

The idea of creating a popularly elected presidency had first been advanced by Sakharov in September 1989. He saw the presidency as a vehicle for taking power away from the old guard Party, as a counterweight to the heretofore all-powerful Politburo, and in the final analysis, as a way of ensuring Gorbachev's political survival by giving him a legally solid base of power.

For months, however, Gorbachev rejected the idea, for reasons that are best known to him, but most likely because he knew that the Party and its Politburo would never accept such a surrender of their authority. Sometime in early 1990, however, Gorbachev did an about-face and embraced the idea of a strong presidency—with the result that now he was the first president of the Soviet Union elected by parliament, with a fixed term of office of five years and a two-term limit. For a society that had never known the rule of law, those changes in the structure and functioning of the government were truly phenomenal. The Politburo and the Central Committee of the Communist Party were now superseded by the new mechanisms of elected power—a presidency and the Supreme Soviet. But Gorbachev still kept his other hat—that of general secretary of the Communist Party of the Soviet Union. If it sounds confusing, it was—even to many who were well versed in the Kremlin's byzantine ways and politics.

Then there was the "Yeltsin factor." As *perestroika* progressed, a beleaguered Gorbachev remained the object of growing criticism not only from the right, i.e., the hard-liners, but also from the left, i.e., the democrats. One of his most vociferous critics was Boris Yeltsin. In October 1987, in a Central Committee session, he had criticized Gorbachev openly and sharply for the first time. Yeltsin charged that *perestroika* was losing momentum and that a "cult of personality" was growing up around Gorbachev in the Politburo. His mention of the "cult of personality" was a chilling echo of the euphemism once used to describe Stalin's dictatorship. When word of this got out, Yeltsin instantly became a folk hero. Ironically, Yeltsin was Gorbachev's former ally whom Gorbachev had yanked out of obscurity in Sverdlovsk, the Urals, where he was a provincial Party secretary, and brought to the capital, in 1985, making him the Party chief of Moscow—the *khozyain* (boss) of the city—and an alternate member of the Politburo. As the capital's boss Yeltsin tried to fight corruption, and his reputation among common people grew. In those early days of *perestroika* Yeltsin portrayed himself as an idealistic bystander, yet he was conniving and dissembling. He felt the taste of power and sought it intensely. He quickly learned the importance of public relations and played the game with surprising skill.

The people loved him because he took on the Party bureaucrats and officials, of whom there were hundreds of thousands in Moscow alone, and began, quite rightly, to criticize the Party privileges. Since his ouster from the Politburo in October 1987, Yeltsin, always a contradictory figure at best, had become more wily, and by 1989 he emerged as a popular politician. His public statements focused on a few simple ideas, and he enjoyed the luxury of being able to criticize and make bold promises without assuming responsibility. His reputation became almost legendary. In the eyes of the people he personified the struggle against corruption and injustices. He was especially popular with the lumpen proletariat, or the working class in the Marxist interpretation. By the spring of 1990, Yeltsin had publicly parted ideological ways with Gorbachev, his former political mentor, and the personal antagonism between them had grown. Yakovlev had once described Yeltsin as "an ultraleftist," and ultraleftists, he wrote, were "the bane of any revolution." "They must be toned down or morally isolated."

Yet, Yeltsin was not isolated, morally or otherwise. In May 1990, as Gorbachev and the Politburo members stood on the Lenin mausoleum to review the traditional annual May Day parade, some demonstrators held up placards with Yeltsin's picture, chanting "Resign" and "Shame." The chant was intended for Gorbachev, not Yeltsin. It was striking evidence that among Muscovites Gorbachev's bête noire was more popular than he. In the heady atmosphere of the spring of 1990, Yeltsin was able to capitalize on the Gorbachev-baiting by portraying himself as un underdog. He exploited the nationalist yearnings of ethnic Russians, posing as the popular champion of the underdog Russians and a defender of Russian sovereignty against Gorbachev and the hated Soviet Communist Party apparat. As a result, on May 29, on the very eve of Gorbachev's arrival in Washington, Yeltsin got elected chairman of the Supreme Soviet, or parliament, of the Russian Republic. He thus staged a spectacular political comeback. While Yeltsin might seem a crass and boorish demagogue to Westerners, to the Russian man in the street, to the proletariat masses, he was a true Russian: a rough-talking, hard-drinking, no-nonsense construction engineer turned Party boss and now the elected leader of Russia's top legislative body. In their eyes, he was one of them, and that was the secret of his political resurrection. For Gorbachev, however, it meant more problems.

Each time I met with Gorbachev, talked with him, or interpreted for him, I saw a different, new Gorbachev. By now he had visibly aged, his hair had gone all gray, but age had added to his statesmanlike posture.

Occasionally flashes of the old Gorbachev came through, as for example during his meeting with Ted Kennedy when he kept referring to Vytautas Landsbergis, Lithuania's newly elected president, as "only a musician." But generally, he was now more reflective, more thoughtful, more philosophical, than the Gorbachev of two years or even one year earlier. And each time I saw him, I couldn't help marveling at the tremendous energy he had, at his stamina and the enormous burden he had assumed and continued to bear.

Having established a personal stake in the shape of future U.S. policy, Gorbachev followed Bush's pronouncements, after he took office, with particular care. A few years older than Gorbachev, Bush had come to office after extensive experience in international relations. As a result, some people close to Gorbachev initially felt that it might prove more difficult to deal with him than with Reagan. Bush was not viewed as a charismatic figure, but rather as a pragmatist in foreign policy.

Gorbachev and Bush agreed in December 1989, in Malta, where they had their first formal minisummit, that NATO and the Warsaw Pact should become instruments of political, instead of military, coordination. Of course, at that point Gorbachev trusted Bush no more than Bush trusted him, although he told Bush that the Soviet Union no longer regarded the United States as its enemy. But Gorbachev needed the American president's goodwill to show at home that the Cold War was now finally over, or almost over. The circumstances of his second trip to America for a full-scale summit meeting with George Bush were very different from those that had surrounded his first visit to Washington, two and a half years earlier. On the home front, Soviet citizens were coming to regard Soviet-American summits as a natural, almost routine affair. The threat of war had been replaced by the threat of domestic economic chaos as the number one preoccupation of ordinary Soviet citizens. Also, there was a strong undercurrent of concern, particularly among older people, about the prospect of a reunited Germany's becoming a member of a hostile military alliance—NATO. At the same time, the American perception of a Soviet military threat had dropped dramatically in the five years that Gorbachev had been in office. According to one poll taken in 1985, 76 percent of Americans thought the Soviet Union was still a serious threat, whereas in 1990, on the eve of the summit, the figure had dropped to 33 percent.

Some of Gorbachev's magic appeared to have worn off for the Americans, however. So much news from the Soviet Union was dark and threatening, as reflected in the Western media. The cover of the *Newsweek* that came out just before the summit showed the Soviet leader taking shelter under a huge but crumbling stone symbol of the Soviet state. "Why Gorbachev Is Failing," said the caption. "A Weakened Gorbachev Arrives in U.S." was another headline in another publication. The *Wall Street Journal* even wondered if this would be Gorbachev's last U.S. summit.

WASHINGTON. MAY 30, WEDNESDAY. DAY ONE.

It was a glorious spring day in Washington. Gorbachev's blue and white jet landed at Andrews Air Force Base at 7 P.M. after a flight from Ottawa, where he had met with the Canadian prime minister Brian Mulroney, ex–prime minister Pierre Trudeau, and other Canadian officials. As at the previous Washington summit, Gorbachev and his entourage were accorded a splendid welcome. The brief ceremony was virtually the same as before. Only this time the American welcoming party was led by James A. Baker 3rd, who had replaced George Shultz as Secretary of State, and it included Jack Matlock, the U.S. ambassador to Moscow, whom Bush had asked to stay on.

Gorbachev's men were basically the same, with a sprinkling of some "new" faces, such as Yuri Maslyukov, a deputy prime minister in charge of the famous Gosplan; the academicians Yuri Osipyan and Stanislav Shatalin, both advisers to Gorbachev and members of the newly established Presidential Council, which had replaced the Politburo; and Alexandr Dzasokhov, chairman of the Supreme Soviet Committee on International Affairs.

The issues to be discussed at the summit lay at the very root of the Soviet-American relationship at this point in time, i.e., ending the division of Germany, the course of change in the Soviet Union, the aspirations of the Baltic peoples, mutual trade, and a significant reduction in the military threat. In short, this was to be a serious summit about serious issues. There would also be a lighter side, however, as Gorbachev would have his first chance to do a little sight-seeing in America. After Washington he was scheduled to visit Minneapolis and San Francisco.

MAY 31, THURSDAY. DAY TWO.

I arrived at the sun-drenched South Lawn of the White House—where Gorbachev had said good-bye two and a half years earlier to Ronald Reagan in the "mushroom rain"—fifteen minutes before the welcoming ceremony. Around the entire perimeter of the White House, flags fluttered in a light breeze: Soviet, American, and the District of Columbia's. The new chief of U.S. state protocol, Amb. Joseph Verner Reed, who had replaced Mrs. Roosevelt with the change in administrations, was bustling about showing everyone where to stand. As I would discover, he was Mr. Perfect Courtesy. I had never met anyone who lavished so much solicitude and attention on people with whom he came in contact as part of his professional duties. He was the right man in the right place.

At exactly ten o'clock, thirty seconds before Gorbachev's black armored Zil came in sight at the other end of the circular driveway, President and Mrs. Bush emerged from the White House and, having reached the driveway, stood at the edge of the red carpet, ten feet from me and Dimitry Zarechnyak, the State Department employee who had stayed on as the presidential interpreter after Reagan left office. Bush cheerfully waved in our direction, exclaiming, "Hi, guys, you rarin' to go?" He hadn't changed in the past two and a half years. It was hard to believe he was sixty-six years old now. In fact, on this occasion he looked even younger than usual. And, he was as friendly and comfortable with everyone around him as he had ever been.

When Gorbachev's limousine stopped and he and Raisa Maximovna emerged from the rear door, the Bushes welcomed them like good old friends, exchanging handshakes and inviting them right away to be introduced to the guests lined up on the South Lawn. Dimitry and I joined them. As the courteous and genial host that he was, Bush made the introductions himself. When they reached Vice President Quayle, Gorbachev exclaimed, "Why, you look quite young!" Quayle retorted, "You, too." Among the Soviets, Quayle had a reputation as a rightwinger and a foe of the Soviet Union, and Gorbachev would set aside time especially to meet with him one-on-one to underscore the point that he had made to Bush in Malta, namely that "we no longer regard one another as enemies," and to try to dispel the vice president's misgivings about the Soviet Union and its foreign policy. Upon completing the introductions, Bush invited Gorbachev to mount the podium. The chief of protocol asked me to stand at the steps of the platform, telling me I was not to go up there "under any circumstances unless invited by the presidents." Their being together on the dais was meant to be a great photo opportunity.

But no sooner had the twenty-one-gun salute begun than Bush turned to me and invited me to join them. Reassured that he could now talk freely with Gorbachev through me, he turned to him and said something I never expected to hear at such a grand ceremony. Pointing to a man, the only one sitting, in a chair in the front row of hosts and guests, he said, "Look. D'you see the man in the chair? It's Armand Hammer. He's dozed off." Indeed, Hammer, oblivious to the gun salute, his head rolled to one side, seemed to be taking a catnap, the solemnity of the occasion notwithstanding. Hammer had told me once that he habitually napped several times a day, which, according to him, miraculously recharged his batteries. Apparently, he thought now was as good a time as any. "He is ninety-two years old," Bush went on. "Next to him is a young woman in a white smock. Can you see her?" Gorbachev looked quizzically at Bush, then at me, then at the woman. He hadn't caught the drift yet. Or maybe he was waiting for the punch line. "She's his doctor and a good companion," said Bush. "He met her not too long ago."

Gorbachev was taken aback but did not show it. "It's a fabulous day today," he said with a grin, switching the subject. "Maybe there is God up there. If so, he is smiling on us."

"Oh, but I thought it was you who brought us this beautiful day," quipped Bush.

The second Washington summit was officially under way.

As the two presidents made small talk, a fife-and-drum corps in red-and-white colonial dress paraded back and forth in front of the platform while playing. They had such determined expressions on their faces that they could have been about to engage in a real battle, and Bush commented, "I wouldn't like to get in their way. These guys could crush you." Then he said to Gorbachev, "If you don't mind, I will say a few words now, and then you will." Gorbachev nodded. "And I want to put glasses on these sixty-six-year-old eyes," Bush added. Gorbachev responded, "I cannot work without glasses either." I sensed that Bush's informality caught Gorbachev off guard. Bush obviously used it to loosen Gorbachev up and put him at ease. Informality would be a theme throughout the summit and would culminate with "no-tie diplomacy" at Camp David.

In his first formal speech of the summit, giving a hint of the most important topics to be discussed, Bush pointedly mentioned the German problem and the need for Soviet reconciliation with Lithuania, while also paying tribute to Gorbachev's achievements. Taking a leaf from Reagan's book, he quoted the words of "one of the world's great men in this or any age, Andrei Sakharov, who said fourteen years earlier, 'I am convinced that guaranteed political and civil rights for people the world over are also guarantees of international security, economic and social progress.' Sakharov knew that lasting peace and progress are inseparable from freedom: that nations will only be fully safe when all people are fully free. And we in the United States applaud the new course the Soviet Union has chosen. . . . We want to see *perestroika* succeed. . . . Welcome, sir."

Gorbachev responded in a similar vein, "The walls that for years have separated the peoples are collapsing. The trenches of the Cold War are disappearing, the fog of prejudice, mistrust, and animosity is dissipating." When Gorbachev finished reading his remarks, he immediately took off his glasses—he used them only when absolutely necessary.

The ceremony with the speeches lasted thirty minutes, and after it was over, Bush took Gorbachev through the Rose Garden to the Oval Office for their first "four eyes, plus two, plus two" meeting, i.e., both presidents, two interpreters, and two notetakers. The latter were national security adviser Brent Scowcroft and Sergei Tarasenko, who was Shevardnadze's top political aide. I noted that the Bush Oval Office was filled with personal mementos and photographs, most of them from the Bush's family album. It seemed more family oriented than even the Reagan Oval Office.

In a wide-ranging philosophical discussion of the future of Soviet-U.S. relations, the role and place of the two countries and means of cooperation between them, Gorbachev spoke honestly of the difficulties he faced at home and tried to convince Bush of the importance of signing a planned trade agreement to make the summit successful. The proposed agreement would, among other things, grant most-favored-nation status to the Soviet Union and lower the tariff rates on Soviet exports to America. For instance the tariffs on a liter bottle of *Stoly* (*Stolychnaya* vodka) would drop by $1.10. The tariff on caviar would be cut in half from 30 percent to 15 percent, etc. Gorbachev hoped that with lower tariffs he could boost Soviet-U.S. trade, which amounted to only an insignificant $5 billion in 1989. Furthermore, a trade agreement would make a favorable impression at home, and that, understandably, was his highest priority at the moment. Approval of the trade accord had been held up on account of the congressional Vanik-Jackson Amendment of 1974, which linked trade privileges to Jewish emigration from the Soviet Union. Congress also threatened to hold up the trade agreement until Moscow lifted its partial economic embargo against Lithuania.

"I need this agreement," Gorbachev told Bush bluntly, looking him straight in the eye.

While Gorbachev refused to promise that the embargo against Lithuania would be lifted, he did tell Bush that he did not intend to use force against the breakaway republic and that he hoped the crisis could be settled through dialogue. Bush responded that the agreement might be signed, but that the required waiver of the Vanik-Jackson Amendment would not be sent to Congress until the administration was satisfied on emigration and on the situation in the Baltic republics. That formula, said Bush, would give Gorbachev a trophy to take home without exposing him, Bush, to charges that he sold out Lithuania or Soviet Jews.

Alone with Bush without their aides, Gorbachev was in a dark mood. Bush, on the other hand, was upbeat and animated throughout the two-hour session. He was particularly interested in the Soviet reforms and concerned over the mounting difficulties Gorbachev was encountering. Gorbachev made the case for cooperation at this particularly difficult time so as to facilitate *perestroika*. Bush agreed it was important to understand one another at a time like this, but did not commit himself to anything specific in this meeting. On the official summit schedule, after this working session Bush was supposed to show Gorbachev his horseshoe pit outside the Oval Office, built at his express request. It was all part of Bush's tactic to loosen up Gorbachev, who never shed his coat and tie and was not sporty. But their session went forty minutes over its planned ninety-minute duration, and Gorbachev begged off because he had a one-o'clock lunch with *"Amerikanskaya intelligentsia,"* as he put it, at the Soviet Embassy. Bush assured him there would be time for games at Camp David, which Gorbachev was to visit on the fourth day of the summit.

When I returned to the Embassy, the guests, or the "American intelligentsia," invited for lunch with Gorbachev had already begun to arrive. "American live icons," however, might have been a more accurate description of the exalted figures in attendance, who included Gregory Peck, Douglas Fairbanks Jr., Jane Fonda, and Dizzy Gillespie. Some of the more prominent guests, such as Henry Kissinger and John Galbraith, had attended a similar meeting with Gorbachev in December 1987. Other of the diverse luminaries included the astronaut Thomas Stafford, the pianist Van Cliburn with his ninety-year-old mother, the science fiction authors Isaac Asimov and Ray Bradbury, the artist Andrew Wyeth, the TV tycoon Ted Turner, and presidents of several American universities and colleges. The television evangelist Robert Schuller substituted for Billy Graham. And there was the ubiquitous Armand Hammer, of course. The guest list had been prepared by the Embassy with due regard for the "wishes of Raisa Maximovna," who wanted to meet "some famous American movie stars."

Before the luncheon I mingled with a few of the famous guests in the lounge. I must say Jane Fonda looked very sexy indeed. With her incredible svelte figure, blond hair, and face without a single wrinkle, she could easily pass for a young woman of twenty-five to thirty, although she was fifty something at the time. She wore a short pink jacket and a miniskirt. The only thing that betrayed her age were her hands. She arrived together with Ted Turner, who was rumored at the time to be her boyfriend. When the good-looking couple exchanged greetings with the Gorbachevs on the receiving line, Raisa Maximovna gave them a quick appraising look and pronounced them a "nice and sweet pair." Ms. Fonda the actress now posed as Ms. Fonda the saleswoman, pitching her famous "Jane Fonda Workout" exercise program to the Soviet first lady. Ms. Fonda wondered how to organize a joint venture to introduce the Soviet people to her system of physical culture. She was ready to do her bit, and she did. Sometime later, she would go to Moscow to promote and participate in the first Russian women's marathon around the Kremlin—not without some help from Raisa Maximovna.

Gregory Peck, on the other hand, struck me as looking much older than he was. His hair was completely gray and his face was heavily lined. And in his eyes was the look of wisdom that comes with age. But he was still tall and handsome. Later, Marshal Akhromeyev, who shared a table with him, told Gorbachev that Gregory Peck had complained that when he was thirty years old he was a well-known movie star, but now that he was almost eighty, he was little known. "But in your case," he told the marshal, "the reverse is true. When you were thirty years old, you were little known, but now that you are over seventy, you are widely known. That's the difference between a marshal and a movie star." (In fact, Akhromeyev was sixty-seven years old at the time, not seventy, as Gregory Peck thought.)

I had a chat with Thomas Stafford, the former astronaut who had participated in the first joint Soviet-U.S. space flight as part of the Apollo-Soyuz space mission in 1975. Naturally enough, the subject was space. He said he firmly believed that by the year 2019, i.e., fifty years after the landing on the moon, the United States would put a man on Mars. Such a goal had recently been proclaimed by President Bush. With Henry Kissinger I briefly discussed—what else?—politics. He reminisced rather warmly about his meetings with Gromyko, for he now remembered me as the interpreter at those meetings and seemed to associate me firmly with the Soviet foreign minister, who had died eleven months earlier, two weeks before his eightieth birthday. Then the always pragmatic Kissinger asked me point-blank whether Gorbachev's hand was now weaker than ever before. I said no, I did not think so, although he certainly faced some formidable challenges at home. Kissinger winced and walked away.

Over a bountiful luncheon of chicken Kiev and caviar in the Golden Room, Gorbachev talked of restless Soviet consumers and Baltic separatists more in the tone of a parent vexed by impatient children and deserving commiseration than of a leader daunted by intermittent crises. His charisma and appeal were as strong as ever. Considering the growing burden of domestic political and economic problems, Gorbachev displayed serenity and self-assurance. He was relaxed and quick to smile and laugh at some of the comments made. He was in total control of himself, although he gesticulated wildly as he spoke, as was his wont. He was even at ease enough to banter lightly on the painful subject of the Soviet economy. "Someone said there can be no half measures in a market economy. It's just the same as being a half-pregnant woman. I said, I agree, but at any rate one has to wait nine months before a child is born. The same is true of the market." Reaction followed immediately from a neighboring table. Academician Stanislav Shatalin, one of the top Soviet economic advisers to Gorbachev, whom he brought to Washington, interjected that some babies are born in as few as seven months. Gorbachev shot back, "Yes, seven months. Shatalin is an advocate of more radical change. But to have a *healthy* child, one has to wait nine months."

The next day I was amazed to read in some of the major newspapers that Gorbachev's performance at this meeting was "rambling, incoherent, muddled, and disjointed." True, he spoke extemporaneously, as he usually did at such gatherings, but that certainly didn't make his remarks "incoherent." To set the record straight, Gorbachev's performance was not at fault but rather the simultaneous interpreter's, whose interpretation of Gorbachev's remarks, frankly, left much to be desired. The interpreter was simply not up to par. He couldn't react quickly enough to keep up with Gorbachev and, as a result, missed many things he said.

The Soviet official in Moscow who was responsible for interpretation assignments at this summit—just another MFA bureaucrat appointed to the job for his "loyal service to the Party" and for no other merits, who had no clue as to what interpretation is all about and who did not even try to conceal his dislike for Gorbachev and his reforms—should have known better than to assign an unseasoned interpreter to do such an important job. I came away from the meeting convinced that it had been done negligently, if not deliberately—to undercut Gorbachev's image. I am not saying that the interpreter in question deliberately sabotaged the interpretation. I know him well, and I know he didn't. He was a good, solid interpreter but a bit slow on the uptake. Still, by now sabotage of Gorbachev's reforms had assumed various forms, and I could not help thinking that this was one of them.

What, for example, were Gorbachev's listeners to make of him when they heard through their earphones, "We, back in our country . . . have been discussing this subject, and I know that you are afraid sometimes and you think that the Russians should somehow quiet down and get down to work, and I believe that it shows that we have not been able to realize our potential . . . and we'll figure out how to proceed in our country . . . and I understood well we cannot proceed like this anymore, so how should we live . . . on the night of March tenth and eleventh, 1985?"

At this point there were animation and laughter in the audience, clearly caused by the mistranslation. Here is what Gorbachev actually said, speaking of intelligentsia back home: "We have now done a great deal in our country to give those who had something important, something meaningful to say to their people—and wanted to say it—a chance to do so. It's true, too, that people are talking their heads off now. You noticed that yourselves. In fact, some of you are even voicing the concern: Are those Russians ever going to pipe down and start working? Probably, this is happening because for a long time things that were pent up in all of us had no outlet. It's an enormous world, after all: 300 million people, 120 languages, that is to say 120 peoples! And that isn't all . . . We will sort out our problems—although we haven't completely managed to yet. But the main point is that having understood our country and our history, the first conclusion we drew for ourselves was that we could not go on living like that any longer. Those words were spoken on the night of the tenth of March, 1985."

What Gorbachev was talking about was the *glasnost* campaign and the reasons why *perestroika* was an imperative. His last remark in this passage referred to the Politburo meeting, convened late at night in the wake of his predecessor's death, Chernenko, at which Gorbachev was appointed chairman of the funeral commission and a day later elected General Secretary of the Central Committee. It was at that late night meeting that the words "we cannot go on living like this any longer" were spoken by Gorbachev for the first time publicly.

Dr. Kissinger, to whom Gorbachev referred at one point as *"moi staryi znakomyi"* (my old acquaintance), grimaced when he heard the interpreter render it as "my old man."

How was Gorbachev's audience supposed to respond to the following drivel, again courtesy of the same interpreter: "I'm sure that especially after these five years, after all . . . ideas and today, which is the decisive moment—I will dwell on it—we have no other way to proceed and there is no turning back"? (Correct translation: "I am convinced: after five years of searching, daring, doubting, and emotional upheavals—and today we're at the peak of all this—there is simply no other way, just as there is no turning back.")

Small wonder then that the audience was left perplexed at what Gorbachev was trying to say to them. Fortunately, though, the interpreter in question did not get another chance to inflict more damage to Gorbachev's image as a speaker. I think the above-mentioned MFA official would have done well to ponder Harry Truman's famous motto: "If you can't stand the heat, get out of the kitchen!" My advice to would-be simultaneous interpreters is this: "If you can't handle it, don't get into the booth!" The next day, when Gorbachev would meet with US congressional leaders in the same room of the Embassy, and at subsequent such meetings with businessmen and other people, Pavel and I would hold the fort by ourselves, alternating every twenty minutes in the booth, to avoid repetition of the incident. Incidentally, something similar happened in Reykjavik, in 1986, during the question-and-answer period at the press conference that Gorbachev gave after his meetings with Reagan and which was carried live by CNN. The Soviet interpreter assigned (by an official in Moscow) to do this part of the press conference was not experienced enough and turned out to be inadequate to the task. He mistranslated some questions, causing miscomprehension and confusion. At one point, Georgy Arbatov, an adviser to Gorbachev, felt it necessary to intervene to correct the interpreter. It was an embarrassment to the interpreter and, more importantly, to Gorbachev's image, and could have been easily avoided had a more experienced colleague been assigned instead.

By the time the luncheon with the "intelligentsia" ended, Gorbachev was late for his second meeting with Bush. Accordingly, he skipped the time reserved for rest and went directly to the White House. The whole summit was like a grueling marathon, except for a one-day stay at Camp David.

When Gorbachev returned to the White House, he brought with him an impressive team of experts, for the subject to be discussed was widely billed as the most important issue at the summit: Should Germany be in NATO or not? Bush wanted it in. Gorbachev didn't. The Soviet Union was not prepared to see a united Germany in the Western military alliance. It preferred to see a neutral Germany or a unified Germany belonging simultaneously to NATO and the Warsaw Pact. But in fact, Gorbachev himself had not yet finally decided what to do about it. Shevardnadze even complained at one point about the need to have "some political direction here." Both Bush and Gorbachev were frustrated. The Soviets could not stop Germany from uniting, and the united Germany would undoubtedly opt for joining NATO. With the collapse of its western buffer, the old Soviet fears of a revived, aggressive Germany had resurfaced. Gorbachev could not afford to look soft on the issue, which had a direct bearing on Soviet security, and he had a weighty bargaining chip on the table: the 380,000 Soviet troops on German soil. Bush had signaled Gorbachev that the West was ready to accommodate Soviet security concerns.

The Soviet team included Eduard Shevardnadze, Sergei Akhromeyev, Evgeny Primakov, Anatoly Chernyaev, Alexandr Bessmertnykh, Anatoly Dobrynin, Valentin Falin, Yuri Maslyukov, Alexei Obukhov, and Georgy Mamedov—the latter was section chief of the USA and Canada desk at the MFA—eleven people altogether. Conspicuous by his absence was Alexandr Yakovlev, who had invariably accompanied Gorbachev on such trips as this until now. Dark hints were dropped among the Soviet delegation that Yakovlev had stayed in Moscow either to keep an eye on the situation in Gorbachev's absence or because he and Gorbachev had major policy disagreements. I had the impression that Yakovlev's place in Gorbachev's entourage had been taken by Evgeny Primakov. A member of the Presidential Council, an adviser to Gorbachev on the press, and an expert on numerous other matters, especially on the Middle East, the sixty-year-old Primakov had day-to-day contact with Gorbachev on a wide range of issues. His star was definitely rising.

The sixty-nine-year-old Anatoly Chernyaev, a longtime member of the International Department of the Communist Party's Central Committee and a specialist on Western Europe with some expertise in American affairs, remained a senior aide to Gorbachev on foreign affairs. Basically, he prepared the necessary material for Gorbachev and did the coordinating for his meetings with foreign leaders and delegations, and in that capacity he always attended those meetings. Alexandr Bessmertnykh, of course, was now the new Soviet ambassador to Washington. By appointing this top-rate expert on American affairs to this job, Gorbachev wanted to signal Bush that he attached paramount importance to further improving relations with the United States. Another major figure in Gorbachev's entourage was Valentin Falin, a former aide to Gromyko, the chief specialist on German issues, and the new head of the Central Committee's International Department. The sixty-four-year-old Falin had replaced the seventy-year-old Dobrynin, who was now a senior aide and consultant to Gorbachev on Soviet-American relations. Dobrynin had the unique distinction of having served as Soviet ambassador to the United States during the tenures of six U.S. presidents and nine secretaries of state—from 1962 to 1986.

Bush's team included Secretary of State James Baker, National Security Adviser Brent Scowcroft, Vice President Dan Quayle, White House Chief of Staff John Sununu, Secretary of Defense Dick Cheney, Deputy National Security Adviser Robert Gates, Undersecretary of Defense Paul Wolfowitz, Director of Policy Planning at the State Department Dennis Ross, who was also James Baker's aide, Senior Director for Soviet Affairs on the National Security Council Staff Condoleezza Rice, and Assistant Secretary of State Raymond Seitz.

The sixty-five-year-old Scowcroft had a reputation as a cautious man who tried to avoid the spotlight, ceding dominance in foreign policy to James Baker. John Sununu, fifty, was viewed as a pragmatist and a loyal Bush supporter. Robert Gates had formerly been a deputy director of the CIA and was a longtime analyst of intelligence about the Soviet Union. He had accompanied Baker on his trip to Moscow not long before the summit and sat in on all the meetings with Shevardnadze and Gorbachev. The youngest person on the American team was Condoleezza Rice; only thirty-five, she was Afro-American and very pretty. A former associate professor of political science at Stanford University, she was invited by Bush to work on the National Security Council as senior director for Soviet affairs. She spoke good Russian and, I remember, during one of her trips to Moscow she met with Marshal Akhromeyev in his Kremlin office. She asked him a lot of pointed questions that had the marshal squirming in his seat. After she'd left, he admitted that he liked her despite her "sharp" questions. He gave her the highest marks for her brightness and incisiveness. When I told him that she habitually read *Krasnaya Zvezda (Red Star)*, the principal Soviet army newspaper, he was astounded, for he himself did not speak or read foreign languages.

When Bush and Gorbachev and their teams sat down and the American interpreter Peter Afanasenko and I took our seats at the head of the oval table, next to the fireplace, in the Cabinet Room, the two presidents put on their earphones and immediately plunged into a spirited discussion of the German issue. Gorbachev spoke about the fears in the hearts of the Soviet people about a resurgent Germany. He said the Soviets lost many lives in World War II and learned a lesson from that. Bush responded that America too had lost many "kids" in the war with

Germany, but today's West Germany was different from the Germany under Hitler. It was now democratic and firmly on the path of steady economic development, a combination that effectively precluded, he said, the danger of an aggressive Germany. Bush reminded Gorbachev that he was "the only one of the two [of them] that was old enough to remember it from being there."

Bush had prepared well for this discussion for he made a strong attempt to convince Gorbachev that this was the crucial moment to acquiesce to the Western plan to "anchor a unified Germany in the NATO security alliance." Gorbachev said the Germans had the right to decide for themselves what alliance they would join after reunification. Bush immediately asked if that meant Gorbachev would go along with a decision to stay in NATO. Gorbachev said, "Yes." But then he asked, in turn, if that also meant that Bush would go along if the Germans said no to NATO. Bush replied, "Yes." But when Bush tried to pin Gorbachev down, he started backpedaling and the conversation got nowhere. Bush and Baker then presented Gorbachev with a list of nine "assurances" to allay Soviet concerns about Germany's becoming a member of NATO. But Gorbachev was not convinced. He suggested that he might be amenable to the idea of "anchoring" a unified Germany in both NATO and the Warsaw Pact.

"You are a sailor," he said to Bush in a friendly aside. "You will understand that if one anchor is good, two anchors are better. So why shouldn't it [Germany] be in the Warsaw Pact?" Then, realizing that this proposal would probably not be taken seriously, he launched into a long and rambling defense. But it was the image of anchors and Bush's response that captured the chemistry of the still-evolving relationship between the two leaders. Bush responded that although he was a naval pilot, not a sailor, he still didn't understand how the other anchor would work. Then Gorbachev joked that "perhaps the Soviet Union should apply to join NATO." Pointing to Marshal Akhromeyev, Bush replied that he doubted that the marshal would agree to serve under NATO's supreme commander, who traditionally was an American. Unsmiling, Akhromeyev agreed with him in the characteristically curt military manner: "*Nikogda!*" (Never). Gorbachev laughed.

Although Bush was careful to explain his reasoning on Germany in full and friendly fashion, no common ground was found, and as a result, no significant progress was made in this meeting. Gorbachev's position was that the German question would not be settled at the negotiating table in the White House, and accordingly he asked that it be removed as a potential irritant for the rest of the summit; he suggested that it be further studied by Baker and Shevardnadze. By proposing putting off the discussion of the German issue, Gorbachev wanted to avoid the appearance of stonewalling, because he was desperate for a trade deal. Without such a deal the summit would not give him the political boost he needed. At the end of the discussion, Bush and Gorbachev agreed to say publicly they now had "a better understanding of each other's positions."

Throughout the entire discussion there was no rancor between Bush and Gorbachev. Occasional tension was defused with humor and laughter. My overall impression of Bush was that he, like Gorbachev but unlike Reagan, was a "detail guy," i.e, he had prepared himself thoroughly on the subject that was to be negotiated and felt at ease discussing minute details and nuances, although his presentation was occasionally somewhat disjointed and rambling and, consequently, difficult to interpret simultaneously. But that was a problem for Peter, my American colleague on my right, to grapple with. My problem was to grapple with Gorbachev's own imperfections as a speaker. During the conversation Gorbachev seemed to me to be a bit less well prepared than he had been in his summits with Reagan; he relied on his aides more. He was noticeably distracted and sometimes even incoherent, as if his thoughts were elsewhere. He was as confident and dynamic as ever, but he did not display the grasp of detail that people had come to expect of him.

Something strange was afoot that I could not help noticing. On the top political level—essentially Gorbachev and Shevardnadze—flexibility and eagerness to forge ahead, in the Vienna CFE (Conventional Forces in Europe) talks, for example, were repeatedly voiced, while on the level of their advisers, essentially top Defense Ministry officials, such as General Omelichev, who was a "new face" on Gorbachev's team and who represented the Soviet Armed Forces General Staff, problems rather than the possibilities of solving them were emphasized when they spoke to their American counterparts.

On our way back to the Embassy, when Gorbachev saw a large crowd gathered to catch a glimpse of him, he told his driver to stop and briefly worked both sides of the street, shaking hands enthusiastically and responding to greetings from the crowd. Gorbachev was clearly motivated by a relish for the adulation he was denied at home, and partly by the knowledge that his "spontaneous" stops were a way of generating television pictures of happy Americans mobbing the Soviet president that might impress the disaffected Soviet people. The shouts and sirens of the nervous KGB, FBI, and Secret Service agents—who were seemingly taken by surprise since they were not informed in advance—mingled with the clapping, shouting, and laughing of the delighted pedestrians. One young man in the crowd, apparently a short one, was jumping up and down trying to see Gorbachev. "Take his picture, take his picture," he shouted excitedly. One woman, who stood within feet of Gorbachev, shouted deliriously into the crowd, "Yeah, I see the birthmark on his head!" It was as if Gorbachev was a rock star being mobbed by fans. The scene was reminiscent of his first spontaneous stop in 1987.

When we reached the Embassy, Mikhail Sergeyevich was in high spirits.

One hour later I was back in the White House, waiting for the Gorbachevs to arrive. I was supposed to act as an escort interpreter for Mikhail Sergeyevich at that most glittering state dinner of the year given in his honor in the State Dining Room. When the Gorbachevs arrived, at 7:15 P.M., they were met at the north entrance by George and Barbara Bush, who first took them upstairs to the Yellow Room in their private quarters for aperitifs. At 7:45, the two first couples came down the grand staircase to the Cross Hall and proceeded to the East Room to form a receiving line. Having been to numerous such occasions by now, I was not surprised to see some familiar faces file by, including Donald Kendall, chairman of Pepsico; George Kennan; Dwayne Andreas, CEO of Archer Daniels Midland; and Billy Graham. In contrast to dinner at 10 Downing Street, almost all these prominent men were with their wives. Most of the American guests were government officials and diplomats, top executives and bankers, senators and judges, politicians and military brass, with a sprinkling of actors and actresses. Jane Fonda was not there, but Jessica Tandy was. The mass media was represented by Hugh Sidey of *Time* magazine and by Tom Brokaw of *NBC Nightly News*.

Fewer Hollywood personalities and more businessmen and bankers were in this crowd than in the one invited by the Reagans in 1987—a reflection of Bush's tastes and friends, to say nothing of his attitude toward politics.

When Bush introduced Judge Webster, director of the CIA, to Gorbachev, the Soviet president said, "Watch us closely. You'll be amazed at many things. And above all, report everything correctly." Webster gave him a big grin and said he would. The next person needed no introduction. It was Armand Hammer. Quite unexpectedly and out of place, he said to Gorbachev, in English, and rather loudly, "Don't worry about Yeltsin—he is a fool!" When I translated, Mikhail Sergeyevich suddenly looked ill at ease; apparently he did not expect such a blunt appraisal of his nemesis, least of all in this place. To smooth out Hammer's tactlessness, he replied that he was not worried, it was a natural process—"one of the costs of democracy." With Kissinger, Gorbachev adopted a skeptical tone, telling him that his "prophecies" about the impending collapse of the Soviet Union would be proven wrong "by life itself." A veritable kaleidoscope of faces passed by Bush and Gorbachev in the receiving line: Attorney General Dick Thornburgh, Chief Justice William Rehnquist, Senator Bob Dole, U.N. Ambassador Thomas Pickering. Everyone wanted to exchange handshakes and some words with Gorbachev.

After the long parade of guests came to an end, Bush invited Gorbachev to proceed to the State Dining Room at the opposite end of the Cross Hall, where thirteen round tables were laid for 130 people. Gorbachev and Bush sat at different tables. Mikhail Sergeyevich was flanked by Barbara Bush on his left, and Carla Hills, chief U.S. trade representative, otherwise known as the trade czar, on his right. I wedged myself in between him and Barbara Bush. Except for George Mitchell, Senate Democratic majority leader, and Walter Shipley, chairman of Chemical Bank, I didn't know who the other five dinner partners at our table were, but they seemed to represent the world of business. I sensed that the seating had been arranged so as to avoid the sort of polemical talk on sensitive political subjects that had arisen at the previous Washington summit when Gorbachev was seated next to Richard Perle, who assailed him with importune questions about the real size of the Soviet military budget. Instead, Bush wanted to surround Gorbachev with businesspeople in the belief that something useful might come out of it for both sides, as he would tell Gorbachev later. President Bush, for his part, was flanked by Raisa Maximovna and the Reverend Billy Graham.

The official speeches and toasts were dispensed with before dinner began. Taking his cue from Reagan, Bush offered in his toast, as befitted a genial host, to share "bread and salt" with the Gorbachevs, in accordance with the Russian custom. He paid a warm tribute to Gorbachev and his reforms and raised his glass to "growing friendship between Soviet and American people . . . and durable peace." Mikhail Sergeyevich in turn invoked Franklin Roosevelt, who spoke of the four freedoms that would prevail in the future world: "freedom of speech, freedom of consciousness, freedom from want, and freedom from fear." Referring to the "long and difficult road that led from Geneva, via Reykjavík, Washington, Moscow, and New York to Malta, and now, once again to Washington," Gorbachev reiterated what he had told Bush in Malta the previous December: the Soviet Union no longer regarded the United States as its enemy and wanted to be partners and even friends with it.

It had been a remarkable evolution in the Soviet-U.S. relationship, and it had happened before my eyes: from confrontation to mutual understanding, to cooperation, to joint action and partnership and even friendship.

After the toasts, some of Mikhail Sergeyevich's dinner companions were curious to hear straight from the horse's mouth, so to speak, about his youth in Privolnoye, where he was born. So, Mikhail Sergeyevich told the story of his childhood. In 1941, when he was ten years old, the family was notified that their father, Sergei Andreyevich, who had gone off to war, had been killed at the front. But then, at the end of the war, after they had already gone through much emotional upheaval, he returned home, safe and sound. Gorbachev's father was no longer alive, but his mother, who was over eighty, was alive and well and occasionally visited him in Moscow. She didn't like it there because it was a big, noisy city, and also because she could see her son only early in the morning and late at night—he was at work most of the time. So, after spending a few days in Moscow, she would go back to her village, Privolnoye.

He himself was a "man of land," of peasant origin. He loved land and, in his own words, "devoted much of myself to it." "Man can fulfill himself on land only," he said. When he was a teenager, he worked in the fields as a combine driver. "Those years after the war were difficult, but I was happy," he went on. His family was poor yet full of enthusiasm and hope for the future. Their hopes were not fulfilled, however. It pained him to realize later on that even though a victorious power, his country could not recover from the consequences of the war for a very long time, and then it began progressively to lag behind the world's development as a result of the "well-known distortions." He did not specify what kind of distortions he had in mind, but I believe it was understood by everyone around the table what he was referring to.

Mikhail Sergeyevich was telling this story calmly, without bitterness in his voice, as if this conversation were taking place in a peasant house, not in the White House.

All the same, the conversation did touch on politics. Somebody at the table wondered who were Gorbachev's favorite Russian political leaders of all time. Without a moment's hesitation, he replied, "Peter the Great and Alexander the Second. They were Russia's greatest reformers." And then, after some hesitation, as if answering the mute question in the eyes of his table partners, he added, "And Lenin."

After dinner, as we made our way out of the Dining Room, Donald Kendall, chairman of Pepsico, came up to Gorbachev and said he would like to discuss something with Gorbachev and President Bush alone. When Bush caught up with us in the hallway, Kendall took us aside and presented what he said was "an idea that would work." He said he had already outlined it to Bush at the dinner table and now wanted Gorbachev to know that he planned to set up a "brain trust" to advise the Soviet president on changing over to a market economy. In Kendall's words, the Americans were prepared to help with practical advice, but didn't want Soviet economists who were long on theory but short on practice to be included in such a brain trust, should Gorbachev find the idea appealing. "Please, no academic economists!" Kendall pleaded earnestly. "Otherwise, they will make a mess of things."

Mikhail Sergeyevich accepted the idea straight off and even mentioned two specific names to be included in such a brain trust on the Soviet side: Osipyan and Shatalin. Although the two were academicians, they had hands-on experience in matters of economy and that's why they had been picked by Gorbachev to be his close advisers as members of the Presidential Council. Kendall was pleased with this choice. He said he had respect for them, they were "sensible and pragmatic people to deal with." Bush said it was an idea whose time had come for the Soviet Union. Gorbachev took advantage of the moment, pulled Bush aside, and buttonholed him again on the trade agreement, telling him that if the U.S. president was serious about wanting to see *perestroika* succeed, he must provide economic help. Bush heard him out but did not commit himself, saying he would see what could be done.

After a concert in the East Room by the opera diva Frederica von Stade and pianist Philip Fortenberry, I returned to the Embassy with the Gorbachevs in their limousine. As we got into the Zil at the North Portico, President and Mrs. Bush stood silhouetted against the brightly lit entrance to the White House, waving good-night.

June 1, Friday. Day Three.

The third day of the summit began for me with interpretation at a breakfast, at 9:30 A.M. at the Soviet Embassy, that Gorbachev hosted for congressional leaders. That morning I worked in tandem with Pavel Palazchenko. We didn't want a repetition of what happened the day before on account of poor interpretation. The meeting was far too important to allow the Soviet leader's remarks to be botched.

In a replay of the 1987 meeting with congressional leaders, Gorbachev reminded the Americans of Soviet strength and prestige to dispel the view in the Western mass media of Soviet decline and weakness. As with the intellectuals and movie stars the day before, he explained why his initial attempts to reform the Soviet economy had failed and tried to get across the idea that there could be no revolution without pain and uncertainty. "Don't be frightened, because that can frighten us, too, if you get frightened," he told the congressional delegation, which included seven senators, George Mitchell, Bob Dole, Alan Cranston, Claiborne Pell, Sam Nunn, Lloyd Bentsen, and Rudy Boschwitz, and five congressmen, Richard Gephardt, Les Aspin, Robert Michel, Dante Fascell, and Bill Broomfield.

"No one can really scare us or scare you—we should be scared of ourselves," continued Gorbachev. His country was failing economically, he said, because the old command system had been dismantled, but no new working system had yet been put in its place. To drive home the point, he resorted to a metaphor: "Our ship has lost its anchor, and therefore we are all a little sick."

Bob Dole raised the sensitive issue of the Baltic states, linking it directly to granting most-favored-nation (MFN) trade status to the Soviet Union. Gorbachev replied that he was not against Lithuania's independence per se, but it should be achieved through a constitutional process, through talks, not through unilateral action. And then he turned the tables on the senators. "Why did you let your administration intervene in Panama if you love freedom so much?" he exclaimed at one point. He then accused Washington of hypocrisy in doling out trade preferences: "You have given MFN to China after [the massacre at] Tiananmen. What are we supposed to do, declare presidential rule in Lithuania?" Declaring presidential rule, of course, was a euphemism for imposing martial law. He also warned that it would be humiliating "if we were to ask or beg something from you."

After the meeting with the congressional leaders Gorbachev went to the White House, slipping in through the "back door," the southwest entrance, unnoticed by the hordes of reporters. It was 11:05 A.M. He and Bush first had a tête-à-tête in the Oval Office at which Gorbachev made another strong plea to Bush to go ahead with the trade accord. At 11:48, they moved from the Oval Office to the Cabinet Room to be joined by other members of both presidents' delegations. The "wall-on-wall" meeting began as soon as they took their seats—the others were already there—and was devoted entirely to arms control.

Almost one year before, on June 20, 1989, five months into his presidency and after an extended period of reappraising U.S. foreign policy,

Bush had finally sent a long message to Gorbachev in which he called for direct contacts, with a view to finding a solution to the pressing issue of a START treaty, which still eluded them. Three months later, on September 18, Gorbachev sent back an even longer message of reply, which Shevardnadze delivered to Bush personally. In it, Gorbachev set out in detail the latest Soviet position on all the remaining arms control issues and made several specific proposals. After saying the two sides had laid good groundwork, he urged Bush to concentrate with him on solving the following crucial problems:

On ABM (antiballistic-missile treaty) and space, Gorbachev proposed putting off the conceptual dispute about whether placing arms in space would enhance strategic stability or instability and concentrating instead on completing and signing the START treaty. In other words, he was proposing to stop arguing about SDI, or "Star Wars," for the time being. On long-range sea-launched cruise missiles, or SLCMs, he called for both sides to compromise to break the long-standing deadlock. As to air-launched cruise missiles, or ALCMs, these and the heavy bombers that carry them should be dealt with as a package so as to preclude the possibility of going over the ceiling of six thousand warheads set at the Washington summit in 1987. On verification, Gorbachev stressed that it was absolutely essential to ensure that the future treaty on strategic offensive arms be strictly complied with. However, the trial verification measures, proposed in Bush's message to Gorbachev, should cover all kinds of strategic arms, not just mobile missiles, as Bush had proposed.

Gorbachev also addressed two more issues: nuclear testing talks and production of fissionable weapons-grade materials. Again, the key here was the development of a mechanism to ensure verifiable reciprocal reductions of nuclear tests and cessation of the production of weapons-grade plutonium. On the Krasnoyarsk radar facility, which had long been a bone of contention, Gorbachev announced the decision to dismantle it altogether, expressing the hope that the U.S. side would reciprocate by addressing Soviet concerns related to U.S. radars in Greenland and Britain.

Last but not least, Gorbachev expressed his readiness to conclude a global and effectively verifiable convention on the prohibition and destruction of chemical weapons, and since the multilateral talks on the agreement were in their final stage, but seemed to lack a sense of purpose, he suggested that the Soviet Union and the United States make a joint appeal for concluding the convention as early as in 1990 or 1991. Gorbachev also addressed in some detail the issue of reductions in conventional armed forces in Europe in the framework of the CFE talks that were under way in Vienna. He welcomed Bush's proposal for an "open skies" regime that would provide for mutual overflights by unarmed aircraft over the territories of the Soviet Union and the United States and their Warsaw Pact and NATO allies for the purpose of monitoring their military activities. It was to become another first in building mutual trust. Trust, but verify.

Gorbachev's letter concluded on a hopeful note: "I think we are now poised on the threshold of producing a mutually acceptable agreement. But you and I together will have to step over that threshold, and we can do so if we take into account each other's fundamental concerns. In closing, Mr. President, I wish to express my readiness to have further exchanges of views on the issues raised and the hope that this will be productive for the cause of peace and security."

That exchange of letters was followed by two more rounds of START talks in Geneva. Round Twelve, in which I participated as an interpreter, lasted from mid-September through the first week of December 1989. I was dismayed to find out that the two sides were as far apart, at the end of the round, on most of the issues raised in Gorbachev's letter as they had been before. Round Thirteen, which opened in January 1990 and went on uninterrupted until this Washington summit, had not produced much progress either, in spite of the face-to-face meeting between Gorbachev and Bush at the "seasick" summit in Malta, in December 1989. They were able to make some headway but not enough because "the devil [was] in the detail," as Richard Burt, the U.S. chief arms-control negotiator at the Geneva talks used to say, and the details were the domain of arms control experts, not presidents. Now it remained to be seen whether the second meeting between Gorbachev and Bush here in Washington would resolve all or any of the major outstanding issues, so that the two sides' experts could finally wrap up the whole thing and the two presidents could call it a good START.

Indeed, by now, before this meeting in the Cabinet Room and after more than forty hours' worth of haggling by experts since the summit got under way, agreement had been reached on only two of the five main issues in a START treaty, a treaty that would actually cut both sides' stocks of long-range arms only by about 30 percent, *not 50*, as was the original intention. (According to some calculations, the nuclear warheads per se were to be reduced by about 50 percent from the existing level, down to 6,000, while the number of strategic nuclear weapons delivery systems was to be cut down by roughly 30 percent—to 1,600. Complications in calculations arose because the United States had 2,200, while the Soviet Union possessed 2,400 such systems, including missiles, bombers, and submarines, i.e., the three types of strategic delivery systems known as the triad. Furthermore, since the United States objected to including SLCMs in the overall agreed ceiling of 6,000 warheads, the actual reductions in these warheads would be much less than 50 percent.)

On both sides the long-range, strategic weapons had assumed a role in political debate that may have exceeded their military significance. Why, Soviet officials said, for example, should Moscow agree to limit its Backfire bombers, as the Americans demanded, when Washington had refused to consider any constraints on its naval arms, as the Soviet military had demanded all along? They also repeated a long-standing argument that the range of the Backfire was too short for it to be considered a "strategic" weapon. Toward the end of the presummit ministerial in Moscow, on May 16–19, involving Shevardnadze and Baker, the Soviet side was willing to declare that the bomber could not be refueled in flight to give it a long-range attack capability, but they were not willing to accept a limit on Backfires assigned to naval strike units.

Now, at this summit the two sides hoped to resolve enough of the remaining thorny issues to agree on a treaty framework and to aim at completing the treaty by the end of the year. They also hoped to issue a joint statement outlining how they might move on to further cuts in a subsequent strategic arms agreement. As to chemical weapons, the two sides had reached an accord to cut their arsenals to five thousand tons.

On conventional arms, although progress had been slow on an agreement cutting the tanks, troops, and other equipment that would be used in a nonnuclear war, Bush and Gorbachev had set a goal of completing this treaty also by the end of the year. But the Soviet stance on conventional forces in Europe was still linked to Moscow's opposition to NATO membership for a united Germany. The Soviet military were opposed to reunification altogether if it would mean the expansion and strengthening of NATO at the expense of the second-strongest conventional force in the Warsaw Pact (i.e., East Germany). Talking at cross-purposes with President Gorbachev, Defense Minister Dmitry Yazov, who would be one of the principal coup-plotters against him some fourteen months later, had stated that the Soviet military would simply not accept a united Germany in NATO, invoking the experience of two world wars. Furthermore, with a much larger conventional force than that of the West, the Soviet military strongly objected to a disproportionate share of the cuts.

At the Cabinet Room meeting, although Gorbachev and Bush did not go into much detail of the arcane business of arms control, their experts did. At the request of both presidents, Viktor Karpov on the Soviet side and Reginald Bartholomew on the U.S. side reported on the status of negotiations in the working group on START, CFE, and the "open skies."

Baker summed up the two experts' presentations, singling out, with the precision and clarity for which he was famous, the remaining three problems: "We believe that noncircumvention [of the future START treaty], the Backfire, and heavy missiles *are* the major issues we must resolve if we are to be able to say we have agreement on the major elements of a [START] treaty." It was also important, he said, to achieve agreement on the goals of future negotiations on strategic arms. He hoped that a joint statement would be signed later that afternoon on the goals of such future talks. To do that, both sides had to reach agreement on the three above-mentioned issues by 5 P.M. that very day. Baker emphasized that if those three issues were to be resolved soon, the presidents had to issue a relevant direction there and then.

In fact, that was all the presidents could do. To my great astonishment, they were not very conversant on the details of arms control, as Bush would admit to Gorbachev in private later that afternoon. Perhaps this was only natural, for it was an extremely complicated and intricate technical subject. Bush admitted he relied on the expertise of such people as Scowcroft and Baker, but said he was sure that Gorbachev had all those details at his fingertips. He was surprised to hear Gorbachev admit that he, too, was familiar with arms control details only in a general way and had to trust his "specialists," such as Shevardnadze. They agreed, however, that the most important thing for them as presidents was to give political direction to their negotiators so they could advance the treaty to completion.

Summing up the exchange, Gorbachev suggested issuing such direction to Baker and Shevardnadze. Bush echoed him, "Let the foreign ministers work on these issues till five P.M. so we could record progress." As Bush spoke those words, he leaned back in his chair and produced from his pocket a piece of paper. "I have received a report," he said, "that Raisa Maximovna [he used her name together with the patronymic, as is customary among Russians but rather unusual for Americans] has just finished speaking at Wellesley College. She was greeted with ovation and applause." On hearing this, Gorbachev was at first taken aback, but his amazement at Bush's changing the subject so abruptly quickly gave way to a broad grin. "Some people say," Bush went on, "that Barbara does not earn her living, and therefore they protest" (he was referring to an incident at Wellesley College near Boston in which the students protested against Barbara Bush's appearance at commencement ceremonies but welcomed Raisa Maximovna Gorbacheva).

Bush was again attempting to put Gorbachev at ease and reestablish a personal rapport with him before proceeding to another subject. The tactic worked. Gorbachev laughed, and so did the members of his team, except Akhromeyev, who could not stand such trivialities. But from this point on, the atmosphere was more relaxed, and the discussion more productive—Gorbachev appreciated personal touches. Later, he would refer to this moment again and again, both privately and publicly. Personal relationships between leaders do indeed go a long way toward shaping relations between the countries they represent.

Bush turned serious again. "I would raise now another item, on 'open skies,' and see your reaction," he said, reverting to arms control themes. This time Marshal Akhromeyev reported on the situation. He was easy to interpret—his expression of thoughts and ideas was straightforward and to the point, without any attempts at philosophizing. But when Gorbachev spoke next, I made an embarrassing blunder, for which I cannot forgive myself to this day.

Speaking of the "open skies" regime under which both sides would be able to overfly each other's territory to verify compliance, Gorbachev went into some technical detail. In discussing the pros and cons of each side's using its own aircraft to overfly the other side's territory, he used a term, *proveryayuschaya storona* (the verifying party), that I knew by heart. I had heard and used it in talks myself a hundred times before. However, another term had an opposite meaning, namely *proveryae-maya storona* (the verified party). The Soviets and the Americans disagreed on whose aircraft should be used for the inspections—those of the verifying party (U.S. position) or the verified party (Soviet position). It was one of the sticking points that prevented further progress.

I misheard Gorbachev. Although I sat only a few feet away from him, at the head of the table, I had to rely on earphones so as to simultaneously interpret from Russian into English. Gorbachev pronounced the ending of the word in question indistinctly, blurring it, with the result that I heard him say (and I translated accordingly) that "the aircraft to overfly territory for inspection purposes should be made available by the verify*ing* party at the disposal of its crew," instead of by the verif*ied* party. When Bush heard my translation, he was startled by the seeming volte-face in the Soviet position.

As soon as I finished translating the sentence, I was in a trap, without my realizing it yet. Bush and Baker turned their heads in my direction (I sat on their side of the table), and I saw puzzlement in their eyes. They could not believe what they had just heard in their earphones, that the Soviet position was now identical to their own. Could it be a case of mistranslation? Alas, it was. To check whether it might be the latest Soviet position, Baker asked Gorbachev to confirm his statement, did he really mean "the verify*ing* party" or was it "the verif*ied* party," stressing the ending in both words. Of course, Gorbachev replied that he was talking about *"proveryaemaya storona"* (the verified party). Everyone now turned their heads to look at me. At that moment I wished the earth could swallow me up. Someone once said that "good interpretation is like air—no one notices it until it is polluted." Nobody notices the interpreter as long as he is doing all right, but the moment he makes a slip, he becomes the focus of attention.

Well, now that Gorbachev had pronounced the sacramental term clearly and distinctly the second time around, I translated it the way it was meant to be, spreading my arms in the process to indicate that it was all my mistake. After the session was over, I went up to Bush to apologize for this blunder. He heard me out, patted me on the shoulder, and quipped, "But you didn't start World War Three!" Gorbachev, too, took it in his stride. "The costs of interpretation," he said graciously, and concluded, "He who does nothing makes no mistakes."

After the morning talks Gorbachev's busy schedule included a meeting with Vice President Quayle and an awards ceremony at the Soviet Embassy in which Gorbachev received the Albert Einstein Peace Prize for his contribution to world peace, the Franklin Delano Roosevelt Freedom Medal for promotion of FDR's "four freedoms," the Martin Luther King Jr. Non-Violent Peace Prize, and the Martin Luther King Jr. International Peace Award. To top off the ceremony, Gorbachev was given the Man of History award, plus five additional peace awards from different groups. Then it was back to the White House for an East Room signing ceremony that would be the cap of an episode of extraordinary international diplomacy at the top level.

Ten minutes before the signing, the fate of a trade deal was still very much in doubt. It was absolutely crucial to Gorbachev that the MFN status be granted by Bush, and so he kept lobbying for it until the very last minute. The ceremony, which was originally scheduled for 5 P.M., was deferred until six o'clock at the request of Gorbachev in the hope that he could himself cajole the Americans into signing the all-important agreement. Even Shevardnadze had failed in his attempts to convince Baker to impress on Bush how important the agreement was for Gorbachev. The Americans responded that Moscow had failed to keep its pledge to enact a law on emigration before the summit, and on top of all else, it had imposed an economic blockade on Lithuania. In those circumstances, they said, neither the administration nor Congress could go ahead with the signing and ratification of the trade agreement.

At 5:45 P.M., after making two stops in the street to wade into crowds, we arrived at the South West Gate to the White House. Bush was waiting outside. He seemed impatient—only fifteen minutes remained before the rescheduled ceremony and he wanted to discuss something urgent with Gorbachev. Bush immediately took him to a tiny elevator, which accommodated only four people: the two presidents, the elevator operator, and myself. Even Gorbachev's lanky bodyguard Medvedev, his constant shadow, was forced to race upstairs to the second floor on foot to rejoin Gorbachev there. During the short ride upstairs, Bush, who was on a first-name basis with the elevator operator, introduced him to Gorbachev as "one of the most important men" in the White House. It was another demonstration of the American president's informal style of dealing with people, whether they were his equals or just plain folk. The operator was visibly pleased and proud to shake Gorbachev's hand.

From the elevator Bush took Gorbachev to the Red Room where, in the remaining fifteen minutes or so, Gorbachev made one last-ditch effort. Photographers captured the moment, in a picture showing Bush in a huddle with Gorbachev standing in the middle of the Red Room, with me between them. Bush was wavering until the very last minute. Later, it would become known that before Gorbachev's arrival in the White House, Baker had reported the inconclusive results of his talks with Shevardnadze, and although Bush had apparently made up his mind sometime that afternoon to go ahead with the trade agreement, he still wanted Gorbachev to pledge to lift the blockade on Lithuania and ensure freedom of emigration from the Soviet Union.

Bush stood, hands in trouser pockets, deep in thought, as Gorbachev tried to work his magic. I must say I was very impressed. He played his cards well. He stressed how important the agreement was to him personally and how it would go a long way toward improving trade relations between the two countries, and how people would not understand if Gorbachev came back home empty-handed. I was interpreting him phrase by phrase, so that Bush would not have to wait long to know what he was saying. It so happened that I was the only interpreter at the moment. My American counterpart was sent for but he arrived too late. After listening to him for several minutes, Bush said slowly, as if weighing each word, "What if we do it this way?" and producing a half sheet of paper from his breast pocket, he asked me to translate the text from sight, "to save time." I took the typewritten paper from his hands and translated it for Gorbachev without pausing to catch my breath. Time was of the essence.

The paper stated that the United States would be ready to sign the trade pact subject to the following private understanding: one, that the Soviet Union would complete as soon as possible and enact legislation on emigration; and two, that Moscow would lift the economic sanctions against Lithuania.

Having listened attentively to my impromptu translation, Gorbachev nodded in agreement and said, "Okay, I agree." Then he added, "Only I want you to know that our Supreme Soviet is currently overburdened with all kinds of bills, and the deputies (MPs or congressmen) simply have no time for everything. But the law on emigration will be passed as soon as possible. . . . This I promise you. As to lifting the sanctions against Lithuania, we will do it, too, although we wouldn't like it to be widely advertised at this time." These words of Gorbachev's must have finally swayed Bush to decide there and then in favor of signing the trade agreement. "So, with this private understanding," he concluded, "I am going to sign the trade agreement today, although my critics will give me hell." This momentous decision by Bush, even though made at the eleventh hour, was a good demonstration of the trust he had in Gorbachev.

Bush said he realized he was opening himself to criticism, perhaps even sharp criticism, from those who opposed such a step. But he would "bear the entire brunt of criticism" and it would not affect Gorbachev, so he didn't have to worry. Gorbachev got the deal probably because he played Bush's game on his own turf, appealing to him *personally* in one-on-one sessions, at dinner and again in private here in the Red Room of the White House, rather than at group negotiations. This tremendous achievement essentially ended the commercial cold war between the two nations.

As we were returning to the Embassy shortly after seven o'clock, Raisa Maximovna couldn't restrain her joy: several times during the car ride from the White House she exclaimed, "It's a great breakthrough, *Mikhal Sergeich!* A great, wonderful achievement! Congratulations!" Mikhail Sergeyevich beamed. Once inside the Embassy lobby, he and Raisa Maximovna were surrounded by Primakov, Chernyaev, Bessmertnykh, Osipyan, and a few other members from his entourage. Mikhail Sergeyevich was positively ecstatic: "Well, it's a great victory that we

have succeeded in persuading Bush. He wavered until the last minute."
Raisa Maximovna joined in, "*Mikhal Sergeich*, make sure that people
[back home] are widely apprised. Let the country know of this victory.
Anyway, everyone should have a drink on this occasion, to celebrate,"
she commanded. "That includes everyone, except the security."

"And except the interpreters. Drinking muddles the brain," I ventured, but she objected, "Yes, that includes the interpreters, too. A drink
will have just the opposite effect—it will clarify the mind."

But to get back to the orderly narration. After Bush told Gorbachev he
would sign the trade accord, they shook hands and Bush asked one of his
aides to bring him a can of spray. Looking at his reflection in the glass
door of a cabinet in the Red Room, he applied the spray liberally to his
hair so "it won't look bad before those cameras," as he put it, then
offered the can to Gorbachev. Mikhail Sergeyevich appreciated the gesture and laughed. Alas, he could not exactly boast a full head of hair.
Bush was rather particular about his own appearance and wanted to
"look [his] best on television." After all, "the signing ceremony," he
explained, "would be televised nationwide and beyond."

And then he threw me a linguistic curve, momentarily putting me
behind the eight ball. Gesturing toward the East Room, Bush said,
"Those guys over there are still behind the curve!" What he meant, of
course, was the "power curve"—that keening arc of fast presidential
decision-making—which indicated that the people in the other room,
who were waiting for the two presidents to appear, were as yet unaware
of the latest top-level decision. Fortunately for me, William Safire—
that language maven and political pundit—came to the rescue. I
remembered one of his *On Language* articles dealing with "power
curve" and came up, a moment or two later, with *virazh vlasti*, in Russian. Mikhail Sergeyevich nodded comprehension. I took out a handker-
chief to mop up the tiny beads of perspiration that had broken out on
my forehead. It wouldn't do to fall flat on one's face in front of the leaders of the two superpowers—it would have been unprofessional if I had
failed in my duty to facilitate the understanding between them. But it
was a close call.

At 6 P.M. sharp, Amb. Joseph Verner Reed, chief of protocol, walked
into the Red Room to invite the two presidents to proceed to the East
Room through the Cross Hall. From now on they were within the cameras' range. "Ladies and gentlemen! The Presidents of the United States
and the Soviet Union!"

The presidents had six documents to sign and the foreign minister and the secretary of state five. Apart from the agreement normalizing trade (which included no public Soviet concessions on Lithuania in keeping with the private understanding), Gorbachev and Bush signed a commitment to reduce long-range nuclear weapons, an important treaty to eliminate most of their chemical arsenals and halt further production of poison gas, and a new five-year agreement on Soviet purchases of American grain, which was of great interest to American farmers.

On nuclear arms, Gorbachev and Bush signed a series of agreements and pointed to progress on the eight-year quest for a treaty reducing the two sides' strategic nuclear arsenals. On chemical weapons, they agreed to cut huge stockpiles to five thousand tons by the year 2002. Destruction would begin by the end of 1992, and at least 50 percent of the stocks would have to be destroyed by the end of 1999. There would be on-site inspections of the destruction, with details to be worked out by the end of the year. In business left over from the days of Brezhnev and Ford, they wrapped up details for on-site inspection of nuclear testing—the verification procedures for two previously existing but still unratified treaties, the 1974 Threshold Test Ban Treaty (TTBT) and the 1976 Peaceful Nuclear Explosions Treaty (PNET). The two treaties banned nuclear explosions with planned yields greater than 150 kilotons—the explosive power of 150,000 tons of TNT.

In his remarks Bush declared, "The world has waited long enough. The Cold War must end. . . . Let's . . . build a more peaceful world." Gorbachev echoed the sentiment, calling for dismantling the "monuments" of the Cold War—"the accumulated arsenals of mutual destruction"—and citing from FDR's "four freedoms" declaration, said that "while liberating the world from fear, we are taking steps toward a new world." In a major move to achieve that goal, Bush and Gorbachev agreed to jump-start the START talks by signing a joint statement that called for new negotiations to begin "at the earliest practical date after the remaining issues are settled and an initial treaty is signed." What was meant by the "initial treaty" was, of course, the long-sought START treaty that Gorbachev and Reagan had once hoped would be signed in 1987–88, more than two years before.

The stumbling block was the same as before the summit: the inability of the two sides to resolve their disputes over limitations on the Soviet Backfire bomber and the SS-18 heavy missile armed with ten warheads that had been of special concern to Americans. But the session was not entirely fruitless: they settled one major dispute, agreeing on a limit of 1,100 warheads on mobile land-based missiles in START. The figure was actually a compromise between a Soviet proposal for

1,200 such weapons and a U.S. proposal of 800. Altogether, the accords signed helped move the superpowers from the "balance of terror" to the steadier ground of the "balance of interests." Bush and Gorbachev also issued a statement pledging to accelerate work toward completion, later that year, of a twenty-three-nation treaty slashing U.S. and Soviet land armies and other nonnuclear forces in Europe—the CFE treaty. The summit had helped to narrow the gaps between the two sides on conventional forces in Europe, but serious, substantive difficulties still remained.

The completion of the START declaration and the signing of the trade and grain agreements cleared away nearly all of the pressing business of the summit. Given his domestic difficulties, Gorbachev needed a successful summit, and he played a weak hand well enough to get one, especially in front of the cameras. Bush was obviously an astute and savvy politician with long experience in foreign policy: he calculated that Gorbachev had enough trouble already and that further undermining him would not serve U.S. interests. He realized Gorbachev had to deal with staggering domestic problems, such as secession, ethnic violence, economic chaos, and now the challenge from Yeltsin, to say nothing of the mounting pressure from the hard-liners, and didn't press for more concessions than Gorbachev had already made. Personal contacts did play an important role in his decision.

What remained to be discussed yet were regional issues, including Afghanistan, the state of *perestroika*, and Soviet-U.S. economic relations. These issues would be taken up directly by the two presidents the next day, Saturday, at the presidential retreat at Camp David.

While her husband was winning over the President, Raisa Maximovna Gorbacheva was getting along just fine with Barbara Bush. Nancy Reagan had always been infuriated by the strong-willed Soviet first lady's proclivity for expounding on Marxist-Leninist doctrine. "Who does that dame think she is?" Mrs. Reagan demanded after one such encounter at a White House dinner in 1987, according to Donald Regan, President Reagan's chief of staff. Mrs. Bush was said to have a quieter way of expressing displeasure, however, known as the Stare. When someone said something that bothered her, she offered a look of granite that showed she was not one to be trifled with or underestimated. She was said to have swiftly set the tone with Raisa Maximovna during the last summit meeting in Washington in 1987. Raisa Maximovna had been told by her staff that the then vice president's wife was a snowy-haired "homemaker type," a far cry from Nancy Reagan, who was described in American mass media as "just a clotheshorse." So when they met, Raisa Maximovna reportedly offered to share a recipe for her favorite blueberry dessert. Mrs. Bush in turn offered her the Stare. "Raisa, do you cook at home?" she asked. Raisa Maximovna replied tentatively, "Well, sometimes." Mrs. Bush supposedly said, "Well, I never cook at home, so let's talk about something else." And the two first ladies "got out of the kitchen" and moved into a discussion about education and grandchildren.

Raisa Maximovna, the sometimes self-assertive costar of previous summit sideshows, threw out her old script on this, her second, visit to the capital city of capitalism and emerged as a graceful and gracious guest. Gone was the woman who once practiced the art of conversation as lecture, peppering the people she met with a mixture of fiats and dogma. Now, instead of simply talking, she conversed. Over the past two days of the summit she had toured the White House family quarters with Barbara Bush, opened an exhibit of religious texts of Russian Old Believers at the Library of Congress with Marilyn Quayle, the vice president's wife, and enlisted the help of the Matlocks' grandson to guide her through the Capital Children's Museum. The child obediently helped her turn the Archimedes' screw, then joined her in a quick game of electronic tic-tac-toe. History did not record who won. Amidst the frenetic socializing of summitry, she found time to pet First Dog Millie, the Bush's English springer spaniel, who sidled up near her leg and basked in the warm words spoken to her in Russian.

And, while their husbands were busy putting the Cold War to rest, Raisa Maximovna and Mrs. Bush did some disarming of their own in a joint commencement speech at Wellesley College. Judging by all accounts from "reliable sources," Raisa Maximovna didn't do too badly with the rest of the people she met on this trip. And in a gesture that brought the third day of the summit to a successful conclusion at the Soviet Embassy, she made it a point at the dinner, hosted that evening by Gorbachev for the president and his wife, to clink glasses with Mrs. Bush.

CAMP DAVID. JUNE 2, SATURDAY. DAY FOUR.

This fourth day of the summit is described in the history of Soviet-U.S. relations in various ways. It is known as either "the Camp David summit" or "the horseshoe diplomacy day" or "the no-tie summit day" or simply as "the day of personal diplomacy." Whatever its official name in history, it was just a beautiful early-summer day, with blue skies and the sun shining brightly overhead.

At 9 A.M. I was at the site near the Reflecting Pool on the Mall from which U.S. Navy helicopters would whisk the Gorbachev party off to Camp David, the presidential retreat in the Catoctin Mountains of Maryland, fifty-five miles northwest of Washington. Gorbachev would fly with Bush in Marine One, the President's helicopter, from the South Lawn of the White House. Raisa Maximovna and Mrs. Bush would follow in a separate helicopter.

When the motorcade pulled up at the lawn next to the Reflecting Pool, the four big, heavy, olive-green flying machines—Sikorsky marine helicopters owned by the U.S. Marine Corps—were ready to take off at a moment's notice. I was assigned to fly on Nighthawk, the biggest helicopter of the four, which could carry as many as twelve passengers. The other passengers on Nighthawk included Secretary Baker and Minister Shevardnadze, Press Secretary Marlin Fitzwater, Soviet interpreters Pavel Palazchenko and Sergei Berezhkov, and six more officials whom I did not know. Although it was a military helicopter, its interior resembled that of a small executive jet. Baker and Shevardnadze sat opposite each other in soft-cushioned chairs separated by a small table of polished wood.

At 9:30 A.M. the helicopter began to shake as its giant rotor blades whirred, and almost instantly it was airborne. I had flown in helicopters before and always enjoyed it, but this was a special thrill. As Nighthawk climbed to a cruising altitude, it offered us a spectacular bird's-eye view of Washington. We flew over such familiar sights as the Grant Monument, the Watergate complex, the John F. Kennedy Center for the Performing Arts, and the Pentagon, which somehow resembled a giant Star of David (minus one side and angle) from above. Baker provided a running commentary for Shevardnadze's benefit, drawing attention to the main points of interest below on the ground. From the air the American capital looked like a huge, skillfully executed mock-up. Most of the time we flew over wooded terrain, occasionally intersected by villages with pretty toylike homes and lawns in which Shevardnadze showed a particular interest, asking who lived in them, how much they cost, who could afford them, etc.

Twenty-five minutes later, Nighthawk landed smoothly in a grassy landing zone inside the gates of the Camp David compound. The site was marked with a small, plain, wooden sign saying simply "Camp #3" and warning would-be trespassers to stay away.

We stepped out of the helicopter and Baker led the way to a podium installed for the benefit of a small army of reporters assembled in the hope of getting a scoop. The scene was tranquil and informal, if you did not count the two marines frantically swabbing the immaculately clean landing pad on the lawn, or about a dozen marines, known as "the side boys," in dress blues, with rifles and Soviet and American flags, or the dozen sailors or so in dress whites standing at attention, or the swarm of security people, or the Soviet and American interpreters nervously waiting for their principals. Two minutes later Marine One landed, and Bush and Gorbachev emerged, squinting in the bright sunlight. They were followed by interpreter Bill Hopkins and President Bush's "football" carrier, and the presumed "football" carrier for the Soviet president, Vladimir Timofeyevich Medvedev, Gorbachev's omnipresent bodyguard. Many presumed he was in charge of *chemodanchik*, the Soviet version of the "football," when the Soviet general secretary turned president traveled abroad.

As Bush and Gorbachev stepped out of Marine One, they were announced and "piped aboard" Camp David; that is, a ship's bell from a U.S. destroyer was rung in the traditional manner. It was a historic bell, for the ship from which it was taken had been part of a convoy that took President Roosevelt to Yalta during World War II in a far different time of Soviet-U.S. relations.

I joined Mikhail Sergeyevich at the foot of the helicopter steps. In response to my question how he felt after the flight, he said he was delighted and enjoyed every minute of it, and with George aboard, he had never feared for his safety. He once admitted that he was not fond of helicopters, and it had taken some persuading on the part of Bush to woo him into Marine One, over the objections of Plekhanov. Gorbachev and Bush may have breached some security rules by flying in the same chopper, but Bush had impressed upon his advisers that it was important to show Gorbachev America from the air so that he could see for himself how beautiful it is. Gorbachev wore a light beige suit. Bush was dressed in gray flannel slacks and a navy blue blazer. Both leaders wore ties, although Bush had asked everyone to leave formal clothes behind in Washington. Bush was said to be never more at ease than when he could play the gracious host at his "dacha" at Camp David, and this was meant to be sort of a private visit. Still, he and Gorbachev wore ties for the benefit of reporters. They would come off once we were inside the presidential retreat.

Reporters immediately fired questions at Bush, asking him about the day's agenda. When he ignored them, they turned to Gorbachev, and I had to shout as I began to translate Gorbachev's remarks so the reporters could hear me better. They wanted to know what ground the presidents intended to cover in their discussions that day. Gorbachev didn't have to be coaxed into talking to reporters. He answered that he and the president were planning to "take a walk all over the planet" and its "hot spots," that is to say, to discuss regional issues and conflicts. Bush interjected they might first "take a walk" on one of Camp David's "lovely trails," and with these words he shepherded everyone off to the golf carts waiting nearby.

Bill Hopkins and I had been put on notice by protocol people that under no circumstances should we try to get in the golf cart with the presidents. "President Bush must be photographed driving President Gorbachev alone, without interpreters," they said. The idea was to create a photo op for history "without any extraneous factors." So Bill and I kept our distance. But when both presidents climbed on board, Bush turned back and shouted, "Why are you standing there, guys? Come on, get in! How can we talk without you?"

Indeed, how could they? Upon hearing those words, the protocol people looked visibly unhappy—all their planning had just gone overboard. Bill and I shrugged and climbed aboard. As soon as we took the rather uncomfortable seats in the rear of the golf cart, Bush issued a command, "Forward, march!" and with his foot pressing on the gas pedal, the cart began to pick up speed.

Perhaps recalling how much Leonid Brezhnev loved speeding around the narrow roads of Camp David in the Lincoln Continental that he had been given by Richard Nixon during his visit there in 1973, Bush asked Gorbachev if he wanted to drive. When the staid Mikhail Sergeyevich demurred, Bush thrust out his hand signaling all golf carts to proceed into the woods and to the log cabins beyond. Our golf cart began a smooth ascent up the hillside and slipped into the greenery, leaving the reporters behind. The two first ladies, the security, and the presidents' personal photographers followed in other carts, including the two men with the "footballs" in their laps.

A few minutes later, Bush pulled up at a house that he called Birch Lodge. It had obviously been selected for the Gorbachevs for its name, since they came from a country where the birch tree is almost a national symbol. Bush explained that the lodge was assigned especially for "President and Mrs. Gorbachev" so they could "freshen up and change into something informal." And, of course, they could relax there as long as they wanted—there was "no need to rush," he added. By now Raisa Maximovna and Mrs. Bush, who drove her golf cart, had arrived at Birch Lodge. Then, Bush continued, they could either drive or walk a few hundred feet down to join him and Barbara at Aspen Lodge—the presidential retreat. Bush then invited Bill and me to take a walk with him to Aspen Lodge.

Camp David is actually a Navy installation. The 143-acre camp is usually used for presidential recreation, but has sometimes been the scene of high-level diplomacy. President Roosevelt, who chose the site and inaugurated the camp in 1942, christened the cool, wooded retreat Shangri-La. He huddled there secretly with Winston Churchill during World War II to devise strategy for the D-day invasion. The legend goes that Sir Winston was once seen in a local tavern at a neighboring village, wearing a bathrobe and working a slot machine. The facts are, as history recorded them, that Churchill was fully dressed and drinking a Coca-Cola. He strolled over to the jukebox, dropped in a coin, and played "The Beer Barrel Polka."

Located an hour's drive from Washington, and nowadays a twenty-five-minute helicopter ride, the camp over the years has received some thirty heads of state and witnessed several epochal events. In 1959, after President Eisenhower had renamed the retreat for his grandson David, Nikita Khrushchev was invited there in an effort to mend the relationship between the United States and the Soviet Union. From those talks, the phrase *spirit of Camp David* was coined to describe what was thought to be a friendlier attitude toward world problems. Initially, however, Nikita Sergeyevich was offended at being invited to what he thought was some makeshift camp in the woods, something along the lines of a Soviet *kemping* (campsite) where visitors who were not accorded full honors were quarantined. When he learned that, to the contrary, it was a mark of distinction to be invited to the American president's "dacha," where visitors, whether foreign or domestic, were rarely admitted, he accepted Eisenhower's invitation.

They say that the Kennedys did not frequent Camp David, but President Johnson liked "to get away from the noise and carbon monoxide of downtown Washington" for "a clearer view of national horizons." It was also a favorite spot for President Nixon, who hosted foreign heads of state at the compound on eleven occasions, including Leonid Brezhnev in 1973. But Camp David's moment of greatest glory came when Jimmy Carter used it in 1978 as the site to launch the negotiations that eventually culminated in a historic peace accord between Prime Minister Menachem Begin of Israel and President Anwar Sadat of Egypt.

Throughout the Reagan era, many of the president's weekly radio broadcasts originated from Camp David, and the Bushes, too, were said to make frequent use of the facilities.

*   *   *

Aspen Lodge turned out to be an unassuming one-story clapboard house painted olive green. It looked rather like a well-made Russian *izba* (a peasant house made of logs). If one didn't know it was the presidential retreat, one would pass it by without a second glance. As we approached the lodge, a beautiful red dog with white spots ran out from around the corner and threw itself under the president's feet. The president introduced the dog as "Millie, otherwise known as the first dog." Millie was followed by Ranger, "the son of Millie," as the president put it. I observed that the mother and son were as like as two peas. But the president disagreed: "Not to me."

Inside, the lodge, with its beamed ceilings, wood-paneled walls, and big windows that looked out on the forest, was spacious and well-appointed. The furniture was in the early-American style; and one window ran the entire length of the spacious drawing room. It overlooked a sun-drenched deck that offered a view of a spacious putting green below, with a gently sloping descent toward the woods. To the right side of the deck and a couple of steps down was a swimming pool in the form of the number 8. Two sofas, arranged in an L-shape, were placed at a direct angle to the window. A few easy chairs were also placed all over the room. The furniture was upholstered in an unobtrusive flowered fabric. In the left part of the house was a small but well-equipped kitchen with a door opening right into the living room. Next to the kitchen was a large round table for six. The chairs were not fancy, but comfortable. And everywhere in the room there were pictures, lots of pictures in all kinds of frames: on tables, in cabinets, on bookshelves, and on the walls. The photographs were personal, from the family album: the president and Mrs. Bush together; the president, Mrs. Bush, and their children; the president, Mrs. Bush, and a multitude of their grandchildren—altogether thirteen. The president fishing with a rod. The president aiming a hunter's rifle.

There was little to remind visitors that the resident of the house was none other than the president of the United States. I could see why Bush enjoyed spending weekends at this place.

The Gorbachevs had not arrived at the lodge yet, and the president invited Bill and me to the sundeck "to enjoy the view." He suggested we change into something less formal, but neither Bill nor I had really expected such informality and had not brought any casual clothes. To get into the Camp David spirit of things, however, we removed our suit jackets and ties. At Bush's gentle prodding, Marshal Akhromeyev, who now joined us, reluctantly took off his jacket and tie, too. A valet carried the jackets away. Then Bush excused himself—he said it was now time for *him* to change into something more casual. He soon reemerged in a white jersey polo shirt, gray casual slacks, and a pair of sneakers. Then Baker and Shevardnadze (who was accommodated at Dogwood Lodge) appeared on the deck together. Like Bush, Baker wore gray slacks and a sky-blue polo shirt. Shevardnadze, like his compatriots, was in his shirt-sleeves but without tie—he had not expected such informality either.

Originally Bush had asked Gorbachev to stay overnight at Camp David, but Gorbachev agreed to only ten hours or so and asked to be taken back to Washington by nightfall. He was worried about developments back home and didn't want to stay out of touch for any lengthy time.

While waiting for the Gorbachevs, Bush went back into the house and brought out a tennis ball. He began to throw it for Ranger. Or maybe it was Millie. Ranger (if, indeed, it was him) chased the ball and brought it back to his master holding it between his teeth. He kept fetching it until the president threw the ball into the swimming pool. The "son of the first dog" ran around the pool wagging his tail, but stopped short of jumping in. "Look," said Bush, "if Barbara comes now, she will forbid him to go in the water." Indeed, Mrs. Bush appeared just as the dog was about to jump in and reprimanded him.

Finally, Mikhail Sergeyevich and Raisa Maximovna arrived, holding hands. She was now dressed in cotton, flowered summer slacks and a dark blouse. Belying her fifty-eight years, she looked youthful and slender— she obviously took good care of herself. Gorbachev had changed into gray slacks and a navy blue pullover. Bush took one look at him and went into the house. A minute later he came back with a short-sleeved white shirt with a logo that said "President" and gave it to Gorbachev. It was close to noon and was getting hot now even here in the mountains. Gorbachev took off his pullover, but did not put on Bush's gift. I thought he felt somewhat constrained to try it on in the presence of others.

Despite Bush's best efforts to put his guests at ease, they still did not feel at home. Drinks were served and then Bush went into the house again and brought out his hunting rifle—apparently an object of considerable pride with him—and suggested that Gorbachev try his hand at shooting. Mikhail Sergeyevich politely declined. He said he had not fired a rifle in a long time and was out of practice. Then he added, "As a matter of fact, we should disarm ourselves!" Marshal Akhromeyev interjected, "Disarm—yes, but not to the end." From his dour mien, it was hard to tell whether he meant it as a joke or was serious.

Then Bush took the rifle back to the house and this time brought out a photo album and began to turn the pages. The album contained photographs of some of the most distinguished visitors to Camp David. Bush pointed to a picture of Brezhnev posing in front of his Lincoln Continental. A grinning Gromyko stood nearby. (A smile on Gromyko's face was a rare sight indeed; in fact, as I typed this work on my computer and ran it through the spell check, it would invariably come up with "replace *Gromyko* with *grimace*" wherever the name of Gromyko appeared, thus making these two words synonyms.) "We no longer make such gifts," said Bush, pointing to the Cadillac. "Everything is much more modest now."

"Can you imagine how hard they fought over this car after Brezhnev's death?" Gorbachev said. "They almost killed one another. That's why we don't need such gifts." Of course, "they" referred to members of the Party top *nomenklatura*, who in their infinite greed and arrogance staked claims to the deceased general secretary's worldly possessions, among which were some forty foreign cars, including a Silver Cloud Rolls-Royce. The conversation inevitably turned to Yeltsin. Bush wondered about the "Yeltsin factor" and how it could impact on Gorbachev. He wondered if Gorbachev was willing to cooperate with Yeltsin or if the antagonism between them was too deep.

Before replying to Bush's question, Gorbachev paused, his eyes becoming cloudy, and looking into the distance, he said that in his opinion Yeltsin was an unpredictable man. Oftentimes, he would change his views and positions. He would say one thing and do another. By virtue of his nature he was a "destructor, not a constructor." He had done nothing to turn things around in the two years that he had been the chief Party boss of Moscow, so it was doubtful that he would be able to do anything in one or two more years to change things, as he had been promising. The populist speeches that he made were intended to win the masses over to his side. Those speeches were written for him by some young cooperators who were paid handsomely. But regardless of his personal feelings, he, Gorbachev, stood ready to cooperate with Yeltsin if the latter would act constructively in the interest of the nation.

Gorbachev spoke in a soft voice and a level tone. He sounded detached and unemotional, as if he were trying to analyze the situation as objectively and impartially as he could. But that was not exactly the case, of course. He *was* emotionally involved. For not only his personal prestige was at stake, but his future as well. Later on, in his travels around the United States, he would revert to the subject of Yeltsin many times, and once in a private conversation with me he let his emotions show. Yeltsin was very much on his mind and bothered him a great deal. Gorbachev predicted that people would lose faith in their new found idol after a couple of years when it became clear that he was incapable of doing anything constructive. Bush listened to him pensively, then abruptly switched the subject and began to tell him about Camp David. He was very good at putting people at ease by changing from delicate subjects to something more innocuous.

After more talk, Bush took Gorbachev back into the house and showed him the "facility to freshen up." When Mikhail Sergeyevich emerged from the bathroom, he took an appraising look around the house, expressing admiration for the "high-quality workmanship" and the "well-thought-out arrangement" of objects and furniture. Everything was so spacious, he remarked to me, that there was no danger of "anybody knocking his head against somebody else's in the hallway." What he meant, I suppose, was that Soviet apartments and houses, even those built for the *nomenklatura* or the party and government elite, were so small, cramped, and poorly designed that this house in Camp David seemed like a palace in comparison. Bush invited Gorbachev to the deck table to "make [him]self comfortable" and "to talk about things." It was not a negotiating table in the classical sense—just a simple white, oval-shaped, glass-top patio table with a huge removable sunshade umbrella and six matching chairs. An omnidirectional microphone was installed in the middle of the table for the benefit of simultaneous interpreters, and six small earphones, dubbed "shells" in our professional parlance, had been placed on the tabletop.

Now, in the rustic, informal setting of Camp David, the two leaders, plus their top aides: Baker and Scowcroft, Shevardnadze and Akhromeyev, were ready to discuss regional disputes, including the stalemated civil war in Afghanistan, the conflict in Cambodia, U.S. complaints about Soviet backing for Cuba, and Cuba's role in supporting leftist rebels in El Salvador. It was an incongruous setting to speak of wars and revolutions and bloody conflicts.

The interpreting at this morning round was to be done by Zarechnyak and Palazchenko, who were seated some thirty feet away under a tree at a tiny table with equipment for simultaneous interpretation that was hooked up to the presidential table on the deck. Since I was not interpreting, I went to explore Holly and Hawthorn, the two adjacent lodges situated, like all the other lodges, within the compound among trees and well-tended shrubs. Holly Lodge is famous as the place where Churchill stayed in 1942 when he paid a secret visit to Camp David. There, I found the other fellow interpreters who, like me, were temporarily "out of business." We caught the latest CNN news report—the reporters were speculating about what exactly was going on inside Camp David, but no one really knew.

By one o'clock, we, the interpreters, went back to Aspen Lodge to see what was happening. The security agents, who stood at some distance from the deck watching the two presidents and their advisers, told us the talks were still in progress, but it looked as if round one would come to an end any minute now. Indeed, at precisely 1 P.M., Bush suggested they interrupt the talks for lunch, to be followed by a period of rest. The talks would then reconvene starting at 3:30 P.M. By this time the two first ladies had returned from a golf-cart trip around the compound. Bush had given advance notice that lunch would be light, since dinner would be hosted sometime later for the Gorbachevs and others in his party who were due to arrive at five o'clock. Raisa Maximovna was clearly disappointed. She whispered to Mikhail Sergeyevich that she was starved after the morning ride in the woods, but he counseled her to be patient and wait for dinner.

"Light lunch" turned out to be hot sorrel soup and seafood served with white Texas wine. Then there were mixed salads, and finally excellent "homemade" ice cream.

The table talk was mostly small. Gorbachev told about his three-year-old granddaughter, *"Nasten'ka"* (little Anastasia). According to him, she would hide herself under the table whenever she took umbrage at someone or something. She was "so funny!" People around the table smiled when he complained that "her grandmother" (who sat on President Bush's right) had spoiled the child by indulging her little caprices. Smiles turned to laughter when Gorbachev told how the little girl enjoyed teasing him about Sobchak, the mayor of Leningrad, who had scored a few political points by publicly criticizing Gorbachev and especially his prime minister, Nikolai Ryzhkov. "Granddad! Granddad! There's your Sobchak again!" she would shout at the top of her voice whenever he appeared on TV.

The story put Bush in a pensive frame of mind and he turned serious. He began to question Gorbachev about Sobchak and Popov (the latter was the mayor of Moscow) and their prospects as national political figures. Gorbachev answered with some reluctance, clearly trying to evade the questions. "The nearest future will show," he concluded, using the well-worn Soviet cliché. Clearly, he did not find the subject to his liking. James Baker the Pragmatic came to his rescue. He started questioning Gorbachev about the state of the Soviet economy, but above all he wanted to know if legislation to permit the sale of land would be passed anytime soon. Gorbachev livened up. No, he said, the question of selling land was not on the agenda as yet, although in practical terms major emphasis was being put on land leasing. He admitted that, as before, the leaseholder still depended on *kolkhozy* (collective farms) because the latter had heavy equipment and machinery at their disposal, such as tractors, harvesters, etc., without which the leaseholder simply could not work the land. However, large stations were to be built that would rent out tractors and other heavy equipment and would repair the equipment owned by leaseholders.

Baker listened with a skeptical expression on his face. "The experience of agricultural development in the United States and other Western countries shows that realistically it is hardly possible to achieve prosperity without having the possibility of buying and selling land," he said.

Gorbachev warmed up to the subject. Once he began to speak about something important to him, especially agriculture, of which he had been in charge at one point in his career, he could not stop. He spoke of the psychology of the Russians, in whose minds the spirit of collectivism had been inculcated for many decades, thus stifling their initiative, their ability to think for themselves. So a whole revolution would have to be carried out in this respect, he concluded. I would hear this theme from him many more times, including in private conversations.

Not long before this visit to the United States, in one of his appearances on Soviet television, he told the story of his trip to Sverdlovsk and Chelyabinsk, the two major cities in the Urals. Obviously carried away by the things he was talking about, he casually remarked, as if in passing, that people from a *kolkhoz* near Chelyabinsk had burned alive a leaseholder simply because he was beginning to prosper. Realizing, however, that he had probably said too much, he abruptly stopped and changed the subject. Now he recounted the same story as an illustration of how difficult it was to change the psychology of people.

After lunch Bush asked Gorbachev if he wanted to get his hands on the wheel and drive a golf cart himself. "*Pochemu bi i net? Ya ved' staryi mekhanizator!*" (Why not? I am an old-time machine operator), Gorbachev exclaimed with brio. (He was referring to the time when he worked the fields as a young boy.) Bush, Gorbachev, Zarechnyak, and I got into the presidential golf cart that was parked in front of the entrance to Aspen Lodge. Mikhail Sergeyevich got behind the wheel, asking Bush to show the way, and stepped on the gas. At first, he drove gingerly. The cart zigged and zagged until he mastered the controls. But then Mikhail

Sergeyevich floored the pedal, the cart lurched forward, and at one sharp turn it began to career. I grabbed the frame with one hand, ready to jump out for dear life. I saw Bush getting tense. Obviously, he, too, felt the cart was about to tip over. Fortunately, all ended well. Mikhail Sergeyevich quickly regained control, applying the brakes just in time to keep us from crashing into a tree. Bush looked slightly shaken and a little pale, but otherwise none the worse for the experience.

After Mikhail Sergeyevich recovered his breath, he displayed his sense of humor: "I hope I will not be accused of an attempt on the life of the president of the United States."

There was another tense moment when Mikhail Sergeyevich started to back up the cart to make a U-turn on the narrow trail and almost hit the tree behind. We all took it stoically. Bush pointed the way down a narrow trail toward yet another lodge with a large swimming pool and suggested stopping there. The marine guards who protected Camp David trained here. Bush took Gorbachev inside. Well-built, muscular young men were exercising on all kinds of equipment, lifting weights, doing karate chops, etc. Bush introduced Gorbachev to their coach, a young-looking, sinewy sergeant. Mikhail Sergeyevich remarked that he seemed too young to be a coach, to which the sergeant replied, with a sense of dignity, that he was already thirty-five years old, "an old man, really, sir." Then Bush introduced the Soviet president to all the other members of the team by their first names. It was amazing how he could remember them all. The secret was simple, however, he told Gorbachev. He exercised with them every time he came to Camp David.

Bush then took Gorbachev to a treadmill and demonstrated his impressive fitness by walking on it fast even at a steep angle. Then he suggested that Gorbachev do the same, but apparently Mikhail Sergeyevich was somewhat out of shape, because after two or three minutes on the treadmill, he was out of breath. He said he preferred riding a floor bicycle because "it's easier." Bush led him to a bicycle nearby, and Mikhail Sergeyevich evened up the score by pedaling long and hard. After this, we returned in the same golf cart to Birch Lodge, where Bush suggested getting some rest before the afternoon's "chat."

The meeting on the deck at Aspen Lodge reconvened at 3:30 P.M., as agreed, and with the same participants: Bush, Baker, and Scowcroft on one side; Gorbachev, Shevardnadze, and Akhromeyev on the other. I was supposed to do the interpreting this time, but Shevardnadze personally reassigned me to take notes instead. It appeared that neither he nor Gorbachev trusted their official notetaker for the Soviet side, Akhromeyev. First of all, the venerable marshal had probably not wielded a pen in the past quarter of a century for anything other than signing orders. He was used to giving orders, not taking notes. More importantly, however, Shevardnadze hinted that the marshal was prone to skew things for his own purposes, and anyway, he was always reluctant to share his notes with the Foreign Ministry, and when he did, they were never complete, and for all those reasons he could hardly be relied upon for accuracy.

I pulled a chaise longue up to the "negotiating" table and found myself seated between Baker and Akhromeyev.

Round two of the informal talks was on. Bush's description of the talks as "just a chat" was perhaps more accurate, for they were held in a nonconfrontational spirit, like an amiable discussion among friends who had achieved a great degree of understanding and had only minor differences to iron out. The two leaders were seemingly sharing their thoughts out loud, without in any way attempting to impose their views upon each other.

Little by little, in response to the atmosphere on that sun-drenched deck, I could almost see Gorbachev relax and could sense the emerging feeling of trust and even empathy between the two presidents. In time, it was bound to lead to something close to partnership in the management of difficult world problems, and it did—in a short while—in the context of Iraq's invasion of Kuwait.

Bush got the ball rolling by asking Gorbachev why nationalism was so rampant in the Soviet Union today. Gorbachev replied that Stalin had created a unitary state and centralism. He did not allow the development of national languages in all the republics, and as a result, resentment began to grow. The resentment developed into nationalism, which gave birth to separatism. Stalin brutally suppressed every manifestation of nationalism everywhere. Even in Georgia. "How did he do it?" asked Bush. "After all, there were cultural traditions, national holidays and so on."

"He did it by revoking their autonomy, both political and economic," responded Gorbachev. "And then he declared there were no more nationalities problems. Under Brezhnev and Andropov this was the slogan: 'Soviet people are one single entity.' It made the situation even worse. And now all this has spilled out into the open."

After a pause, Bush turned to the subject at hand, the regional issues.

First was Afghanistan. Even though Moscow had withdrawn its forces from that country by February 1989, as Gorbachev had promised, i.e., almost one and a half years before, the conflict there continued unabated. Rival factions were now fighting for power among themselves. And both Moscow and Washington continued to give military aid to the warring parties.

Bush and Gorbachev discussed ways of helping the warring parties reach a political settlement, set up a neutral and nonaligned regime that would not be radical, hostile, or detrimental either to the Soviet Union or the United States, and establish a broad-based coalition government or a transitional authority during a U.N.-supervised transitional period to organize elections. Bush assured Gorbachev, for the first time, that the United States would then be ready to consider stopping its military aid and withdrawing its military equipment from Afghanistan—to send a clear message that serious efforts were being made to end the conflict. The hang-up, however, was the resistance forces, or the mujahedeen, who were opposed to Najibullah, the president of Afghanistan, installed by Gorbachev's predecessors. Gorbachev conceded he and his people were having a hard time with Najibullah, who had lately been making increasing demands on Moscow. But a transitional authority, in Gorbachev's view, should start the election mechanism, and that was the most important thing at this stage. Baker floated the suggestion that in the meantime Najibullah should perhaps play the role of "acting president," so as to show the Afghan resistance that the transitional authority would be real. Najibullah knew that after the elections he would have to step down, because by his own estimate he controlled only 35 percent of the population, while 65 percent were under the control of the mujaheddin, and that meant that he would hardly be reelected president.

The important thing was that Bush and Gorbachev agreed that the Afgans themselves should elect a coalition government. They further agreed that such elections "should be organized and held in the Afghan style," i.e., without any imposition from outside, as had been done in Angola and Nicaragua, but with the U.N. and the Islamic Conference playing a full role. Both leaders further agreed that during the supervised transitional period Najibullah could stay in office and even participate in the elections, because he had a right to, but he should be cautioned not take advantage of this to strengthen his hand. The key to success was compromise on all sides.

Next the two presidents discussed Ethiopia. Tens of thousands of people were dying there of hunger caused by a drought and the civil war over Eritrea, a province that had been fighting to secede from Ethiopia. Bush and Gorbachev discussed ways of resuming food shipments for the starving people, which had been interrupted because of the intensified hostilities. The presidents drafted a joint appeal for humanitarian relief and agreed that American humanitarian relief supplies would be delivered by Soviet planes. The joint operation would be a gesture to illustrate the two superpowers' concern for the plight of the starving people.

After Ethiopia, they discussed South Africa, where President de Klerk and opposition leader Nelson Mandela were advocating peaceful negotiations to eliminate apartheid. The Soviet and U.S. presidents felt they could contribute to a peaceful development there, then they turned to Angola, where they agreed to call for elections and national reconciliation after a long civil war.

On Korea, Gorbachev and Bush agreed that South and North Korea should seek a peaceful dialogue to solve the problem of reunification. Gorbachev pointed out that the first political step toward this goal had been taken by the United States when it announced the reduction of its forces in South Korea, which had been present there under the U.N. flag since 1950. Like Bush, he expressed his concern over the absence of an agreement between the IAEA (International Atomic Energy Agency) and the PDRK (People's Democratic Republic of Korea) regarding IAEA nuclear safeguards designed to prevent the proliferation of nuclear weapons. North Korea was trying to build a nuclear bomb, and this was exacerbating the already tense situation in the Korean peninsula.

Gorbachev said Moscow was seeking ways to cooperate with South Korea in the economic sphere. This had caused North Korea to react nervously, "although," said Gorbachev, "we told Kim Il Sung [the PDRK leader], 'Nothing is changing . . . our informal contacts with South Korea do not constitute diplomatic recognition, but are merely a reconnaissance to promote dialogue.' " Moscow still provided economic aid to the North Korean regime by helping it build nuclear reactors. Bush said he was concerned about Kim Il Sung's actions and intentions. The North Korean leader did not show any signs of moderation or desire for openness. He had an enormous military force at his disposal and instigated instability in the peninsula. Bush said that he and his advisers believed that Gorbachev was doing a positive thing by trying to cooperate with South Korea. The discussion of the sensitive subject of the two Koreas was inconclusive, however.

"The walk across the hot spots of the globe," as Gorbachev put it, did not bring any immediate solutions to regional issues, but it was certainly an important step toward a meeting of minds.

The talk was definitely a success in building trust between the two leaders. This was due in no small measure to Bush's ability to persuade the meticulous Gorbachev to loosen up and shed some of his wariness along with his suit jacket as they sat chatting on the veranda of Aspen Lodge. As Gorbachev would later admit to me in a private conversation,

"Well, this Bush! He is really good at putting people in the right frame of mind." History was made that day in the way diplomatic talks were conducted.

At the end of the day about thirty more Soviet and American officials flew up in helicopters from Washington for an early dinner hosted by the Bushes. Before joining them, however, Bush took Gorbachev for a walk to practice with him what might be called horseshoe diplomacy. "Come with me. I'll show you the trails and a playground," Bush said, and led the way down a narrow path through the putting green into the forest. They were trailed by a small army of security agents. Soon they reached the playground, equipped with parallel bars and a pit for horseshoes—the President's favorite game. Bush suggested that Gorbachev try his luck first.

Gorbachev took a horseshoe, aimed, tossed it, and . . . hit a ringer on his first try. It was the first time in his life that he had played the game. I had never seen him so relaxed as at this moment. Bush, rumored to be supremely competitive, was visibly impressed. Ironically, he himself missed a ringer.

After Gorbachev's triumph, Bush announced that he was hungry and, taking Gorbachev by the arm, steered him toward Laurel Lodge where dinner was to be hosted. All the newly arrived officials, both Soviet and American, wore suits and ties despite Bush's insistence all along that ties were not necessary.

Laurel Lodge is a spacious log cabin with a conference room, a living room, and a dining room. It was used, as Bush explained to Gorbachev, to receive larger groups of people, both for talks and for informal lunches or dinners.

Before dinner began, at 6:15 P.M., aperitifs were served during a "happy hour" to help the Soviets and Americans socialize. The guests and the hosts broke up into small knots, and soon the reception room was a steady din of sounds. At dinner, which was informal, Bush complained in his speech, "I wanna tell you, these meetings haven't been all sweetness and light. It's very important for me to do well in sports. I like to win. So you can imagine how I felt when I learned that my visitor— throwing a horseshoe for the first time—got a ringer." Then Bush reached under the table, pulled out the "lucky" horseshoe, hastily mounted on a plaque, and presented it to Gorbachev amid general laughter. Gorbachev responded that he would hang it over the door of his home "for luck," as Russian custom demanded.

After dinner, Gorbachev took Bush aside and asked me to tell him he wanted to discuss something important, "in private." Bush said, "Of course, no problem," and suggested that we step out onto the veranda. Gorbachev asked if credits might be available. He assured Bush that he was ready, of course, to get them on general conditions and pay the interest—"everything as it should be." The country badly needed credits, he said, and *he* really needed them. The figure he mentioned, several billion dollars, made Bush pensive.

After some reflection, Bush responded that he saw a political problem with Gorbachev's request, namely Lithuania. But he hoped that the business community would go along with providing credits, in spite of this problem, if they were sure reforms would be in place. Bush said that he had invited bankers and prominent businessmen to the White House dinner two nights before so they could hear firsthand how things were in the Soviet Union regarding the implementation of reforms. In short, he said, he would try to talk about it with the people concerned.

The dinner was now over, and the guests began to file out of Laurel Lodge onto the veranda. It was 7:50 P.M. and time to go back to Washington.

Before they left Camp David, Bush took Gorbachev back to Aspen Lodge "to freshen up." Bush put on a jacket and a tie, saying he didn't want to appear in casual dress in front of reporters. Gorbachev also put on his suit jacket "to look decent in front of those reporters," who waited for them outside the Camp David gate. Then he couldn't find his tie, so I lent him mine.

Bush asked Gorbachev if he wanted to drive the golf cart again so the reporters outside would get his picture at the wheel—it would be a great photo op. Gorbachev did not have to be coaxed. He got behind the wheel and this time drove more confidently and not so fast. Practice makes perfect. When we arrived at the front gate, Bush suggested that Gorbachev turn the cart around in front of the reporters—"they'll go wild over it." Mikhail Sergeyevich knew the name of the game and, skillfully executing a smart U-turn, pulled up right in front of the amazed crowd of reporters. They cheered him wildly, as the president had promised.

Then, the two presidents answered several questions that the reporters shouted at them. They all wanted to know how the day had passed. Gorbachev stressed that in the discussions with Bush throughout the day they had established a personal rapport—something important for a constructive approach to solving problems. "It was an important day" to him personally. Bush agreed with Gorbachev's assessment. He expressed optimism about future cooperation in dealing with the world's problems. He believed that the situation did not appear as if "the glass is half-empty," but rather as if "it is half-full, and even more than half." Of course, they had not solved all the problems in one day, but to him the important thing was that they had a lot of common ground, that they did not accent the differences, but looked at the problems in hopes of developing a common position and finding common solutions. The only thing that was wrong and had upset him, admitted Bush, was that the Soviet president had beat him at his own game of horseshoes on his first ever try.

As Mikhail Sergeyevich answered questions, I had to shout while translating his answers—there was too much noise from the reporters. When it was Bush's turn to answer, I translated his responses simultaneously into Gorbachev's ear, but I did it loudly enough so that Raisa Maximovna, who stood next to him, could hear my translation, too. She always wanted to be in the know.

Marine One took off at 8:30 P.M., and all the other helicopters followed a couple of minutes later, one after another, taking the hosts and their guests back to Washington. We arrived in Washington at nine. Upon his return to the Embassy, Gorbachev convened all his advisers and briefed them on his "informal chats" with Bush. He said he was pleased and satisfied with the events of the day. Our interpreters' troika, Palazchenko, Berezhkov—who, too, had been a notetaker in Camp David talks—and myself, labored until two o'clock in the morning, dictating our notes to the Embassy typists. Mikhail Sergeyevich wanted to see the transcript on his table first thing early in the morning. As far as I know, the officially designated "notetaker," Marshal Akhromeyev, never showed his transcript to Shevardnadze.

WASHINGTON. JUNE 3, SUNDAY. DAY FIVE.

The final event of the summit, a joint press conference, took place this beautiful Sunday morning. In the history of Soviet-U.S. summits, this was the second joint Soviet-U.S. presidential conference (the first was in Malta six months before). Gorbachev and Reagan had never held joint press conferences.

Now, Gorbachev and Bush sat side by side at an imposing table in the East Room of the White House, facing the reporters and cameras. For me, this was an exciting moment, perhaps the crowning performance of my career as a simultaneous interpreter. Not only did I have the honor of interpreting what the leader of one of the world's two most powerful nations had to say to probably his largest audience ever—the press conference was broadcast live on radio and television around the world—but I did it into English, and that was a special thrill. The greatest difficulty, perhaps, in translating Gorbachev was his uncanny ability to *plesti kruzheva*, to "weave the lace," as he himself put it once so elegantly.

After the press conference, when Gorbachev got off the podium, one of the reporters asked him if he was going to take his horseshoe home and throw it at his pesky rival, Boris Yeltsin. Gorbachev smiled mischievously, enjoying the image. I translated his answer: "No, I will leave it at home, but remember this—I got a ringer on my first try, so I am a pretty good shot." And then, after the farewell ceremony with a twenty-one-gun salute, an honor guard, a red carpet—in short the whole works—the Gorbachevs were off, in their customized presidential jetliner, Il-62M, on an unofficial visit to the Twin Cities of Minnesota.

The trip to the Twin Cities was in part a romantic excursion into the American heartland, a chance for the Gorbachevs for the first time to see something of America. It was also conceived as a lesson in capitalism for Gorbachev. It was all about money—how to make it, use it, trade it, sell it, and spread it around in the market. Gorbachev was expected to pick up some free-market tips from visiting a working farm and Control Data, the mainframe-computer maker. One important event in the Gorbachevs' seven-hour whirlwind tour was Mikhail Sergeyevich's address to leading American businessmen, including such magnates as Dwayne Andreas, Donald Kendall, Lee Iacocca, and Roger Smith.

In his speech Gorbachev told the executives that they need not fear investing in the Soviet Union while the country was undergoing economic reform, although he acknowledged that *perestroika* had produced difficulties. "Those companies that remain on the sidelines now will remain observers for years to come," he told them. He urged his audience to be patient while the Soviet Union developed financial and legal mechanisms: "Please understand that certain things that you have had for decades, perhaps even centuries, are new to us. We are just beginning." One thing Gorbachev didn't talk about was that communism was better than capitalism, as Khrushchev had done some thirty years before.

It was amazing to hear some of the businessmen at this meeting propose a number of concrete projects for cooperation only two days after Bush and Gorbachev had signed the trade agreement in Washington. American businessmen took the bull by the horns right away. Of course, it is one thing to propose and another to dispose. A multitude of obstacles were still in the way of such cooperation.

Perhaps the most remarkable aspect of Gorbachev's trip to the Twin Cities was the incredibly warm welcome he received from Minnesotans. Braving the cool, forty-nine-degree, gray, drizzling weather that strangely enough was known in these parts, according to our host, Minnesota governor Rudy Perpich, as a "Siberian cold front," Mikhail Sergeyevich and Raisa Maximovna created a sensation wherever they went.

Surrounded everywhere by screaming, adoring crowds with TV and video cameras who chanted, "Gorby, Gorby," including one man on stilts dressed as Uncle Sam and waving a Soviet flag, Gorbachev accomplished what he needed to. He won the West, or at least the Midwest, without a shot.

Several times in his visit Gorbachev stopped his motorcade so he could clamber out of the Zil and shake hands with eager, cheering Minnesotans. At one stop, two admirers handed Raisa Maximovna a sign that featured a heart and the message "We love Mikhail and Raisa Gorbachev." Other people offered other encouraging words on the placards they held high along the motorcade route: "Go *Glasnost*," "President Gorbachev, Keep Hope Alive," "We're With You, Gorby." One sign defied adequate translation, it lauded Gorbachev as a "Cool Dude."

There were a lot of signs in Russian. One said, *Gorby, zarulivai k nam na vecherinku* (Gorby, drop by for a party). When Gorbachev read it, he remembered a sign he saw out of his car window on the way from the airport in Ottawa. It said, also in Russian, *Gospodin Gorbachev, zakhodite na pivo k nam. Besplatno!* (Mr. Gorbachev, stop in for a beer. It's free!). Mikhail Sergeyevich regretted then that he saw the sign too late. Otherwise, he said, he would have stopped the car and dropped in. Then there was an unexpected sign in Russian: *Ot zagnivayuschego kapitalizma k protsvetayuschemu sotsialismu!* (From decaying capitalism to thriving socialism). Another sign next to it read, *Gospodin Gorbachev, kapitalism zagnivayet, a kak pakhnet!* (Mr. Gorbachev, capitalism is decaying, but how sweetly it smells!).

Finally, there was this sign: *KGB ubiyitsa narodov!* (KGB is the murderer of peoples). In reaction to this placard, Raisa Maximovna rolled down the window in defiance of all security regulations and stuck out the sign that somebody had given her earlier: "Gorby and Raisa, we love you!" The crowd went wild with delight. She enjoyed the episode so much that later, even in Moscow, she would recount it again and again.

Most of the time, Raisa Maximovna just kept both her hands pressed against the window on the other side of the car. "Gorby, go home!" she read aloud when the car passed by one of the signs. Mikhail Sergeyevich asked me, "What does it mean?" I said it meant that he wasn't welcome here *(otpravlyatsya vosvoyasi)*. But Raisa Maximovna demurred, "Why, no! Maybe they mean to say they realize how tired Mikhail Sergeyevich is and advise him to go home to rest." As if to prove her point, she added, "Look, they are holding this slogan with one hand, while with the other they are waving at us in friendly greeting." Mikhail Sergeyevich was confused by this interesting interpretation.

I noticed that M.S. often acted either on impulse or at the urging of Raisa Maximovna. "*Mikhal Sergeich,* go out. You must mingle with *people,* not only with officials. People love you," she would say each time at an opportune moment. She was undoubtedly "the woman behind the successful man." Whatever people might have said about her, she was a real friend and even a mentor to her husband.

M.S. asked me to alert him when I saw the largest crowd, so he could stop to pump hands. I did so when I spotted a large crowd of several thousand people, somewhere near the state capitol in St. Paul. Some Baltic-American nationalists in the crowd were waving Lithuanian, Estonian, and Latvian flags. They chanted, "*Da* to negotiations! *Nyet* to occupations!" But even they seemed good-natured in their criticism. A group of young people, who were probably students, standing nearby drowned out their chant with a counterchant from some beer or cigarette commercial, something about "tasting good." Another group included demonstrators who were protesting Soviet policy in Afghanistan and Azerbaijan. Gorbachev ignored them. He stopped the motorcade and plunged into the crowd only when portable highway signs displayed "Welcome to President Gorbachev" in English and Russian. At one point, while extending his hand across the top of his Zil to shake hands with people on the other side of the car, he got it stained—the car top was splashed with dirt from the rain. A woman in the crowd saw it and handed him what she said was a white "gorbychief" to wipe off his hand. I learned later that these handkerchiefs went for three bucks each—a good lesson in capitalism for Gorbachev. The enterprising Americans struck while Gorbachev was hot. Ironically, the handkerchiefs were made . . . in China.

I had followed Gorbachev into crowds several times before, in Washington, London, Bonn, and Ottawa, but nowhere had I witnessed such an enthusiastic and spontaneous welcome as here in the heartland of America. It was something incredible. People were wildly waving hands at Gorbachev, trying to catch his eye. They were reaching out to him, trying to touch him as if he were a deity. And above all, they were shrieking. Especially young people. Gorbachev asked them how they were, how long had they been standing there? Some had been there as long as five hours waiting for him to pass by in the hope of shaking his hand. "I see you're cold," he remarked to one young woman who was dressed in a light summer frock and had turned blue with cold. But the woman was happy: "It's worth it," she replied. The crowd asked, "How do you like it here?" Gorbachev responded, "Very good. It feels just like being at home. Only you live better than we."

At the end of our visit to the Twin Cities we had almost one hour at our disposal, and while the motorcade was circling the airport to while away the time, Mikhail Sergeyevich compared notes with me about the incredibly enthusiastic welcome extended to him by the people of Minnesota. He and Raisa Maximovna sat holding hands in the backseat of the Zil. He was relaxed and informal. He admitted that he had never expected anything like this. The Washingtonians gave him a warm welcome, of course, but the Minnesotans broke all records in terms of hospitality, warmth, and enthusiasm, he said. In general, the Americans were such a spontaneous and ingenuous lot. Unlike other people, they did not feel shy in displaying their emotions. "Hm, look at that!" he would exclaim every time we passed a friendly crowd. And he would shake his head in wonderment.

In the conversation, it came up that Mikhail Sergeyevich and I were *zemlyaki*, that is to say, fellow countrymen from the same part of Russia. I told him I had spent my entire childhood in Kislovodsk, a resort town about one hundred miles from Stavropol, where he had been the Party boss for almost twenty years. He had warm memories of Kislovodsk, he said. He enjoyed visiting it when he was the first Party secretary of the Stavropol region.

The Stavropol region is the main resort area of the country, famous for its mineral spas, watering places, and health resorts. This blessed, sun-kissed land with its mild and dry winters and cool, pleasant summers had a concentration of dachas, sanatoriums, and special medical centers for the *nomenklatura*, which were, of course, inaccessible to the common people. For decades, the Kremlin leaders, apparatchiks from the Communist Party Central Committee, ministers, Party bosses from major cities and regional Party committees, KGB and Army generals, came here to *otdokhnut'* (rest) at the watering places, with their wives and children.

As the region's governor Gorbachev met the most important visitors in person. He accompanied them to their luxurious mansions and visited them from time to time, thus establishing intimate relations with them. In so doing, he collected invaluable information; playing host to the top leaders while they were on vacation was not the same thing as seeing them in Moscow at meetings of the Central Committee being one of the faceless mass of regional and provincial Party secretaries. Andropov was among the top leaders who regularly came to Krasniye Kamni (Red Rocks), a sanatorium for the Party elite in Kislovodsk. In Krasniye Kamni, Andropov usually occupied a secluded residence with tight security. He did not receive anybody, except for his KGB generals and Gorbachev. Thus Gorbachev became a protégé of Andropov, who saw great promise in the relatively young regional Party secretary. When Fyodor Kulakov, the Politburo member in charge of agriculture, died in 1978, Andropov immediately proposed Gorbachev as his successor in the thankless job. By now Gorbachev was firmly associated in the Politburo members' minds with pleasant and useful weeks of rest and vacation. They also remembered that he was exceptionally young by their standards. Why, he was young enough to be their son. Hence he was not dangerous as a rival.

As a result, on the evening of August 19, 1978, a special train bound for Baku made an unexpected stop at the railroad station of Mineralniye Vody, a town not far from Kislovodsk. Leaning on the arm of the chief of his personal bodyguards, Leonid Ilyich Brezhnev himself, accompanied by his top aide, Konstantin Chernenko, stepped out onto the platform, which was surrounded by KGB guards. The party was met by Andropov, who was vacationing in Kislovodsk at the time, and Gorbachev. This historic meeting would radically alter the course of history some dozen years later. The four men who came together in the small railroad station in the North Caucasus that evening were fated to succeed one another in the future as head of the Party and state. One of them was ordained by fate to destroy the Soviet Communist Party. Gorbachev's transfer from Stavropol to Moscow was decided in just a few minutes. Exchanging handshakes with the young secretary from Stavropol, Brezhnev mumbled, "Agriculture is very important. You are a specialist. Save it." Gorbachev said firmly, "I'll do my best."

After brief farewells with Governor Perpich and other officials, we were airborne once again, bound for the City of the Golden Gate Bridge. The clouds had somewhat dissipated by now, and we could see the setting sun. It was almost eight o'clock—5 A.M. by Moscow time.

SAN FRANCISCO. JUNE 3, SUNDAY. SAME DAY.

As soon as the plane was airborne, Mikhail Sergeyevich dozed off. He was exhausted. He roused himself for the brief welcoming ceremony at the San Francisco airport, but when it was over, at close to eleven o'clock at night, all he wanted was to be driven as soon as possible, together with Raisa Maximovna, to the consulate-general, which was to serve as their residence for the night. He did not want any of the officials to accompany him. He simply was not up to it. But to my surprise, he invited me to ride with him and Raisa Maximovna in their car—he knew that I had no independent means of transportation.

On the way to town Mikhail Sergeyevich stifled yawns several times and apologized to me each time he did so. Raisa Maximovna restrained herself. The eleven-hour time difference between San Francisco and Moscow, the morning press conference in Washington, and the hectic events of the day had all taken their toll. It was amazing that he had such stamina. I myself, a younger man, was terribly tired and could hardly wait to go to bed. In spite of being exhausted, however, the Gorbachevs displayed a hefty dose of curiosity about the city where they were to spend one day. They wanted to know more about San Francisco and asked me to tell them everything I could. I stressed that it was considered to be one of the four most beautiful cities in the world, with a year-round even climate, and that it was called a "window on the world," just as Leningrad was called a "window on Europe." We discussed the latest earthquake that had struck the city a year earlier. We talked about the skyscrapers they built in America.

When I mentioned that about half a million people of Russian origin lived in the San Francisco area and there was a place in the city itself known as the Russian Hill, Gorbachev interrupted me, "That's exactly the reason why I decided to come here of all other places in America. I had a choice, of course, as to where to go to. I was advised to go to Hollywood. But what would I do there? One of ours [i.e., one of our people] went there once, and what's the use?" He was obviously alluding to Nikita Khrushchev, who visited Hollywood on his first trip to the United States in 1959 and was not even allowed to see Disneyland, but was shown a cancan instead, which prompted him to observe that "Soviet people prefer to look at a person's face, not at his or her derriere."

"There are many Slavs here, after all," mused Mikhail Sergeyevich. "Genes! It's an amazing thing. They remain for generations. That's why I decided to come here to stir them up." The main purpose of his visit here was not to meet with Slavs, of course, but with a group of powerful California businessmen to convince them to do business with the Soviet Union. On the other hand, he could have done it in Los Angeles just as well, so there must have been something to his nostalgic observation about the Slavic genes. Shortly before we reached the residence,

Mikhail Sergeyevich stifled yet another yawn and asked Medvedev at what time he was supposed to meet with Reagan the next day. Medvedev said it was supposed to be a breakfast scheduled for 9:30 A.M. Gorbachev thought for a while and then said that the breakfast should be canceled and the meeting with the Reagans moved to ten o'clock and shortened to no more than half an hour. He and Raisa Maximovna were too tired, he said, to begin the day so early.

When the Reagans were mentioned, Raisa Maximovna touched my arm, indicating she was addressing me and wanted my individual attention, and unexpectedly began to speak about Nancy. I sensed that the subject of the American former first lady still touched a raw nerve in her, and that in spite of her fatigue she needed to express herself to someone who had indirectly witnessed the evolution of their relationship over several years. "You know," she began, "last time they wrote so much about her and me not getting along, making it seem like we almost hate each other. This is really absurd. What have we got to do with that? Why, we don't know any state secrets. We have nothing to share between the two of us. We are so different. She does her own thing and I do mine. It really is absurd what they wrote about us. And what do *you* think, Igor Dmitriyevich?" she asked, turning to face me. I squirmed in my seat.

I responded that one had to understand the way the mass media operated in Western countries, especially in America. Such personalities as the first ladies of the two superpowers could not fail to evoke enormous public interest, and for that reason the mass media followed every step they made in the hope of generating a scoop to attract their readers or viewers. Such stories helped sell the papers after all. People were interested in gossip—people were people. "Yes," she said, "but why should they make up things? She and I, we are not leaders. We are just wives."

"Tomorrow we are going to meet again," she continued. "But I don't know what we should talk about. I wonder what she is doing nowadays." Those were her last words on the delicate subject. Mikhail Sergeyevich smiled like a sphinx but said nothing.

As the car sped along, I drew their attention to the road, which was divided into lanes that were separated by protruding metallic bumps. Seeing a puzzled look on their faces, I explained that these were to improve safety—the bumps helped keep drivers awake. Raisa Maximovna observed that nothing of the kind existed in the Soviet Union. "American marvels," remarked Mikhail Sergeyevich.

Even here inside the car we could smell that the air was suffused with the distinctive fragrance of California, which prompted Raisa Maximovna to ask the driver to roll down the window so she could "inhale it deeper." Whenever she wanted to say or ask something, she would touch me by the arm or incline her head toward mine to catch my attention. Occasionally, she would address me by my first name and patronymic. Mikhail Sergeyevich on the other hand always preferred to address his associates by their first names (if he knew them well, that is), using the second-person singular *ty* (you), like *tu* in French, rather than *vous*. The striking thing was that during private moments like this the first couple of the Soviet Union was totally devoid of what was aptly described by somebody as *komchvanstvo* (Communist conceit or arrogance), a malaise so characteristic of most Soviet leaders of the past. The two of them behaved as normal people. They were not like those pompous automatons who look down on their subordinates or simply do not stoop to talk to them. In my professional life I had met many such people among Soviet leaders.

By now the motorcade had reached the consul general's residence on one of the many hills of San Francisco. It was about eleven-thirty at night, but the street in front of the residence was brightly lit. Members of the mass media were alerted by Gorbachev's arrival. The tiresome reporters, corralled in the roped area across the street from the consulate, shouted several questions at Gorbachev when we got out of the car, but he waved them off, invoking tiredness, and retired inside the residence to rest for the night.

JUNE 4, MONDAY. DAY SIX AND LAST.

At five minutes to ten I went inside the red brick mansion of the consul general in the affluent neighborhood of Pacific Heights. Mikhail Sergeyevich and Raisa Maximovna were already up, and he was pacing the room in anticipation of meeting the Reagans. He asked Chernishev and me to go out to meet them outside the gate. The consulate, with roses climbing up its facade and a forest of antennas on the roof, was cordoned off for security, and reporters were kept at arm's length behind police lines across the street. However, elite representatives of the mass media were allowed near the residence gate, where they took up strategic positions to film the event. On the adjacent streets and nearby lanes, citizens of San Francisco were craning their necks to catch a glimpse of the two presidents and their wives. It was a picture-perfect day: a golden sun in the nearly cloudless azure skies, the balmy temperature in the midseventies, and a light breeze from the bay.

The Reagans arrived in a navy blue Jaguar at ten on the button and stepped out of the car, dazzling us with Hollywood smiles. Despite the vicissitudes of life—the bullet wound he had received almost ten years ago, a recent fall from a horse, and removal of the benign tumor—Ronald Reagan had not aged a bit over the two years since I had seen him last in Moscow in 1988. He looked dapper in his well-tailored charcoal gray suit. With his hair grown back after the operation he'd undergone after falling from a horse and injuring his head (the hair still jet-black, without any hint of gray, which made me wonder if he dyed his hair), well-tanned skin, and the same upright bearing, he looked dashing and young for his age. And, he would turn eighty next February! Nancy, too, looked just great. She seemed younger and prettier than ever. Did they both know the secret of the fountain of youth? Was their good health due to the absence of the burden of the affairs and concerns of state? Or was it simply due to the beneficial effects of the wholesome California climate and the famed California lifestyle? In fact, Reagan was on a liquid diet, as he would tell Gorbachev later, and according to him, it made him feel much better. Nancy's appearance would prompt Raisa Maximovna to remark to her, with a tinge of envy in her voice, how good she looked. Nancy would be visibly pleased to hear the compliment coming from her, perhaps the first such compliment she'd heard from the Soviet first lady. Nancy was twelve years younger than her illustrious husband.

The former first couple took time to shake hands with those of us who constituted a kind of small welcoming committee: "How are you? It's been a long time!" The ex-president's charisma was still very much in evidence. After these initial greetings, we invited them inside the mansion where, in a spacious living room on the ground floor filled with bouquets of flowers, Mikhail Sergeyevich greeted Ronald Reagan with a bear hug, and Raisa Maximovna and Nancy embraced. Gorbachev's attitude had changed overnight. While the night before he had said he was not in the mood to meet with the Reagans for more than half an hour, he would get so carried away reminiscing with them that the meeting would actually last forty-five minutes, causing him to be late for his important appearance at Stanford University.

After greeting Reagan, Gorbachev took him by the arm and steered him gently outside onto the balcony, which overlooked the beautiful island-studded San Francisco Bay with the Golden Gate Bridge glittering in the sun on the left and the infamous Alcatraz rising steeply out of the sparkling blue waters. They were followed by Nancy and Raisa Maximovna. They all stood there about five minutes, drinking in the magnificent view. Unexpectedly, Raisa Maximovna briefly held hands with Nancy.

The sight of the terraced houses down the hill, or to be more exact their tiled roofs, terraces, and patios, evoked enthusiastic comments. But then Reagan spotted a pretty girl in a reclining chair on a patio below and drew Gorbachev's attention to her. The unsuspecting girl was sunbathing topless. She seemed totally oblivious to being an object of admiration by none other than the two presidents and their wives. Mikhail Sergeyevich, however, appeared somewhat embarrassed. "What is she doing there?" he asked. Reagan explained with a mischievous smile that it was a typical example of the California lifestyle, "a laid-back lifestyle, as we call it here." After surveying the panorama some more, Gorbachev took Reagan back into the living room for a "chat." Mikhail Sergeyevich and Reagan made themselves comfortable on a sofa, sitting next to each other. At Raisa Maximovna's suggestion, the two first ladies occupied two separate armchairs, placed a few feet away at a direct angle, so they "will not interfere with [their] husbands' conversation." She seemed to want to draw a line between the role of their husbands as presidents and their own as their wives, which was quite in keeping with what she had told me in the car the night before. The two of them carried on a separate conversation, and they seemed to get along pretty well, despite Raisa Maximovna's earlier apprehensions that they would have nothing to talk about.

In Gorbachev's eyes the point of this meeting was not so much to discuss anything of substance as to create an excellent photo opportunity. He and Reagan reminisced over tea and coffee about their five meetings in Geneva, Reykjavík, Washington, Moscow, and New York and chatted about the results of the summit with Bush. Reagan gave high marks to Gorbachev for his handling of the delicate question of German reunification and Lithuania and encouraged him to stay the course in *perestroika*. The reporters were let into the room in two waves—the first time to record the bear hug, and the second time to record Gorbachev awarding Reagan a Medal of Honor for the aid provided to the Soviet Union in the aftermath of the earthquake in Armenia in December of 1988. After the Reagans left, the Gorbachevs got into the Zil for the drive to Stanford, where former secretary of state George Shultz and two thousand students were waiting for them in the auditorium.

About an hour later, when the motorcade reached Stanford University, Gorbachev got out of the car and looked around. What he saw was a huge, sprawling, beautiful campus with tall and mighty palm trees and Spanish-style buildings with characteristic red- and orange-tiled roofs, like haciendas. The sun, the sheer beauty of the place, and the exotic fragrance exuded by evergreen shrubs, which I mistook for boxwood, and other tropical plants, all this caused Gorbachev to remark to Shultz, who was there to greet him, "Well, George, I see that you now live in paradise." Shultz was now a professor at Stanford where he headed the Hoover Institute of War, Revolution and Peace located on campus. The institution has the world's largest collection of materials on the Russian revolution, outside Russia itself. Shultz had played a major role in persuading Gorbachev to visit Stanford.

What seemed like the entire student body (by my estimate, at least ten thousand) turned out on the quad to welcome Gorbachev. They stood like two solid walls with only a narrow passage for him to pass through. The students represented all races: white, black, red, and yellow. A storm of cheers greeted Gorbachev when he appeared, and as he strolled down the human passage in the shade of eucalyptus trees, occasionally plunging into the crowd to shake hands, the cheers grew in intensity. Gorbachev waved and shook hundreds, if not thousands, of hands. People were applauding, reaching out to touch him, and simply screaming, especially young women. The tumultuous welcome had a magical effect on Mikhail Sergeyevich, who took fifty minutes to work the crowds of young people amid screams of "Gorby! Gorby!" before he got to the main building of the Graduate School of Business. It was like a mass hysteria or induced mass hypnosis.

The high point of Gorbachev's visit to Stanford was his address at Memorial Auditorium before some two thousand students and guests, most of whom had obtained their coveted seats through a random drawing. In the frenzy for tickets, those who were not among the lucky winners had to buy tickets from scalpers, who were rumored to charge from a minimum of $250 for an upper-balcony seat to as much as a whopping $1,400 for front-center seats. Local entrepreneurs were quick to exploit the hysteria that surrounded the Soviet leader's visit. Thus, some ten thousand "Gorby" T-shirts had been sold, but Gorbachev didn't get any royalties. That was capitalism in action.

When he appeared in the spacious auditorium, Gorbachev was introduced by Stanford University president Donald Kennedy as "the architect of a great world transformation." Unlike previous occasions when he did a lot of ad-libbing, this time Mikhail Sergeyevich strictly adhered to the written text that I had translated for him in Moscow. In this carefully considered speech, Gorbachev charted a new path and called for cooperation in wide-ranging areas. The speech was peppered with kind words for Stanford researchers and scholars. Gorbachev cited joint Soviet-American research on high-temperature superconductivity, a phenomena that he said would soon revolutionize technology. He quoted the nineteenth-century Russian writer Alexandr Herzen's description of the Pacific Ocean as "the Mediterranean of the future," apparently meaning to say that ideas and technologies were born here in California. But he also sounded a note of caution about the relationship between the Soviet Union and the United States: "I am under no illusion as to the possibility of a faster rapprochement or convergence of our two societies. They are quite different. For many years they have been developing in different directions. They will probably never be fully alike. Indeed, there is no need for that." And he called for tolerance, which he said was "the alpha and omega of a new world order." Most importantly, Gorbachev told this academic audience, "The Cold War is now behind us—let us not wrangle over who won it."

The speech lasted twenty-five minutes and was greeted by a thunderous standing ovation.

Then Shultz took the podium. He sang the praises of Gorbachev calling him "a great leader" who had established "a unique place" in history and "a man of action and ideas" who had a key part to play in the drama of forming a new world order. Not one for flowery speeches, Shultz stopped in the middle of his monotone remarks, turned directly to Gorbachev, and said, "You light up the landscape with your ideas. You are a great leader. You have a key part to play in this drama. We need you, Mr. Gorbachev." Shultz concluded his passionate panegyric to another round of thunderous applause. I sat next to M.S. on the podium behind the lectern, and as he listened to the translation of Shultz's remarks through his earphones, Mikhail Sergeyevich looked overwhelmed. Here he was, beleaguered on all sides, fighting for his political life at home, when a man of Shultz's stature reached out and offered him this heartfelt statement of support. At one point, he raised a hand to his eyes and brushed away what I thought was a tear—or, perhaps, it only seemed so to me.

After the speeches, I added to Gorbachev's star quality, quite unwittingly, as if he needed it. When he was asked by Robin Kennedy, wife of Stanford president Donald Kennedy, how he was enjoying his visit here, Mikhail Sergeyevich, never at a loss for words, exclaimed, *"Potryasayusche!"* This expression of extreme delight can be translated into English by many different words. The temptation being too great to resist, I decided to flaunt my knowledge of what I knew was a current student "vogue word" and, accordingly, translated *potryasayusche* as "It's awesome!" Mrs. Kennedy was delighted: "I wish the students could hear it! That's just the word they love. Thank you, President Gorbachev, for the future—ours and our children's."

Before he left the campus, students presented him with two gifts.

One, an abstract enamel on wood, was appropriately called *Creation of Peace*, and the other was an oil painting, also appropriately enough called *The Peacemakers*, which depicted a pair of dolphins nuzzling in outer space. The artist said he had used recycled diapers instead of a brush. Gorbachev seemed to cringe with embarrassment, but politely thanked the artist for the gift.

By now Gorbachev was running a full hour behind schedule, departing from Stanford at 2:05 P.M. He was supposed to go back to his residence for a private lunch and thirty minutes of rest, but on the spur of the moment he decided to skip lunch and go straight to the Fairmont Hotel, where he was to appear before an audience of West Coast businessmen. Since I was on the podium with him during and after the speechmaking, he invited me to keep him company during the ride back to San Francisco. Raisa Maximovna had a program to sightsee around the city on her own, and he obviously wanted someone at his side with whom to exchange impressions.

Once inside his Zil limousine, he suggested I sit next to him in the backseat. The only other Soviet in the car, besides the driver, was Medvedev, who occupied a jump seat, with his back to us. The road was rather long—fifty-five miles or about sixty minutes of driving—so this was an extraordinary opportunity for me to talk in private with the president of the Soviet Union. The conversation was a spontaneous reflection of his feelings and thoughts on a broad range of subjects. Everything he said became etched in my memory, and I hastened to set it down on paper later that same day. Also, I played the "mental recording" of the conversation in my head so many times afterward that I can reproduce it even now almost word for word. So, let's go to the "tape."

The moment we hit the freeway in the direction of San Francisco, Mikhail Sergeyevich exclaimed, "What a welcome! That was really something! Simply stupendous! I never even expected anything like this. After all, this is Stanford—a citadel of imperialism!"

I.: Indeed, that was incredible. Perhaps even more enthusiastic than in Minneapolis. The amazing thing is that no one brought them together, no one organized them. They came of their own free will.

M.S.: I, too, perceived it to be a spontaneous expression of feelings. True, here and there I noticed groups of protesters, but they didn't really count. In general, Americans express their feelings very freely. Especially here, in California. It must be due to the propitious climate.

I.: The climate, yes. But I don't think that is the only thing. Traditionally and historically, Americans respect freedom and always welcome it, wherever it may be. And, they associate you with the advent of freedom in the Soviet Union.

MS.: Yes, our people have been kept in bondage far too long. This is true even today. It's a difficult thing to change the psychology of people. How many generations have grown up in our land without any idea of what freedom is. Well, all right—we are going to change all this, little by little. If *perestroika* is to succeed, we've got to turn around the brains of our people. Our heads are still clogged with far too many stereotypes that have been drummed into several generations of our people.

I.: Mikhail Sergeyevich, if I may be frank with you—we now have a new species of man, what they call in the West *Homo sovieticus*, a whole new generation of people who are devoid of initiative and full of inertia. It seems to me that the root of the problem lies in the fact that, unfortunately, it is not possible to change their psychology overnight. In general, we, Soviet people or Russian people for that matter, are known for our proclivity to go from one extreme to another while avoiding the golden mean. As far as I know, this has been the case throughout our history. What we are witnessing now is a case in point: some are pro-*perestroika*, others are opposed to it.

M.S.: That is why I am trying to act so as not to alienate either the former or the latter, although by nature my sympathies lie with democrats. Otherwise, nothing good will come of it. We must stop messing things up. There's been enough mess as it is.

I.: What do think of the results of your visit? Are you satisfied? On the whole, my impression is that the Americans are pleased.

M.S.: I am pleased, too. We have accomplished a thing or two. You were present in the White House when President Bush was still doubting whether he should sign the trade agreement, weren't you?

I.: Yes, I was.

M.S.: We consider it a great victory—the signing of the trade agreement. Never mind that for the time being it doesn't amount to much in practical terms. But in the future, we will show what we can do. My advisers, too, believe that the visit has been a success. But you saw for yourself how all this was happening, how the talks with Bush were proceeding, how they treated us. In general, Bush is a cautious man, and I do appreciate what he did. It was his personal decision [to sign the trade agreement]. Do you remember what he said? That his critics would castigate him, but that it shouldn't make me worried? That he would take it all upon himself?

I.: Why do you think he decided to do it?

M.S.: He is an intelligent man and a farsighted politician. He understands that if they don't help us now, no one knows how all this may turn out. As a matter of fact, this [summit] meeting was in jeopardy: there were too many of those back home who didn't want it. They said that the timing was wrong, that I was going to go on a junket around the world while the country was going through hard times. They said that all the Americans wanted was to grab a piece of the action for themselves. But I told them that I had to go, that it was in our interest. It was difficult to argue with them. There's an awful lot of naysayers back there who don't really want to see improved relations with America or others. Give them half a chance, and they will do real damage.

I.: Mikhail Sergeyevich, I wonder if you find it easier to do business with Bush than with Reagan.

M.S.: Bush is quite different. Unlike Reagan, he knows the issues well. He tries to get a handle on them before he makes a decision. Clearly, he works hard. I myself read four hundred to five hundred pages a day. I get tired, of course. But one is supposed to know the issues. How can it be otherwise? What kind of president would I be if I didn't know the issues! But as to Reagan, he just loved telling jokes. He didn't like to go into details. When it came to details, he would turn the floor to Shultz. He was the one who always came to his rescue. But I decided at one time not to overemphasize this characteristic of his. I thought, "let him do it his way—you can't really change him." The most important thing was that he moved toward an accommodation with us. But the credit for that belongs to Shultz, not to him. There's an intelligent man for you, you know. He understands everything right. Without him there would not have been any agreements with the Americans. . . .

I.: What do think of your meeting with Reagan today? Has he changed over this time?

M.S.: The meeting went off very well. It was even longer that I had expected. But Reagan is the same, he hasn't changed.

I.: Did he tell you any jokes this time?

M.S.: Not really a joke, but some kind of anecdote. For him, jokes and one-liners are a part of his nature. But he looks great for his years. How old is he?

I.: I think he is nearing eighty. . . . He has a strong constitution. . . .

M.S.: Yes, he is now resting from his labors. But he says he follows everything that goes on, including the developments in our country. He believes we owe it to him and to his policies that we made our changes.

I.: Mikhail Sergeyevich, the trade agreement is a good thing. But what about the arms control agreements? It seems to be tough sledding, especially in Vienna.

M.S.: It's a complex issue. There's a divergence of opinion among the experts. But the important thing is that we should not rush things—or else we will screw it all up. Everything is changing so abruptly in Europe. We must make very careful calculations of everything. That's why our military is saying we should not be in a hurry. We'll see. We will try to reach agreement. On strategic arms, perhaps toward the end of this year. As to Vienna, it is Germany that stands in the way. Did you notice that when we were discussing the unification of Germany, Bush had a pensive air? It seems to me we managed to sway him, plant a seed of doubt as to whether he is right. In any case, we made him ponder over our position. All this is not so simple, after all. We have to think of our own security. But they are not thinking far ahead. So I hope the seeds that we planted with them will grow shoots.

I.: Mikhail Sergeyevich, may I draw your attention: we are now passing along the San Andreas Fault—it's on the left. It is predicted that if there is a powerful enough earthquake here, the entire state of California will split away and either sink under water or float in the sea as an island. It is believed that it will happen sooner or later.

M.S.: Earthquakes are a terrible disaster. Look what happened in Armenia. California is such a blooming land. There is so much of everything concentrated here: industry, agriculture. Why, it's like a whole country! You know, in Stanford I felt an irresistible urge all along to put aside the written speech and start ad-libbing. I could hardly restrain myself. But I had to stick to the speech. It was a very important speech, very well thought-out. So I couldn't digress from it. Well, it's okay. I think I can express myself more freely at lunch [with businessmen, at the Fairmont Hotel]. In fact, I often get carried away if I am not stopped. But no one ever tells me about it.

I.: Generally speaking, Americans are not known for liking long speeches. They believe the average attention span is half an hour. They prefer discussions, exchanges of views.

M.S.: With us, it's impossible. What can one say in half an hour? There's so many things that need to be said!

I.: Mikhail Sergeyevich, as you know, they're showing a heightened interest in the figure of Yeltsin. Bush himself questioned you about him. What do you think, is it really possible to make a transition to a market economy "painlessly," as Yeltsin says? Or, do you think it's impossible?

M.S.: I already said, including to Bush, what kind of man he is. He is a destroyer, not a builder. Soon, people will see it for themselves when in a year or two they will see that he won't be able to do anything. It's rubbish—a "painless" transition to a market system. This is sheer populism and nothing else. But when it comes to making things happen, it will turn out that there is nothing he can do. Why, I did say already—what did he do in the two years that he had been in Moscow [as mayor]? Nothing! It's the same now. A demagogue, that's what he is!

After a pause, Gorbachev pointed through the window to the motorcycle cops who were escorting our car. Roaring by on their powerful Harley-Davidsons, with huge black helmets on their heads and in black leather outfits, the cops made a strong impression on Gorbachev.

M.S.: Look how efficiently they work—in such a well-coordinated fashion! I've been watching them for a long time now. Excellent teamwork. Now they pass us—and this at the speed of 130–140 kilometers per hour—block access lanes to traffic from one side of the road, and then pass us again. Well done! Excellent work!

I.: Their motorcycles have 160 horsepower. They block traffic just for a few minutes, long enough for the motorcade to pass by, and then they unblock it. It is efficient.

M.S.: It's the opposite of what we have back home. There, they would block traffic half an hour before we [Politburo members] pass by. In the meantime, they prevent the drivers from going anywhere, and the drivers would curse us in general and Gorbachev in particular. It would not be a bad idea for our security people to learn from the Americans. We should really take a leaf out of their book [pointing to a cop whizzing by on a motorcycle].

I.: But they have these great highways that we don't have. Look! Five lanes each way. No streetlights, no obstructions. These roads are a matter of pride for America. . . . They realized the advantage of having good roads a long time ago. And now they are just reaping the benefits. . . .

M.S.: Roads require a lot of money. Where shall we get it?

I.: That's correct. But these outlays yield return sooner or later. After all, it is not only America, but other countries, too, that have excellent roads. . . .

M.S.: I wish it were the only problem we had. But I can understand why the people here are so cheerful and carefree. They have the sun all year round. It's paradise on earth!

A few more moments etched themselves in my memory. During the ride from Stanford, M.S. looked out of the window and tried to read aloud the signs on the road and on the houses that we passed. He read them as a German would—that is, he read every letter exactly as it was written.

He asked me how he was doing and whether his pronunciation was correct. When an escort police car passed us with the words "Highway Patrol" painted in large white letters on its rear, he read it as "Heegvai Patrool," accenting the last syllables in both words. I said Americans would not understand him. He then explained, in a sort of apologetic tone, that he had studied German at school a long time ago and had never had a chance to learn English. He then asked me to correct him each time he mispronounced the words on signs. That was his first lesson in English—"on the run," so to speak.

At one point he startled me by exclaiming in Latin, seemingly without any reason, *"Homo homini lupus est"* ("Man is a wolf to man"), adding a touch of mystery to the way his mind operated. I saw a mischievous twinkle in his eyes as he said it. Although he didn't explain what prompted him to think of this maxim or to whom he was referring, I think, in retrospect, that he may have been referring to his political opponents back home, because he used it in the context of our conversation about those people back home who were either opposed to his reforms or were pulling in a different direction.

He surprised me again later when he started to recite extensively a poem by Lermontov, *Mtsyri*. I was amazed to hear him declaim in a solemn voice, as if before a theater audience—and this from a man who had spent most of his life in Party and government work! He said that whenever he and Raisa Maximovna came to Pyatigorsk (which is another spa in the Stavropol region under his former jurisdiction), situated not far from Kislovodsk, they would make it a point to visit the places frequented by Lermontov. He was especially fond of *Mtsyri*, one of the great Russian poet's most famous poems.

An hour later, the motorcade reached the city and the Fairmont Hotel. Mikhail Sergeyevich put on his salesman hat to "sell" his reforms to American business leaders, urging them to invest in the Soviet Union where major reforms—economic, legal, and industrial—"will make it easier for you to bring home your profits," as he put it. His speech, which he delivered in front of a bank of Soviet and American flags, was met with a standing ovation by a crowd of about 250 business executives crammed into the Venetian Room. There, the governor of the State of California, the Honorable George Deukmejian, and the mayor of the City and County of San Francisco, the Honorable Art Agnos, as well as the San Francisco Chamber of Commerce, together with the International Foundation for the Survival and Development of Humanity, hosted a lavish luncheon in honor of Gorbachev.

The grand affair was sponsored by such giants of American business as AT&T, Apple Computer, Bank of America, Bechtel Group, Chevron Corporation, Hewlett-Packard Company, Transamerica, Wells Fargo Bank, and more than 150 other major West Coast enterprises. Gorbachev pointedly thanked the U.S. business community three times during his talk for its work in the Soviet Union. He cited California and western U.S. businesses as those best poised to reap the profits of promising new Soviet-American business relationships. Specifically, he spoke of the conversion of Soviet defense-related industries and cooperation between the Soviet Union and the United States in areas such as space and science as holding special promise for California business. For example, he said, the Soviet aircraft industry was looking forward to a profitable joint effort with Americans and Israelis on a "gigantic project to build a plane . . . which is a remarkable result of cooperation."

But during his talk, Gorbachev repeated a theme he had delivered in Minnesota on Sunday: that the Soviet Union would be watching "those who are willing to cooperate at this time . . . who may be risking something . . . and those who stand on the sidelines." The implication was that the risk takers would have "many more opportunities" in trade in the years to come.

The Soviet president told the audience about major changes he was backing, including legislation to encourage joint ventures and to allow foreign ownership and management within the Soviet Union, as well as laws that would ensure that foreign businesses would be afforded protection and repatriation of profits. He said business leaders could anticipate the convertibility of the ruble far sooner than expected—"within a shorter period of time." But he didn't give any hint of a time frame. The ruble's nonconvertibility into dollars and other major hard currencies remained a principal reason why many American businesses were reluctant to enter the Soviet marketplace.

Gorbachev conceded that he had made mistakes in the early stages of Soviet economic reform and painted a picture of a nation in the most difficult stages of transition, urging U.S. business to recognize the huge transformations occurring in the Soviet Union during the switch from communism to what he called "a market economy." As in Stanford, his speech lasted for about forty minutes, leaving him little time to answer questions, which were submitted in writing. But unlike Stanford, he didn't have a text to follow—he spoke impromptu, as he said he would, and got carried away, just the way he liked it. Before the luncheon ended, the two famous computer pioneers Steve Wozniak and John Sculley of the Apple Computer Corporation persuaded Gorbachev to accept a desktop Macintosh. Mikhail Sergeyevich was embarrassed and said he didn't know what to do with it, then relented and said, all right, he would give it to his daughter, who perhaps would pass it on to her daughter.

After the luncheon and a brief rest at the consulate building, President Gorbachev and his wife were to depart for the San Francisco airport whence they would fly back home. At about six o'clock, Mikhail Sergeyevich and Raisa Maximovna emerged from the residence onto the street. They were instantly bombarded with dozens of shouted questions from the reporters who had been keeping watch over the red-brick mansion from across the street. Mikhail Sergeyevich asked me what it was they wanted to know, but in the din of the excited reporters' voices I couldn't possibly pick out a single coherent question. So I guessed and told him that I thought they wanted to know his impressions of San Francisco. When Mikhail Sergeyevich walked across the street, together with Raisa Maximovna, to talk to the reporters, I was awfully relieved to hear the first question was indeed about the Soviet president's impressions of San Francisco. "It's a fabulous city! I always wanted to come here and I never had a chance, until now," Gorbachev exclaimed with brio. "You're just fortunate to live here. If I were President Bush, I would even levy a tax on you for the beauty in which you live, and for the air that you breathe. It's simply fantastic!"

Next, Raisa Maximovna shared her impressions. She was no less enthusiastic in expressing her delight with the stay in San Francisco, "short as it [was]." She briefly recounted her adventures at Fisherman's Wharf, where she decided to take a ride in one of the famous San Francisco cable cars. The operator—also a woman—was so flabbergasted when she saw who her passenger was that she forgot for an instant driving the cable car and offered instead to take the Soviet president's wife to a friend of hers, a hairdresser who would do her hair for free, in the punk style if she wanted—"she would be happy to do something for the Soviet first lady!" The reporters wondered in chorus what kind of hairstyle she would have preferred, if she had accepted the invitation. Raisa Maximovna smiled coquettishly and parried the question, without missing a beat, "Why, don't you see I already have a new hairstyle?"

Later, on the way to the airport, she would return to the subject of hairstyles. She would laugh and say, "Well, Mikhail Sergeyevich, perhaps I should have really had my hair done à la punk! What do you think?" He laughed but said nothing. But she persisted and, touching my arm, addressed the same question to me: "And what do *you* think, Igor Dmitriyevich?" What do you say to the first lady when she asks you a question like that? Well, I said it would be quite a sensation if she did it, but she didn't really need it, her present hairstyle was just too good to be changed. Flattery didn't get me anywhere, of course, but I could tell she was pleased.

At 6:30 P.M., after the brief encounter with reporters, we boarded the cars and the motorcade departed for the airport. Who could have known then that it would be the last ride of the Gorbachevs through the streets of America as president and first lady? I was privileged to accompany them in their Zil all the way to the airport, and so I had yet another opportunity to observe them at close range as two human beings, rather than as the top leader and his spouse. We were still within the city limits, and people on both sides of the streets through which the motorcade passed waved at us in a friendly fashion. In breach of all security regulations, Mikhail Sergeyevich opened the window on his side, leaned out, and waved back at people. Raisa Maximovna did the same on her side. When the motorcade reached the official city boundary line, the San Francisco motorcycle escort stopped and the police dismounted. They had done their duty. From this point the motorcade would proceed without an escort. Gorbachev leaned out of the window and loudly thanked the cops for "a job well done!" I had to shout the translation at the top of my lungs through the open window, so all the cops for whom the compliment was meant could hear it. The cops waved back.

Now we were well on the way to the airport.

Raisa Maximovna was full of impressions of what she had seen and heard that day during her lightning tour of San Francisco, and she wanted to share them. She told about her visit to Chinatown, about the exotic smells there, about the Chinese who lived there. Then she switched the subject again, and this time she spoke of . . . homosexuality. "It turns out there are special neighborhoods in San Francisco where homosexuals live, where there are all kinds of establishments especially for them, so it is easier for them to meet one another. Maybe, it's the climate that is conducive to this, too!"

At these words, Mikhail Sergeyevich interjected, "It's like on a different planet." His mind was elsewhere, however. He was deeply impressed by the nice homes with garages and manicured lawns. They were so different from anything in Russia, he said. He must have been thinking of the enormous gap in living standards that separated the Soviet Union and the United States, while militarily both countries were equal, more or less. Raisa Maximovna must have read his thoughts, for she changed the subject, picking up where Gorbachev had left off—the American homes.

R.M.: I understand most people in America can afford homes like these. As for us, we are still very far from this. There's hope only if *perestroika* succeeds. It's just unbelievable what Stalin and his ilk did to our country.

M.S.: Zhenya [Evgeny] Primakov keeps talking about how modest Stalin was. What kind of modesty was it if he had thirty dachas all over the country?

R.M.: Mikhail Sergeyevich and I are blamed for living too sumptuously, for having two dachas. But the president is supposed to have two dachas: one near Moscow, another in the South of Russia. We are not asking for more, you know. It's quite enough for us. Why, Stalin, the "modest one," had no less that thirty dachas! And they all had to be maintained: domestics, gardeners, and so on—all of those people had to be kept there! All year round! 'What if Stalin suddenly decided to come!' Even though he'd never been to most of them. And the maintenance costs were very high. Is that what is called modest?

I.: It is certainly absurd to talk about modesty in his case. The fact that he wore boots and a tunic or a sackcloth shirt means just nothing. Anyway, how can one talk about his modesty if he killed millions and millions of innocent people!

M.S.: Moreover, whenever he was going to make a trip by train to the South, to the Crimea, soldiers, armed with rifles and submachine guns, were lined up every hundred meters [yards] all the way along the tracks from Moscow to Simferopol, to ensure his safety and security! The railroad stations in Moscow and Simferopol were closed down for this period of time—crowds of people collected there. Is that modesty? Well, all right, we are going to change all this! It has to be done!

I wished the road to the airport were longer, so we could talk more! But we were now just a few minutes away, and after hesitating, I decided to ask Gorbachev a question only he could answer.

I.: Mikhail Sergeyevich, you remember, perhaps, that at the table in the White House, during the dinner, you mentioned that your favorite historical figures in Russia were Peter the Great, Alexander the Second, and Lenin. The reason why it is Peter the Great is clear. He was a great reformer. But why Alexander the Second?

M.S.: [after a pause] Because he was a democrat.

On that encouraging note the motorcade reached the presidential aircraft. The Gorbachevs boarded their plane to fly to Moscow as a choir sang a Russian rendition of "I Left My Heart in San Francisco."

*   *   *

Gorbachev's journey across America for the first time was an eye-opening and enlightening experience for him. He was able to see more of the American people and got a glimpse of that quintessential "American dream"—the homes that he liked so much. They tugged at his heartstrings and planted promising seeds in his soul.

His visit took place at a time when the summit excitement was no longer fed by Cold War tensions. The electricity generated at past superpower summits by the prospect of mortal enemies edging inch by inch toward peace was now missing. This time the meetings were between two world leaders whose nations were fully at peace, but had conflicting interests and needs. The once grand gesture was replaced by negotiations over money and politics.

One of the major accomplishments of the summit was the creation of an atmosphere in which the leaders could get together almost routinely, without any prospective spectacular agreement or deep crisis to justify a meeting. Ideally, summit meetings should cease to be isolated pageants of accord or encounters of great moment. They should become more frequent, more businesslike, and routine. The establishment of a more casual, personal relationship between Bush and Gorbachev was the crowning achievement of this summit. There was every reason to expect that the Soviet Union and the United States would become partners, if not allies, in diplomatic, economic, cultural, and social spheres.

Moreover, after what initially appeared as a doubting period, Bush had apparently now come to view Gorbachev as more likely to foster peaceful relations with the United States than any other potential Soviet leader. Over the previous year he had gone from saying, "We can't base our policy on one man," to stating flatly, "This is our guy." An emphasis on personal relationships was a hallmark of Bush's diplomatic style, and whatever their political differences, he generally sought to cultivate friendships with foreign leaders with whom he had to negotiate. In the end, Gorbachev was no exception. Consequently, there was one weighty reason for optimism for the future: the extraordinary understanding and trust between the two men. Even as they differed on issues, they displayed respect, even deference, for each other—proof that both wanted to keep reconciliation going. With Gorbachev, Bush was firm but considerate, careful to avoid gloating, and stressed mutual benefits. He had all the trumps, but he didn't play them. Gorbachev played equal in an unequal position.

Although they did not write the final chapter on Germany, they pledged deep cuts in nuclear and chemical arms, and Bush offered Gorbachev the most-favored-nation status—a sign of his willingness to meet the Soviet leader's urgent economic and political needs. And thus, when they put pen to paper on that memorable Friday evening of June 1, 1990, they put an end to the forty-odd years of the Cold War.

CHAPTER SIX

EMERGENCY SUMMIT

Gorbachev-Bush Helsinki Summit, 1990

After Iraq's invasion of Kuwait on August 2, 1990, and intense, almost daily consultations over the phone and exchanges of messages between Foreign Minister Shevardnadze and Secretary of State Baker, President Bush proposed to President Gorbachev that they get together for a brief working summit to discuss coordination of further, possibly joint action against the aggressor. After some initial hesitation, Gorbachev agreed, and the decision was announced on Moscow television on September 2.

The venue for this extraordinary summit, Helsinki, was chosen because of its proximity to Moscow. Bush was conscious of how busy Gorbachev was at the time and that he had his hands full with domestic problems: the five-hundred-day plan for the transition to a free market system, known as the Shatalin Plan, was nearly complete, and a session of the USSR Supreme Soviet was scheduled to be convened in a week's time, beginning September 10, to discuss the plan with a view to adopting it. It was to be a momentous event in the life of the country, the most important domestic development since *perestroika* had been proclaimed five years earlier, and Gorbachev, quite understandably, was reluctant to travel far from the Kremlin. Yet, he knew that something had to be done about the blatant Iraqi aggression if his policy of new thinking was to be credible in the eyes of the international community.

This working summit was prepared in record-breaking time—in a little more than a week. It was also the briefest summit meeting ever between Soviet and American leaders. For those reasons, it was dubbed by the mass media "a minisummit" or "a snap summit." Its purpose was to demonstrate to the world community, and above all to Saddam Hussein, that the two superpowers were united in their condemnation of the Iraqi aggression against defenseless Kuwait and, more importantly, that they were determined to punish the aggressor, deny him his ill-gotten gains, and thereby discourage any would-be adventurists from following suit. It was also important to avert an attack on Saudi Arabia by Hussein's troops.

The immediate purpose of the emergency meeting in Helsinki, however, was for Bush to gain Gorbachev's acquiescence for a massive troop buildup that the United States contemplated in the Gulf region.

Gorbachev's initial response to the Gulf crisis was understandably cautious, for Iraq was an old Soviet ally in the Middle East and the Soviet Union was still bound to it by a treaty of friendship, cooperation, and mutual assistance. If this crisis had broken out a few years earlier, Moscow would have sided with Iraq. But now that the Cold War was over, Gorbachev and the Soviet leadership were anxious to demonstrate their concern for upholding the international rule of law. The day after the aggression against Kuwait was launched, Jim Baker interrupted his visit to Mongolia to fly to the Moscow Vnukovo airport where he and Shevardnadze issued a historically unprecedented joint Soviet-U.S. statement condemning Hussein's action and proclaiming cooperation in dealing with the aggression. But Moscow faced some difficult choices. The fate of the eight thousand Soviets working in Iraq as experts, including a group of military advisers on loan, was in danger. And, the Soviet leadership was reluctant to be seen by the rest of the world as siding with the United States against its ally.

Bush had acted more decisively after the invasion: he authorized, almost immediately, the freezing of Iraqi assets in the United States and instructed the U.S. fleet in the Indian Ocean to move into the Gulf. When it became clear that the efforts of the Arab states to find an "Arab solution" would be unsuccessful, Bush would not rule out the use of force to eject the aggressor from Kuwait. To demonstrate his credibility, he ordered an airborne division to move to Saudi Arabia, together with F-15 fighter planes. Britain, too, sent its fighter planes and an aircraft carrier to the Gulf. In the month since the Iraqi invasion, the United States had assembled in the region troops and matériel in numbers and quantities that were unprecedented in the post-Vietnam period. According to the U.S. secretary of defense, Dick Cheney, more than one hundred thousand American troops were already stationed there, plus the British, French, and others. This impressive display of military might could be used to restore international legality and to protect oil supplies. But Bush also needed international political support, above all, that of the Soviet Union, to forge a united front against Iraq.

In the month since Iraq's seizure of Kuwait there was neither war nor peace in the Persian Gulf. The United Nations, led by the United States with Soviet, British, and French support, passed a resolution condemning Iraq for its action and calling for total withdrawal from and immediate negotiations with Kuwait. Later, it passed another resolution, 661, imposing economic sanctions against Iraq, but without enforcement provisions. When it became clear that Saddam Hussein was flagrantly flouting the U.N. sanctions and continued to defy the world community, Baker and Shevardnadze agreed, through "telephone diplomacy" and exchanging messages, to propose in the U.N. Security Council yet another resolution to give effect to the sanctions by enforcing them through "appropriate means commensurate with specific circumstances." Britain and France, too, supported such a resolution, and on August 25, the Security Council adopted it.

The unparalleled extent of cooperation between the Soviet Union and the United States in this crisis must have spurred Bush to propose an unscheduled summit with Gorbachev to consolidate and strengthen this encouraging trend. The prevailing opinion in Moscow at the time was that something would result from the political and economic sanctions already imposed by the Security Council and the military show of force, but that things would not end in war. Thinking that what was needed now was additional diplomatic efforts to settle the crisis, Gorbachev went to Helsinki.

HELSINKI. SEPTEMBER 8, SATURDAY. DAY ONE.

After a short, uneventful flight from Moscow, President Gorbachev's plane landed in the Helsinki-Vantaa airport at 6:40 P.M. local time. It taxied up to the terminal and came to a stop right next to Air Force One, the presidential jumbo jet. Bush had arrived earlier that day, in the morning. Secretary Baker's Boeing 707 was parked nearby. Baker had arrived in Helsinki straight from Cairo and would depart the next day, after the summit, for Brussels to brief NATO allies on the summit results.

Gorbachev's entire entourage, including MFA people, were lodged on the ninth floor of the Palace Hotel overlooking the Gulf of Finland. He himself and Raisa Maximovna, who invariably accompanied him on all foreign trips, stayed at the Soviet Embassy, as usual.

According to the schedule, Gorbachev would be welcomed at the airport by President Koivisto of Finland and would have dinner with him later that evening. No English-speaking interpreter would be needed at either event. The Finnish-speaking interpreter, a young, diminutive

Russian fellow from the Soviet Embassy in Helsinki, who specialized in this "exotic" language, was already here on the tarmac to do the interpreting at the welcoming ceremony. So I decided to leave for the hotel right away without waiting for the ceremony to begin.

In contrast to Moscow's blue skies and sunny weather, the Finnish capital was heavily overcast and it was drizzling. On entering the room reserved for me at the Palace, I turned on the TV set to watch the arrival ceremony, which was being broadcast live on CNN. After watching Gorbachev leave the airport with President Koivisto, I went to the hotel restaurant for dinner. The restaurant was almost empty, but shortly it began to fill with members of Gorbachev's team, who had arrived from the airport.

During dinner, Sergei Tarasenko, chief aide to Shevardnadze, joined me and a few of my colleagues at our table. He told us that a message addressed to Gorbachev had just arrived from Saddam Hussein, saying basically that the Soviet Union was no longer a superpower and it was demeaning for the Soviets to echo the voice of American imperialists. The USSR ought to know better, the message went on, and join the Arab cause in this hour of trial on the side of Iraq to oppose the imperialist USA. According to Tarasenko, Hussein's message to Gorbachev did not contain a single constructive proposal or idea. His game plan was simple: to try to split the American and Soviet leaders on the eve of their meeting. The plan failed, of course. Unsurprisingly, several months later, on the very first day of the coup against Gorbachev in Moscow in August 1991, Hussein would be the first, along with Gadhafi, to send congratulations to the putschists.

SEPTEMBER 9, SUNDAY. DAY TWO AND LAST.

At 9:55 A.M. Gorbachev's motorcade departed for the Presidential Palace, the official residence of the president of Finland, where the emergency summit was to be held. The Soviet president's team of advisers included most of the people who usually accompanied him on visits to other countries, namely Academician Evgeny Primakov, member of the newly formed Presidential Council; Marshal Sergei Akhromeyev, chief military adviser to President Gorbachev; Anatoly Chernyaev, chief foreign policy aide to the president; Vitaly Ignatenko, the president's new press secretary, who recently replaced Arkady Maslennikov; and Alexandr Bessmertnykh, the current Soviet ambassador to Washington. It also included Alexandr Belonogov, who had been the Soviet permanent representative to the United Nations until the summer of 1990, when he was recalled to Moscow and made a deputy foreign minister in charge of Middle East affairs; Alexei Obukhov, who had also been promoted, to the post of deputy foreign minister in charge of American affairs; Vladimir Chernishev, Soviet chief of state protocol; and Valentin Falin, chief of the CPSU Central Committee's Department on International Affairs. Once again, the notable absence was that of Alexandr Yakovlev. It was the second time, to my knowledge, that he hadn't accompanied Gorbachev on a foreign trip. It appeared his star was on the wane. Palazchenko and I were assigned to do the interpreting for Gorbachev.

When the motorcade pulled up at the palace gate and Gorbachev got out of his car, he was pelted with questions from reporters, mostly American. By prior agreement with Bush, however, he declined to answer them, and together with Raisa Maximovna, he made a beeline for the entrance. Once inside, they were greeted by President Koivisto and his wife. They escorted the Gorbachevs to the second floor to a room adjacent to the larger Yellow Salon. The Yellow Salon itself was an ornate room with polished parquet floors carrying the imprint of a Russian craftsman from 1872. Bush, who had arrived a few minutes earlier, was already waiting in another room on the opposite side of the Yellow Salon. The two presidents were very much like two boxers in a ring just waiting for the gong to sound for round one.

At 10:02 A.M., the doors at both ends of the Yellow Salon opened, and Gorbachev briskly moved toward Bush, who came out from the opposite room. They met in the middle of the room and, beaming, exchanged a hearty handshake for the benefit of the cameras. Gorbachev did not arrive with empty hands. He had a gift for Bush: a hand-drawn framed cartoon showing the nasty Cold War knocked out, while they both triumph as fighters in a ring. He held up the picture for all to see and presented it to Bush in full view of the reporters. After posing for more photos, Bush and Gorbachev went into an adjacent, smaller room for a one-on-one meeting, which went on for almost three hours.

The result was an agreement to draft a joint statement on Iraq. The original Soviet version had been prepared by Belonogov while the two leaders were in their tête-à-tête. He ensconced himself in a corner of a small room reserved for the use of Gorbachev's delegation in the palace and wrote the draft on a pad that he placed on his knees. The original U.S. version was drafted by Dennis Ross, an aide to Secretary of State Baker. Ross was said to be a very capable man who could work like a thinking computer: take notes as a meeting went on, make an instant analysis for the record, and offer his suggestions and ideas, if asked. I had seen Ross in action at Camp David and was impressed by his efficiency.

With Gorbachev and Bush busily discussing what should be done about Saddam Hussein, and Shevardnadze and Baker having a meeting of their own, their respective advisers didn't have much to do until the afternoon meeting. They stayed in two small rooms at opposite sides of the palace. Gorbachev's men included Belonogov, who was finishing his draft, Primakov, Akhromeyev, Bessmertnykh, Obukhov, and Georgy Mamedov of the American desk at MFA. I joined them for lack of anything better to do, because it had been decided between Palazchenko and me that I would interpret for Gorbachev and Bush at the second round of talks in the afternoon. So for the next two and a half hours, I observed these men at close range.

While Belonogov was totally absorbed in his task, the rest of Gorbachev's advisers gathered in a circle around the stocky Primakov, who shared his impressions of Saddam Hussein. He had met the ruler of Iraq for the first time in the late 1960s as a *Pravda* correspondent in the Middle East. Hussein was not yet president, but he had already become an influential member of the Iraqi leadership. About this time the treaty on friendship, cooperation, and mutual assistance between Iraq and the Soviet Union was being prepared, which treaty Moscow did not repudiate even after Iraq's aggression against Kuwait.

Primakov assured us that Saddam was not a madman in the common sense of the word, but a wily, cunning, perfidious, and above all, extremely brutal man. Even in those early years when he was just beginning his political career, he had all the proclivities for becoming a dictator. He possessed a firmness that often turned into cruelty and a strong will bordering on stubbornness, a readiness to charge toward his goal, whatever it was, regardless of obstacles or the price.

Primakov had met Hussein again as recently as a couple of years ago, after the end of the war between Iraq and Iran, and discussed with him his plans for the future. Hussein's primary ambition was to make Iraq a regional first-rate power (with Soviet arms supplies and military advisers, he hoped) so as to eliminate what he regarded as detestable regimes in Saudi Arabia and Syria whom he considered his archenemies. Even now, according to Primakov, despite the presence of American troops on Saudi Arabian soil, those two countries were facing a threat of aggression from Iraq. As to Syria, Hussein boasted that he was in a position to stage a revolt there, even a coup, anytime, to overthrow the hated President Assad, just by lifting his finger.

Primakov clearly preferred to steer a middle course in the current crisis. The most important thing, in his view, was to try to find a political solution. By contrast, some in the Soviet Union advocated activating the treaty on mutual assistance to help Iraq. An internal struggle was going on inside the Soviet leadership over what position to take, with the military clearly opposing any moves to act in concert with the United States and the international community to punish the aggressor. Gorbachev's plan was for a political solution. Yet, a sizable number of Soviet military advisers were in Iraq, many of whom were close to the top echelons of power in Baghdad. How could they not have known about Hussein's plans to invade Kuwait? Why were they still in Iraq? Why had they not been withdrawn yet? I had taken the liberty to ask this question of Shevardnadze after one of his telephone conversations with Secretary Baker a couple of weeks before the summit, late in August.

For one thing, Shevardnadze said, besides the military advisers, six thousand Soviet civilian experts or "specialists," to use the then current Soviet terminology, were in Iraq. The Iraqis let it be known that if the Soviet military advisers were withdrawn, they would not let those six thousand experts leave and would hold them as hostages, just like the many thousands of other foreign citizens then in Iraq. Granted, this was a good reason to show caution, yet the nagging question remained: Was such a position morally justified when other nations were taking a strong stance against Saddam Hussein despite their citizens' being held as a "live shield," or hostages, to protect him against a possible Western attack?

Two other members of the Soviet team, Bessmertnykh and Mamedov, had also made a trip to Baghdad a couple of years before and met with Hussein. Mamedov had always impressed me with his realistic approach to politics. He talked sense, he was intelligent, and he was a rising star on the MFA diplomatic horizon.

Mamedov added a few extra touches to the portrait of Hussein. He was even more blunt in his characterization of Hussein than Primakov. He thought that no self-respecting political leader should consider himself bound by any treaty with Hussein, because he was the kind of person who would go to any lengths to achieve his personal ambitions. He had been thwarted in his attempts to conquer Iran, or at least to chop off a chunk of its territory. Yet, that failure did not dampen his greed. He decided for the time being to put Iran on the back burner and turn his attention to smaller neighboring countries such as Kuwait to grab their riches and continue his expansion by swallowing up more Arab sheikhdoms and emirates. That, of course, was a sober, realistic assessment of the man who had brought about an international crisis.

The talk soon turned to the sorry state of the Soviet economy, and Bessmernykh and Akhromeyev had an argument. Bessmernykh blamed Prime Minister Ryzhkov for the breakdown of the economy over the last five years. He thought Ryzhkov should have resigned a long time ago. Akhromeyev sharply disagreed. He said it was not Ryzhkov but the people who were to blame. "People got out of hand," he insisted, and refused to work as they used to in the past, "especially under Stalin, when there was order in the country." What was needed was discipline, a "firm hand," he said.

While I couldn't agree with Akhromeyev's prescription, his diagnosis had merit. Most of the Soviet people did not seem willing to embrace a new market-oriented economic system. Sadly, when a Soviet collective farmer wanted to get out of his *kolkhoz* to lease a piece of land and work it on his own, his fellow collective farmers would come down hard on him because he wanted to become an independent operator. "Why," they said, "he just might get rich if he became a private farmer, while we would still remain poor!" "No," they said, "let him stay what he is— poor, like the rest of us!" Alas, such was the psychology of the average *Homo sovieticus*, the collective farmer, among others. A story, known to almost every Russian, illustrates the point:

Once upon a time, God came to a peasant to tell him he would grant any wish he might have, but on one condition: that he, God, would do exactly the same for the peasant's neighbor but twice as much. The peasant scratched his head in reflection and said, "In that case, you'd better gouge out my left eye."

The most difficult thing about *perestroika*, Gorbachev once admitted, was to "turn around the brains of our people."

Next, I had a little argument of my own with the marshal. I had known Akhromeyev since the 1987 Washington summit and had closely followed the increasingly fierce public polemics in the press between him and Georgy Arbatov over the role of the Soviet military-industrial complex, and I was interested to hear what he had to say on the matter at hand, as a top military man and adviser to the Soviet president. I asked, "Sergei Fyodorovich, what do you think of the Iraqis as fighters? One should assume, I suppose, that the Iraqi army would be no match for the Americans?"

By asking a question like that I also wanted to test the limits of *glasnost*, to see how someone in his position would react. Akhromeyev had been directly responsible for arming and training Iraqi officers, and my question must have touched him to the quick. He began vehemently to defend the Iraqis. He said he could not agree with me. For one thing, many Iraqi officers had received excellent training in the Soviet Union, he said. Their army was equipped with some of the best Soviet weapons, and they knew how to use those weapons. Besides, the Iraqi army, including its rank-and-file soldiers, had solid experience in the fighting against Iran, and that was by no means an unimportant factor.

He paused, darted a quick look at me, then said that the American troops assembled in Saudi Arabia had no such experience, and they were "hirelings" [nayemniki] anyway. He conceded that their matériel and equipment were good, but so far the Iraqis enjoyed an advantage in tanks. Even if hit from the air, they would not be destroyed right away. "So I wouldn't say that the Iraqi army is that much inferior to the Americans," concluded Akhromeyev.

That was a startling conclusion. It flew in the face of the facts and reality as I knew them. The marshal's sympathies clearly lay with Iraq. But then, maybe he knew something I didn't?

I pursued the question further: "What if Hussein used his chemical missiles, would that change substantially the course of hostilities?" Akhromeyev mulled over the question, then answered with disarming frankness that, in his view, chemical weapons were a weighty factor in the equation, and even if the Americans targeted the sites where they were stationed and tried to take them out from the air in one strike, the consequences and losses for the Americans would be too great. And that, according to him, could cause a backlash from the American public at home, and Bush's popularity would sharply plummet. In these circumstances, the use of chemical weapons would achieve the desired results, at least from Hussein's point of view, he added. It was an interesting opinion. I tried delicately to steer him to the subject of Soviet military advisers and asked why they were still in Iraq. But he evaded the issue and remarked only that they were not taking part in Iraqi combat operations.

After this, Akhromeyev sulked and shortly repaired to another room, taking Primakov with him. Those of us who remained exchanged glances. The differences between the diplomats and the military were not imaginary.

When his meeting with Bush had ended and the two leaders had addressed a few reporters' questions, Gorbachev came in our room and sat down at a small table. We clustered around him. He was full of impressions of his talks with Bush, and he seemed eager to share them with the rest of his team without delay.

"On the whole, we had a good conversation," he began. "Toward the end we started to address each other on a first-name basis. He called me Mikhail, and I called him George." Gorbachev said such informality helped them to deepen their personal relationship. He was exuberant about Bush's recognizing the legitimacy of a Soviet presence in the Middle East, something that was important, he stressed. He said he had extracted a promise from Bush that the U.S. troops would not remain in the Gulf area indefinitely and, consequently, would pose no threat to the Soviet Union on its southern borders. This assurance was important to the Soviet military in general, and to Akhromeyev in particular, for the marshal had earlier expressed strong misgivings on that score. Akhromeyev still did not trust the Americans, even after visiting the States so many times, both with Gorbachev and without him.

Having said this, Gorbachev complained that "they [the Americans] do not understand us," that "they" were not aware of all the consequences and implications in the event they decided to undertake military operations. "Well, suppose they hit Iraq, then what?"

A vexed look was on his face as he said this. To him, it was not merely a rhetorical question. He had to make the critical decision there and then on what position he should take in his next meeting with Bush some two hours from now. It seemed he had not made up his mind yet. Still, one could feel that he was leaning in favor of a peaceful, diplomatic way out of the crisis, even though such an approach would clearly be counterproductive under the circumstances. It would only give Hussein time to ensure his protection with a "live shield" of foreign hostages and to close Arab ranks by appealing to their nationalist feelings and thus turn their anger against the Americans. It would only strengthen his position in the Arab world.

Shevardnadze on the other hand was a little bolder in his approach. He knew as well as Gorbachev, on the basis of intelligence information and from debriefing some of the high-ranking Soviet officials who had previously visited Baghdad, that Saddam Hussein was confident that even if the Soviet Union would not support his adventure directly, at least it would not oppose him. Such presumptuousness on the part of the Iraqi ruler bothered Shevardnadze. He believed that the Soviet Union had to do something more drastic.

This impromptu meeting of Gorbachev and his advisers did not come to any conclusions because Raisa Maximovna appeared. She took her husband's arm, saying, "*Mikhal Sergeich*, it's time to go," and led him out of the room to join the Bushes in the State Room for lunch and another photo session. The photographers never had enough pictures, they always wanted more.

As the first couples were lunching with President Koivisto, I had lunch in the Pink Room with Pavel Palazchenko. As we sat there talking, Sergei Tarasenko rushed in looking for us. He had the latest version of the American draft joint statement on two pages, which he said Gorbachev wanted to see translated into Russian as soon as possible. We divided the text in two equal parts and tossed a coin. I won the toss and got the first page. Pavel got the second. Fifteen minutes later, the translation was ready in handwritten form.

To understand a few of the finer points of the final text of the joint statement eventually agreed upon by Gorbachev and Bush, it is instructive to follow how the American draft was revised in places by the Soviets. The original U.S. version read:

1. With regard to Iraq's illegal invasion and continued military occupation of Kuwait, President Bush and President Gorbachev issue the following joint statement:
2. We are united in the belief that Iraq's aggression must not be tolerated. No peaceful international order is possible if larger states can devour their smaller neighbors.
3. We reaffirm the joint statement of our foreign ministers of August 3, 1990, and our support for United Nations Security Council resolutions 660, 661, 662 [the number 663 was inadvertently omitted from the text but later restored], 664, and 665. Today we once again call upon the government of Iraq to withdraw unconditionally from Kuwait, and to free all hostages now held in Iraq and Kuwait.
4. Nothing short of the complete implementation of the Security Council resolutions is acceptable.
5. Nothing short of a return to the pre–August 2 status of Kuwait can end Iraq's isolation.
6. We call on the entire world community to adhere to the sanctions mandated by the United Nations, and we pledge to work, individually and in concert, to ensure full compliance with the sanctions. The United States and the Soviet Union further agree that the current situation does not warrant any exceptions in embargo provisions against Iraq.
7. The United States and the Soviet Union further agree that any such imports must be strictly monitored by the appropriate international agencies to ensure that food reaches only those for whom it is intended.

8. Our preference is to resolve this peacefully, and we will remain united against Iraq's aggression as long as the crisis exists. However, we are determined to see this aggression end, and if the current steps fail to end it, we are prepared to consider additional ones. We must demonstrate beyond any doubt that aggression cannot and will not pay.

9. Once our objectives mandated by the U.N. Security Council resolutions mentioned above have been achieved and we have demonstrated that aggression does not pay, the Presidents will direct their Foreign Ministers to work with countries in the region and outside it to develop regional security structures and measures to promote peace and stability. It is essential to work actively to resolve all remaining conflicts in the Middle East and Persian Gulf. Both sides will continue to consult each other and initiate measures to pursue these broader objectives at the proper time.

After the short luncheon at the Presidential Palace was over, the entire delegation returned to the Embassy and went into a huddle without wasting a minute. Gorbachev invited all those concerned to a room on the second floor to work on the U.S. version of the text. As he read the translation, he nodded in approval. He liked the basic thrust of the proposed text. But at paragraph 8, where it said "we are prepared to consider additional ones [steps]," he grew pensive. After a while he said that in his opinion this phrase actually meant that the United States could act alone to take such additional measures as it might deem necessary and, allowing for its growing impatience, such measures would most likely be military ones. "That's why," he said, "we should dampen their ardor and add here a phrase *under United Nations control.*"

It occurred to me that obviously the United States would not accept such a phrase because it might limit the scope of actions that it might eventually want to take. But the U.S. could certainly agree to act *in accordance with the U.N. Charter*—under Article 42 or 51, for example. Accordingly, I suggested this idea on the spur of the moment, and it was supported by Belonogov, the principal Soviet drafter, and accepted by Gorbachev, who said that he liked it. Developing my idea further, he argued aloud that if the United States went ahead with military operations, invoking Article 42 or 51 of the U.N. Charter, it would then act legitimately within its framework, and at the same time the phrase would "leave us room for our own interpretation" of such actions. "That way," he concluded, "both the wolves would be fed and the sheep would be alive." It was decided to include the phrase in the text.

It was almost 3 P.M.—time to return to the palace for the second round of talks with Bush and his team of advisers.

*　　　　*　　　　*

Five minutes later, we all were back in the Presidential Palace. This time the talks were held in the Yellow Salon, in a larger group, without ceremony or photographers. It was to be strictly business. The Soviet side was represented principally by Gorbachev, Shevardnadze, Primakov, Akhromeyev, and Bessmertnykh. Chernyaev and Tarasenko were the notetakers.

Besides Bush, the most important U.S. representatives at this meeting were Jim Baker, Brent Scowcroft, John Sununu, and Condoleezza Rice, who had been promoted, after the last Washington summit some three months before, to become the president's assistant on Soviet affairs and National Security Council chief expert on the Soviet Union. Marlin Fitzwater and Dennis Ross were the U.S. notetakers. The two presidents and their advisers made themselves comfortable in chairs, grouped in a semicircle. Bush and Gorbachev sat by the wall under a painting depicting a green forest. They were separated by a small low table on which two omnidirectional microphones were set up for the benefit of us, the simultaneous interpreters.

Bush was the first to speak: "We have no secret agenda for this meeting. We have had a good discussion this morning. Welcome."

Gorbachev: I welcome your colleagues. All of us have been working with them continuously and successfully. I don't know about Mr. Fitzwater, though, whether or not he's changed for the worse. [Gorbachev was poking fun at the corpulent White House spokesman, who looked like a genial Nikita Khrushchev. Gorbachev was still smarting from Fitzwater's offensive description of him, in the spring of 1989, as a "drugstore cowboy" and did not fail to take this opportunity to needle him.]

I, too, agree with the president that we had a thorough discussion. My colleagues on our side will read the record of that discussion. It is important that in these trying times for international relations we have cooperated and worked together, relying on support from the United Nations and the world public opinion. This is a great achievement if you will recall the 1967 crisis and the way it developed at the time. Although the situation now is difficult, we have been able to cope with it so far. We have noted today that what has been achieved makes it possible to say that some of the strategic objectives have already been reached. We have jointly condemned the aggression and we have hindered the possibility [for the aggressor] to act further with impunity. We have agreed on an embargo and on the need to preserve an important source of oil resources.

On the basis of this, we can say that we already have some major accomplishments to our credit, and the next phase now would be to enforce compliance with the Security Council resolutions, in particular resolution 661. So during the next stage of the crisis we will be acting from a position of strength rather than weakness. There are some hotheads out there who insinuate that we are acting from a position of weakness. But surely, that's not the case. The president and I have considered a number of alternatives concerning further development of events, and we did so in a very productive manner. . . .

Speaking about the joint statement, I have studied it, and I will now comment on it.

We have some comments to make on page one, some clarifications, if you will. The word *illegal* before *invasion* [in paragraph 1] should be deleted. There are no legal invasions after all, even though Hussein yesterday tried to prove otherwise [an obvious reference to Hussein's letter to Gorbachev].

Bush: Okay.

Gorbachev: Second, the paragraph on the first page [paragraph 6] that says, "We call on the entire world community . . . ," and to the end of the first phrase, "to ensure full compliance with the sanctions." I suggest making a full stop here and deleting the rest. The word *full* means that there are no exceptions.

As to the next paragraph [6a], we propose adding the following: *At the same time, the Soviet Union and the United States recognize that U.N. Security Council Resolution 661 permits, in humanitarian circumstances, the importation of food into Iraq and Kuwait;* and further down in the text [of paragraph 7], where it is important to stress that *such imports must be strictly monitored by the appropriate international agencies,* perhaps we should also say something about children, that priority must be given to them, and that food must reach only those for whom it is intended, something like *with special priority being given to meeting the needs of children.* The next phrase [paragraph 8], "Our preference is to resolve this [crisis] peacefully. . . ," and still further down, where it says "additional ones" [steps], add, *consistent with the U.N. Charter.* That is to say, we will, once again, have recourse to the United Nations. And then it will be a strong statement.

Bush: I would call on our lawyer to work on it. It will be a very strong statement. . . . I think it will have a strong positive impact.

The exchange was followed by more drafting work. More amendments and subamendments were proposed, considered, discussed, and either accepted or rejected. All this was done in a remarkably businesslike and cooperative spirit. It took the two leaders forty minutes to reach final agreement on the text. The statement was extraordinary in that Bush and Gorbachev did the nitty-gritty drafting by themselves, something that does not happen often at the top level, and especially by leaders of the two superpowers. Both men were pragmatists and did not disdain to do what they might have entrusted their advisers or experts to do for them. With this major piece of business out of the way, Gorbachev, relief clearly discernible on his face, cheerfully uttered in English, "Well." Bush reacted instantly.

Bush: Ronald Reagan liked to say "well." I understand he will be in the Soviet Union soon. He has great affection for you. He believes he got your relationship going. [Reagan was indeed going to visit the Soviet Union at Gorbachev's invitation, in the third week of September.]

Are there any other matters that are of interest to you? We for our part would like to discuss some questions relating to the Soviet Union, and how we can have positive influence. I would think we will work together better on economic questions in Eastern Europe and the Soviet Union. I will welcome your ideas on that score . . . all the more so that you have now reached a crucial stage in your reforms. . . .

Gorbachev: Very good. "Well," as Ronald Reagan used to say indeed. You are right in saying that we have reached now the most crucial stage in the framework of our reforms. This accounts for all the political passions that are running high in our society. So far we have been able to keep them within the framework of discussions. But all too often, the debates are getting too heated. Still, so far we have been able to avoid global [sic] clashes or civil war.

[Gorbachev talked about his country going through tough times, what with its "complex society" facing so many problems: political, social, economic, and so forth. Then he continued:]

Our society now seems to understand the necessity of making a transition to the market [economy]. It understands that if we are to achieve it, we must have a different situation in the economy, that new entities must emerge in our economy. Where will all this come from? This will come from changing the relations of ownership. There will be a difficult process of denationalization. . . . We already have privatization in various forms. . . .

Well, then, the most important thing is that despite all these numerous problems and our complex society, we are well on the way to market-oriented relations. This can push up the prices. And so there is a clash of opinions on how we should proceed toward the market. Should the market set the prices, or should it be done centrally? Academician Shatalin's group believes that first and foremost it is necessary to go through a period of stabilization, and later on the market itself will determine the prices. But that means that we must withdraw surplus cash and add it to the market. So there is a debate going on about this program. Our plan provides for a transition to the market to begin on October 1.

Bush: When you submit this plan to the republics, will they have to approve it?

Gorbachev: They will make their comments, and then it will mean an okay.

Bush: How long is the time frame?

Gorbachev: Four to five months for stabilization, so as to start introducing price changes after that. And, the actual entry into the market—1991–92; that is to say, a year or a year and a half from now. And then, this process will continue to develop. Our people fear soaring prices and unemployment. Our society has been accustomed to believing that somebody else will do the thinking and make decisions for them. But now they have to make decisions for themselves. This may seem strange to you. So we'll have to exert enormous efforts to set this process in motion. We may have to take unpopular steps. But we can no longer delay it further. Unless radical steps are taken now, there will emerge a threat of disintegration. The choice is simple: either we act decisively now, or we'll face an economic chaos. We intend to follow this path.

For that reason, we need understanding. But that's not enough. We must also have financial possibilities for maneuvering, so that we can satisfy the consumer, so that people will feel that although the prices are changing, the situation in the market is changing for the better. And so, we hope for financial assistance and products from Western countries. . . . We'll need credits . . . not at high rates, but not for free. We'll return them, that is the credits and loans—in short, the financial aid—in a few years' time. But the first stage is crucial in our reform, the first four or five months. And here, your position would be of great importance. I hope when Baker comes to the Soviet Union [Secretary Baker planned to pay a visit starting the following night, September 10, and through September 13], we'd like to hear some specific approaches and views on this score. This moment has now arrived.

After questioning Gorbachev some more about his plans for the Soviet economy, Bush suggested discussing specific projects for cooperation in the economic sphere. He offered to send U.S. governors to the Soviet Union to share their experience in running their states. Such experience, he said, would be helpful to Soviet republics. Bush was also concerned about the problem of power sharing between the center and the republics, especially now that many of them had proclaimed their sovereignty. Gorbachev explained that although the republics had indeed proclaimed sovereignty, they had nothing to support it with. Many simply did not have the resources. They were beginning to realize that their sovereignty was hollow, empty, and they were increasingly conscious of the need for the center, i.e., the central government in Moscow, to retain the basic functions of governing the country. This involved above all the regulation of finances, money circulation and so forth.

Turning to specific projects in which interested U.S. companies could provide assistance, Gorbachev suggested that these could include exploration and development of oil reserves, specifically the oil field near Arkhangelsk, and implementation of a joint project for developing a Soviet-American-Israeli aircraft for which the fuselage would be built by the Soviet Union, the engine by the United States, and the cockpit by Israel.

Bush heard him out attentively and said that a high-level delegation of fifteen American businessmen led by the secretary of commerce, Robert Mosbacher, would be in Moscow on September 13–14 and would have some proposals to make for specific joint projects. It would be the first time, he said, that such a high-level delegation of so many prominent U.S. businessmen would be visiting the USSR. Hopefully, something concrete would come of it.

Anyway, Bush stressed that he would not object to providing assistance to the Soviet Union. As to financial aid, the question was already being studied by experts, said Bush.

The animated discussion continued until almost 5 P.M., at which time the two presidents decided to call it a day. The second and last meeting of the minisummit was over, and both leaders were satisfied with its results. Now they were expected at Finlandia Hall for a joint press conference scheduled for 5:30. The discussion was basically between Bush and Gorbachev, with Baker participating and interjecting comments more actively than did Shevardnadze. Primakov and Akhromeyev contributed to the discussion rather sparingly. Scowcroft also made a few remarks.

The U.S. side seemed generally well disposed and receptive to Soviet ideas and suggestions. At the same time, the Soviet side seemed somewhat constrained and embarrassed about having to discuss aid, especially after its recent public declarations that the Soviet Union "does not need any assistance from the West." Such pronouncements had been made by Shevardnadze and Primakov, among others, just a few months before. The economic situation was deteriorating rapidly. Apparently, it was so bad that all considerations of national pride had to be set aside to make a plea for aid. Otherwise, the reforms would simply fall apart, spelling an end to *perestroika*.

In making this appeal, Gorbachev stressed that *perestroika* was necessary for the West no less than for the Soviet Union. He hinted at the possibility of a coming dictatorship, a "strong hand" taking over and reversing everything he had achieved so far in international relations, should the reforms fail. And, he stressed that if this came about, the West and the United States had better be prepared for a new arms race, a new rise in tensions, in short, a revival of the Cold War. But he never said so explicitly.

After the meeting broke, Bush wanted to tie up some loose ends in light of the upcoming press conference. In a stand-up conversation with Gorbachev, he wondered what the Soviet president thought about their next meeting—to discuss, and possibly sign, a START agreement—which was being planned for later that year. Gorbachev replied that it was something to strive for, his intention to that end had not changed. Bush mulled over his reply and said, "All right, this is what we'll tell the reporters then. But it would be more realistic to assume that the next meeting would most probably take place sometime early next year." (In fact, the next meeting of the two presidents did not take place until the middle of the following year, i.e., at the end of July 1991, in Moscow, when they would finally sign the START treaty—barely three weeks before the coup d'état against Gorbachev).

Gorbachev knew that the START treaty would not be completed before the end of the year, all pledges to the contrary notwithstanding. He was coming under increasing pressure from his military, most of whom were resisting further progress in Geneva. By this time, Yazov, Kryuchkov, and Co. were having second thoughts about the wisdom of making drastic cuts in the Soviet nuclear arsenal. They could not stomach what they perceived as the impending loss by the Soviet Union of its superpower status. The military felt that the ground was slipping from under it and was using the technical details in verifying compliance with a treaty as an excuse for dragging its feet.

Judging from the backstage utterances by Akhromeyev, the differences between the Soviet military and political leadership over the future of their strategic and conventional forces were growing. The generals still harbored deep-seated suspicions that the United States and

NATO had "insidious designs on the Soviet Union." They considered it intolerable that their political leadership was willing to accept extensive verification and on-site inspections of both conventional armaments and strategic nuclear weapons. They singled out Shevardnadze for special criticism, accusing him of disarming the Soviet Union unilaterally. That was a serious charge.

By now, everyone concerned knew that the Geneva talks had hopelessly bogged down in technical details, and only a forceful political decision at the very top could help break what amounted to a virtual impasse. However, Gorbachev was at present forced to give his undivided attention to economic problems and reform at home and, as a consequence, slackened his vigilance vis-à-vis the military.

Gorbachev and Bush agreed to meet in Finlandia Hall in thirty minutes, after which Gorbachev withdrew to the room reserved for the Soviet delegation to exchange impressions about the second and last round of talks with Bush. In his words, the Americans were willing to go to any length to secure "our continued support" in the Gulf. "As for us, we haven't given up anything, we've stuck to our guns." He looked around the room to see the reaction, then went on to say how important it was that Bush had promised economic aid. "It is very, very important," he stressed, involuntarily mimicking Thatcher. "Western support, especially from the USA, is needed now as never before. Without such support, we won't be able to drag our economy out of the quagmire."

After this meeting the Soviet and U.S. delegations left the Presidential Palace for the joint press conference.

Finlandia Hall is a big, white, modern conference building, where the first Conference on Security and Cooperation in Europe (CSCE) took place in 1975 and where thirty-five heads of state of Europe, Canada, and the United States signed the Helsinki Act.

After entering the building and waiting in a VIP lounge, we were ushered up a narrow staircase to the stage and found ourselves in the wings. There, a few moments later, we were joined by President and Mrs. Bush. In the obligatory small talk, M.S. noted it was good that "Barbara and Raisa Maximovna" had spent some time together, sight-seeing in Helsinki. Mrs. Bush replied that unfortunately they had not been able to tour the harbor in a pleasure boat, as originally planned, because she didn't want to be seen back home having a good time "while the American young men are suffering from heat and uncertainty in Saudi Arabia." That was as close as Mrs. Bush came to discussing politics. R.M. said nothing, and M.S. tried to change the subject.

At this point, Bush beckoned a brawny, young black man, with an attaché case in his right hand, from among his retinue and asked Gorbachev if he remembered Bill. M.S. gave the young man one look and demonstrated his phenomenal photographic memory. He said, yes, of course, he did remember Bill and asked him if he still pumped iron in the Camp David gym. When I translated, Bill was awfully pleased and smiled back broadly. "Yes, sir," he answered curtly, in the military fashion.

At 5:30, the Finnish chief of protocol asked the two presidents to get ready to go to the stage as an announcer's voice resounded through the conference hall: "Ladies and gentlemen! President Bush and President Gorbachev!" The two presidents walked toward a table with a battery of microphones in the center of the stage. They were followed by their respective spokesmen, Ignatenko and Fitzwater, who mounted two lecterns flanking the table. Their job was to alternately give the floor to reporters for questions. I took the chair behind and slightly to the left of Gorbachev. Zarechnyak sat behind and to the right of Bush. The hall was packed. Gorbachev estimated there were at least seventeen hundred correspondents, among whom were many familiar faces: the indefatigable summit veteran UPI reporter Helen Thomas, CNN's Charles Bierbauer, *Izvestia*'s Stanislav Kondrashov, *Pravda*'s Thomas Kolesnichenko.

The press conference went off well, but not without a little hitch. Halfway through it, as Bush was speaking, his microphone suddenly stopped and the interpretation (it was simultaneous, from the booths) as well. Bush struggled with his earphones, apparently thinking that was the problem. Gorbachev turned back to me and asked me to help Bush, as if I knew how. I approached Bush to explain that something was wrong with his mike, not the earphones. Bush took a whack at it, but it didn't help. "*A ty yesche raz udar', Djordj,*" Gorbachev suggested, and I translated, "Hit it again, George!" Bush whacked the mike again and this time it worked. A little later, the same thing happened to Gorbachev's mike. He raised his right hand over the mike, as if to follow Bush's example. "Well, shall I hit it, too?" he said, and when I translated this remark loudly from the stage, the audience exploded in laughter. But the mike came back on by itself, without encouragement from the presidential fist.

The hour-long press conference ended at 6:45 P.M. With that the Helsinki emergency summit was over.

Bush was the first to leave Helsinki to fly back to Washington. He was followed by Baker, who went to Brussels to report to NATO allies on the results of the summit. Half an hour later, after a brief farewell ceremony at the airport, Gorbachev's Ilyushin-62M took off, bound for Moscow. Initially, the plan had been to stay in Helsinki overnight, but due to unforeseen circumstances, which I will explain below, he decided to cut short his stay.

What did the emergency summit accomplish? was the question on everyone's mind as we flew back home from Helsinki. Most importantly, this was the first time since the end of World War II that the Soviet Union and the United States had sent a clear message to the world that they were determined to cooperate, as partners, to solve a military crisis. The presidents' joint statement demonstrated that the Soviet Union and the United States were no longer on opposite sides.

Despite the diminishing status of the Soviet Union as a superpower and all its domestic problems, it still retained its veto power in the Security Council of the United Nations, and if it had wanted, it could certainly have resorted to this to cause mischief, as it had done so many times in the past during the Cold War.

What were Gorbachev's motives in joining the United States in a partnership?

Moving from declarations of cooperation to actual partnership was new thinking in action. Gorbachev wanted to maintain his image as a great international statesman who had consigned the Cold War to the ash heap of history. And he certainly deserved enormous credit for this. He was also eager to demonstrate that the Soviet Union was still a power to be reckoned with, whatever assertions to the contrary may have been made, such as Saddam Hussein's charge that Moscow's support for American actions in the Gulf indicated the decline of the Soviet Union as a world power. Obviously, economics played a role, too: the USSR badly needed an infusion of Western economic assistance, particularly investments.

Above all, the emergency summit was another major milestone in the continuously evolving relationship between the Soviet Union and the United States from hostility and enmity at the height of the Cold War to cooperation and, now, to partnership. In their joint press conference, both leaders repeatedly called on Hussein to back off, contending that Iraq's already deep political and economic isolation was now even deeper because of the new Soviet-American unity that had emerged as a result of this one-day summit. It was curious to hear Gorbachev first deny the need to resort to military force to bring Iraq to its knees, even if peaceful methods would not work, while agreeing, later, to use "all necessary means" toward that end. That was yet another sign of the evolution of his own thinking. Clearly, only military force would dislodge Iraq from Kuwait.

Last but not least, at the press conference Gorbachev also emphasized that "today's meeting has ensured unity of action not only in the Security Council, but to a large extent unity in the world community—this is unprecedented solidarity." He also stressed his intention to closely and actively cooperate within the Security Council of the United Nations, a hint that if all else had failed, he would support the United States should it decide to act militarily.

And he did. On the afternoon of November 29, 1990, the Soviet Union, represented by Foreign Minister Shevardnadze, would vote, in a special meeting of the U.N. Security Council presided over by Secretary of State Baker, in favor of resolution 678, authorizing the use of force to expel Iraq from Kuwait.

After we returned to the Embassy from the press conference, and while Gorbachev was giving an interview to Soviet television on the second floor, I was told Gorbachev had just decided to cut short his stay in Helsinki and return to Moscow. The decision took everyone by surprise. I tried to find out what had happened, but no one seemed to know.

I remembered that the Supreme Soviet of the USSR was scheduled to meet in the Kremlin the following day, September 10. Gorbachev was expected to address the Supreme Soviet, but not necessarily at its opening session—he could certainly do it either in the afternoon of the same day or on the following day. But now at the Embassy, we were told to pack our things as quickly as we could and be ready to leave for the airport in half an hour. Dark hints were dropped here and there that something unusual was afoot in Moscow, and later the following picture emerged.

On the day of the summit, several paratrooper units from as far away as Leningrad and other remote areas were unexpectedly moved to Moscow—ostensibly to help with harvesting the potato crop. Under different circumstances, it would have been routine for Soviet soldiers to be used as a free labor force. Students and even white- and blue-collar workers often worked once or twice a year in the fields to help collective farmers with harvesting. But in this case, while the paratroopers had indeed been sent to the fields near Moscow, they were in full combat gear with automatic weapons. Nobody at the Embassy or in Gorbachev's entourage seemed to know what was going on at home and what it all meant. Or, maybe they knew but pretended they didn't.

When I heard the confused whispering in the corners of the Embassy hall on the second floor, I had a foreboding that something was going to happen. All kinds of things seemed to have happened in Moscow before when Gorbachev was out of town. The growing resentment of Gorbachev's reforms and heretofore hidden resistance from the Party, the old guard in the KGB, the military, and the military-industrial complex who saw their grip on power slipping was an open secret. In Moscow, just before Gorbachev left for Helsinki, the possibility of a coup was rumored.

All of us rushed back to the hotel to pack our bags and return to the Embassy speedily to leave for the airport together in a motorcade. Shortly, at 8:15 P.M., we were on our way back to Moscow.

We landed at Vnukovo-2 at about midnight (there is a two-hour time difference between Helsinki and Moscow). Zil limousines and numerous official black Volga cars were out on the tarmac to take everyone to their homes. I got home well after midnight.

What I learned in the next few days confirmed my worst suspicions. According to one version of events, an abortive coup attempt had been made against Gorbachev. The coup plotters, whoever they were, decided at the last minute to take advantage of Gorbachev's absence from Moscow to try to depose him, much as Khrushchev had been ousted twenty-six years before. But either because they had miscalculated or failed to coordinate their actions properly, or simply because someone blew the whistle on them, the coup did not materialize.

According to another version, a group of Communist Party hard-liners and disgruntled military and KGB generals decided to bring pressure on Gorbachev to abandon the plan for the five-hundred-day market-oriented economic program—drawn up and scheduled to be introduced on October 1—by doing a little muscle-flexing and sending armed paratroopers to "harvest potatoes."

This second version implied there must have been a stormy showdown between Gorbachev and the hard-liners before the Helsinki summit, and he was presented with an ultimatum: soft-pedal on the reforms, get rid of Shevardnadze, who was a thorn in their flesh, and give the top positions to hard-liners or else. The names of those hard-liners, which were shrouded in mystery at the time, later became well-known to the whole world. They were Gennady Yanayev, Valentin Pavlov, Boris Pugo & Co., and most importantly, Minister of Defense Dmitry Yazov and KGB chairman Vladimir Kryuchkov. They were the ones who would stage the real coup d'état against Gorbachev on August 19–21, 1991.

Being a skillful tactician, Gorbachev must have decided, after receiving information about the impending coup, to do a tightrope act to stay in power and steer a middle course for the sake of preserving *perestroika* and making it irreversible. He wanted to keep the wolves satisfied and the sheep alive. He fed the wolves by appointing Yanayev as vice president, Pavlov as prime minister, and Pugo as minister of police. But he failed to keep the sheep alive or, to be more precise, his closest comrades-in-arms. In a dramatic gesture some three months later, the proud Eduard Shevardnadze would resign because of his irreconcilable differences with the military, warning, as he did so, of a "coming dictatorship." And, Alexandr Yakovlev, the other staunch supporter and loyal associate of Gorbachev, would be quietly pushed to the sidelines.

After Helsinki, Gorbachev seemed to lack the energy and the vigorous sense of direction he had once had. While in the West the Soviet leader was still viewed as a bold and visionary statesman whose foreign policy initiatives had changed the world, in the Soviet Union the father of *perestroika* and *glasnost* was coming across as hesitant and indecisive, more at home in Communist Party intrigue than in the new, more open politics he had done so much to create. Soon after his return from Helsinki, Gorbachev would swerve to the right, then back to the left, in an attempt to steer a middle course. Little did anybody know then, including Gorbachev himself, that a real coup was barely ten months away.

CHAPTER SEVEN

REAGAN'S SOVIET REUNIONS

Ex-President's Nostalgic Journey to Moscow, 1990

MOSCOW. SEPTEMBER 16, SUNDAY. DAY ONE.

It had been drizzling since early morning. The overcast sky and the gloomy weather, which had set in in Moscow at the beginning of September, inspired in me a sense of melancholy and made me long for sunny California. California was on my mind because on that Sunday, September 16, Moscow was preparing to welcome Ronald Reagan, former governor of the state and now a resident again after leaving the White House. Some three months earlier, at the beginning of June, in San Francisco, Gorbachev had invited him to come to the Soviet Union together with Nancy on an informal visit. Reagan readily accepted the invitation to revisit Moscow, which he had not been able to see properly during his first, historic visit here in 1988. I was assigned to act as his interpreter.

Now that the Cold War was over, Reagan's trip here had the feel of a nostalgic journey, a return to the site of a past glory. Surely, one of the most euphoric moments of both his and Gorbachev's careers and of their relationship must have been the Moscow summit of 1988 when the general secretary was still enjoying Gorbomania and Reagan, a life-long anticommunist, had the pleasure of visiting the "Evil Empire" and finding that it was no longer so evil.

Reagan was arriving a week after Gorbachev's return from the one-day summit with Bush in Helsinki. As I said in the previous chapter, the Soviet Union was then facing one of the most momentous decisions in its seventy-three-year history: whether to proceed with the dismantling of the Communist system by going ahead with a radical economic reform in accordance with the five-hundred-day plan. The plan had been developed by a group of top economists headed by the academician Stanislav Shatalin, with Grigory Yavlinsky, the thirty-seven-year-old economic whiz kid said to be its chief architect, and it provided for a phased transition to a free market system in five hundred days. The plan, if approved by the Supreme Soviet, would come into effect on October 1. The time had come for a clear break with the legacy of the 1917 Bolshevik revolution.

On this Sunday afternoon of September 16, as I approached the MFA building on Smolenskaya Ploschad (Smolenskaya Square), where I was supposed to be picked up by an official car to go to Sheremetievo-1 airport to welcome Reagan, I saw a big crowd moving from Gorky Park in the direction of the Kremlin. The mob was chanting, "Resign! Resign!" Some of the demonstrators were beating kitchen saucepans with spoons and making a lot of noise.

A passerby told me that a huge rally had just taken place near Gorky Park where the participants had demanded the resignation of Prime Minister Ryzhkov. Nikolai Ivanovich Ryzhkov was said to be opposed to the rapid introduction of a free market—a burning subject that was under discussion in the nation's principal legislature. Ryzhkov was not opposed to a market-oriented economy per se but advocated a slow transition and had stated so in a speech before the Supreme Soviet in May. Still, in the public eye, he was associated with antimarket forces.

But the main reason for the demonstration that day was really the shortage of even the most basic foods, medicines, and consumer goods. The old system of production had been destroyed and a new one had not yet been put in place.

The demonstration was an alarming sign of how rapidly things were falling apart.

I arrived at Sheremetievo-1 an hour before Reagan's plane was scheduled to land. As I waited in the Deputies' Lounge, as the VIP room on the second floor was called, with a small group of Soviet and U.S. welcomers, I felt a rush of adrenaline. I was excited at the prospect of working once again with Reagan, especially in combination with Gorbachev.

I'd expected that Reagan would bring an interpreter of his own, but since he was now out of office, he apparently was no longer entitled to an official American interpreter. That was understandable. But what I could not understand was why the top-ranking official delegation of the U.S. Congress, led by Senate Republican minority leader Bob Dole, which paid an official visit to Leningrad and Moscow only a couple of weeks earlier and met with Gorbachev and Yeltsin, had not brought an American interpreter with them, although I was glad and honored to act as their interpreter.

So now, as in that case, an interpreter was provided by the host country. On the other hand, Reagan as a former president was entitled to no fewer than eighteen bodyguards.

In the Deputies' Lounge, apart from members of the American advance party, there was the affable, as usual, Anatoly Fyodorovich Dobrynin. He was said to be almost a personal friend of Reagan's. There was Ambassador Matlock with his wife, Rebecca. And there was Vadim Medvedev, a member of Gorbachev's new Presidential Council. One of the less noticeable figures in the now defunct Politburo, who had been in charge of ideology, he always struck me as a gloomy individual devoid of charisma. Why he was picked by Gorbachev to extend a welcome to Reagan at the airport on his behalf I do not know.

The Reagans had flown into Leningrad the day before, on September 15, from Gdansk, Poland. Earlier, the former president had addressed the Polish Sejm in Warsaw, and before that he had visited Bonn and Berlin. In Leningrad, he was greeted by Mayor Anatoly Sobchak. Then, he and Nancy toured the famed Hermitage Museum, did sight-seeing at the Palace of Catherine the Great in the town of Pushkin near Leningrad, attended a service at the Alexander Nevsky Monastery, and took a walk down Nevsky Prospect—Leningrad's equivalent of Fifth Avenue. In short, Reagan toured the major sights of the Palmira or the Venice of the North as a real tourist with no official meetings to think about.

As scheduled, at 6:15 on the dot, the plane landed. The aircraft was decidedly not presidential in appearance. Short, small, and "paunchy," painted the color of an egg yolk, with a bright green tail, it was a far cry from Air Force One. It was difficult to imagine that Reagan would arrive in a plane like this, but my puzzlement dissolved when I spotted the words inscribed in large letters on the tail: *FORBES,* and in smaller letters, *Capitalist Tool.* Ambassador Matlock explained that the private Boeing 727 had belonged to the late Malcolm Forbes, the celebrated American billionaire who had been a great personal friend of the Reagans. The *Capitalist Tool* was put at the disposal of the Reagans for this trip by Forbes's son.

The aircraft had scarcely come to a stop when a boarding ramp was wheeled out to its side, the door was opened, and Ambassador Matlock ran up the stairs. A minute later, the two familiar figures emerged in the plane's doorway. Ronald Reagan wore a light beige raincoat. Nancy Reagan was dressed in a lilac wool suit. As he descended the ramp, Reagan supported Nancy by the forearm. At the foot of the ramp, during the inevitable round of handshakes, Reagan greeted me with his familiar "It's good to see you again," accompanied by a firm handshake. But his eyes did not exude the magnetism and the irresistible charisma they had in the old days. I would say he looked somewhat confused and at a loss. I wondered if it was jet lag, but he had visibly declined, even in these past three and a half months since San Francisco. As the world would later learn, Reagan was suffering from the early stages of Alzheimer's disease.

The welcoming ceremony was short and simple, without pomp or circumstance, appropriate for a private citizen. Then the Reagans were taken to Spaso House in the Old Arbat, just as in 1988. My presence there that evening was not required, so I walked back home.

SEPTEMBER 17, MONDAY. DAY TWO.

Weeks before Reagan's visit his people had requested that he be given an opportunity to address a session of the Supreme Soviet, the national legislature. They were firmly told that was impossible because that very day Gorbachev would be appearing before the parliament to deliver the keynote address on the transition to a free market economy. The Soviet people would not understand, or so the officials said, if Reagan was allowed to speak there on the same day. Instead, they suggested that Reagan address one of the committees of the Supreme Soviet, specifically the International Affairs Committee. Some officials were evidently loath to provide the nation's loftiest rostrum to Reagan from which he could "lecture" the Soviet populace on the virtues of capitalism. Aware only too well of his ability to attract broad masses and win their sympathies and hearts, the authorities obviously feared that his prestige would only rise among the common Soviet people, who—thanks to the now irreversible *glasnost*—would be watching his speech on television and could thus form their own opinion of this "notorious" American president. Just the day before, I had even heard some people in the top echelons grumble that it would be too great an honor for Reagan even to be allowed to address one of the committees, and for that matter, he should be grateful that he was allowed to speak publicly at all. The denial of the Supreme Soviet platform was a great disappointment to Reagan, but since he had no alternative, he accepted the offer to speak before the International Affairs Committee. He wanted to become the first American president, albeit with the prefix *ex*, to appear before one of the Supreme Soviet committees. His appearance would raise the bar of relations between the two countries one notch. Something like this would have been unthinkable even two years earlier.

I met the Reagans at Spaso House in the morning and barely had time to glance at Reagan's twenty-four-page speech I would be translating before the motorcade left for the Kremlin. In the Kremlin, at the central entrance to the yellow building of the Supreme Soviet, which is near Spasskiye Vorota (the Spassky Gate), the protocol officer of the Supreme Soviet was waiting with a concerned expression on his face.

The four of us—Ronald and Nancy Reagan, the protocol officer, and I—had already passed through the central door and mounted the stairs in the lobby to take the elevator to the fourth floor, when suddenly a breathless Fred Ryan, one of Reagan's closest aides, caught up with his boss, blurting out excitedly, "We are not going any further, Mr. President! The KGB stopped our people! They are not letting them in!" He was referring to the other members of Reagan's group. But before Reagan had time to react, the Kremlin security guards—seeing that one of Reagan's assistants had broken through their protective lines and reported to him what had happened, and realizing that they had over-stepped the mark—relented and let in the other Americans. Ryan was pleased. "It's all right now, Mr. President. We can go," he said. The moment the elevator doors shut, Reagan exclaimed in a deliberately loud and clear voice, raising his head toward the ceiling as he did so, apparently for the benefit of the walls, "This must stop if they want friendship with us! The KGB must not be allowed to do this to our people! We must send them a clear message about that!"

But things did not go beyond that. Reagan forgot this little incident the minute he stepped out of the elevator and would never bring it up again, either with Gorbachev or with Yeltsin. He was in a rather genial and conciliatory mood.

This incident wasn't just happenstance. It was but one in a whole series of similarly petty incidents clearly intended to poison the atmos-phere of steadily improving relations between the Soviet Union and the United States. They were obviously orchestrated by someone higher up. This reminded me of another incident that had occurred just a few days before Reagan's arrival. Concurrently with Secretary Baker, a large dele-gation of American businessmen came to Moscow, in keeping with Pres-ident Bush's promise to Gorbachev in Helsinki to send them to share their experience in entrepreneurship.

While Baker and Robert Mosbacher, the U.S. secretary of commerce, who led the delegation, were having talks with Gorbachev in the Kremlin, a "competent comrade"—no less than a KGB general who had accompanied Gorbachev to Helsinki and who was in command of the presidential security detail in the Kremlin on the day of the talks with the Americans—vented his anger at Americans, in defiance of all diplomatic etiquette. He said too many of "these Americans," meaning those from Baker's security detail, were allowed into the waiting room next to Gorbachev's office where the talks were under way. "They must be taking us for Zulus or something!" blazed the general. "When we go over there, they don't let us inside the White House!" Then he loudly ordered, to no one in particular, "Let them get out of here!" and added a few strong expletives. When he spotted me in the room, he insisted that I translate his bombast for the Americans.

I retorted that I was not his subordinate, but a diplomat working for a different agency and would not translate his order, for it could have undesirable political consequences. One should have seen his face at that moment. I thought he was going to have a stroke there and then. The general accused all MFA people, and the MFA as a whole, of conniving with American "insolence." "But for the MFA," he railed, "they would not even have set foot in here!" And with those words the general stormed out of the room, slamming the door behind him. The Americans, of course, understood everything without translation. Body language is universal.

I believed that the "competent comrade" had made a spectacle of himself on instructions from Plekhanov, who had come out from the adjacent room and stood in a corner quietly watching as the general ranted. All orders concerning security came from Plekhanov. Was he the one who was orchestrating all those incidents behind Gorbachev's back, so as to cast a shadow on him? He could well have been, for he, like Kryuchkov and Yazov, would be one of the plotters against Gorbachev in the failed coup d'état in August of 1991.

When we entered the conference room on the fourth floor where Reagan was to speak, fifty-odd people were sitting on either side of a long wooden table. They did not applaud as Reagan entered. In the main, these were the members of the International Affairs Committee, but among them were quite a few men in military uniform. The more familiar faces around the table included Anatoly Dobrynin; Valentin Falin; Valentina Tereshkova, the first woman cosmonaut; and David Kulgutinov, the well-known Kalmyk poet.

The meeting was opened by the committee chairman, Alexandr Dza-sokhov, one of the former top Party ideologues and a member of the Presidential Council, promoted to this job by Gorbachev. In his brief introductory remarks, he reminded those present that Reagan's presidency had begun in 1981 "with a vision of our country as one that was covered with thunderclouds, a country that was the source of trouble to the whole world." But by the time he left office in January 1989, Reagan, as Dzasokhov emphasized, had formed a "different and fair image of the Soviet Union." Thus introduced, Reagan, followed by me, approached the lectern, positioned directly under a portrait of Karl Marx. The photographers had a field day. In 1988, it was Lenin, now it was Marx, but Reagan took it in stride. He never gave Marx a second look. He simply ignored him.

For the next forty-five or fifty minutes, standing shoulder to shoulder with Reagan behind the lectern and taking turns speaking into the microphone, I expounded, in consecutive interpretation into Russian, the quintessence of Reagan's philosophy, presented in his inimitable fashion. Reagan's performance, in words and gestures, could only be called vintage Reagan. For that reason, I think, it deserves to be presented in greater detail. Reagan began in his bedtime-story mellow voice:

"In America, there is a folk story about a man named Rip van Winkle who lived long ago. One day, it seems, Rip van Winkle fell asleep under a tree. When he did wake up and looked about, he did not recognize anything, because all had changed in those twenty years. Nowadays, if Rip van Winkle were to fall asleep in the Soviet Union, he would only have time for a very short nap before finding that everything had changed!"

Reagan paused, in anticipation of a reaction from the audience. There was none. The deputies, such as Valentin Falin, sat with stony faces. Unperturbed, Reagan went on with his speech. As he did during his official visit to Moscow in 1988, he spoke in the tone of a kindly teacher, lecturing Soviet students politely on the basics of freedoms and the marketplace. In his words, over the two years and four months since his first and last official visit to Moscow in May–June 1988, so many changes had occurred in the Soviet Union and the world that he was beginning to understand how Rip van Winkle must have felt. He noted the extraordinary cooperation of the United States and the Soviet Union in standing up to Saddam Hussein's aggression in Kuwait, the reduction of American and Soviet armaments, the end of the Soviet war in Afghanistan, and last but not least, the fall of the Berlin Wall as the symbol and monument of the Cold War.

Reagan continued, "And, here in the Soviet Union . . . you have embarked on a program of economic and political reforms that has surprised and sometimes stunned a curious and watching world. During my last visit here I met with the students of Moscow State University. I said to them that the key to progress is freedom, freedom of thought, freedom of information, freedom of communication. Under your *glasnost* policy those freedoms have begun to flower. But of course, having a little bit of freedom is like being a little bit pregnant—it isn't possible. One must be entirely free to think bold, even heretical, thoughts and to communicate them. And one must be free to acquire information from any source. . . . When we turn on our television sets and see on the evening news broadcasts of your street rallies and parliamentary debates, we know we are seeing a new Soviet Union in the making. . . . These are yeasty times; times of ferment. . . . With your reforms, you have embarked on the right course, the democratic course."

Still, Reagan's audience didn't react. The deputies remained just as impassive as they were at the outset, although a few, almost, it seemed, in spite of themselves, appeared fascinated with what the speaker was saying. Small wonder that Reagan had been denied the lofty platform of the entire Supreme Soviet. He had just proved that he would not have failed to take advantage of such an opportunity to win new friends and influence Soviet people.

Referring to Gorbachev's trying to negotiate a treaty giving more autonomy to the Soviet Union's ethnically diverse republics, thirteen of which had recently declared some form of independence, Reagan warned, "Freedom can bring out passions between groups of people that may boil over. When they do, cool and calm decisions are called for by leaders, so as to lower temperatures all around," he said, raising his finger. "As you find a reformulation of the relationships in your union, you will find there is a period of uncertainty and tension. Differences can be resolved in ways that are fair to all, but reason must prevail over passion." He recalled the "wrenching and terrible" civil war fought in the United States in the previous century, and he sounded a note of warning lest such a sad experience be repeated in the Soviet Union.

Speaking of such democratic processes as free elections, Reagan stated that "no one has a monopoly on truth. No person, no one group, no government. Each and every individual has something to contribute to the process of seeking truth."

Reagan then offered his prescription for economic troubles. He was obviously under the illusion that America's experience could easily be transplanted to Russian soil, which, of course, is far from the case. "In some ways political changes are easier than economic ones," he said. "At least they will seem to yield results more quickly because they will be so visible. . . . Major economic reforms, on the other hand, show results less quickly. . . . Like a large ocean liner, an economy cannot make a one-hun-dred-eighty-degree turn with the speed of a motorboat. To go from a so-called command economy, as you have had for several decades, to a fully functioning market economy takes time and perseverance. There will be disappointment and discouragement at times. There will be trials and errors. But if you have the courage to persist, you will create an economy within which all can prosper."

He spoke of the market economy and the law of supply and demand in simple terms and extolled the role of the entrepreneur.

Reagan admitted that he felt "tempted to look ahead—as if I had a crystal ball—to try to glimpse at our relationship five years from now: I see gradual but steady reductions [in arms] as we find new ways to work together on matters where our goals are similar. For example, the Soviet Union's cooperation in the international effort to counter the unwar-ranted Iraqi invasion of Kuwait shows our mutual understanding for the need to prevent the spread of conflict in a volatile region of the world. . . . We both have powerful tools of war. Neither of us wants to use them; however, we can use the knowledge about them to help blunt or head off regional conflicts or reckless acts of renegades. Together, our great size can be used in the service of all mankind to persuade those whose passions have reached the danger point to cool down again. And, is it too much to dream that within these next few years, we will begin to plan to one day reach the stars together? The peoples of both our lands—especially the young people—have it within themselves to do these things, and more."

In retrospect, some of Reagan's predictions appear to be quite accu-rate: arms reductions are continuing and new areas of cooperation are emerging, especially in the exploration of outer space—for example, the docking of the U.S. space shuttle *Atlantis* and the Russian space station *Mir*. What Reagan failed to predict, however, was the total collapse of the Soviet Union and the eruption of internal, not international or regional, conflicts and fratricidal wars in Europe and Africa.

Having begun with an American fairy tale, Reagan ended on an upbeat note, with a quotation from Russian classical literature: "Chekhov once wrote in *Uncle Vanya* about the power of faith in bringing about better times. He said, 'Our life will grow peaceful, tender, sweet as a caress. I believe. I *do* believe.' Today, you are rebuilding your society's institutions so that all of your people can have a life one day 'sweet as a caress.' Your building materials will not be bricks and mortar, but faith;

faith in yourselves to accomplish what must be done. Great things must be done, but you are no strangers to great deeds or to challenges in which the future of your whole land is at stake. With the same determination you used to repulse an invader nearly fifty ears ago and that you use to send men and women into space today, you will succeed. Thank you and God bless you."

During the fifty minutes of the speech and frequent pauses, which I filled in with interpretation, the audience fidgeted in their seats and occasionally whispered to one another or gazed at the walls. Once, Reagan read the same passage twice, though, surprisingly, he didn't seem to notice it. To avoid embarrassing him, I modified it a little bit in translation the second time to make it sound as if it were a new paragraph.

Reagan's traditional "Thank you and God bless you" was followed, at last, with polite applause. The loudest applause came from Nancy, who sat in the side row of chairs in front of the lectern, together with Ambassador Matlock. But the applause was not universal—the people in military uniforms greeted the speech with a frown. They were clearly jarred and disturbed by Reagan's advice. Someone muttered under his breath, but loudly enough so I could hear from where I stood at the lectern, "What makes him think he can come here and lecture us? He should not have been allowed to come here in the first place. Let him go back to his Evil Empire." In the eyes of people such as these, America had always been the focus of evil. They were incapable of dismissing the enemy image that had sustained them for so many decades as their raison d'être. Had it been in their power, the golden dream of Chekhov's Sonya—about life "sweet as a caress," of which Reagan spoke—would never come true. These people were incorrigibly wedded to the bad old ways.

One high-ranking Soviet official once admitted to me in a candid private conversation that "perestroika will not succeed unless everyone who is older than sixteen is shot. Don't get me wrong," he hastened to add. "I am not a bloodthirsty person and do not wish anybody's death. I am second to none in supporting perestroika, and I use this metaphor just to emphasize the point that it can be carried out only by very young men and women who do not bear the heavy burden of the past, not by people of our generation." Those words were spoken early in 1988. Well, it was a point of view, and glasnost was already in progress.

From the Kremlin we returned to Spaso House, then Reagan departed for the Kremlin again for the high point of his trip, a meeting with Gorbachev. But before that, he had a short meeting with Anatoly Lukyanov, chairman of the Supreme Soviet, who would later have a major role to play in the coup against Gorbachev. When Lukyanov casually mentioned "a common European home" in the context of "steps toward unification of the two Germanies," Reagan rather startled him by saying, "When you mentioned Germany, perhaps it is careless of me, but I remembered a joke that some people in East Germany created when the Wall was still there. It's a joke about Honecker. You see, Honecker was attracted by a lovely young lady, and while courting her, he asked her, 'What can I do for you?' And she said, 'Tear down that Wall!' He said, 'Tear down that Wall?' Then he thought and said, 'Oh, I see why—you want to stay alone with me.' "

Lukyanov clearly did not appreciate the joke; he gave Reagan a disapproving look and switched the conversation to another topic.

The meeting with Gorbachev was the main reason for Reagan's visit to Moscow. By now, it seemed, Reagan had come genuinely to like him. He asked me lots of questions about Gorbachev, how he was, what he was doing, that sort of thing. Like Margaret Thatcher, he also asked me how I thought he, Reagan, could help Gorbachev and what specifically could America do to help with the reforms.

From Lukyanov's office we drove across Ivanovskaya Square to the Council of Ministers Building where Gorbachev's office was located. We were escorted in a small, creaky elevator, which probably dated from Lenin, to the third floor to Room 3, whose double doors were wide open. I followed Reagan into the spacious and cavernous office of the president of the Soviet Union. It was the same office that I had visited so many times before, but it had recently been renovated and refurbished with new furniture that was said to have been made by special order in Italy. Now, a handsome desk made of dark cherry wood with a massive polished top stood near a window. In the place of the long T-shaped table covered with green baize, which Gorbachev had inherited from his predecessors, was a sleek oval conference table with heavy leather chairs on both sides of it.

Gorbachev greeted Reagan with a warm embrace in the middle of the room. He hugged him twice, patting him on the back. Reagan readily reciprocated. Then the two men clutched each other by the forearms, like two good old friends, and stood like this, creating a photo opportunity for the benefit of the photographers packed into the room and for posterity. Gorbachev seemed genuinely glad to meet once again with the man with whom he was destined by fate to alter the course of world history.

After some chitchat about the weather, we were seated at the oval table and the reporters and everybody else were ushered out. During the first half hour that Gorbachev and Reagan spoke, I was the only other person in the room, the proverbial "third man in the middle," a situation that would surely have been deemed inadmissible when Reagan was president. It brought to mind the situation in 1974 when Nixon, who was still president, came to Moscow and had one-on-one talks with Brezhnev in the presence of a Soviet interpreter, Viktor Sukhodrev, only. For reasons known best only to him, Nixon had neglected to bring his own, American, interpreter, and was subsequently heavily criticized. Of course, Nixon was then the incumbent president, while Reagan was now out of office.

I believe the talk, which was held in a congenial, relaxed, and friendly atmosphere, is of special interest to students of history in that Reagan was obviously intent, with the zeal of a missionary, on convincing Gorbachev of the virtues of capitalism and democratic government, and also because it marked an important stage in the evolution of Gorbachev's thinking on the topical subjects that were discussed. As the host, Gorbachev started the ball rolling by paying tribute to Reagan for his contribution to better relations between the two superpowers.

Gorbachev: Welcome, Mr. Reagan. Well, I am very glad to see that our agreement about your coming here has come to fruition. Now you are here, and not only as a tourist, but as somebody who has made a major contribution to the betterment of Soviet-American relations. I am sure you must have sensed by now, during your stay here, that President Reagan enjoys a great respect in the Soviet Union. We hold you in enormous esteem.

Reagan: Yes, indeed. It was clear from the very start of my arrival here. I am very proud of this and consider it an honor to have been given such a cordial welcome. . . . You know, I remember our first meeting in Geneva. We were then two in the room, with our interpreters. And I said to you then, "We may be the only two men in the world who together can bring about world peace."

Gorbachev: Yes, I confirm those words. Yes, indeed, they were actually spoken. And, those were not mere words—they were followed by actual deeds. It was difficult to begin then. . . . Without Geneva and everything that followed, nothing would have changed in the world so far.

Reagan: I know you have come up against some technical difficulties, especially in the changes you propose to make in your economy. If we can be of any help, we will be glad to give it, because it would bear out our common aspirations and will be a contribution to world peace.

Gorbachev: I am very glad that you have been succeeded in the office of president by your associate George Bush. We have been able to continue, without excessive procrastination, the policy whose foundations you and I had laid in Geneva at that time.

Reagan: Well, George was very much part of it when I was president. He was vice president then. I am also glad he's continuing this policy now.

Gorbachev: You did a great deal to make sure that he took over from you to carry the torch. I realize it is not an easy thing to do. After all, what was so different about Reagan's policy? Well, what made it different was the fact that he was capable of a new vision of future prospects, and that enabled us to turn to a new strategy in our relations. But if we had begun to present each other with lists of grievances, we would not have advanced too far. We had to cross over whole decades of mistrusting each other. . . . Now we are having a session of the Supreme Soviet under the guidance of parliament chairman Lukyanov. I have made a speech there today at the outset of the meeting, in which I said that we have reached a turning point where it is necessary to make a transition to a market [economy]. It is not an easy transition, particularly in our society with its problems and peculiarities.

Reagan: I think later on we will discuss this subject. Now I would like to make some suggestions about it. . . . I wonder if the fifteen republics you have here form one nation.

Gorbachev: At present, this question is the focus of attention here. Yes, indeed, we are fifteen republics, fifteen peoples. But at one time, all of them were united on a unitary basis [i.e., a state system characterized by centralized governing of administrative and territorial units], even though a federation was formally proclaimed. Now we are proceeding with reforming our union, so as to restore more sovereignty for the republics, to give them more rights. But there seems to be some kind of competition going on: Who can get the best deal? And, when it came to the economy, they saw that all the questions are closely interwoven here, that over this time such strong links have formed among the republics that these links cannot be broken, if we want to preserve the union and our entire society.

I am told that while speaking on this subject today in the International Affairs Committee of the Supreme Soviet, you cited the relevant experience of your own country.

Reagan: Yes. We have fifty states united into the United States. It has been like this virtually from the very beginning, although at one time there was a civil war between our states. This system has been working for more than two hundred years. Our constitution explicitly states that our national government has certain rights and powers over the states.

But according to our constitution, our states also have certain rights and powers, and the national government cannot interfere.

Gorbachev: We are moving in the same direction. Only we want to achieve this without fighting.

Reagan: I would suggest you look quietly at our system to see where and how the division is between the rights and powers of the states and the federal government so that no problems arise here. In the United States, if a man has killed somebody on a street, he is punished in accordance with the state laws where he lives. And, he is tried in a state court by a state judge. It is true also to some extent of local communities and towns. They all have their rights. The federal government cannot tell the local government where to put road signs or traffic lights. It is decided by the city government. This is in our constitution.

I don't want to seem like somebody who gives unwanted advice or sticks his nose in your affairs. But I would point out that other than federal laws, we have state and local laws. But you have a constitution, like each nation has, where we greatly differ in that all these constitutions are a document which tells the people what they can do, while our constitution is alone in the world, because it is a document where it says, "We, the people, tell the government what its limits are and what it can do." Perhaps, a look at our constitution will be of help to you.

Gorbachev: Yes. I must say that the experience of your constitutional arrangement and the functioning of your institutions at federal, state, and local levels is something that we are thoroughly analyzing, and we are using quite a few elements from there. As this system continues to develop further, we will embrace your time-honored experience where it involves the division of responsibilities between federal, state, and local authorities.

At this point, the double doors were thrown wide open, as if by command, and Dobrynin, Matlock, Fred Ryan, and another Reagan aide, Mark Weinberg, walked into the room, joining us at the table. The conversation now continued in a larger format.

Reagan (to Gorbachev): I was interested to hear from you about your plans to give land to farmers and the kind of problems you have here, how you solve them. Our two countries have vast land territory. . . . I would suggest the difference between us and you is that your government is the farmer in collective farms while in our country the individual farmer is the owner.

Gorbachev: Now our government is no longer the farmer. We are going through a period of transition.

Reagan: . . . In our country, what we did with the land was to set up a land grant program. The government owned the entire land before that, and people began to come to the government asking for land. And the government decided to give them land on the basis of their promise to farm it, build homes, and grow crops, and granted them millions of acres of land, so that they could farm it successfully. Today we produce enough food not only for ourselves, but also enough to sell it abroad to the hungry of the world. . . .

Gorbachev: As a matter of fact, until now we have not given our *kolkhozniki* [collective farmers] real freedom. For this reason, it is difficult to judge their potentialities for work. There is an interesting observation here. We have several thousand excellent *kolkhozi* [collective farms], *sovkhozi* [state farms] and *agrofirmi* [agro-firms]. So what is the matter? Why is it that they operate successfully? The point is that these collective and state farms are headed by people who don't give a damn about laws. They don't pay any heed to them, and they act in spite of them just to get the job done, all in a good cause. I myself was confronted with this in Stavropol where I come from. I even had to stand up for those people to keep them from being sent to prison. They did not work for themselves but for the common good.

So collective farmers have not had the requisite freedoms so far. But our reform program envisages granting them total freedom so that the farmer could have his own farm, if he wished so, and work as he thinks fit. We will be encouraging it. At the same time, the attitude toward this varies from area to area. For instance, the Baltic republics agree with such an approach, but Southern Russia and the Ukraine want to keep their collective farms, although there does seem to be a willingness to lease land, set up cooperatives, in short—to give people certain freedoms. . . .

I remember President Reagan used to say "Well" when he wanted to change the subject of conversation. Perhaps we should say "Well" now?

Reagan: . . . Well, not quite. The important thing is that people have pride in owning land. You can feel it when you fly over our cities, towns, and villages and see rows upon rows of homes. These are the homes of working people who live there and own the land on which they stand. There is something about it that adds to patriotism of people who are proud to own land. . . .

Gorbachev: I think what we have done calling it socialism, the model that we have created, suffers from one serious shortcoming, namely the alienation of people from land and from the means of production—something that killed all initiative in them, all incentives to work. Up to a point, such an economic system was capable of coping with some problems. But if this process is to be developed and intensified, it is necessary to operate in the framework of democracy and economic freedoms. So, this model of socialism proved inadequate for the purpose. We are now working on how to integrate the idea of socialization with the idea of private initiative. Perhaps in so doing we'll be riding for a fall, but the reality is such that this particular system of socialism has become deeply rooted. If we fail to take it into account, we can do a lot of foolish things in the next century, too.

So, it is necessary to create legal conditions for a choice. We want to create a mixed economy. But to this end, people must be given the possibility of choice. This is what I spoke about today at the session of the Supreme Soviet.

Reagan: There is something I have overlooked that you should do in your country. In case you decided to give land to people, so anybody would pick any land to own, you should remember that your people would also want to look at some areas that have beautiful forests, lakes, and so forth. And then the government should proclaim such areas as national parks or forests. In the United States, there are millions upon millions of acres where people cannot claim this land as their own. These areas belong to the entire people as national parks or forests. They are owned by the people through their government. . . . For instance, there is a place called Yosemite National Park. It is known for its waterfalls, thick forests, mountains, and so forth. It is a place of pride in California. The government built roads there, motels and hotels and campsites and rents them to visitors to encourage them to come to enjoy the beauty of the park. No one is allowed to change it or claim any part of its land.

What do you want to do with the land that has beautiful landscapes? You have vast territories of such land.

Gorbachev: We, too, have national parks. Only we call them national reserves. . . .

At this point, Gorbachev hurriedly scribbled on a piece of paper, "Time to finish?" and slipped it under the table to Dobrynin. Dobrynin imperceptibly nodded, and one minute later Gorbachev smoothly brought the meeting to an end.

Gorbachev: Mr. President, we will continue our conversation later tonight, at dinner. But here an unfortunate situation has arisen. The problem is that for the fourth day in a row Raisa Maximovna has had a temperature of thirty-eight degrees [Celsius]. She's been quite prostrate in bed all this time. It is some kind of infection, but the doctors have been unable so far to determine what it is exactly. She's feeling very bad. That's why she won't be there tonight. But I will be there, and so will someone else. So we'll have a talk then.

Reagan: I am sorry about that. I hope she will soon recover, though.

The meeting was over, or almost over. Reagan would not have been Reagan if he had left the table without telling a joke.

Reagan: I would be remiss if I didn't tell you a joke about the way our people look at land. Texas is our biggest state. It has ranches that take up hundreds of thousands of acres of land. Sometimes rich farmers from Texas or the ranch owners go to New York to have some fun. And, of course, there are ladies of the evening who want to meet them. So one of these girls one evening meets one of these Texas ranchers and asks him, "How big is your ranch?" And the rancher says, "Thirty-five acres." And the girl says, "Thirty-five acres! And you call it a ranch!" And then the rancher says, "Yeah, but it's the whole of downtown Dallas!"

Reagan was obviously in the mood for humor that day. During the meeting, he reminisced about a trip to Ireland he had once undertaken, linking it somehow to his first meeting with Gorbachev in Geneva. "Incidentally," he said at one point, "it was like my first trip to Ireland, where a guide took me to a cemetery and showed me the tombstone on the grave of one man. The tombstone had an inscription that read, 'Remember me as you pass by; For as you are so once was I; But as I am you, too, will be; So be content to follow me.' But some Irishman had scratched on the stone, beneath the inscription, the following: 'To follow you I am content; I wish I knew which way you went.'"

Gorbachev only shook his head in bewilderment and extended his hand across the table to shake Reagan's. Generally speaking, he did not seem to relish jokes the way Reagan did. But this time he gave as good as he got, telling a joke of his own on the topic of the day: "President Mitterrand has a hundred mistresses. One of them has AIDS, but he doesn't know which one. President Bush has a hundred bodyguards and one of them is a terrorist, but he doesn't know which one. And President Gorbachev has a hundred economic advisers. One of them is smart, but he doesn't know which one."

Before parting until evening, Gorbachev and Reagan exchanged autographs, at Reagan's initiative. Reagan produced from his folder a picture that showed him and Gorbachev together, walking about in Red Square with St. Basil's Cathedral in the background, and asked him to sign it.

The picture dated back to 1988 when Reagan had visited Moscow as president. Then he gave Gorbachev a book containing his, Reagan's, selected speeches in Russian and inscribed it for him.

Reagan got in his Zil and returned to Spaso House to rest. I went home for a little rest of my own. I figured that, as usual, I would have to work at the informal dinner perhaps even harder than at formal meetings or talks, and consequently I should eat something at home. But, as luck would have it, the refrigerator was empty—a grim reminder of the reality outside the Kremlin walls. It was useless to go to a food store because of the interminable lines and the lack of choice—only the most basic staples were available and to get them one had to stand in interminable lines. I didn't have time for that. However, it was all for the best, as on this occasion, unlike most, I would have ample opportunity to partake of the meal that Gorbachev offered his guests.

Toward evening, I returned to Spaso House only to discover that no one in Reagan's entourage was quite sure yet whether Nancy would go to Gorbachev's private dinner party. I heard some speculation that given the nature of Nancy and Raisa's relationship, Mrs. Reagan might suspect that Mrs. Gorbachev's sickness was diplomatic in nature. But all questions were answered when, at 6:45, holding hands, President and Mrs. Reagan together solemnly descended the main staircase from the second floor. Nancy was dressed in a black, gold-embroidered brocade suit. Her black stockings and high-heeled shoes dramatically emphasized her youthful figure. She appeared in high spirits, and the first thing she asked me, seemingly nonchalantly, was how was "Raisa's health" and whether she was feeling any better.

The dinner was for a strictly limited number, and only two cars departed from Spaso House that evening: the Zil with the Reagans and a Volga with a man from protocol, an American security agent, and a physician. Since Reagan did not have a physician on this trip, the Soviets thought it prudent to provide one. Reagan invited me to join him and Nancy in their limousine "to keep [them] company." I was delighted to accept. By now I had come to feel quite comfortable with Reagan and felt sufficiently at ease to maintain a conversation and even to ask questions. I took the jump seat opposite Nancy in the backseat, and Reagan's personal bodyguard took the other jump seat, facing Reagan. The bodyguard never let Reagan out of his sight. Nancy wondered aloud where exactly we were being taken. She hoped we were being driven to Gorbachev's private home, which he had built with his own money in Lenin Hills, as she had heard. I could neither confirm nor deny it, as I myself was in the dark until the last minute as to where we were going—the location was kept secret not only from the Reagans, but from Soviet personnel, too.

When Reagan first ran for president in 1980, I often heard a catchy election slogan that was popularized by the ingenious managers of his campaign: "Win Just One for the Gipper!" I knew what "a gip" was, or "a gyp artist," but I didn't have a clue what "a gipper" was unless it was a person who "gipped." But then, it would have been a poor name for a presidential hopeful. I was intrigued, but hadn't had a chance to find out the origin of the word or why Reagan was called the Gipper until now.

No sooner had we departed from Spaso House than Reagan started to talk about movies and reminisce about the days when he was a Holly-wood actor. I told him I was a movie buff and that as an interpreter I had always been curious to know why he was referred to as the Gipper with a capital G and who or what "a gipper" was. My question must have touched the right chord in him, for it set his mind on reminiscences that he would continue to share with Gorbachev later at dinner. He told me, with relish and feeling, like the real raconteur that he was, the story of the origin of the phrase.

The way Reagan told me the life story of one of America's football heroes, George Gipp or "the Gipper," as he was affectionately known to his fellow players, made me want to see the film, *Knute Rockne, All-American*, made in 1940, in which Reagan played the part of the Gipper. I must say I had never seen Reagan so emotional, either in public or in private, as when he was telling me the story of the Gipper. I said I would see it with-out fail at the first opportunity. Alas, I said, I didn't have it on videocas-sette here in Moscow, but I had another movie on videocassette, where he played a major role, and I said I was going to see that as soon as time per-mitted. Reagan brightened up and asked what the title of the film was. I said I didn't remember, but he played the part of a RAF pilot in World War II, shot down behind the German lines, whereupon Reagan instantly iden-tified the film as *Desperate Journey*. He said he had costarred with Errol Flynn in that picture and told me its plot with gusto and brio, and that it was made to "inspire and encourage our people fighting the Germans."

Then, our conversation took a somewhat unexpected turn as Reagan began to complain that in his time the press has been unfair to him. When he was president, he said, they often accused him of "sleeping on the job" in the White House. But, of course, it was "sheer nonsense!" he fumed. "On the contrary, they were the ones who slept!" He remem-bered that whenever he went somewhere in his plane, he would come out of his cabin and walk into the press section, and the reporters would be asleep, as a rule. "It appeared *they* slept on the job. I myself never slept on the job in the White House," he concluded firmly. All this was said with disarming simplicity and conviction. Nancy chimed in, as if trying to justify her husband in my eyes, that [her] "husband was always in his White House office before nine o'clock in the morning, and he *never* slept on the job. I know it. But why did those reporters lie? They never walked into the Oval Office the way I did—unexpectedly."

Our car turned onto a tree-lined boulevard with a long row of government villas for top VIPs, which overlooked the sprawling panorama of the city, with the Moskva River at the foot of the hills. The villas were concealed from the curious eyes of outsiders behind tall yellow solid-stone walls and green iron gates that were well protected by KGB units round the clock. A few minutes later the car stopped at the gate of Guesthouse 40. I knew it was formerly Khrushchev's villa. The massive steel gate, painted olive green, was opened by two guards in KGB military uniforms, and our Zil pulled up in front of the two-story mansion.

I saw Dobrynin standing on the brightly lit steps and, through the doorway, inside the hallway, the stout figure of Mikhail Sergeyevich, with a big bouquet of pink roses in his hands. Raisa Maximovna was nowhere to be seen. When the Reagans got out of the car and mounted the steps, M.S. came out of the hallway, took a step forward, and greeted them warmly. He handed the flowers to Nancy and exchanged handshakes with Reagan and with me. Turning to Nancy again, he apologized to her on behalf of Raisa Maximovna for "being unable to come on account of her sickness." Then, with the gesture of the host, he invited us to follow him.

We found ourselves in a small drawing room. The furniture was simple: a round wooden coffee table, a love seat, and three chairs. M.S. motioned to the love seat and chairs and suggested that everyone sit where he or she would feel most comfortable. Ronald and Nancy sat down on the love seat, holding hands all the time, as usual. M.S. first eased himself into a chair, then changed his mind and asked Nancy to exchange seats with him and joined Reagan so the two of them could sit next to each other. Nancy raised her eyebrows and seemed about to say something, then thought better of it, shrugged her shoulders, and changed seats.

I often wonder how politicians and diplomats would start a conversation without the weather. If it didn't exist, it would have to be invented. When no one really knows what to say for starters, as it was in the Kremlin when Reagan and Gorbachev met earlier in the day, the weather always comes in handy.

And so, the Reagans and Gorbachev exchanged, once again, small pleasantries about California weather. On the basis of his one-day experience there, M.S. seemed to believe that California was blessed with "eternally beautiful and sunny weather." But Reagan demurred, "It rains not only in Leningrad or Moscow, but in California, too." This served as a prelude to "polite conversation," with no set agenda or list of items to be discussed. But in the free and easy conversation that followed, they also exchanged views on some political and economic matters.

After a while we proceeded to the dining room. This small, unpretentiously furnished room had a table set for five. M.S. motioned the Reagans to their seats first, then Dobrynin and I sat down, I on Reagan's left, Nancy on his right. Dobrynin sat next to M.S. We were waited upon by a strong-looking unsmiling blond young man wearing a black suit, white shirt, and black bow tie, with a military bearing—almost like a character from a James Bond movie. Wines were served by another young man who was just as strong-looking and just as unsmiling, and who also wore a black suit and bow tie. He, too, had an erect bearing. They looked as if they were twin brothers who got their training at the same school—the *devyatka*, the Ninth Directorate of the KGB responsible for presidential security. I decided that the "wine captain's" rank was no less than that of a KGB captain. Lucky for me, several times during the dinner Gorbachev noticed that I was interpreting nonstop, both ways, thus having no chance to eat. And then, he would stop in the middle of a sentence and turn to Dobrynin to ask him to interpret so I could dine That was a nice human touch.

The first question Nancy asked, when we sat down, was, "Where are we? Is it your own home?" "No, it isn't," replied M.S., "we're in a government guesthouse." Nancy seemed disappointed. She had clearly anticipated being invited by Gorbachev to his home. Judging from the questions that the Reagans asked Gorbachev throughout dinner, they were rather interested in his personal life. For instance, Reagan asked M.S. bluntly how old was he. M.S. replied that he had half a year to go before retirement on a pension: "In this country people retire on a pension at sixty." "Then you are still just a kid," quipped Reagan. M.S. savored the compliment. His lively brown eyes flashing, he said that he, too, thought it was premature for him to retire on a pension, for he intended to carry on his cause unless he was "asked to go."

In contrast to the Reagans, M.S. did not seem inclined to discuss his personal life, saying the the country was now going through such a period of uncertainty—the transition to a market economy, interethnic relations, the problem of the Union's breaking up—that he literally had

353

"no time to catch [his] breath." He complained that he had absolutely no time left for himself. All his private time, if any, was used up by the "business of *perestroika.*"

Nancy Reagan made light of his serious mood, apparently attempting to loosen him up. If he was so busy, then why did he look so great and, judging from his looks, why was he in very good shape? she wondered. M.S. mulled it over and responded that it was due to three factors. First, it was the genes that he had inherited from his parents. His parents "were of the soil—they were peasants." Second, "the tremendous moral support of [his] wife," on whom he "could always rely." To buttress this statement, he quoted Balzac's famous line: "Behind every successful man there is a woman." At these words the Reagans exchanged affectionate glances. Ronald said he understood him well, while Nancy coquettishly cast down her eyes.

"And the third factor," continued M.S., bending a finger, "is my faith in the chosen cause—the cause of *perestroika*. If I didn't believe in it, I would not have started it. These are the three factors that I believe keep me in good shape," he concluded, and directed the conversation to Raisa Maximovna, lamenting her sickness. "She's been hospitalized all this time, poor thing," he said.

Reagan nodded sympathetically and said he was sorry for her, but Nancy did not react, saying nothing.

While on the subject of health, M.S. complimented Reagan on how good he looked despite his injury and queried him about the reasons for his good looks. Gorbachev suggested this must surely be due to the same factors of which he had just spoken. And here I heard, from the lips of Reagan himself, the story of the attempt on his life. Yes, indeed, Reagan said, he remembered very well that day in 1981, two and a half months after he took office. He would never forget that day.

It happened quite unexpectedly. But things like that always happen unexpectedly, he continued. He had just finished making a speech at some important gathering and was almost at his car outside the Hilton Hotel in Washington when he heard what he thought sounded like several firecrackers. "I remember saying, 'What the hell is that?'" said Reagan. The next thing he remembered was his Secret Service bodyguard hurling him with terrible force into the back of the limousine and jumping on top of him, covering him with his body. Only then did he feel pain in his chest, but he attributed it to his being pressed down on the driveshaft on the floor—"the bodyguard was a big fellow." He also remembered telling the bodyguard to get off him, because it hurt as though one of his ribs was broken. Then he saw blood on the floor and realized that he was seriously hurt. But he didn't feel acute pain until a moment later, when he suddenly realized that he couldn't breathe, and he started to panic a little; then the bodyguard told the driver to head to a hospital. The surgeons later extracted from his body the bullet that had lodged within two and a half inches of his heart. But the wound had since healed and never bothered him. He had soon virtually forgotten all about it.

This whole thing had a lighter side, too. Later, when Nancy visited him in the hospital, he told her, "Honey, I forgot to duck." As Reagan told the story, Nancy added that his sense of humor did not abandon him even in those critical moments. While in the hospital, he teased the doctors who were taking care of him, "Tell me that you are all Republicans." Reagan concluded the story by saying that "the job of a president is dangerous" because there would always be "some crackpot out there willing to kill if only to immortalize himself in history." But he held no grudge against John Hinckley, who was just "a mixed-up young man" who tried to assassinate him "to show his love for some actress." He even asked the Lord on the day he was wounded to forgive the young man and heal him of whatever "demons" tortured him.

None of those present that night imagined that a month and a half later a would-be assassin would target Gorbachev, too. On November 7, 1990, during the demonstration on Red Square on the occasion of the Bolshevik revolution, an obscure engineer from Leningrad would attempt to shoot him with a sawed-off gun that he had concealed under his jacket. But when he whipped out the gun and aimed it at Gorbachev, who stood atop the Lenin Tomb less than 150 yards away, a policeman spotted him and grabbed his arm before he could squeeze the trigger. Two shots were fired harmlessly into the air, and the would-be assassin was arrested, while Gorbachev did not even leave the Tomb.

Reagan reminisced about his triumphal appearance at MGU, the Moscow State University, in 1988. "Imagine," he said with a broad grin on his face, "they put me then at this rostrum under Lenin. It was his bust on a very tall pedestal—about fifty feet tall! And so I looked back and up at him, sighed, and read my speech. And when I finished, there was big applause in the audience. The students were applauding, standing on their feet. I looked back at Lenin again—and he cried!" M.S. smiled enigmatically, but said nothing. "Only then did I heave a sigh of relief," said Reagan with a mischievous smile.

Nancy steered the conversation to the first meeting of the two leaders in Geneva five years before. "I think," she said, as if addressing her words to me and Dobrynin, "I think that these two men were destined to meet at this juncture of history, and they found they had a lot in common in spite of all the differences. My husband always wanted peace, and as soon as a new man appeared in the Kremlin, Mr. Gorbachev, he realized that he could get along fine with him. And that's how it happened. The whole world owes it to them. It was the right combination of two leaders at the right time."

M.S. nodded in acknowledgment. Indeed, he said, he also felt then—and, in no small measure, thanks to such a competent and experienced ambassador as Dobrynin—that the time had come to change "our course in the foreign policy arena," and that he should meet with "Mr. Reagan." The interests of peace demanded it. "And now, look how far we have advanced! But without that first meeting no one knows what would have happened in the world today. I then understood that Mr. Reagan is a man of peace." Reagan nodded his assent, and Nancy solemnly proposed a toast to "these two men who have given the world so much!"

It was a moving moment. Everyone rose and clinked glasses. After we sat down again, Reagan recalled the difficult and thorny path traveled by the two countries since the Geneva summit. He made it a point to use again his favorite Russian saying, *Doveryai, no proveryai* (Trust, but verify). This adage would never become obsolete, he said. It would always retain its relevance and topicality because that is the way the world is made. M.S. responded that he was confident that someday their "two countries would trust each other on the word of honor, without verifying," and then this proverb would become obsolete.

Reagan told Gorbachev that on the way to the Soviet Union he had stopped in Berlin where he visited the Wall. Given a chisel and a hammer, he "chiseled off a piece of the Wall." Everyone around applauded and he "felt very good." And he muttered, as if to himself, "It was damned hard." Nancy added that earlier, in 1989, when the Wall was destroyed, they were given a piece of it for their ranch in California. The piece weighed some six tons and was about five feet tall. M.S. said he, too, had been given a piece of the Wall, "although rather small." "But generally speaking," he said, this was "the most important event in the postwar Europe. . . . We decided not to interfere in this process. If that is what the peoples want, then that's the way it should be."

An entry in my diary reminded me that in a speech in Berlin in 1987, a few months before the Washington summit, when the light was just beginning to gleam at the end of the long tunnel of the Cold War, Reagan challenged Gorbachev, saying, "Mr. Gorbachev, open this gate! Mr. Gorbachev, tear down this Wall!" Then, Moscow called the challenge a provocation. But two years later, with domestic turmoil buffeting the Soviet government and change sweeping across the rest of Eastern Europe, Gorbachev dropped his support for the aging East German leader, Erich Honecker, paving the way for the collapse of the Wall on November 9, 1989.

Reagan delicately wondered if Gorbachev was writing anything or keeping a diary. He said that he himself had just finished writing his memoirs, which were due to be published the following October or November. M.S. replied evasively. No, unfortunately, he had not been writing anything since he became general secretary of the Party in 1985. He simply didn't have time for that, and besides it "just didn't occur [to him]." To this, Reagan remarked, in a friendly way, that sooner or later M.S. would have to write his memoirs. But then he would find it more difficult to remember exactly what had happened and when, because all the events could get mixed up in the head, unless he kept a diary. He, Reagan, had been keeping such a diary for a long time, from the very first days of being in the White House. When he was still the governor of California, near the end of his second term, he couldn't recollect some events no matter how hard he tried. Everything got mixed up in his head, especially the dates, to say nothing of details. So he had learned a lesson from this, and ever since, every night before going to bed, he wrote about what had happened that day, with whom he had met, what had been discussed, what decisions had been made, and so forth. In his memoirs, he said, he devoted much attention to him, "President Gorbachev," and if he had omitted something he hoped that "President Gorbachev would fill the gaps in his own memoirs."

Nancy remarked that it was best not to rely on her husband because he had "a lot of gaps in his memoirs, and Mr. Gorbachev must fill them," especially with respect to "their meetings and personal relations." I found Reagan's admission of his poor memory interesting in light of his defense in the Iran-contra scandal that he simply didn't remember certain conversations and meetings concerning the affair that shadowed much of his second term and tarnished his credibility. Reagan survived the scandal, pleading memory gaps.

The talk wandered around many subjects, but finally turned to movies, which were obviously Reagan's pet theme. M.S. struck the right chord by asking him how many films he had acted in. Reagan began to talk, with great animation, about his acting career, saying he had appeared in fifty-six films altogether. M.S., too, it turned out, knew a thing or two about movies, saying he had seen a lot of them, not only Soviet films, but American ones as well. He even remembered seeing one film with Reagan in it, but forgot its title. After a couple of leading questions, it turned out, by a strange coincidence, that he was talking about *Desperate Journey*. Reagan repeated for M.S.'s benefit everything he had told me about the movie: why it was made and so forth.

M.S. wondered whom the Reagans considered the stars of today. Reagan thought for a while and then replied that he personally didn't know any contemporary "so-called stars." "Well, to be sure, there are no stars today," said Reagan. As to movies nowadays, they were simply "trash." In his days in Hollywood, they used to make "real movies," with a system of seven big studios, and the way things were done then the actors were real stars.

M.S. did not seem entirely satisfied with this answer. He wanted to know whom specifically Reagan would call real stars of that epoch. This time Reagan responded without hesitation, "Well, Spencer Tracy, of course. Now, he was a truly great star!" M.S. shifted his inquiring eyes to look at Nancy. She smiled and said diplomatically that as far as she was concerned, there were "only two" stars of the American cinema of her time: "Spencer Tracy and . . . Ronald Reagan!"

After dinner M.S. invited us back to the drawing room "for tea." At tea, Reagan inquired, ever so delicately, what kind of relations Gorbachev had with Yeltsin, but M.S. only said, "We are cooperating."

At nine o'clock, M.S. rose from the couch, where he had sat again together with Reagan, thus announcing that the dinner was over. He warmly hugged Reagan twice and then embraced Nancy, kissing her twice on both cheeks. Dobrynin, too, bussed her on the cheeks. An obligatory exchange of gifts followed. M.S. gave Reagan a box wrapped in gift paper and Nancy a huge bouquet of roses—the same one he had handed her when they arrived and that she had put aside before dinner. Nancy gave him, "for Raisa," a flat little box in a blue wrapping. My impression, probably erroneous, was that in the absence of Raisa Maximovna that evening, Nancy had felt much more at ease than usual; she seemed in a positively elated mood.

SEPTEMBER 18, TUESDAY. DAY THREE.

It was the last full day of Reagan's stay in Moscow. The next day he would be leaving for Rome to have an audience with the pope. Reagan's schedule for the day turned out to be rather heavy: at 10 A.M., participation in a round table discussion with students at MGU; at 2 P.M., a luncheon that he hosted for Gorbachev at Spaso House; and finally at 4

P.M., a meeting with Boris Yeltsin, although officially this meeting was not on the program. That concluded the formal part of the visit. The departure was set for early the next morning.

At 10 A.M. sharp, the Zil carrying Reagan pulled up at the bottom of the steps leading up to the main entrance to MGU, or Moscow State University, on the side where the huge building faces the Moskva River. At the entrance, we were greeted by Logunov, the rector, or president of the university, who escorted us to the auditorium.

The high-ceilinged room was not large and was so crammed with people that there was not enough room to swing a cat, as the Americans would say, or for an apple to fall, as the Russians put it. The original plan was for Reagan to meet with fifteen students only, but quite a few journalists and reporters were in the auditorium, as well as some people whose purpose in being present was not immediately clear. I assumed they were faculty members. Reagan was offered a seat at a huge round table placed in the center of the auditorium. Then Logunov made a few welcoming remarks, after which Reagan made a short introductory statement:

"Thank you very much. It is a great pleasure for me to be back here at this university. I cherish fondest memories of my visit here in 1988. When I was here last time, I made a formal speech, but today, I think, we will have a more lively and interesting dialogue and discussion. But before that I hope I can share with you some thoughts. First, a serious one. To those of you who are the students here I wish to say that these are the better years of your life. So I hope you will take every advantage of the opportunities here to study hard and use the time to get a good education.

"As I appear here today, I remember my college days in Eureka, which was where my family lived not too far away. My brother went to that college, too. I studied economics there, and I had the time of my life then in those days. It was then that I made some of the best friendships and learned some of the lessons that later on were helpful in life. And the friendships and lessons that you get here will stay with you for most of your lifetime. So take every advantage of your present time here. It is a special time in your life.

"As we learned recently, there are few things in life that are permanent. What is today may not be there tomorrow. Some great changes are now taking place here in your country and in the whole world. New opportunities and freedoms develop each day, and I hope they will be irreversible in your country. As future leaders you will be confronted with challenges that will face your country in the next century, and I wish you well. Now I will take up your questions. But please, give your name, where you are from, and what is your field of studies."

Here are some of the students' remarks and questions, and Reagan's answers, which give an idea of what stirred the souls and minds of the younger generation of Soviet students then and of Reagan's reaction now that he was out of office:

Question: What was your main achievement when you were in the White House? And what were the best years in your life?

Reagan: To answer this question about my years in the White House, my administration in Washington did its best to tell our people that things would never be as good as they were unless they had faith. I thought there was a great desire in the hearts of people for spiritual revival. And I am very happy and proud that our people in America have restored their faith and patriotism. As a result, we had great economic restoration. Furthermore, I felt we had to get the government out of the way so as to give freedom to people to restore the economy. It worked. I am blessed, I believe, because I have enjoyed some of the best years in my life during my college days, during the Great Depression.

Question: First, how do you manage to keep in such a great psychological and physical shape? And secondly, do you owe your successes to the good team of people that you selected?

Reagan: To answer your second question first, what kind of people I selected as my team. You see, I did not want people who wanted to land a job in the government. I wanted people who were already successful in their life and jobs, people who were willing to give up better salaries in order to serve their country. As to your other question, physically, I was always interested in athletics. . . . How do I keep in psychological shape? I don't know how to answer. But I will explain it in the words of Abraham Lincoln. He said at one point that he couldn't perform his duties in office even for fifteen minutes if he didn't know that he could always call upon one who is wiser and stronger than everybody else. He meant God, of course. And during my years in the White House I understood very clearly why he said it, because I saw I had the same need to call upon Him who is wiser and stronger than the rest of us.

Question: Yesterday you had a meeting with President Gorbachev and you discussed numerous issues. What were the most interesting issues that you discussed, if it's no secret? And also, are you satisfied with the discussion?

Reagan: Yes. I am glad we had that meeting between us. We discussed questions that your parliament has before it today: the economic reform, the ideas of free enterprise. I believe we had a good understanding of what has to be done to implement those ideas in order to improve life for the people of our two countries.

Question: What are your personal impressions of Sakharov? And what do you think of the role of one single individual such as Sakharov in history?

Reagan: I believe the entire history [of the world] demonstrates that great and important changes for the benefit of all mankind are the result of actions and statements of individual people who stand above the crowd. It is true today, too. There are people who dare make proposals that benefit us all eventually. I have the greatest respect for Dr. Sakharov.

Question: What is the area in Soviet-American relations that should be developed most rapidly to make further progress? And, what do you think Soviet students should do to improve ties with the Americans who study at MGU?

Reagan: I would respond first to your second question about establishing closer ties between the students. I would encourage both sides to have more exchanges of students that you send to our educational institutions and our students who come here to study. This will serve to have a better understanding between our peoples.

As to your first question, I believe with respect to the economic changes proposed here that economy is one such area from the standpoint of farmers becoming the owners of land, cultivating it and selling the produce on the market, rather than the government being the owner. I think your president understands this. We are ready to support any steps that will lead to the development of initiative of your people and the establishment of a private sector. I discussed it with President Gorbachev and compared it with our country. I believe people have a right to own land in their country. Prior to this, one cannot realize the sense of patriotism and pride that comes when you own land.

Question: You said you had studied economics as a student. Can you say the American economic way is right also for the Soviet Union?

Reagan: I believe in the system of private enterprise. Nothing so far has changed this belief of mine. . . . You may be wondering what you will do after you complete your education. Don't get upset, if you don't know yet. I studied economics in college and got a degree. I don't know about your schools here, but we have drama groups in our schools which put on plays onstage. I was not interested as much in economics when I graduated from school as I was in the theater. I always wanted to get into the world of entertainment. So my first job I landed after college was a radio sports announcer. In those days radio was a new thing, and people loved to listen to baseball and football matches over the radio. But I hungered for the theater, and eventually it led me to Hollywood where I became an actor. So do not feel discouraged if you don't know what to do. It'll come to you in time, as it did to me.

Question (from the young lady seated next to Reagan): I am a student at the department of history and I major in studies of Germany. I wonder what you, as an experienced politician, think about the European problems such as the unification of the Germanies. On the one hand, it is a system with an authoritarian regime, while on the other—a system with true democracy. Do you think this alliance may be dangerous for the future of democracy in the world?

Reagan: I strongly believe that the two Germanies must unite. At the same time I can understand how people look back at the history of war and feel concern. I have been to Germany two times, and while there I saw the horror camps where there was a lot of violence during the war, people were tortured and killed. Today they still keep those camps with the photographs of the horrors that were committed there. They keep them so that children would see those horrors and learn, so it would never happen again. I think that people in Germany and the whole civilized world rejected that dark past and that democracy is there to stay.

Question: Mr. Reagan, imagine a situation where you are the president of the Soviet Union. What would be your first step?

Reagan: I would do the same things that President Gorbachev is trying to do: create private property and free enterprise, which have been so beneficial in our country.

Question: As president you attempted to reduce the size of the government bureaucratic machine. But the first rule of any bureaucracy is to entrench itself as part of the government machinery. Do you think you succeeded?

Reagan: I would give you one example from the history of our so-called free and independent nation. It was during the war. There was a big warehouse filled with lots of file cabinets that contained lots of government papers and documents. The research showed, however, that all those papers were not important, in fact they were obsolete. They had no use or historic value. I was then an officer in an Army Air Corps intelligence unit, and we needed those file cabinets for our documents. So we asked the government for permission to destroy those obsolete papers and give us the right to use the file cabinets. Then, one day, we get this reply from the government through the proper channels, and so forth: "Permission granted provided copies are made of each paper destroyed."

*   *   *

Bringing the discussion to a close, Logunov thanked Reagan for this "interesting and instructive story," and then, as if demonstrating *glasnost* in action, he said, "I understand that you, Mr. Reagan, like jokes. So I have a joke to tell. It relates to the time in our history when the choice of the path for the development of Russia was made. Here is the gist of it:

"A revolutionary lands in jail at the time of the czar, and he is guarded there by a prison guard. Some time passes and the situation changes. This time it is the prison guard who is in jail and the revolutionary guards him—that was after the [1917] Revolution. Then some more time passes, and both the revolutionary and the former prison guard land in jail—that was the time of repressions [in the late 1930s]. Finally, the latest period, closer to our time. They meet again, and this time the former revolutionary sells *pirozhki* [small stuffed pastries] in the street while the former guard looks at him and says, 'Why did you have to go to all that trouble—do you think the czar would have forbidden you to sell *pirozhki?*'

"So I think we should not keep our guest of honor any longer. I would like to give you, Mr. Reagan, a book, but unfortunately it is in Russian. It is about the founder of this university, Vassily Lomonosov."

Reagan: Thank you very much. Unfortunately, I do not speak Russian, but would venture to make a suggestion today. It is too late for me to go back to school, but all the young people, I think, should learn the languages of our two countries, the languages of each other, so as to cement the friendship between our people.

The formal part of the round table meeting ended at 11:05 A.M. to stormy applause from the audience. But Reagan's visit to MGU was not over yet. Unexpectedly for everyone, and above all for his hosts, he expressed a desire to "get to know the students closer" and to see for himself the conditions in which they lived, and so he asked to be taken to the students' cafeteria. After an initial hesitation the hosts obliged.

When Reagan walked, unannounced, into the cafeteria on the second floor, accompanied by his aides and bodyguards, he was not recognized at first, and the people in the cafeteria did not pay any attention to him. But a few moments later, when it dawned on them who had just walked in, the students and the service staff, who were mostly women dressed in white frocks, began to turn their heads in our direction, and a murmur of surprised exclamations rose above the tables. "Look, it's Reagan, Reagan!" Spontaneously, the students stood up and gave Reagan a big round of applause. Reagan raised his right hand and waved at them in acknowledgment. Then he made a little speech, urging the students to do their best to take advantage of the opportunity to study here and at the same time enjoy their time within the university. In the absence of a microphone or a bullhorn, I had to put together the palms of my hands at my mouth to amplify the sound of my interpretation, so that everyone could hear it.

Then, pointing to the open door leading to the kitchen, Reagan began to relate the story of how he looked for a job after he finished his studies. His family was poor, he said, and he could not count on them. "Finally, I landed the best possible job one could wish at the time—a dishwasher in a girls' dormitory!" When I finished interpreting this, a burst of laughter and another round of applause followed. He was cheered especially loudly by the women dishwashers who were standing in the doorway to the kitchen. The Great Communicator certainly knew how to strike the right chord in the hearts of these ordinary people. One of the women nudged another and said, "He's really something else, isn't he!" Reagan cut a fine figure, indeed. In spite of his almost eighty years and the fact that he did look older now than even three months before, he still had a dashing appearance.

At the exit from the university building Reagan was waylaid by a group of students holding placards high up in the air with exhortations to support democracy in the Soviet Union. Many were waving Soviet and American flags. At first, it wasn't clear what their intentions were and what they wanted, and Reagan's bodyguards visibly tensed. But then, on seeing Reagan emerge from the university, the demonstrators cheered him with "stormy, lengthy, and continuous applause turning into a standing ovation," to use the worn-out cliché. Only now it was an unorchestrated, spontaneous manifestation of feeling.

These students were not among the privileged few admitted to the round table with Reagan, and they simply wanted to express their warms feelings toward him. Responding, Reagan lifted his hands up in the air, clasped them together in the gesture of a victorious pugilist, and regaled the crowd with a dazzling Hollywood smile. He felt on top of the world. In his eyes, this spontaneous demonstration was tangible evidence that his preaching had had the desired effect.

Reagan at MGU had an extraordinary ability to communicate with young people and preach to them the good old values to which he was so dedicated. According to him, those values made him "somebody in this life," enabling him to make the long and difficult journey from washing dishes to becoming president of a great country. Communication came to him easily and naturally. He spoke to people in a simple, understandable language with a clear preference for dialogue, not monologue. This manner of speaking and his attitude drew people to him. With his jokes, stories, and earnest exhortations he aroused in people the hope for a better future and a faith that if one embraced his values, precepts, and advice with regard to private property and free enterprise, success would be assured. The only question in my mind was how soon would the seeds he had planted begin to germinate and would they sprout on Soviet soil at all?

From the university we returned to Spaso House for a formal luncheon in honor of Gorbachev hosted by the Reagans. As in 1988, the luncheon was held in the grand ballroom. The head table for both the hosts and the "hero of the event" was set up at the very entrance to the ballroom, in breach of all protocol rules, because Gorbachev was expected to leave at three o'clock to get back to the momentous Supreme Soviet session, which was debating the five-hundred-day economic reform plan. Gorbachev had asked to be seated closer to the door so that he could "slip out unnoticed," in the English style, as the Russians say.

Seated at the head table were, counterclockwise, Reagan, Gorbachev, Nancy Reagan, Ambassador Matlock, the wife of Deputy Foreign Minister Alexei Obukhov (who sat at the next table, representing the foreign minister—Shevardnadze could not attend the luncheon because he was occupied with his counterpart from Saudi Arabia, who had arrived in Moscow to discuss the Gulf crisis and establish diplomatic relations with Moscow, which was a historic event in itself). Next to her was Ivan Laptev, the new chairman or speaker of the Soviet of the Union (the upper chamber of the Supreme Soviet). The circle closed with Rebecca Matlock, who sat on Reagan's left. My seat was between Reagan and Gorbachev. Among the other guests whose faces were familiar and who were seated at other tables were the wife of the late Andrei Sakharov, Elena Bonner, whose name must have been on the American Embassy's list of guests who had a standing invitation to all such social functions; the newly elected mayor of Moscow, Gavriil Popov; and his counterpart from Leningrad, Anatoly Sobchak.

Gorbachev arrived in his black Zil limousine at the entrance to Spaso House at exactly two o'clock. He was alone, without Raisa Maximovna. I met him in the entrance hall and helped him off with his navy blue raincoat—it was still raining. He appeared to be agitated; he said that he had just addressed a session of the Supreme Soviet and had not yet cooled down from "yet another battle." And a battle it was: when Gorbachev told the Supreme Soviet that the pace of introducing market reforms and all their implications needed to be carefully considered once again before "plunging into an abyss," he was nearly booed off the rostrum. With the characteristically Slavic penchant for going from one extreme to another, the deputies were now split into two hostile camps. Some demanded that Gorbachev act immediately, invoking Napoleon's famous line, "First start a battle, and then we'll see," while others were up in arms, opposing any further reforms.

The session was on a lunch break now, and M.S. asked me to remind him when it was three o'clock, so he could leave, otherwise he would "get carried away talking with Reagan." I escorted him to the grand hall where the Reagans, the invited guests, and reporters were assembled to greet him. Reagan and Gorbachev embraced again and proceeded to the dining room, supporting each other by the elbow, like good old friends. Reagan had been advised that the Soviet president's time was strictly limited and decided to exchange speeches at the beginning rather than at the end of the luncheon. And so Reagan, as the host, rose to speak first. I had been given a copy of his remarks well in advance and had the rare luxury of preparing the translation carefully and even writing it down in my pocket notebook. All I had to do now was read in Russian the translation of Reagan's remarks, although I could still not afford to relax my attention even for a moment, for Reagan might ad-lib.

As Reagan approached the podium and I followed him, I could sense that everyone was eager to hear him firsthand, as if he and no one else could and should say something that reflected the truth of the moment, the meaning of his having yet another meeting with Gorbachev. After thanking the Matlocks and the Gorbachevs for their hospitality, Reagan summed up in a memorable metaphor just how far U.S.-Soviet relations had advanced in the past few years. "And yes," he said, referring to yesterday's private dinner with Gorbachev, "I did use the phrase *Doveryai, no proveryai*, but this time he didn't put his hands over his ears!"

After the laughter died down, Reagan continued:

"When we sat down in front of that fireplace in Geneva, we were filled with high hopes that we could begin to eliminate the mistrust which for so many years—for far too many years—had been part of the relationship between our two great nations. And in the past few years we have made great progress in doing exactly that. To be sure, much remains to be done. But there is a new and very encouraging level of cooperation and communication between us now, which I have every confidence will serve the world well. Who would have thought that the warmth of that fireplace in Geneva would melt the ice of the Cold War?"

Reagan ended his remarks by proposing a toast to Gorbachev and to "the continued friendship of the Soviet and American peoples."

M.S. had warned me in advance that his reply would be off the cuff. I asked him to try to speak in shorter sentences, so as "to maintain contact with the audience," and he readily agreed. However, M.S. did get carried away several times during his remarks, and then I had to wait till he paused for breath and use the slightest opportunity to get in the translation. What always gave me the greatest jitters was the fear that somehow I would not remember some word or would lose the connection between words or phrases, so I whipped out my notebook and scribbled furiously when he spoke in long sentences. Like Reagan before him, he emphasized that the two of them had been the first to "lay bricks in the edifice of present-day good relations between our two countries" and that "positive changes would hardly have occurred in the world had it not been for that first meeting between [them] in Geneva." He, too, proposed a toast: "To the health of President and Mrs. Reagan and to the further development of good relations between the Soviet Union and the United States."

Each toast was followed by a burst of applause. Each time all rose to their feet, clinking glasses, and each time the room resounded with the Russian *"Na zdorovye!"* and the English "To your health!" Each time the guests and the hosts emptied their glasses all together. Reagan leaned forward at the table to get closer to my ear and, lowering his voice so that the others would not overhear, asked me to coach him on how to say "To your good health" in Russian. He repeated, in an undertone, the Russian phrase several times after me until I was satisfied that he pronounced it correctly, and then he stood up and loudly toasted, *"Za vashe zdorovye!"* It turned out quite well. His actor's training came in handy.

I sat shoulder to shoulder with Reagan at the table and I couldn't fail to notice his oversize cuff links. They were gold, square, and had the form of a calendar with engraved numerals and the date March 4. The numerals on the cuff links were set with deep red garnets resembling the seeds of the pomegranate. Reagan sensed my curiosity and told me the cuff links were Nancy's present to remind him of their wedding anniversary. "She doesn't like it when I forget our memorable date, March fourth, 1952," he explained. He wore them only on days that were particularly important, such as this day, he said, when he and Nancy were out together. These were his favorite cuff links, said Reagan. He caught Nancy's glance and raised his hand for her to see that he was wearing these special cuff links. She laughed. "I gave them to him so he wouldn't forget our wedding day," she explained to Gorbachev. I probably intrigued Reagan, and especially Nancy, when I ventured that one year from now he would have to replace the garnet with a ruby because, I said, the ruby was associated with the fortieth anniversary of the wedding, which they would be celebrating next year. For a second I saw a glimmer of interest in Nancy's eyes and she asked me if I believed in astrology. When I shook my head, she lost interest.

M.S. was a gracious guest. He conversed alternately with Nancy and Reagan, occasionally turning to Matlock with questions. He spoke with him in Russian, of course, without my assistance, and then the ambassador had to interpret their conversation back into English for the benefit of Nancy, who was seated between him and Gorbachev. When M.S. was busy talking with Nancy and Matlock, Reagan maintained the conversation with me. On a more serious note, and as if in continuation of the conversation in the Kremlin, he told me in detail about the division of powers between local and federal government in the United States, about local, state, and federal taxes. When M.S. finished discussing something with Nancy, I recounted the contents of my conversation with Reagan. M.S. showed a lively interest in the subject and pressed Reagan for further details. He wondered what Reagan thought of the function of taxes in general and particularly of their division as applied to Soviet realities, i.e., to relations between the center and the republics within the framework of the new union treaty the work on which was already in progress, with his active involvement.

Reagan drew a historical parallel, recalling that in his youth, way back in the 1930s, he voted for Roosevelt because he believed then that Roosevelt had the right tax policy. At that time he, Reagan, was a Democrat. But later the Democrats changed so much, he said, that their policies no longer appealed to him and to many others, and he decided to go over to the Republican camp. Ever since, he had been a hard-core Republican. "Strange as it may seem," he said, "but the Democrats even under Roosevelt had inflated the government machinery at the expense of the people so much so that as a result they antagonized and alienated a lot of people."

Reagan invited Gorbachev to come with "Raisa" to his Ranch Del Cielo in California on an unofficial visit at least for a few days—"far from the mundane hustle and bustle." M.S. was noncommittal, however; he certainly wanted to visit Reagan's ranch, he said, "even if it's only for a few hours," but simply couldn't do it now because he was "so very, very busy. I must accomplish the cause that I began, the cause of *perestroika.*" After his goal was achieved, he said, he would be able to retire, and then he and Raisa Maximovna could come to visit the Reagans.

At three o'clock I reminded M.S. that it was time to leave, but he lingered another fifteen minutes before saying good-byes. When the moment of parting came, Reagan presented him with a bottle of Iron Horse, vintage 1987. He remembered that Gorbachev had liked it when he had been in Washington for the 1987 summit. He said this particular brand of champagne was produced in small quantities in a valley in California along the Russian River, and most of it was intended especially for the Reagans' table. M.S. embraced Reagan and then Nancy for the last time, kissed her on both cheeks, and saying *"Do sleduyuschei vstrechi"* (Until our next meeting), headed to the exit. With some emotion in his voice, Reagan responded, "Good-bye, our friend!" Then the Reagans escorted him down the steps in silence, and with that, their nostalgic Moscow reunion was over.

As I escorted M.S. farther down the hallway to the cloakroom, I asked how the session of the Supreme Soviet was doing. He said it was progressing "rather acutely" because many opposed the proposed market-oriented course. Before getting in the car, he asked me to apologize to the Reagans once again for his hasty exit and to explain the circumstances. When I later complied with this request, Reagan was understanding, saying he realized full well that Gorbachev's presence at the session was absolutely imperative "so he could steer it in the right direction." Indeed, much of the success of the reforms ultimately depended on Gorbachev personally.

That afternoon I had more work cut out for me: a meeting with Yeltsin.

At 4 P.M., a small motorcade departed from Spaso House in the direction of Belyi Dom—the Russian "White House"—which stands on the Krasnopresnenskaya Embankment, with its facade facing the Ukraina Hotel across the Moskva River. Across the road from the White House is another landmark edifice—the tall, glass-paneled building of CMEA (Council for Mutual Economic Assistance). The third side of the sprawling White House faces the new, two-storied, red-brick building of the U.S. Embassy, which became so well known to the world in 1986 when the Americans discovered it was infested with "bugs" of the distinctly man-made variety.

The motorcade turned off Kalinin Avenue and, ascending a ramp, pulled up at the plaza in front of the central entrance to the huge white building. This was the Russian parliament that had been dubbed the White House on the principle that the Americans had their White House in Washington, so "why shouldn't we have one here, in Moscow?" Actually, it was called the White House for its white marble exterior. The building's construction had been completed some fifteen years earlier, after twenty years of work. The massive building was designed when Soviet architecture was still dominated by Stalinist monumentality intended to symbolize the permanency of the socialist system and its vitality for millennia to come. The stairway descending toward the river at the front of the White House appears to take up as much space as does half the entire building. I often thought how something else—something functionally necessary and useful—could have been built in its place, such as an underground garage or just a park with trees. Anyway, this house was built to accommodate the Russian republic's parliament, which was called the Supreme Soviet of the Russian Federation.

But in June 1990, after he was elected chairman of the Supreme Soviet of the Russian Federation, Yeltsin installed himself here, making it his headquarters from which to rule Russia—one of the constituent republics of the USSR.

Thanks to Matlock's fast-driving chauffeur, Andy, who drove the Cadillac, which the ambassador so kindly lent to me, I arrived at the White House first. When I stepped out of the car to wait for Reagan, it was drizzling, but no marquee or canopy sheltered visitors from the rain. When Reagan arrived, he was welcomed at the entrance by Yeltsin's first deputy. The man said his name was Khasbulatov. He attempted to say a few words of welcome in broken English, but Reagan did not recognize the babble as English and asked me, rather loudly, I am afraid, "Who is this guy?"

I repeated the man's words in English for Reagan's benefit, although I didn't have a clue as to who the man was, for I had never heard his name until now. Reagan gave him a sidelong glance and confined himself to a brief "Hello."

But Ruslan Imranovich (only later did I learn his first name and patronymic) was a tenacious man. He said something else in English. This time Reagan told him bluntly that he was sorry, but he did not understand him and would he please speak through the interpreter? Khasbulatov explained, now in Russian, that he would lead us to a side elevator inside the building to take us to the fifth floor where Yeltsin's office was located. While we rode in the elevator, Reagan's aides and bodyguards, except for the one who always stayed at his side, ran up the stairs—the elevator was not spacious enough to accommodate Reagan's entire party.

In a bizarre move three years later, on October 3–4, 1993, this small, unprepossessing man, Ruslan Khasbulatov, acting in concert with

Alexandr Rutskoi, another former top lieutenant of Yeltsin's, would lead the extremists who barricaded themselves inside the White House, supported by a small private army, to challenge Yeltsin in an armed rebellion. The White House building would be shelled from tanks and attacked by troops—on Yeltsin's orders—and heavily damaged, the rebellion crushed, Khasbulatov, Rutskoi, and their confederates arrested (but later released), and the charred White House would become known, at least for a while, as the Black House.

Yeltsin met Reagan outside the entrance to the conference room on the fifth floor. They exchanged handshakes, but no bear hugs, although Yeltsin took great pains to demonstrate his affability and friendly feelings for Reagan, perhaps more than was warranted by the situation. He even made a feeble attempt to embrace Reagan, but this gesture was not reciprocated. This was their second meeting. Their first had taken place under peculiar circumstances when Yeltsin visited America in 1989. Reagan was then in a hospital in Rochester where he was undergoing treatment for a serious head injury after falling from a horse. Naturally, there could be no substantive conversation then, and the meeting was perforce brief and of a purely protocol nature.

And so, after a polite exchange of handshakes in the hallway outside the conference room, Yeltsin invited Reagan inside, with an exaggerated grand gesture of the host. All the time he seemed determined to play the part of a warm and gracious host, but his awkward manners, clumsy movements, and unrefined language revealed he still had a long way to go to polish his public image. He motioned Reagan and the rest of his party to the long, white, highly polished table of Karelian birch in the middle of the room with matching chairs on both sides and took a seat opposite Reagan. Yeltsin was flanked by Khasbulatov and by two more men whom I assumed to be his aides. Ambassador Matlock sat next to Reagan on his right, I on his left, and Mark Weinberg and Fred Ryan brought up the flanks at both ends of the table.

Yeltsin's approach at the time, however schematic and vague, to revolutionary political and economic reforms was based on the Shatalin-Yavlinsky five-hundred-day plan. Gorbachev had backed away from his original endorsement of the plan, saying the timetable for its implementation was unrealistic and that it should be reconciled with another plan developed by Prime Minister Ryzhkov's Union government. However, Yeltsin declared that his government, i.e., that of the Russian republic, would implement the five-hundred-day plan in the Russian republic, starting on October 1, 1990. As a result, the split between Gorbachev and Yeltsin widened even more, and the specter of dual power in the Soviet Union began to seem like a real possibility.

Such was the background to the conversation between Reagan and Yeltsin.

After welcoming Reagan, Yeltsin presented him with a framed charcoal drawing depicting a medium-range missile on a wooden wagon being pulled by a sickly-looking horse along a muddy road. A soldier with a doleful face sat dejectedly on top of the missile. Yeltsin explained that the drawing symbolized Russia, which was backward in everything, but had sophisticated nuclear missiles that were now being taken, on a bad road, for destruction, in compliance with the INF treaty that he, Reagan, had signed with Gorbachev in 1987. Accepting the gift, Reagan quipped, "I am glad to have it. But if this drawing had been made in my country, they would have depicted *me* on top of the missile." After a pause Yeltsin said, "The new Russia intends to get rid of both, that is to say of missiles and bad roads."

Reagan expressed his intense interest in what he referred to as "Yeltsin's five-hundred-day plan," saying, "It will be a great step for your country."

Yeltsin replied, "Thank you. . . . The plan boils down to the following. Over the seventy-three years [of Soviet rule], the supercentralization and the Party's monopoly on power have led to what we call a deformation of society. But we realized that we could not go on any longer living and developing like this, that we had to look for new ways out of this situation.

"The *perestroika*, of course, did give a certain impetus to *glasnost* and democratization. Unfortunately, no bold steps were taken in the economy, something that has now brought it to a dead end, because the forces essential for the creation of a market economy have not been released. Seeing that the Union, the center, refuses to give up its positions and wants to keep everything in its hands—whereas this has not yielded any positive results so far—the new parliament and government of Russia decided to take a more independent approach and adopted a Declaration of the State Sovereignty of Russia but within the Union. The difference between the central government's program [of economic reform], which envisages centralization during the transition to the market, and *our* five-hundred-day plan consists in the fact that our program stipulates that everything will emanate from the bottom to the top, from republics to the state; the center will retain only some elements of power. . . .

"Here then are some basic elements of our program:

"First, the new constitution of Russia is based on new principles.

When drafting it, we analyzed very carefully the history and Constitution of the United States and the constitutions of other countries. . . . Our Constitutional Commission meticulously studied the works where human rights, to which you devoted so much time and effort, are examined at the international level. Second, we divided the powers between Russia and the center and even dispensed with most of the Union ministries. Third, from the rigid, vertical planning inherent in the command-administrative system, we are turning to horizontal links. Russia will now conclude bilateral treaties with each republic, as well as treaties with other countries at the international level.

"In a word, self-dependence and renunciation of the dogmas that have been imposed upon us for more than seventy years now—this is what it's all about. Subsequently, we are going to take a number of serious steps in keeping with the laws enacted in Russia. First of all, these are the laws on land and ownership, which provide for private ownership, including land. This position of principle is a new fundamental change for the first time since 1917. I am talking about a mixed economy, a market economy. True, there still remain some orthodox people who got used to thinking in slogans over these many decades. They contend that we now want to build capitalism. But we believe there are not so many of them, and they are not of the same importance as before.

"Bearing in mind the fact that the market transition program, as drafted by the Union government, did not meet with approval either among the people or in the Supreme Soviet of the USSR, we have developed our own, Russian, program, and on that basis we proposed to President Gorbachev the formulation of the five-hundred-day Union program."

Yeltsin then went on to describe in detail the four stages of the program and got so carried away that he did not realize that Reagan had endeavored several times to get in a word edgewise. An exasperated Weinberg took advantage of a Yeltsin pause for breath to cut in. Addressing him simply as "Mr. Yeltsin," and speaking in a voice louder than normal, Weinberg said politely but firmly that the president had something to say, too, so that the meeting would not become a monologue. When I translated this into Russian, Yeltsin seemed genuinely perplexed. Spreading his hands widely, he said, "Well, all right. But the president himself asked me to tell him about our program. So I'm telling."

After this little episode, the monologue turned into a dialogue.

Reagan: You mentioned the part that I am most interested in, that is private ownership of land and enterprises. I think it is where the great difference is between us. In our country with its vast territory, our government made a plan some time ago to parcel up the land into farm-size plots. We told the people, "If you promise that you will farm this land, it is yours." It was the land grant. That way the land was distributed to people who wanted to farm it, grow crops, and sell the produce at the market.

Then there is the private sector and small businesses. Our country is known in the world for big industries and big plants, but it is actually small businesses that play the main role in our economy. The entrepreneur has ideas, he sets up businesses and helps the economy prosper. Over the eight years that I was president, we created 19 million new jobs, and most of them were created by individual entrepreneurs, people who are shopkeepers, bakery owners, et cetera, not the big plants and factories.

Yeltsin: We want to enact a law on entrepreneurial activities, so as to free people from government shackles.

Reagan: Did you note our constitution and the difference between it and all the constitutions of other countries of the world? All the other constitutions are a document where the government tells the people what they can do. But our constitution is a document which says, "We, the people, tell the government what it can do."

Yeltsin: The Russian constitution will be the same.

Reagan: Only three words, "We, the people," and what a difference! I would give you one example of entrepreneurial activity.

There was a young lady in our country who graduated from university. For years she wanted to be a classical pianist, but she developed arthritis of the hands and so she could not play the piano. But she could make good home cookies—we call them brownies. And, to make some money, she began to sell those cookies through a neighborhood grocery. In a few years she had thirty-five people working for her, making cookies and selling them. So last year, she made a profit of one and a quarter million dollars!

Yeltsin: When Senator Dole was here [in early September], he asked if he could participate in entrepreneurial activities here and whether he could invest his capital. I told him we would be glad to offer him various opportunities—Russia is rich, strong, and solvent—so he could safely invest in Russia. In view of the fact that now Russia has its own internal and external policies, I think the United States would do well to pay greater attention to the serious changes in the realignment of forces in the [Soviet] Union.

As to your story about that girl, there are a great many men and women in Russia who would be willing to try their hand at commerce, even though over the past seventy-three years people have forgotten how to sell.

Reagan: These people have ideas, and if given an opportunity, they will put them to good use. I am sure you will accomplish a great change.

The conversation lasted only forty minutes, and although Yeltsin was eager to carry it further, Reagan appeared tired. At 4:40 P.M. he stood up, thus signifying the end of the meeting. At 5 P.M., he had his last event to attend—a meeting with his compatriots, the employees of the U.S. Embassy; and he wanted to get back first to the residence to pick up Nancy before driving to Tchaikovsky Street where the U.S. chancellery is.

Yeltsin saw Reagan to the door, and after exchanging perfunctory handshakes, they parted, never to see each other again. We went down the elevator, and the same man who had met Reagan downstairs, Khasbulatov, escorted him now to his car, but this time he didn't try to speak English. I got into the backseat of the Cadillac, and Andy drove me back to Spaso House where I said good-bye to Reagan until the next day.

A witty joke was making the rounds in Moscow in the fall of 1990. It described in a nutshell the evolution of the views of the principal leaders of the Soviet state over the seventy-three years of its existence and illustrated their differing approaches to eliminating obstacles in the way of building a "radiant and glorious future"—communism. But after this meeting with Yeltsin, it occured to me to give it a new punch line.

According to the joke, Lenin, Stalin, Khrushchev, Brezhnev, and Gorbachev are traveling together by train into communism. Suddenly, the train stops somewhere in the middle of the Siberian taiga and the engineer says that it has come to the end of the track. Lenin stands up and makes a little speech: "Comrades, don't worry. I know what is to be done in order for us to continue our journey into communism. In principle, it is necessary to look into my theoretical works, such as 'Two steps forward, one step back.' They contain the answers to all the questions. But first, we need to send for peasants in the nearest village to cut timber and make the ties. After that, we must send for workers in the nearest city and ask them to make rails and lay the track. Everything will be *khorosho*, okay, then, and we will continue our journey into a radiant future."

Now Stalin gets up and says that the engineer and the track-layers should be shot because they are definitely wreckers and saboteurs. After that everything will be all right and the journey can continue. Then Khrushchev jumps up and suggests that the engineer be first rehabilitated, then they should all drive off the end of the track to see what happens. "No!" booms Brezhnev. "We must all stay in the car, draw the blinds, sit down, rock it back and forth, and pretend that we are moving. You'll see—it will feel good."

Finally, it is Gorbachev's turn. "I suggest we call a meeting to redefine everything and then announce the restructuring of the train, a change of the crew, and the extension of the ties, and then we'll see what happens."

At this point, Yeltsin unexpectedly comes out of the taiga and tells them, "I know how to get out of this situation. Everybody get off the train—no more journeying to communism. We'll turn it around and roll it back to the future—toward capitalism."

In fact, Yeltsin had not openly disavowed communism until July 12, 1990, when he announced—at the 28th (and the last) Party Congress— his resignation from the Communist Party of the Soviet Union, which had already been losing support among its rank-and-file members. Some thirteen months later, after the abortive coup against Gorbachev in August 1991, Yeltsin, acting as the elected president of the Russian republic, would ban the Communist Party, which constituted the base for the coup plotters, from operating on its territory.

September 19, Wednesday. Day Four and Last.

At the request of Reagan's aides, his departure from Spaso House for Sheremetievo-1 was scheduled at 8:45 A.M.—on the same day Reagan was to have an audience in Rome with His Holiness the Pope John Paul II. At eight-thirty, I was already inside the imposing yellow mansion in the very heart of the Old Arbat. Before leaving, the Reagans wanted to have their picture taken with the group of the Soviets who had been busy all these days making sure that the visit proceeded as smoothly as possible: the protocol officers, the security men, and even the drivers. "Unless they have any objections," quipped Reagan in his usual style.

On the way to the airport, Reagan sprang a surprise on the Muscovites. When the motorcade left the confines of Sadovoye Koltso, or the inner ring road, it started to pick up speed, forcing other traffic aside to the curb. Reagan noticed this and asked me to tell the driver not to break the speed limit on his account. The driver obeyed and eased up on the gas, so it took the motorcade forty minutes, instead of the normal twenty or so, to reach Sheremetievo airport. The drivers of all the other cars and trucks on the road did not dare to overtake our motorcade, nor could they, because the lead police cars took up all the lanes. As a result, a tail of cars and trucks trailed behind us for several miles. What color-ful epithets the drivers of those vehicles must have bestowed upon Rea-gan, who hadn't the slightest inkling of the consequences of his desire to abide by the law like all other mere mortals!

The farewell ceremony at the airport was as short as the welcoming cer-emony. No speeches were made, no salutes were fired, no honor guards marched by. The Reagans were brought in the Zil right up to the board-ing ramp of the *Capitalist Tool*, where Medvedev and Dobrynin with his wife were already waiting. The Reagans said their good-byes, and Rea-gan paused to shake my hand and thank me for "a job well done." Then, he went up the ramp, supporting Nancy by the elbow, a black attaché case in his hand. At the top of the ramp they paused, holding hands, then turned around to wave at us. That was the last I saw of them, and that is how I remember them, standing together on that ramp, holding hands.

That was their last visit to the Soviet Union.

The summits described in these journals were the major milestones on the way to ending the Cold War, and ending the Cold War was not easy. But with a series of gradual steps taken by Gorbachev and his Western counterparts—primarily Reagan and Bush—and with several successive reciprocal gestures of trust and goodwill, the insanities of the nuclear menace were finally ended. The momentous START I Treaty, which reduced Soviet and U.S. strategic nuclear arms by 50 percent, was signed on July 31, 1991. It was followed by the START II Treaty, signed on January 12, 1993, which made even deeper cuts in the Soviet and U.S. nuclear weapons arsenals. Numerous other treaties and agree-ments, especially on arms control, such as the CFE agreement and the CW (chemical weapons) convention, have also been concluded and signed since the relevant talks started in the 1980s.

The world has now all but forgotten that only a few short years ago the hands of the so-called Doomsday Clock—which has appeared monthly since 1947 on the cover of the *Bulletin of the Atomic Scientists*, published in Chicago—were set at three minutes to midnight; that's how dangerously close the world had come to nuclear Armageddon. Since then, the risk of global nuclear war has been significantly lessened, and the world is a much safer place now—in many respects thanks to the crucial summits described in this book.

EPILOGUE

THE SUN HAS SET
ON GORBACHEV . . . OR HAS IT?

On a cold and miserable Western Christmas evening, December 25, 1991, Mikhail Sergeyevich Gorbachev, the last general secretary of the Soviet Communist Party and the first and last president of the Soviet Union, spoke on the phone, for the last time in his official capacity, with President Bush, informing him that he would be resigning in two hours. He said "Good-bye" to him, in English, and assured him that the friendship between them would always remain. Then, at 6:55 P.M. Moscow time, five minutes before he went on television to announce his resignation, he signed a decree transferring the right to use nuclear weapons to the president of Russia, Boris Yeltsin, thus abdicating "the nuclear button." At seven o'clock, he made the resignation speech relinquishing the presidency of the Soviet Union.

The red hammer-and-sickle flag that had been flying over the Kremlin government building since 1917 was lowered almost at the same time as Gorbachev spoke, and a white-blue-red tricolor, symbolizing Russia, was hoisted in its place. The Soviet empire had collapsed and the old regime had dissolved. The Soviet Union was no more. Mikhail Sergeyevich Gorbachev was now a private citizen. The sun had set on him.

Two days later, on the morning of December 27, when Gorbachev arrived at the Kremlin intending to give a farewell interview to Japanese journalists in Room 3—which had been his office for more than six and a half years—he was startled to discover that the nameplate on the wall next to the door of his office, with the inscription "President of the USSR, M.S. Gorbachev," was gone. He was told by new security guards that his office was already occupied. Indeed, inside, Boris Nikolayevich Yeltsin himself was sitting behind what had been until now Gorbachev's desk.

The Russian government headed by Yeltsin had promised Gorbachev that it would give him at least a couple of days before it took up residence in this venerable seat of the country's power, but this was Yeltsin's way of slighting and humiliating Gorbachev. Gorbachev had been his political nemesis since they parted ways in 1987. He was also the first Soviet leader ever to agree to step down voluntarily and to peacefully turn over power to the president of a new independent state on the map of the world, to be known as the Russian Federation.

Gorbachev's fall from power inspired many commentators to take his historical measure, and many focused on his missteps and shortcomings. But I would rather focus here on his achievements, on his contribution to ending the Cold War and establishing a genuinely warm personal relationship with his Western counterparts, above all with President Reagan, President Bush, and Prime Minister Thatcher of the Anglo-Saxon world, to say nothing of other leaders such as President Mitterrand and Chancellor Kohl. For Gorbachev as a man of history does not deserve the accusations and needs no vindication.

Gorbachev will go down in history as one of the great reformers of all time. He is a towering historic figure of great courage and intellectual energy and capacity, although his downfall was perhaps inevitable because he presided over a transition in his country—always the most difficult period in the life of any country. The political and economic reforms he had introduced at home had ground to a halt because of the increasing resistance of the Party, the KGB, and the military, because they threatened the entrenched interests of the ruling class of Soviet *nomenklatura*. This resistance, covert and passive at first, grew into direct sabotage and culminated in a coup d'état against Gorbachev on August 19–21, 1991. As I watched the coup unfold on a TV screen, weak and dazed from the seven-hour-long heart surgery I had just undergone, I prayed. I prayed for my country and for my people. I prayed for Gorbachev and his family who were being held incommunicado at their summer residence in Phoros, Crimea. I prayed that the despicable bunch of men, who represented no one but themselves and whose time had run out, would fail in their attempt to turn back the clock of history by restoring the old System. My prayers were answered. The coup failed.

Eventually, Gorbachev realized that he had to *remake* the system, not just reform it, and do so without provoking civil war. That realization, unfortunately, came too late. But the seeds of democracy he had planted did bear fruit, and that was why the coup failed. He gave the Soviet people freedom of speech and expression, freedom of worship, and freedom from fear—the fear of persecution. He gave them liberty. In that sense, he was a great liberator.

He may go down in history as the man who destroyed the Soviet system by mistake, which may explain his downfall, but his reform programs consciously and deliberately discredited and undermined the old Soviet system: its stultified and stultifying ideology, its command and administrative economic structure, its reliance on fear to keep people in obedience, its lies and violence, its empire ruled by brute force, and its foreign adventures in the Third World. For this alone he deserves the Nobel Peace Prize, which he was rightfully awarded. He sought a more decentralized and flexible economy, eventually embracing privatization and a market economy. He wanted to ensure politics would be more participatory, and to that end he arranged the first-ever free elections in the Soviet Union.

Gorbachev's vigorous pursuit of change was enough to delegitimize the old system and sap its strength, but not to save it. He had let loose a political unraveling he could not stop. The idea was to break the backbone of the totalitarian monster. And he did. To his everlasting credit, he let this occur and never resorted to the brutality of the past. He stood his moral ground, held to his vow never to use violence and to look for solutions to all problems through *political* means—and for that, too, he deserves the Nobel Prize.

He also deserves praise for his tactical brilliance. He maneuvered between the zealots of right and left, trying to convince each side that he was shielding it from the excesses of the other. He maintained a balance between them that averted a civil war, while the tide inexorably flowed in the direction of reform. So when a coup was attempted against him, the hard-liners had been much too weakened and the trend of democratization in Soviet society had become too strong for the coup to succeed. But when the hard-liners were defeated, his balancing act was over. Still, the peaceful revolution he had unleashed, every bit as important in its impact as the one in October of 1917—only in reverse—was now well on track and irreversible. The main purpose of his life was fulfilled.

Some say that Gorbachev was too indecisive. But the fact remains that Gorbachev would have been toppled, even as late into *perestroika* as in 1990, by a decision of the then still powerful Politburo or a plenum of the Party's Central Committee had he tried any precipitous action. Even some three months before the August putsch the hard-liners were still capable of bringing back the old order by force and returning the Baltic states to the USSR. They could very well have rebuilt the Iron Curtain and put up another Berlin Wall. But Gorbachev prevented them from doing this by his skillful maneuvering. He never tired of repeating, "This country cannot be reformed overnight, otherwise there would be bloodshed."

Now in retrospect, we realize how right he was. He said that the [Soviet] economy could not be plunged into the market overnight, that the transition should be gradual and "painless" to the people, that it was not the speed but direction that was most important. He never neglected the social dimensions of such a transition to a market-oriented economy, after more than seventy years of the command-administrative economy, that could stop and even reverse the forward movement.

Gorbachev's accomplishments in foreign policy are truly great and numerous. Perhaps his greatest achievement is that he took his country away from the impending conflict with the West and almost single-handedly curtailed the ruinous arms race, thereby creating a golden opportunity to reallocate resources to peaceful uses. In so doing, he managed to keep at bay the Party, the military, and the KGB while Soviet society at large grew used to the ideas of democratization and demilitarization. He had perspective. Thanks to his common sense and political courage, too, Russia today has no more expensive clients such as Cuba or Angola or Afghanistan. But most importantly, it has *no more enemies*—perhaps for the first time in its history.

That even honest men must one day exit the world political scene is a truism, as is the fact that gratitude does not extend to political realities. So one could very well shrug off Gorbachev's exit from the political scene and simply say that his time ran out. Yet I think these truths do not apply to Mikhail Sergeyevich Gorbachev. Let everyone ask himself how his or her judgments have changed since March 1985. Who could have believed then that the Cold War, for one thing—with its concomitant arms race, disarmament, détente, rearmament and dangerous brinkmanship—would end in just a few years' time? It then seemed so deeply rooted in the minds of men that no one could do anything to reverse it. It took Mikhail Sergeyevich Gorbachev to accomplish *three miracles* and thereby turn the world upside down.

First, he exposed the irrationality of the seemingly reasonable ideological rivalry between the two superpowers and their policy of nuclear deterrence. When the spiral of the arms race continued upward and when, from one summit to another, the division of the world appeared to be increasingly natural, the thought would sometimes cross my mind: What would happen if one of the sides suddenly said it no longer wished to play this game? It took a courageous man from Stavropol to make the play of my fancy a reality.

Second, the end of the Cold War came without war or great bloodshed. To be sure, Gorbachev is not the only one to be credited with this—it takes two to tango, as the saying has it. But without the tactical adroitness and ingenuity of Gorbachev, without his ability again and again to get on top of the rapidly evolving situation and steer the course of reforms in the right direction—would the collapse of what Ronald Reagan called the Evil Empire have been so relatively peaceful? After all, none of the previous empires, whether Roman or Ottoman or British or any other, had fallen without war or destruction. If someone had predicted that the Soviet empire would collapse and avoid colossal cataclysms in the age of supersophisticated conventional arms and nuclear weapons, he would have been ridiculed in those early days of 1985 when Gorbachev had just become the leader of the Soviet Union.

Third, Gorbachev brought Russia back to Europe. The bonds that had linked Russian history to European history seemed to have been cut forever—so alien, unnatural, and unacceptable to the West was the brutal and bureaucratic imperialism of Moscow. Gorbachev preached reconciliation, peace, and what he called "common human values and interdependence." He returned to people in the Soviet Union their real voice, and the Westerners saw that the Soviet people were part of them, part of the whole of humanity.

What has happened to these three accomplishments of Gorbachev? Two of them already belong to history. Without them, the third one would have been impossible—the return of Russia to Europe. To be sure, this enterprise will be long and difficult. But the hope remains that no more Berlin Walls will ever be built again. At the origin of this hope stands Gorbachev.

Gorbachev's place in the pantheon of outstanding statesmen has been assured. Of one thing I have no doubt: The farther away the river of time will carry the watershed events in the Soviet Union of the second half of the 1980s and early 1990s, the more prominent and impressive the role of Gorbachev will appear to be as the symbol of the Great Reformation. I have a feeling that we have not heard the last from him. He is not the kind of statesman who could ever quietly fade into history. His political career is far from over. It is quite possible that he will rise again and stage a political comeback, and once again the sun will shine on him. It has never been power for its own sake that he cares about. Power is transitory, and he knows it. He is ready, capable, and willing to undertake another mission: to revive his country, bring it back to normalcy, and restore to its people a feeling of human dignity. Russia needs him at this critical juncture of its tormented history, for he is the individual best equipped to effect more important changes, peacefully, without violence or bloodshed. Russia needs an enlightened and experienced leader—now more than ever before.

Who knows, maybe one day the incumbent president of Russia, whoever he may be, after having been soundly defeated at the ballot box, upon arrival in the Kremlin to clean out his desk in what is now his office, will find a new nameplate on the door, one that will say, "President Gorbachev, Mikhail Sergeyevich."

History's ways, like God's, are unknowable.

INDEX

ABC-TV, 148, 182
ABM Treaty, 35, 102, 108, 124–28, 137, 256
    observance of, 116
    Reagan and, 103, 159
    Soviet interpretation of, 124
    Soviet-U.S. joint statement on, 116–18
    START and, 116–18, 120
Academy of Sciences, USSR, 112, 199
Adams, John, 92
Adams, Robert, 83, 86
Adelman, Kenneth, 69
"adversaries," "competition" vs., 65–66
Afanasenko, Peter, 48, 72, 73, 126, 127,
    151, 248, 250
Afghanistan, 112–13, 118, 139, 275
    Bush and, 96–97, 279–80
    Geneva Agreements on, 144–45
    Gorbachev on, 103–4
    Reagan on, 80, 103–4
    Soviet withdrawal from, 41–42, 103–4,
        112–13, 143–44
    warring factions in, 279–80
    Yakovlev and, 196
Aganbegyan, Abel, 83
Agnos, Art, 302
agriculture, 276–77, 346–48, 361, 373–74
agrofirmi, 346
Air Force One, 54
Akhmatova, Anna, 170
Akhromeyev, Sergei Fedorovich, 43, 50, 53,
    67, 68, 83, 119, 192, 206
    in arms control working group, 107–9,
        113, 116, 124–34
    at Helsinki summit, 312, 314, 316–17,
        318, 321, 325, 326–27
    at Washington summit II, 243, 247, 248,
        249, 260, 272–73, 275, 278–79, 284
Albert Einstein Peace Prize, 261
ALCMs (air-launched cruise missiles), 256
Alexander I, Czar of Russia, 223

Alexander II, Czar of Russia, 253, 306
Alexander Nevsky Monastery, 335
Alexei, son of Czar Nicholas II, 227, 306
Alexi, Patriarch of All Russia, 163
All-Union Institute of Scientific and Tech-
    nical Information, 199
Altman, Robert, 85
Americanology, Soviet, 88
Americans, 298–99, 300
    Gorbachev's meetings and encounters
        with, 82–88, 121–23, 242–43,
        250–51, 286–88
    KGB hostility toward, 338
American Sovietology, 88
amerikanisti, 54
Amvrosiyevich, Eduard, 60
Anastasia, Grand Duchess of Russia, 227
Andreas, Dwayne, 180, 251
Andrews Air Force Base, 138, 139
Andreyeva, Nina, 147
Andropov, Yuri Vladimirovich, 28, 148, 289
Andy (chauffeur), 370, 375
Angola, 34
Anne, Princess of England, 228
Anti-Defamation League, 92, 93
Anyone for Denis?, 210–11
Apollo-Soyuz space mission, 243
Apple Computer, 303–4
Arab world, Persian Gulf war and, 309–32
Arbat district, Moscow, 142, 157, 336, 376
Arbatov, Georgy, 95, 246, 316
Archer Daniels Midland Co., 180, 251
Argumenti i Fakti, 187
Arias peace plan, 78
Armacost, Michael, 112
Armenia, 188, 199, 300
Arms Control and Disarmament Problems
    Department (UPOVR), Soviet, 125
Army Band, U.S., 64
Asimov, Isaac, 242

INDEX

Aspen Lodge, 270–71, 272, 275, 281, 283
Aspin, Les, 255
Assad, Hafez, 314
astrology, 171, 368
AT&T, 303
Atlantis, 341
August coup (1991), 312, 331–32, 338, 380, 381
"awesome," "*potryasayusche*" as, 296
Azerbaijan, 287

Backfire bombers, 258, 265
Baker, Howard, 49, 62
Baker, James A., 3rd, 337–38
    at Camp David talks, 276–77
    Gorbachev and, 276–77
    at Helsinki summit, 309, 310, 311, 314–15, 321, 324, 325, 328
    at Moscow summit, 158
    at Washington I summit, 62, 68, 90
    at Washington II summit, 248, 258, 259, 260–61, 262, 268–84
Baltic republics, 238, 255, 382
    see also Lithuania
Balzac, Honoré de, 354
Bank of America, 303
Bartholomew, Reginald, 259
BBC, 111, 182, 217
Bechtel Group, 303
Begin, Menachem, 271
Belgium, 71
Bellow, Saul, 90
Belonogov, Alexandr, 312–13, 314, 320
Benjamin Franklin Room of White House, 106
Bennett, William, 123
Bentsen, Lloyd, 255
Beresford, Philip, 220
Berezhkov, Sergei, 165, 268, 284
Beria, Lavrenty, 142
Berlin, Sir Isaiah, 223–24
Berlin Wall, 156, 174, 196, 233, 356–57
Bessmertnykh, Alexandr, 43, 67, 110, 180, 247, 263, 312, 314, 315–16, 321
Bialkin, Kenneth, 92
Bierbauer, Charles, 328
Billington, James, 94
Biryukova, Alexandra, 231
BKD (Grand Kremlin Palace building), 154, 158, 162–63, 169, 197
blinis, 119
Bogart, Humphrey, 118
Boldin, Valery, 69, 76–77, 192, 206
Bolshoi English-Russian Dictionary, 65

Bonner, Elena, 175, 365
Borovitsky Gate, 153
Boschwitz, Rudy, 255
Boulevard Ring, Moscow, 157
bracketing of disputed phrases in treaties, 116–17
Bradbury, Ray, 242
Brahms, Johannes, 100
Braithwaite, Sir Rodric, 223
break dancing, 157
Brezhnev, Leonid Ilyich, 26, 32, 146, 172, 270, 274
    decline of, 27–28
    Khrushchev and, 45
    as public speaker, 33, 38–39
Brezhnev doctrine, 188, 196
Brokaw, Tom, 56, 111, 251
Broomfield, Bill, 255
Brubeck, Dave, 90, 174–76
Bukharin, Nikolai, 86
Bulletin of the Atomic Scientists, 377
Bunche, Ruth, 94
Bundy, McGeorge, 83
Bunny (protocol assistant), 120
Burt, Richard, 257
Bush, Barbara, 63, 68, 99, 252, 259–60, 270–71
    Raisa Gorbacheva and, 266–67, 327
Bush, George:
    Afghanistan and, 96–97, 279–80
    Camp David talks and, 267–84
    chemical weapons and, 96
    Ethiopia and, 280–81
    Gorbachev and, 15, 307–8, 344–45
    Gorbachev's views on, 298–99
    at Helsinki summit, 309–32
    at Malta summit, 257
    open skies proposal and, 257
    popularity of, 317
    Reagan and, 49, 323
    Soviet MFN status and, 261–63, 283, 308
    in state dinner conversation with Shevardnadze, 94–98
    as Vice President, 49, 116
    at Washington I summit, 62, 65, 68, 81, 92, 93, 94–95, 100, 101, 118–21
    at Washington II summit, 233–308
business interests, U.S., 136, 285, 302–4
Butch Cassidy and the Sundance Kid, 174
Byrd, Robert, 91, 102, 175

Cabinet Room of White House, 76, 77, 124, 130, 133, 134, 248, 255–61
California, 291, 299, 300, 353

Cambodia (Kampuchea), 113, 275
Camp David, 267–84
    see also Washington summit II
Canada, 193–94
Canterbury, Archbishop of, 223
Capitalist Tool, 335, 377
Carlucci, Frank, 49, 81, 106–7, 127, 145,
    158, 159, 160, 178, 179
Carter, Jimmy, 19, 81, 146, 271
Casablanca, 118
Case Communications, Inc., 204
Castro, Fidel, 203
Catherine (the Great), Empress of Russia,
    109
Catoctin Mountains, 268
Center for Defense Information, 83
Central America, 77–78
CFE (conventional forces in Europe),
    256–57, 377
Chaplin, Deputy Foreign Minister, 44, 45
Charles, Prince of Wales, 62, 220, 229
Charles I, King of England, 198
Chebrikov, Viktor, 75, 231
Chekhov, Anton, 341–42
Chelyabinsk, 277
Chemical Bank, 252
chemical weapons, 52, 96, 256, 377
Cheney, Dick, 94, 248, 310
Chernenko, Konstantin Ustinovich, 28,
    148, 245, 289
Chernishev, Vladimir, 54, 68, 150, 154,
    292, 313
Chernyaev, Anatoly Sergeyevich, 43, 83,
    181, 193, 213, 247, 263, 312, 321
Chervov, Nikolai, 47
Chevron Corp., 303
China, People's Republic of, 214, 233, 255
Churchill, Sir Winston, 20, 70, 197
City of the Yellow Devil, The (Gorky), 25
class struggle, theory of, 188
Cliburn, Van, 100–101, 242
CNN, 19, 87, 171, 183, 217, 246, 312, 328
Cohen, Stephen, 83, 86, 88
Coldstream Guards, 222
Cold War, 140, 152, 162
    class struggle theory in, 188
    danger of mutual miscalculation in,
        69–70
    end of, 15, 16, 252–53, 257, 307–8; see
        also Washington summit II
    irrationality of, 382
    Persian Gulf war and, 310, 313, 329
collective farms (*kolkhoz*), 277, 316,
    346–48

Collet, Sir Christopher, 216, 217, 223
Committee for State Security, USSR, see
    KGB
communism:
    "human face" of, 234
    Marxism-Leninism and, 56, 57, 104, 214
    theory of class struggle in, 188
Communist International (Komintern), 163
Communist Party, U.S., 163
Communist Party, USSR:
    Central Committee of, 28, 29, 30, 76,
        163, 182, 235, 313
    constitutional powers of, 141, 234
    General Secretary of, 32
    Gorbachev and, 29
    ideological conservatism of, 142
    19th Conference of, 182
    1988 conference of, 213
    27th Congress of, 219
    Yeltsin and, 376
    see also Politburo, CPSU
Communist Party of Great Britain, 215
comprehensive test ban treaty (CTBT)
    talks, 145
Congress of People's Deputies (USSR),
    187, 208
Constitution, USSR, Article 6 of, 141, 234
Constitutional Commission, 373
Contadora Group, 78
Contras, Nicaraguan, 78
Control Data Corp., 285
conventional forces in Europe (CFE),
    256–57, 377
Coolidge, Calvin, 135
Cooper, Gary, 165
coup d'états, attempted:
    August 1991, 312, 331–32, 338, 380,
        381
    September 1990, 331–32
CPSU Bulletin, 187
Cranston, Alan, 102, 144, 255
Creation of Peace (painting), 297
Crowe, William, 49, 63, 93, 233
C-SPAN, 19
CTBT (comprehensive test ban treaty)
    talks, 145
Cuba, 195, 203, 275
Cuban missile crisis, 126
CW (chemical weapons) convention, 377
Czechoslovakia, 42

Daily Mirror (London), 207
Daniil, Prince, 162
Dead Souls (Gogol), 174

Debussy, Claude, 100
defense and space (D&S) talks, 108
de Klerk, F. W., 281
Democratic Party, U.S., 368
De Niro, Robert, 83
Denmark, 20
Denver, John, 83
Depression, Great, 360
Desperate Journey, 351, 358
Deukmejian, George, 302
DiMaggio, Joe, 102
dissidents, Soviet, 158, 162
Dobrynin, Anatoly Fedorovich, 133–34,
    149, 158, 181, 247, 248, 335, 338,
    346, 348, 352, 353, 355–56, 358, 377
    at Washington summit I, 50, 54, 60–61,
    67, 68, 101, 119, 124
Doctor Zhivago (Pasternak), 115
Dokuchayev, General, 45
Dole, Robert, 63, 69, 102, 175, 252, 255,
    334–35, 374
Donahue, Phil, 29
Donaldson, Sam, 148
Doomsday Clock, 377
doveryai no proveryai (trust but verify), 70,
    71, 110, 356, 366
Dubinin, Yuri, 54–55, 116
Dzasokhov, Alexandr, 238, 339

earthquakes, 149, 300
East Room of White House, 69, 72–74,
    87–91, 101, 251, 264–65, 284–85
economic reform, Soviet, 162, 205–6, 225,
    316
    agriculture and, 346–48, 361, 373–74
    Reagan's views on, 339–41, 344–46,
    361–62
    Supreme Soviet and, 28, 81–82, 146,
    238
    and transition to market economy, 254,
    300, 309, 323–25, 339–41, 365–66,
    382
    Yeltsin and, 371–73
Edward, Prince of England, 222, 223, 228
Eisenhower, Dwight D., 83, 94, 271
Eisenhower, Susie, 83
Elizabeth II, Queen of England, 215,
    220–30
El Salvador, 275
Elton, Lady, 224
Emerson, Ralph Waldo, 73
emigration policy, Soviet, 67, 111, 241–42
Engels, Friedrich, 178
Eritrea, 280

Ethiopia, 34, 280–81
Étude-Tableau (Rachmaninoff), 100
Eureka, Calif., 359
European-Soviet economic cooperation,
    196
Evert, Chris, 92, 93
"Evil Empire," Reagan and, 79, 165–66,
    168, 169, 183, 333, 342, 383

Faceted Chamber (Granovitaya Palata),
    Palace of Facets, 164–66
Fairbanks, Douglas, Jr., 242
Fairmont Hotel, San Francisco, 297, 302–4
Falin, Valentin, 192, 195, 247–48, 313, 338,
    339
farmers, 276–77, 346–48
Fascell, Dante, 255
F-15 jet fighters, 310
Figaro, Le, 142
Finlandia Hall, 325, 327
First Moscow State Institute of Foreign
    Languages (*Inyaz*), 25
fissionable weapons-grade materials, 256
Fitzwater, Marlin, 268, 321, 328
five-hundred-day program, 300, 309, 331,
    333–34, 371–73
Flynn, Errol, 351
Foley, Thomas, 102
Fonda, Jane, 242, 243
Forbes, Malcolm, 106, 335
Ford, Gerald, 83, 146
foreign policy, Soviet, 26, 196, 213–14
"Formation of New Features in Everyday
    Life of Kolkhoz Peasantry" (Gor-
    bacheva), 104
Fortenberry, Philip, 254
"four freedoms," 261, 265
France, 310, 311
Franco, Francisco, 94
Franklin, Benjamin, 109
Franklin Delano Roosevelt Freedom
    Medal, 261
Friendly Persuasion, 165
Frolov, Ivan, 206
"front-loading," 144
Fulbright, William, 83

Gadhafi, Muammar, 190, 312
Galbraith, John Kenneth, 242
Garbo, Greta, 44
"Garden of Gethsemane, The" (Paster-
    nak), 175–76
Garwin, Richard, 83
Gates, Robert, 248

Geneva Agreements on Afghanistan
(1988), 144–45
Geneva arms control talks, see START
George V, King of England, 229
Georgia, nationalist movement in, 220,
230, 231, 279
Gerasimov, Guennady, 181
German Democratic Republic (GDR)
(East Germany), 42, 188, 356–57
see also Berlin Wall
Germany, Federal Republic of, in NATO
discussions, 237, 246–50, 258, 362
Gillespie, Dizzy, 242
Gipp, George, 351
glasnost:
    Big Lie and, 142
    definition of, 29
    emigration policy under, 111
    government revelations under, 187
    Persian Gulf war and, 316–17
    Politburo opposition to, 75
    social change under, 51
"glasnost brigade," 74–75
Glitman, Maynard, 71
Gogol, Nikolai, 174
Golden Room of Soviet Embassy, 82–83,
86, 113, 118–19, 244
Gorbachev, Mikhail Sergeyevich:
    accomplishments of, 379–84
    on Afghanistan, 103–4
    Andropov and, 289
    appearance of, 28, 31
    attempted coup (1990) and, 331–32
    August coup (1991) and, 312, 331, 338
    autograph given by, 184
    Baker and, 276–77
    body language of, 40
    on Bush, 298–99
    businessmen's meeting with, 285,
        302–4
    at Camp David summit, 267–84
    childhood of, 253
    civil war averted by, 380–82
    Cold War ended by, 382–83
    crisis announced by, 51
    debating style of, 80–81
    disarmament and, 35–36
    evolution in thinking of, 16
    on expansionism charge, 78–80
    five-hundred-day plan and, 309
    Germany-in-NATO issue and, 246–50,
        258
    glasnost and, 29
    granddaughter of, 276

Gromyko and, 31
Guildhall speech of, 213–19
at Helsinki summit, 309–32
human rights and, 111–12, 140
Hussein and, 309–12
importance of, 15–17
impromptu encounters with public by,
    121–23, 250–51
informality of, 292, 318
INF Treaty signed by, 73–74
international support for, 51–52
interpreters for, 38–40
Iraq and, 309–32
and KGB, 75
land ownership and, 277
on land reform, 346–48
Lithuania blockade issue and, 234, 237,
    262–63
at London summit, 187–231
Lukyanov and, 343
market economy transition and, 254,
    300, 309, 382
and Marxist view of West, 161–62
MFN recognition sought by, 261–63,
    283, 308
at Moscow summit, 141–86
Mugabe's meeting with, 27, 30–37
as negotiator, 80
Nixon on, 11
Nobel Prize for, 381
on nuclear-free world, 35–36, 218
on nuclear weapons, 35–36
perestroika and, 29–30, 166
Politburo and, 27–28, 74–75, 234–35
in preparation for Moscow summit,
    145–48
presidency issue and, 234–35
prompt books and, 33
on Reagan, 299
Reagans' interest in personal life of,
    353–57
reasonable defense sufficiency doctrine
    of, 52
resignation of, 379–83
Russians admired by, 253
San Francisco visited by, 289–308
SDI and, 35–36, 159–60
on socialist model, 347–48
Soviet military and, 52–53, 185
speaking style of, 33–34, 38–40
at Stanford, 294–97
START treaty and, 117–18, 256–58,
    265–66
as Stavropol secretary, 288–89

Gorbachev, Mikhail Sergeyevich, (cont.)
  Supreme Soviet and, 365
  as Supreme Soviet Presidium chair-
    man, 189
  term of office for, 212
  Thatcher on, 11
  Twin Cities visited by, 285–89
  U.S. as viewed by, 161–62
  U.S. popularity of, 74, 87–88, 121–22
  vernacular language used by, 38–39
  at Washington I summit, 41–140
  at Washington II summit, 233–308
  Yeltsin and, 56, 235–36, 251–52,
    274–75, 358, 371–73, 379–80
  as youthful, 28
Gorbachev, Sergei Andreyevich, 253
Gorbacheva, Anastasia, 276
Gorbacheva, Raisa Maximovna:
  Barbara Bush and, 266–67, 327
  at Camp David, 271–72, 273, 276
  "conspicuous consumption" of, 198
  criticisms of, 55, 57–58, 198
  dress of, 55, 57–58, 135, 163–64, 198,
    216–17, 273
  as educated woman, 56
  as first Soviet First Lady, 55–56
  George Bush and, 118–20
  "glamornost" of, 207
  granddaughter of, 276
  health of, 348, 350
  at Helsinki summit, 311, 313, 318–19
  on husband's fame, 184
  influence of, 56–57
  informality of, 292
  Jane Fonda and, 243
  KBG and, 57
  at London summit, 198, 202, 207–8,
    213, 223, 229
  Marxism-Leninism and, 56, 57, 104
  Nancy Reagan and, 56–57, 63–64,
    104–6, 170–71, 266–67, 291–94,
    350, 358
  personality of, 56, 58
  as "Red Little Star," 58, 202
  in San Francisco, 289–306
  Thatcher and, 36–37, 192, 198, 199,
    213
  Twin Cities visited by, 285–89
  at Washington summit I, 55–57, 68, 74,
    83, 86, 91–92, 94, 104–6
  at Washington summit II, 259–60
  Yeltsin and, 56
Gorbachev–Reagan summit, see Washington summit I

Gorbomania, 16, 123
Gore, Albert, 106
Göring, Hermann, 21
Gorky, Maxim, 25
Gosplan (Soviet Planning Authority),
  238
Gowry, Lord, 223
Graham, Billy, 86–87, 90–91, 251
Graham, Katherine, 47, 153
Graham, Philip, 16
Grand Kremlin Palace building (BKD),
  154, 158, 162–63, 169, 197
Great Britain, see London summit
Great Fire of Moscow (1812), 164
Greenland, 256
Gromyko, Andrei Andreyevich, 28, 77, 158,
  274
  Gorbachev and, 31, 148
  interpreters and, 22, 25–26, 150
  Kissinger and, 84
  at MFA, 25–26
  Reagan and, 149, 150–53
  retirement of, 189
Gromyko, Lydia Dmitriyevna, 150–52, 171
Grozny, Ivan, 164
GUM, 167
Gumilev, Nikolai, 170

Haig, Alexander, 69
Hammer, Armand, 92–93, 113, 163, 180,
  240, 242, 251–52
Harriman, Averell, 83
Harriman, Pamela, 83
Hawthorn Lodge, 275
Helms, Jessie, 81
Helms, Richard, 90
Helsinki Act, 327
Helsinki summit (1990), 309–32
  accomplishments of, 329–30
  economic cooperation discussed at,
    323–26
  immediate purpose of, 310
  press conference after, 328
  Soviet team for, 312–13
  UN sanctions and, 311
  US-Soviet joint statement in, 319–24
Hermitage Museum, 335
Herzen, Alexandr, 296
Heseltine, Sir Michael, 223
Hewlett-Packard Company, 303
Hills, Carla, 252
Hinckley, John, 355
Hitler, Adolf, 64
Holdsworth, Sir Trevor, 204, 223

Holly Lodge, 275–76
homosexuality, in San Francisco, 305
Homo sovieticus, 298
Honecker, Erich, 188, 269, 357
Hopkins, Bill, 48, 110–11, 116, 169, 270–71
House of Commons, Yakovlev's meeting with MPs at, 195–96
Howe, Sir Geoffrey, 190, 191, 192, 195, 200–201, 206, 223
Howell, David, 195
human rights issues, 175, 191
    Gorbachev's reaction to, 111–12, 140
    in London summit, 191, 201, 209
    in Moscow summit, 153, 156, 158–59, 177, 179
    in Washington summit I, 111–12, 140
Hurd, Sir Douglas, 206, 233
Hussein, Saddam, Persian Gulf war and, 309–12, 318, 339

Iacocca, Lee, 285
"I Cannot Forgo My Principles" (Andreyevna), 147
ICBMs (intercontinental ballistic missiles), 130–31, 137
Ignatenko, Vitaly, 312, 328
"I Left My Heart in San Francisco," 306
India, 22
INF (intermediate-range nuclear force) missiles, 42–43, 70–71
INF (intermediate-range nuclear force) Treaty, 136, 139
    arms reduced by, 70–71
    Bush's support for, 95
    signing of, 68–69, 72–74
    Supreme Soviet and, 81–82, 146
    U.S. ratification of, 81, 82, 102, 146
Institute for USA and Canada Studies, 95
Institute of World Economics and International Relations, 112
Intermezzo (Brahms), 100
International Affairs Committee of Supreme Soviet, 334–42
International Atomic Energy Agency (IAEA), 281
International Foundation for the Survival and Development of Mankind, 143, 302
International Institute for Strategic Studies, 218
interpretation:
    of locutions, 39–40

    to or from native language, 21
    types of, 21
interpreters:
    background of, 23
    importance of, 19–20, 97–98
    nervousness of, 22–23
    occupational hazards of, 19
    press treatment of, 30–31
    simultaneous, 244–46
    skills of, 21–22
    translators compared with, 20–21
    at UN, 22–23
Inyaz (First Moscow State Institute of Foreign Languages), 25
Ipatiev House, 227
Iran-Iraq war, 95–96, 113
Iraq, 309–32, 341
    Kuwait invaded by, 279, 309–32
    Shevardnadze and, 95–96, 309–11
    UN and, 95–96, 309–11, 320–22, 329–30
Ireland, 317–32
Islamic Conference, 280
isle Joyeuse, L' (Debussy), 100
Israel, 325
Italy, 71
Ivan IV (the Terrible), Czar of Russia, 164
Izvestiya, 30, 142, 204, 328
Izvestiya TseKa KaPeSS, 187

"Jane Fonda Workout" exercise program, 243
Jews, Soviet, 67, 111, 241–42
John Paul II, Pope, 376
Johnson, Lynda Bird, 69
Joint Chiefs of Staff, U.S., 159, 233

Kaiser, Robert, 92, 93
KAL-007 shoot-down incident, 69
Kamentsev, Vladimir, 68, 192, 199, 206, 223
Kampelman, Max, 49, 69, 80, 91, 93, 125, 126, 127
Kampuchea (Cambodia), 113, 275
Karpov, Viktor, 69, 116, 124, 125–26, 170, 259
Kendall, Donald, 251, 253–54, 285
Kennan, George F., 83, 86, 251
Kennedy, Donald, 294
Kennedy, Edward M., 233, 237
Kennedy, John F., 16, 126, 227
Kennedy, Robin, 296
Kensington Palace Gardens, 219

KGB (Komitet Gosudarstvennoi Bezopasnosti) (Committee for State Security), 28, 122, 162, 203, 211, 214, 285, 331, 338
  border troops in, 219
  British operations conducted by, 191
  Gorbachev and, 75
  popular fear of, 142
  Reagan and, 157–58, 337
  security provided by, 49–50, 53–54
Khasbulatov, Ruslan Imranovich, 370–71
Khomeini, Ayatollah Ruhollah, 96
Khrushchev, Nikita Sergeyevich, 30, 50, 56, 187, 205, 271, 290
  Brezhnev and, 45
Khrushcheva, Nina, 56
Kim Il Sung, 281
Kirilenko, Andrei, 28
Kirillov (KGB agent), 46
Kirillova, Irina, 198, 204, 216
Kirkpatrick, Jeane, 90, 94
Kislovodsk, 23, 288, 289
Kissinger, Henry, 83, 88, 91, 158, 242, 243–44, 245
  Gromyko and, 84
Knute Rockne, All-American, 351
Kohl, Helmut, 37, 380
Koivisto, Mauno, 311–12, 313, 319
Koleshlichenko, Thomas, 328
kolkhoz (collective farms), 277, 316, 346–48
komchvanstvo, 292
Komintern (Communist International), 163
Komsomol (Communist Youth League), 154
Kondrashov, Stanislav, 328
Korchilov, Igor:
  Akhromeyev confronted by, 316–17
  background of, 23–25
  education of, 25–26
  Gorbachev's accomplishments summarized by, 379–84
  Gorbachev's first encounter with, 27–40
  Gorbachev's long San Francisco conversation with, 297–306
  at Helsinki summit, 309–32
  at London summit, 187–231
  mistranslation episode of, 260–61
  at Moscow summit, 148–86
  in Reagan-Gorbachev Moscow reunion, 333–78
  as Shevardnadze's interpreter, 60–140
  at Washington summit I, 41–140
  at Washington summit II, 233–308
  as Yeltsin's interpreter, 370–75
Korea, People's Democratic Republic of (North Korea), 281
Korea, Republic of (South Korea), 281
Korotich, Vitaly, 83
Kosygin, Alexei Nikolayevich, 26, 28
krasnaya, krasivaya vs., 167–68
Krasnaya Zvezda (Red Star), 248
Krasniye Kamni (Red Rocks), 289
Krasnoyarsk radar facility, 256
Krokholev, Oleg, 48, 104, 170
Kropotkinskaya Street, 145
Kruchina, Nikolai, 76–77, 113, 192, 206
Krylov, Ivan, 72
Kryuchkov, Vladimir, 63, 77, 204, 321, 331, 338
Kulakov, Fyodor, 289
Kulgutinov, David, 338
Kuwait, 279, 309–32, 339, 341

Landsbergis, Vytautas, 237
Laptev, Ivan, 365
La Rocque, Gene, 83
Laurel Lodge, 282
Lawson, Nigel, 210
Lenin, Vladimir Ilyich, 29–30, 83, 87, 115, 167, 169, 214, 253, 306
Leningrad, 335
Leninism, international revolution and, 213–14
Lennon, John, 84
Lermontov, Mikhail, 302
Levin, Carl, 144
Libya, 190, 201
Ligachev, Yegor Kuzmich, 75, 147, 175, 182, 231
Light of the World, The (painting), 198
Lincoln, Abraham, 73
Linhard, Robert, 125, 126
Literaturnaya Gazeta, 142
Lithuania, 234, 237, 240, 241–42, 246–50, 262–63, 283
Logunov (MGU rector), 359, 363
Lomonosov, Vassily, 109, 174, 363
London, 194, 201–2, 212, 216
London summit (1989), 187–231
  arms sales issue in, 200–201
  economic issues in, 205–6
  Guildhall speech in, 213–19
  Namibia settlement and, 200
  Soviet delegation for, 192
  spying issue and, 191
Lukyanov, Anatoly, 231, 342–43

McDonald's, 141
McLennan, Gordon, 215
Macmillan, Harold, 197
McNamara, Robert, 83
Madison Hotel, 44, 46–47
Magna, Utah, 71
Mailer, Norman, 83
Malik, Yakov Alexandrovich, 99
Malta summit (1989), 252–53, 257
Mamedov, Georgy, 247, 314, 315–16
Mandela, Nelson, 281
Map Room of White House, 133
Marine One, 268–69, 284
market economy, *see* economic reform, Soviet
Marks & Spencer department store, 220
Marshall, Michael, 195
Martin Luther King Jr. International Peace Award, 261
Martin Luther King Jr. Non–Violent Peace Prize, 261
Marx, Karl, 154, 214, 339
Marxism, 161–62
Marxism-Leninism, 56, 57, 104, 214
Mary, Queen of England, 22
Maslennikov, Arkady, 312
Maslyukov, Yuri, 238, 247
Matlock, Jack, 49, 79, 91, 110, 150, 151, 158, 185–86, 238, 335, 346, 365
Matlock, Rebecca, 91, 335, 365
matreshki, 157
Maxwell, Robert, 199
Maxwell Communications, 199
Mayne, Michael, 202
Medvedev, Vadim, 335, 377
Medvedev, Vladimir Timofeyevich, 33, 219, 231, 262, 269, 291, 297
Mehta, Zubin, 91
Mexico, U.S. immigration restrictions on, 67
MFN, *see* most favored nation status
MGU (Moscow State University), 171, 173, 355–65
Michael of Kent, Prince, 212
Michel, Bob, 255
Middle East, 96, 113, 200–201, 309–11
MiG-29 jet fighters, 33
Mike (Secret Service agent), 46, 50
military spending:
    Soviet, 52, 162, 219
    U.S., 52
Millie (First Dog), 267, 272, 273
Mineralniye Vody, 289

Ministry of Foreign Affairs (MFA) of USSR:
    African Desk of, 33
    Diplomatic Academy, 26
    under Gromyko, 25–26
    Press Center, 180–81
Minneapolis, Minn., 285–88
Minsky (dog), 49–50
Mir, 341
missiles:
    air-launched cruise, 256
    Geneva talks and, 69–71
    intercontinental ballistic, 130–31, 137
    intermediate-range nuclear force, 42–43, 70–71
    Pershing II, 42
    reduction of, 129–30, 131, 257–58, 265–66
    sea-launched cruise, 256
    SS-18, 265
    SS-20, 42, 70
    submarine-launched ballistic, 130–31, 137
    see also ABM Treaty; INF Treaty; START
Mitchell, George, 233
Mitterrand, Franáois, 57, 212, 380
Monde, Le, 142
Mongolia, 310
Mosbacher, Robert, 325, 338
Moscow, 145–46, 157, 158, 164, 236, 333–77
Moscow News, 142
"Moscow Nights," 101
Moscow Olympics (1980), 146
Moscow State University (MGU), 171, 173, 355–65
Moscow summit (1988), 141–86
    euphoric aspects of, 33
    human rights issues in, 153, 156, 158–59, 175, 177, 179
    KGB incident at, 157–58
    Kremlin dinner in, 163–66
    Nancy Reagan and Raisa Gorbacheva in, 170–71
    "peaceful coexistence" debate in, 177–80
    planning for, 143–45
    public relations campaign in, 166–69, 172–74
    Reagans' arrival in Moscow for, 150–56
    Reagan's Russian television apperance in, 172–74
    SDI discussion in, 159–60

Moscow summit (1988), (cont.)
    START treaty and, 146–47, 160,
        176–77
    state protocol modified for, 162–63
    U.S. delegation for, 150–53, 158
most favored nation (MFN) status, 255,
    261–63, 283, 308
motorcycle cops, 301
Mount Vernon Restaurant, 44
Moynihan, Daniel Patrick, 63
Mozambique, 34
Mtsyri (Lermontov), 302
Mugabe, Robert, 27, 30–37, 233
mujahedeen, 97, 103, 144, 280
Mulroney, Brian, 238

Najibullah, Mohammed, 280
NAM (non-aligned movement), 27, 35, 37
Namibia, 200
Napoleon I, Emperor of France, 164, 223
nationalism, in Soviet Union, 279
National Security Council, U.S., 248
NATO (North Atlantic Treaty Organiza-
        tion), Germany issue in, 70, 237,
        246–50, 258, 326–27, 328
NBC Nightly News, 251
Netherlands, 71
Nevsky, Alexandr, 162
Newman, Paul, 83
Newsweek, 142, 153, 237–38
new thinking:
    foreign policy in, 26, 196, 213–14
    interdependence concept in, 214
    international attention on, 51
    Thatcher's endorsement of, 208–9
New York Times, 23, 122, 142
Nicaragua, 77–78
Nicholas I, Czar of Russia, 158, 223
Nicholas II, Czar of Russia, 56, 212, 227, 229
Nikonov, Viktor, 180, 231
Ninotchka, 44
Nitze, Paul, 49, 67, 69, 80, 91, 158
    in arms control working group, 107–9,
        113, 116, 124–34
Nixon, Richard M., 11, 45, 49, 76, 123,
        146, 172, 270
Nobel Peace Prize, 381
nomenklatura, 274, 275, 288, 380
Novy Mir, 83, 86, 87, 115
Norwegian Sea, Soviet submarine sinking
    in, 220
nuclear arms accords, 81–82, 102–3,
        124–33, 337
    see also specific treaties

nuclear testing, 110, 256
Nunn, Sam, 63, 144, 255
Nuremberg trials, 21

Oak Room of Soviet Embassy, 84–85, 113,
        114, 119, 134
Oates, Joyce Carol, 83
Obraztsova, Elena, 114–15
Obukhov, Alexei, 69, 71, 126, 247, 313,
        314, 365
Ogarkov, Nikolai, 125
Ogonyok, 83, 142
oil reserves, development of, 325
Old Arbat district, Moscow, 142, 157, 336,
        376
Olympics, Moscow (1980), 146
Omelichev, Bronislav, 250
Ono, Yoko, 84
open skies proposal, 257, 260
Ortega, Daniel, 78
Osipyan, Yuri, 238, 254, 263
Oval Office of White House, 66–67, 77,
        102, 124, 241–42, 255
Owen, David, 195

Pacific Heights, 292
Pakistan, 97, 144–45
Palazchenko, Pavel, 73, 144, 213, 215, 246,
        254, 268, 275, 284, 313, 314, 319
Parris, Mark, 80
Parshin, Lev, 190, 195
Pasternak, Boris, 170, 171, 174, 175
Pavlov, Valentin, 331
Peace at Brest, 115
"peaceful coexistence," debate on, 177–80,
        188
Peaceful Nuclear Explosions Treaty
        (PNET) (1976), 265
Peacemaker, The (painting), 297
Peck, Gregory, 242, 243
Pell, Claiborne, 255
PepsiCo, 251, 253–54
Peredelkino, 171
perestroika, 166
    beginnings of, 26, 29–30
    Bush and, 242
    coup and, 323, 332
    definition of, 29
    five-hundred-day plan in, 309
    "human face" provided by, 234
    INF Treaty and, 85
    as irreversible, 218
    1988 Party conference and, 213
    Politburo opposition to, 74–75

popular mindset and, 316
U.S. businessmen and, 285
Western distrust of, 209
Western interests in, 326
Yakovlev and, 61, 94, 372
Yeltsin and, 235–36
Perestroika (Gorbachev), 75
perevoploscheniye, 21, 23
Perle, Leslie, 92, 93, 97
Perle, Richard, 93, 94, 98, 252
Perpich, Rudy, 286, 289
Pershing II missiles, 42
Persian Gulf war, 279, 309–32
Peter I (the Great), Czar of Russia, 253,
    306
Philip, Duke of Edinburgh, Prince, 221,
    222, 223, 224, 228
Phoros, 380
Pickering, Thomas, 252
Pinsky (dog), 49–50
pirozhki, 176, 363
Pisarev, Dmitri, 11
Plekhanov, Yuri, 120–21, 338
plutonium production, Soviet, 218
Podgorny, Nikolai, 26, 228
"Podmoskovnie Vechera," 101
Poland, Carter's interpreter incident in, 19
police dogs, 49–50
Politburo, CPSU, 27–28, 182
    in decision-making process, 30
    elected power and, 235
    paperwork of, 76
    perestroika opposition in, 74–75
    presidency issue and, 234–35
    replacement of, 238
    Tbilisi incident and, 230–31
    Yakovlev on, 61
political prisoners, Soviet, 111, 175
Pollock, Richard, 224
Popov, Gavriil, 276, 365
"power curve," 264
Powell, Colin, 49, 69, 127, 158, 178, 179
Pozner, Vladimir, 29
Pravda, 23, 30, 31, 131–32, 147, 189, 190,
    206, 314, 328
Presidential Council, Politburo replaced
    by, 238
Presley, Elvis, 23–24
Primakov, Evgeny Maximovich, 112, 192,
    195, 206, 247, 263, 306, 312,
    314–15, 317, 321, 325, 326
Privonoye, 253
proverbs and fables, Russian, 65, 70,
    72–73, 154–55, 168, 173, 184, 208

Pugo, Boris, 331, 332
punctuation, treaties and, 128

Quayle, Marilyn, 267
Quayle, Dan, 239, 248, 261

Rachmaninoff, Sergei, 100
Radio Liberty, 111
Ranger (Bush's dog), 272, 273
Rather, Dan, 70
Rayner, Lord, 223
Razumovsky, Georgy, 231
Reagan, Maureen, 69
Reagan, Nancy:
    appearance of, 151, 350
    astrology as interest of, 171, 368
    health of, 134
    in Leningrad, 335–36
    Raisa Gorbacheva and, 56–57, 63–64,
        104–6, 170–71, 266–67, 291–94,
        350, 358
    reunion of Gorbachev and, 333–77
    Ronald Reagan and, 354, 367–68
    at Washington summit I, 63–64, 68, 74,
        91–92
Reagan, Ronald, 11–15
    Afghanistan and, 80, 103–4
    Alzheimer's disease of, 336
    assassination attempt on, 354–55
    attention span of, 80
    Berlin Wall and, 156, 356–57
    as campaigner, 168
    at Camp David, 271
    capitalist values promoted by, 336
    on communism, 79
    on contemporary films, 358
    debating style of, 80–81
    and "Evil Empire," 79, 165–66, 168,
        169, 183, 333, 342, 383
    Forbes and, 335
    on "friendly persuasion," 165
    on Germany, 362
    as the Gipper, 351
    Gorbachev on, 299
    as Great Communicator, 72, 151–52,
        155, 364–65
    humor of, 72–73, 78–79, 82, 165, 349,
        355
    International Affairs Committee
        speech of, 334–42
    and KGB, 157–58, 337
    on land ownership, 346–48
    on Lenin, 154
    on local vs. federal powers, 346

Reagan, Ronald, (*cont.*)
  on Marx, 154
  memoirs of, 357
  at MGU, 355–65
  at Moscow summit, 141–86
  Nancy Reagan and, 354, 367–68
  own presidential achievements identified by, 360
  on *perestroika*, 342
  on private enterprise, 361–62
  religious views of, 184
  Russian proverbs used by, 70, 72–73, 154–55, 168, 173, 184
  in San Francisco visit, 291–94
  SDI and, 35, 159–60, 169, 176
  Soviet emigration policy and, 67, 156
  Soviet expansionism charged by, 79–80
  on Soviet republics, 345–36
  on Soviet reunion trips (1990), 323, 333–77
  Soviet TV appearance of, 172–74, 336
  "Star Wars" speech by, 69
  trust-but-verify policy of, 70, 72
  on U.S. Constitution, 346
  at Washington summit I, 41–140
  Yeltsin and, 370–76
"red" as "beautiful," 166–67
Red Rocks (Krasniye Kamni), 289
Red Room of Soviet Embassy, 118, 119, 349
Red Room of White House, 100, 262–63
Red Square (Krasnaya Ploschad), 155, 166–69, 349, 355
Red Star (*Krasnaya Zvezda*), 248
Reed, Joseph Verner, 239, 264
Regan, Donald, 266
Rehnquist, William, 252
Republican Party, U.S., 355, 368
Retton, Mary Lou, 93
Reykjavík summit (1986), 35, 41, 51, 52, 57, 70, 75, 118, 123, 124–25, 246
Rice, Condoleezza, 248, 321
Ridgway, Rozanne, 49, 67, 110, 158, 178, 180
Rodgers, William, 69
Romanoff jewels, 220
Romanov family, 227–28
Roosevelt, Eleanor, 21
Roosevelt, Franklin Delano, 133, 134, 252
Roosevelt, Selwa, 54–55, 58–62, 66, 89, 120–21, 148
Rose Garden of White House, 241
Ross, Dennis, 248, 313–14, 321
Rostropovich, Mstislav, 90

Rowny, Edward, 49, 80, 158
Royal Air Force, British, 192
Royal Gardens Hotel, 193, 194
Russia, post-Soviet, 379–84
Russian-Americans, Gorbachev welcomed by, 286–87
Russian language, 166–67, 173
Russian proverbs, Reagan and, 70, 72–73, 154–55, 168, 173, 184
Russian republic, in Soviet Union, 371–73
Rust, Mathias, 53
Rutskoi, Alexandr, 371
Ryan, Fred, 337, 346, 371
Rybakov, Yury, 111
Ryzhkov, Nikolai Ivanovich, 32, 231, 276, 316, 334, 371

Sadat, Anwar, 271
Sadovoye Koltso, 145, 181, 376
Safire, William, 264
Sagan, Carl, 83
Sagdeyev, Roald, 83
St. Basil's Cathedral, 349
St. Catherine's Hall (Grand Kremlin Palace), 158
St. George's Hall, 185
St. Paul, Minn., 285–88
Sakharov, Andrei Dmitriyevich, 111, 143, 235, 240, 361
  human rights issues and, 175
SALT II Treaty, 146
Samoilovich, Georgi, 191
San Andreas fault, 300
Saudi Arabia, 200–201, 310, 317, 365
Savoy Hotel, 201
Scherbakov, Igor, 45, 48, 148
Schuller, Robert, 242
Scowcroft, Brent, 83, 241, 248, 259, 275, 278, 321, 325
Sculley, John, 303
SDI (Strategic Defense Initiative), 35, 106–9, 256
  Gorbachev and, 35–36, 159–60
  Reagan and, 35, 159–60, 169, 176
  Reagan's "Star Wars" speech and, 69
  in Washington summit I discussions, 106–9, 132
Secret Service, U.S., 47, 49–50, 53–54, 158
Seitz, Raymond, 248
Senate, U.S., INF Treaty and, 81, 82, 146
Shatalin, Stanislav, 238, 244, 254, 323, 334
Shatalin Plan, 309
Shevardnadze, Eduard Amvrosiyevich, 50, 51, 54, 70

Afghanistan and, 41–42, 96, 112–13
Geneva agreements signed by, 144
Gulf crisis and, 365
at Helsinki summit, 309–11, 314–15,
   318, 321, 325, 326
INF treaty and, 42, 74
Iraq and, 95–96, 309–11
at London summit, 192, 199–201, 206,
   219, 223
at Moscow summit, 149–50, 158, 181,
   182
new thinking of, 26
on nuclear testing, 110
in planning for Moscow summit,
   143–44
predecessor contrasted with, 69
SDI and, 95, 106–9
September coup and, 331, 332
in state dinner conversation with Bush,
   94–98
at Washington summit I, 58, 59–68, 77,
   79, 85, 89–90, 100, 101, 114–18,
   122, 123, 124, 133–35, 138–39
at Washington summit II, 258, 259,
   261, 262, 268–84
Yakovlev and, 66
Shevardnadze, Nanuli Rozhdestvenna, 171
Shifter, Richard, 110
Shipley, Walter, 252
"Short Course of the History of the
   CPSU," 35
Shulman, Marshal, 83
Shultz, George, 49, 55, 70, 80, 155
   ABM treaty and, 116–18
   Afghanistan and, 41–42, 112–13
   Geneva agreements signed by, 144
   INF treaty and, 42–43
   in Moscow summit, 158, 176, 178–79
   in planning for Moscow summit,
      143–45
   Shevardnadze and, 109–10
   at Stanford University, 294–97
   START treaty and, 116–18
   at Washington summit I, 58, 63, 67, 68,
      77, 81, 87, 103, 108, 114–18,
      133–35, 138–39
Shultz, Helen, 62
Sidey, Hugh, 251
Simpson, Alan, 63, 69, 102, 144
Slavs, in U.S., 286–87, 290
SLBMs (submarine-launched ballistic mis-
   siles), 130–31, 137
SLCMs (sea-launched cruise missiles), 256
Slyunkov, Nikolai, 180, 231

Smith, Carolyn, 48, 94, 148
Smith, Roger, 285
Smolenskaya Ploschad, 334
Sobchak, Anatoli, 276, 335, 365
Solzhenitsyn, Aleksandr, 170
South Africa, 33, 281
Soviet Americanology, 88
Soviet embassy, Washington, D.C.:
   Golden Room of, 82–83, 86, 113,
      118–19, 244
   Oak Room of, 84–85, 113, 114, 119,
      134
   Red Room of, 118, 119, 349
Soviet-Indian agreements, 27
Sovietology, U.S., 88
Sovietskaya Rossiya, 147
Soviet Union (Union of Soviet Socialist
      Republics):
   agriculture in, 276–77, 346–48, 361,
      373–74
   August coup (1991) and, 312, 331–32,
      338, 380, 381
   British investment in, 205–6
   chemical weapons in, 52
   cynicism in, 29–30
   dissolution of, 379–81
   economic reform in, see economic
      reform, Soviet
   economy of, 162, 225
   emigration of Jews from, 67, 111,
      241–42
   espionage and, 191
   "expansionism" charge and, 79–80
   five-hundred-day program for, 300, 309,
      331, 333–34, 371–73
   foreign policy of, 26, 196, 213–14
   free elections in, 187
   generals of, 326–27; see also specific
      military personnel
   glasnost in, see glasnost
   human rights in, see human rights
      issues
   land ownership in, 276–77
   market economy transition in, 254,
      323–25, 365–66
   MFN status for, 255, 261–63, 283, 308
   military forces reduced in, 218–19
   military-industrial complex of, 316
   military spending in, 52, 162
   nationalism in, 279
   office of president in, 234–35, 379
   perestroika in, see perestroika
   Persian Gulf war and, 309–32
   psychological bondage in, 297–98

Soviet Union (*cont.*)
   realistic news in, 51
   republics of, 345–46
   September coup (1990) attempted in,
      331–32
   see also KGB; Politburo, CPSU; *specific
      agencies*
Soviet-U.S. Joint Statement on Iraq, 317–32
sovkhozi (state farms), 347
Space Research Institute, 83
Spain, 205
Spaso House, 145, 157, 162, 165, 170,
      174–76, 181, 336, 337, 342, 350,
      358, 365, 369
Spassky Gate, Kremlin, 166, 337
Spiegel, Der, 142
SS-18 nuclear missiles, 265
SS-20 nuclear missiles, 42, 70
Stafford, Thomas, 242, 243
Stalin, Joseph, 20, 142, 147, 150, 187,
      203–4, 229, 316
Stanford University, 294–97
Staraya Ploschad, 76
Staropeskovsky Pereulok, 157
START (strategic arms reduction treaty)
      (1991), 36, 116–18, 120, 146–47, 160,
      176–77, 256–58, 265–66, 326, 377
START II (1993), 377
Star Wars, *see* SDI
State Dining Room of White House,
      92–100, 251–53
Stavropol region, 288, 347
Stevens, Ted, 91
Stewart, James, 92, 93
Stolychnaya vodka, 241
Strategic Defense Initiative, *see* SDI
Strathclyde, Lord, 192
Style Wars, 57–58
Styron, William, 83
Sukhodrev, Viktor, 26, 344
Sullivan, Kathleen, 91
summits, *see specific summits*
Sununu, John, 248, 321
Supreme Soviet, USSR, 28, 81–82, 146,
      158, 238, 336–42, 373
   Reagan's speech in, 334–42
Suslov, Mikhail, 28, 193
Sverdlovsk, 277
SWAT teams, 62
Syria, 314

Tandy, Jessica, 251
Tarasenko, Sergei, 241, 312, 319, 321
tariffs, 241

Tartars, 164
Tbilisi, 220, 231
Teller, Edward, 90, 94
10 Downing Street, 196–99
   dinner at, 206–13
Tereshkova, Valentina, 175, 338
Texas, 349
Thatcher, Denis, 192, 201, 206–7, 210–12,
      223
Thatcher, Margaret Hilda, 15
   Armenian earthquake and, 199
   Brezhnev and, 38
   Britain's "mini-*perestroika*" and, 225
   capitalism promoted by, 219
   as charismatic, 207
   "common European home" and, 218
   dress of, 192, 193, 197
   dynamic and forceful personality of,
      224–25
   free enterprise and privatization sup-
      ported by, 225, 226
   Gorbachev and, 11, 31, 36–37, 188–89,
      199, 213, 219
   interpreters for, 198
   as "Iron Lady," 37, 189
   jokes about, 189, 210
   KGB activities and, 191
   at London summit, 187–231
   nuclear weapons and, 36–37, 219
   perestroika and, 208–9, 218, 230
   as prime minister, 189
   Raisa Gorbacheva and, 36–37, 198, 199,
      213
   Soviet reforms supported by, 224–25
   speaking style of, 210
   speeches by, 208–10
   term of office for, 212
   Thatcherism and, 226
Third Congress of Peoples' Deputies,
      USSR, 234
Thomas, Helen, 328
Thornburgh, Richard, 252
Threshold Test Ban Treaty (TTBT) (1974),
      146, 265
Tiananmen protests, 255
Time, 29, 184, 251
Times (London), 23, 142, 191
Tocqueville, Alexis de, 15, 99
Tower, John, 69
Tracy, Spencer, 358
trade agreements, 241
Transamerica, 303
translators, interpreters compared with,
      20–21

Treasury Department, U.S., 47
Tretyakov Gallery, 171
Trudeau, Pierre, 238
Truman, Harry, 246
Trump, Donald, 106
Trump, Ivana, 106
trust-but-verify summit, *see* Washington
    summit I
Turner, Ted, 242, 243

Ukraine, 164
Ulyanov, Mikhail, 83, 114–15
Uncle Vanya (Chekhov), 341–42
United Nations, 280
    Charter of, 320
    interpreters at, 21–22
    Iran and, 95–96
    Iraq and, 95–96, 309–11, 319–22,
      329–30
    resolution 598 in, 95
    resolution 661 in, 322, 331
    Security Council of, 311, 322, 329, 330
    Soviet-U.S. unity in, 329
United States:
    business interests of, 136, 285, 302–4
    division of powers in, 345–46, 368
    Gorbachev on, 161–62
    Gorbachev's popularity in, 74, 87–88,
      121–22
    Mexican immigration restricted by, 67
    military spending in, 52
    national parks system in, 348
    Slavs in, 286–87, 290
    see also specific agencies and people
UPOVR (Department of Arms Control
    and Disarmament Problems), 125
uranium production, 218
USIA (United States Information Agency),
    91
USSR Academy of Sciences Institute of
    World Economics and International
    Relations, 112
Ustinov, Dmitry, 28

Vance, Cyrus, 88
Vanik-Jackson Amendment (1974), 241,
    242
van Reigersberg, Stephanie R., 48
VE-Day, 114
verification issues, 256, 260–61
Victoria, Queen of England, 204, 223
Vienna CFE talks, 250
Vishnevskaya, Galina, 90
Vlasov, Alexandr, 231

Vnukovo-2 airport, 148, 149, 231, 331
Voice of America, 111
von Stade, Frederica, 254
Votkinsk, 71
Vremya TV program, 143, 162, 172
v tselylakh, translation problems of, 127

Wall Street Journal, 238
Walnut Room of Kremlin, 30
Walters, Vernon, 94
Warsaw Pact (Warsaw Treaty Organiza-
    tion), 22, 237, 249, 258
Washingtonians, Gorbachev's impromptu
    encounters with, 121–23, 250–51
Washington Post, 47, 92, 102, 142, 153
Washington summit I (1987), 41–140
    Afghanistan and, 103–4, 112–13
    arms control discussions in, 81–82,
      102–3, 124–33
    human rights issues in, 111–12, 140
    interpreters for, 47–48
    Nancy Reagan at, 63–64, 68, 74, 91–92
    public relations activities in, 82–88
    regional issues in, 77–78
    SDI and, 106–9, 132
    security for, 45–47, 49–50, 53–54,
      121–23
    Soviet-U.S. relations and, 69–71, 74–75
    START discussions in, 116–18, 124–33
    trust-but-verify policy in, 110
    U.S. participants in, 48–49
Washington summit II (1990), 233–308
    arms control issues in, 255–61
    credits proposal at, 283
    economic brain trust established at,
      253–54
    Ethiopia and, 280–81
    Germany and, 246–50, 258
    Gorbachev's poor interpreter in,
      244–46
    "intelligensia" at, 242–44
    Korchilov's translation error in, 260–61
    Korea and, 281, 282
    Lithuania issue in, 255, 262–63, 283
    presidential press conference at, 284
    regional disputes and, 275, 279–80
    South Africa and, 281
    Soviet domestic issues and, 233–38
    trade discussions in, 241–42, 261–63
    verification issues in, 260–61
    White House dinner in, 251–53
"we," Thatcher's preference for, 210
Weatherill, Bernard, 196
Webster, William, 251

Weinberg, Mark, 346, 371
Weinberger, Caspar, 91, 106, 158
Wellesley College, 259
Wellington, Duke of, 222–23
Wells Fargo Bank, 303
Westminster Abbey, 201–2
White House (Russia), 369, 371
White House (U.S.):
    Benjamin Franklin Room of, 106
    Cabinet Room of, 76, 77, 124, 130, 133,
        134, 248, 255–61
    East Room of, 69, 72–74, 87–91, 101,
        251, 264–65, 284–85
    Map Room of, 133
    Oval Office of, 66–67, 77, 102, 124,
        241–42, 255
    Red Room of White House, 100,
        262–63
    Rose Garden of, 241
    State Dining Room of, 92–100,
        251–53
Wick, Charles, 21
Widmung (Schumann–Liszt), 100
Will, George, 91
Windsor Castle, 220–30
Winter Garden, 27, 163
Wolfowitz, Paul, 248
Woodward, Bob, 47
World War II, 114, 133, 134, 135–36, 139,
    248–49, 253
Wozniak, Steve, 303
Wright, Jim, 63, 69, 102
Wyeth, Andrew, 242

Yakovlev, Alexandr Nikolayevich, 43, 50,
    51, 54
    Afghanistan and, 196
    background of, 193–94
    in Canada, 193–94
    Eastern Europe policy and, 196
    glasnost and, 142
    humor of, 194, 195, 203, 212–13
    as ideology chief, 141–42
    at London summit, 189, 192, 193–95,
        203–4, 206, 212–13, 219, 223
    at Moscow summit, 158, 175, 181
    Party apparatchiks hatred of, 203–4
    perestroika and, 61, 194, 332
    as Politburo member, 61, 193
    on Stalin's crimes commission, 203–4
    at Washington summit I, 60–61, 67, 79,
        101, 119
    on Yeltsin, 236
Yalta Conference (1945), 20
Yanayev, Gennady, 331, 332
Yavlinsky, Grigory, 334
Yazov, Dmitry, 53, 145, 158, 176, 181, 231,
    258, 326, 331, 338
Yekaterinburg, 227
Yellow Salon of Presidential Palace,
    Helsinki, 313, 320
Yeltsin, Boris Nikolayevich:
    Communist Party banned by, 376
    in Congress of People's Deputies, 187
    five-hundred-day plan and, 371–73
    Gorbachev and, 56, 235–36, 251–52,
        274–75, 358, 371–73, 379–80
    Hammer on, 251–52
    perestroika and, 235–36
    popularity of, 235–36
    Raisa Gorbachev criticized by, 56
    Reagan and, 371–75
Yosemite National Park, 348
Young, Lord, 199
Young Communist League (Komsomol),
    154
Younger, George, 199, 201, 306
Yunost, 142

Zaikov, Lev, 231
Zalygin, Sergei, 83, 86, 87, 114–15
Zamyatin, Leonid, 190, 223
Zarechnyak, Dimitry, 48, 155, 239, 275,
    277
"zero option," 71
Zimbabwe, 27, 33